Virginia Woolf and the Anthropocene

Virginia Woolf – Variations
Series editor: Derek Ryan

Recent books in the series
Virginia Woolf and the Anthropocene
Peter Adkins

Virginia Woolf and Capitalism
Clara Jones

Forthcoming
Virginia Woolf – Objects, Things, Matter
Laci Mattison

Virginia Woolf and Transnationalism
Shinjini Chattopadhyay

Virginia Woolf and the Anthropocene

Edited by Peter Adkins

EDINBURGH
University Press

Edinburgh University Press is one of the leading university presses in the UK. We publish academic books and journals in our selected subject areas across the humanities and social sciences, combining cutting-edge scholarship with high editorial and production values to produce academic works of lasting importance. For more information visit our website: edinburghuniversitypress.com

© editorial matter and organisation, Peter Adkins 2024, 2025
© the chapters their several authors 2024, 2025
© BP plc 2024, 2025 for illustrations in Chapter 5

Edinburgh University Press Ltd
13 Infirmary Street
Edinburgh EH1 1LT

First published in hardback by Edinburgh University Press 2024

Typeset in 11/13 Adobe Sabon by
IDSUK (DataConnection) Ltd

A CIP record for this book is available from the British Library

ISBN 978 1 3995 1668 6 (hardback)
ISBN 978 1 3995 1669 3 (paperback)
ISBN 978 1 3995 1670 9 (webready PDF)
ISBN 978 1 3995 1671 6 (epub)

The right of Peter Adkins to be identified as the editor of this work has been asserted in accordance with the Copyright, Designs and Patents Act 1988, and the Copyright and Related Rights Regulations 2003 (SI No. 2498).

Contents

List of Figures	vii
Acknowledgements	viii
Series Editor's Preface	ix
Abbreviations	x
Notes on Contributors	xii

Introduction: Reading Virginia Woolf in the Anthropocene   1
Peter Adkins

PART I: IMAGINING CLIMATE

1. Virginia Woolf and Anticipations of the Anthropocene   35
   Christina Alt

2. Cosmopolitan Anthropocene: The Convergence of Transnationalism and Climatic Consciousness in Virginia Woolf's *The Years*   56
   Shinjini Chattopadhyay

PART II: MATTER AND MATERIALITIES

3. Outside the Anthropocene: The Subject of Virginia Woolf   79
   Claire Colebrook

4. 'Mud and dung': Virginia Woolf's Environmental Mattering of War   99
   Molly Volanth Hall

5. Following the Oil: Virginia Woolf, Vita Sackville-West and Imperial Extractivism   118
   Peter Adkins

PART III: WRITING EXTINCTION

6. Hearing Beyond Extinction: The Inhuman Comedy of Virginia Woolf's *Between the Acts*   143
   Rasheed Tazudeen

7. The Rat or the Flower? Decomposed Being(s) in the Holograph Draft of Virginia Woolf's *The Waves*   163
   Shilo McGiff

PART IV: MORE THAN HUMAN ENCOUNTERS

8. Darwinism, Dogs and Significant Otherness in Virginia Woolf   189
   Saskia McCracken

9. Virginia Woolf's 'bewildering world'   210
   Derek Ryan

PART V: OUTSIDERS, ASSEMBLAGES AND ACTIVISM

10. 'Suspending the sky': Virginia Woolf and the Brazilian Indigenous Worldview of Ailton Krenak   231
    Davi Pinho and Maria A. de Oliveira

11. Staging Collective Action for an Anthropocene Audience in Virginia Woolf's *Between the Acts*   248
    Kelly Sultzbach

Index   270

Figures

5.1	Official Anglo-Persian Oil Company photograph of an oil pipeline climbing the Iman Reza Ridge, included by Vita Sackville-West as an illustration for *Twelve Days*. Reproduced by the BP Archive.	128
5.2	Photograph of the Anglo-Persian Oil Company oilfields on the horizon, included by Vita Sackville-West as an illustration for *Twelve Days*.	129
7.1	Virginia Woolf, *The Waves: The Two Holograph Drafts*, Holograph Draft 1.1.	169
7.2	Virginia Woolf, *The Waves: The Two Holograph Drafts*, Holograph Draft 1.7.	171

Acknowledgements

First thanks must go to the contributors to this volume. Their hard work, collegiality and brilliant ideas made editing the book a truly enjoyable experience. I am grateful for the wonderful chapters they produced. I am hugely grateful to Derek Ryan for inviting me to edit a volume in the series and for his unwavering encouragement, advice and patience during the whole process. Thanks, too, must go to Jackie Jones, Elizabeth Fraser, Susannah Butler and the team at Edinburgh University Press for all the support and help they have provided throughout. I am grateful to the anonymous reviewers who helped strengthen and improve the book at an early stage. Many thanks to Sarah M. Hall for her meticulous work as copy editor for the volume.

I am also very grateful to Ian Woods, the manager of the BP Archive at the University of Warwick, for digging through old photographs on my behalf and for giving permission to use them in my chapter. These photographs are used courtesy of BP plc.

Thanks, too, must go to Amy C. Smith and Laci Mattison, the respective organisers of the 31st and 32nd Annual International Conference on Virginia Woolf. The panels on Woolf and the Anthropocene at these conferences were invaluable opportunities for contributors to present their work, enter into dialogue with one another and receive comments and questions from the broader Woolf community. It is no exaggeration to say that this book bears the fingerprints (or paw prints) of the Woolf community at large.

Thanks to colleagues and friends in Canterbury, where this book began, and in Edinburgh, where it was completed.

Final and most important thanks, as ever, go to Maddi and Wallace.

Series Editor's Preface

Virginia Woolf's 1937 BBC radio broadcast 'Craftsmanship' memorably describes how words live '[v]ariously and strangely, much as human beings live, by ranging hither and thither, by falling in love, and mating together' (*E6* 96). Her awareness of 'their need of change', their attempt to convey 'many-sided' truths (97), was strongly felt when she was composing her own works. In one diary entry, jotted down on Boxing Day 1929 as Woolf was 'blundering on at The Waves' (her seventh novel), she remarks: 'I write two pages of arrant nonsense, after straining; I write variations of every sentence; compromises; bad shots; possibilities' (*D3* 275). Itself one of those many-sided words, 'variations' famously characterise Woolf's Bloomsbury circle, this time – with an echo of her description in 'Craftsmanship' – 'on the theme of sex, and with such happy results' ('Old Bloomsbury', *MOB* 57).

This series, *Virginia Woolf – Variations*, explores the multiple ways in which Woolf's words, through their abundant variations upon theme and form, speak to urgent critical debates of the twenty-first century. Covering topics as diverse as 'the Anthropocene', 'Capitalism', 'Transnationalism', 'Objects, Things, Matter' and 'Health Humanities' (to name only a handful of the titles commissioned), its volumes present innovative, agenda-setting research by international scholars into the lasting historical, political, ethical and theoretical significance of Woolf's modernist aesthetics. Whether revisiting familiar questions from a fresh perspective or shifting our focus to new concerns, the books explore how Woolf's writing continues to incite provocative arguments about what it means to be human in the strangeness of a variously inhuman, posthuman or more-than-human world.

Derek Ryan

Abbreviations

AHH	*A Haunted House and Other Short Stories*
AROO	*A Room of One's Own*
BP	*Books and Portraits*
BTA	*Between the Acts*
CDB	*The Captain's Death Bed and Other Essays*
CE	*Collected Essays* (4 vols)
CR1	*The Common Reader*
CR2	*The Common Reader, Second Series*
CSF	*The Complete Shorter Fiction*
D	*The Diary of Virginia Woolf* (5 vols)
DM	*The Death of the Moth and Other Essays*
E	*The Essays of Virginia Woolf* (6 vols)
F	*Flush: A Biography*
FR	*Freshwater*
GR	*Granite & Rainbow: Essays*
JR	*Jacob's Room*
L	*The Letters of Virginia Woolf* (6 vols)
M	*The Moment and Other Essays*
MD	*Mrs Dalloway*
MEL	*Melymbrosia*
MOB	*Moments of Being*
MT	*Monday or Tuesday*
ND	*Night and Day*
O	*Orlando: A Biography*
PA	*A Passionate Apprentice*
RF	*Roger Fry: A Biography*
TG	*Three Guineas*
TTL	*To the Lighthouse*
TW	*The Waves*
TY	*The Years*
VO	*The Voyage Out*

Additional abbreviations in this volume only:

FMS   *Flush* manuscript draft
TWHD   *The Waves: The Two Holograph Drafts*

Notes on Contributors

Peter Adkins is Lecturer in Modernist Literature at the University of Edinburgh. He is the author of *The Modernist Anthropocene: Nonhuman Life and Planetary Change in James Joyce, Virginia Woolf and Djuna Barnes* (2022) and co-editor of *Virginia Woolf, Europe and Peace: Aesthetics and Theory* (2020), and has written widely on modernism, the environment and posthumanism.

Christina Alt is Lecturer in Twentieth-Century Literature at the University of St Andrews. She is the author of *Virginia Woolf and the Study of Nature* (2010) and a treatment of modernist nature writing for the co-authored book *Land Lines: Modern British Nature Writing, 1789–2016* (2022), as well as articles on H. G. Wells's engagement with ecology and early twentieth-century conceptions of anthropogenic climate change. She is currently working on a monograph on modernism and ecology, tentatively titled *Modernist Roots: Early Ecology and Modernist Literature in Britain (1900–1945)*.

Shinjini Chattopadhyay is an Assistant Professor at the University of North Carolina-Chapel Hill. Her monograph-in-progress, *Plurabilities of the City*, investigates the construction of metropolitan cosmopolitanism in modernist and postcolonial novels. She is the author of several book chapters and journal articles which have been published in *James Joyce Quarterly*, *European Joyce Studies*, *Joyce Studies in Italy*, and *Modernism/Modernity Print+*.

Claire Colebrook is Edwin Erle Sparks Professor of English, Philosophy, and Women's, Gender, and Sexuality Studies at Penn State University. She is the author and editor of many essays and books, including *Who Would You Kill to Save the World?* (2023), *Posthumous Rites and Inhuman Life* (co-edited with Jami Weinstein, 2016), *Twilight of the Anthropocene Idols* (co-authored with Tom Cohen and J. Hillis Miller, 2015), *Sex After Life: Essays on Extinction*

Volume Two (2014), *Death of the PostHuman: Essays on Extinction Volume One* (2014), *Deleuze and the Meaning of Life* (2010) and *Irony* (2003). With Tom Cohen, she is editor of the 'Critical Climate Change' and 'CCC2 Irreversibility' book series.

Molly Volanth Hall is a Lecturer in Literary Arts and Studies at the Rhode Island School of Design. Her monograph in progress is entitled *Base Matters: Modernist Environments of War and Empire* and she is co-editor of *Affective Materialities: Reorienting the Body in Modernist Literature* (2019). Her work can be found in *ISLE: Interdisciplinary Studies in Literature and Environment*, *The Journal of Literature and Trauma Studies* and several edited collections.

Saskia McCracken completed a PhD thesis on Virginia Woolf's Darwinian animal tropes at the University of Glasgow. She is co-editor of *Beastly Modernisms: The Figure of the Animal in Modernist Literature and Culture* (2023) and has published widely on Virginia Woolf. Her transcription of the earliest manuscript draft of Woolf's *Flush: A Biography* will be published in the forthcoming Cambridge edition of the novel.

Shilo McGiff is an interdisciplinary artist, literary critic and editor living in Ithaca, New York. She is a co-conspirator at the Woolf Salon Project and guest editor of the 'Portmanteau Woolf' issue of the *Virginia Woolf Miscellany*. She is co-editing the forthcoming *Routledge Companion to Virginia Woolf*. She holds a PhD in English Literature from Cornell University.

Maria A. de Oliveira teaches at the Federal University of Paraíba and is the author of *Women's Representation in Virginia Woolf's Works: A Dialogue between Her Political and Aesthetic Project* (2007). Recent publications include *A Prosa Poética de Virginia Woolf* [Virginia Woolf's Poetic Prose] (2021), the co-edited volume *Conversas com Virginia Woolf* [Conversations with Virginia Woolf] (2020) and *Vozes Femininas* [Feminine Voices] (2020).

Davi Pinho is a professor of English Literature at Rio de Janeiro State University and the author of *Imagens do feminino na obra e vida de Virginia Woolf* [Images of the Feminine in Virginia Woolf] (2015). His co-edited volumes include *Eros, Tecnologia, Transumanismo* [Eros, Technology, Transhumanism] (2015) and *Conversas com Virginia Woolf* [Conversations with Virginia Woolf] (2020).

Derek Ryan is Senior Lecturer in Modernist Literature at the University of Kent and author of *Bloomsbury, Beasts and British Modernist Literature* (2022), *Animal Theory: A Critical Introduction* (2015) and *Virginia Woolf and the Materiality of Theory: Sex, Animal, Life* (2013). He is editor of *The Cambridge Companion to Literature and Animals* (2023), co-editor of several collections including *Cross-Channel Modernisms* (2020), *Reading Literary Animals* (2019) and *The Handbook to the Bloomsbury Group* (2018), and co-editor of the forthcoming Cambridge Edition of Virginia Woolf's *Flush: A Biography*.

Kelly Sultzbach is Professor of English at the University of Wisconsin, La Crosse. Her books include *The Cambridge Companion to Literature and Climate* (co-edited with Adeline Johns-Putra; 2022) and *Ecocriticism in the Modernist Imagination: Forster, Woolf, and Auden* (2016). She has published widely in the fields of ecocriticism and modernist studies, most recently in *Modernist Cultures* and *Green Letters*.

Rasheed Tazudeen is Lecturer in English at Yale University and the author of *Modernism's Inhuman Worlds* (2024), as well as articles on modernism, the nonhuman and the environment in *Modernism/modernity*, *Parallax*, *James Joyce Quarterly*, *Victorian Literature and Culture* and *Studies in the Novel*.

In memory of Susan Stanford Friedman (1943–2023)

Introduction: Reading Virginia Woolf in the Anthropocene

Peter Adkins

Early on the morning of 27 June 1927, Virginia Woolf witnessed the end of the world. Standing at the top of Barden Fell in the Yorkshire Dales, Woolf saw a world being drained of life, recording in her diary how the 'colours [of the landscape] faded; it became darker & darker [. . .] We had fallen. It was extinct. There was no colour. The earth was dead' (D3 143). Woolf registers a moment where human history and geological time seem to collide, as humans lose their individual outlines and instead are identifiable only by an essence of their planetary being: 'we were like very old people, in the birth of the world – druids on Stonehenge' (D3 143). And as the solar eclipse drew to an end, for this is what Woolf (alongside Leonard Woolf and a small party of friends) had been witnessing, she describes being left with a feeling of 'relief' (D3 144). As Woolf writes, 'We had been much worse than we had expected. We had seen the world dead. This was within the power of nature. Our greatness had been apparent too' (D3 144). Woolf's diary entry speaks to what Hilary Thompson describes as the way in which total solar eclipses offer writers 'a glimpse of planetary life's extinction' and thereby hold the potential to generate 'new routes of perception' in the Anthropocene.[1] Yet, Woolf's journal entry, with its twists and turns reflecting the immediacy of the diary form, also speak to the knots and ambiguities around agency in the Anthropocene. If it is within the power of 'nature' to kill the 'world', then it raises the question of who *exactly* is acting and who is being acted upon (since what constitutes 'nature' is clearly more than 'the world'). At the same time, the human observers seem to both stand within and beyond this dying world, looking on as ancient sentinels, both immensely powerless and powerful at once. This feeling of 'greatness' is vertiginous, indeed, even vertigo-inducing, as Woolf describes the party of watchers as having been 'much worse' than expected.

This confluence of the personal, the impersonal and the planetary would be much refined and developed by the time Woolf's vision of the 1927 total solar eclipse was reworked into an essay entitled 'The Sun and the Fish' for *Time and Tide* the following year. Describing how 'the sky, which was the object of so many million thoughts, assumed greater substance and prominence than usual', Woolf's essay describes a scene in which the human subject loses all familiarity, becoming 'no longer in the same relation to people, houses and trees' but 'related to the whole world' (*E4* 520).[2] Yet, it is this impersonal 'world' (within which Woolf has firmly situated the human) that is at risk, becoming, as the moon passes through the sky, 'frail; brown; dead; withered' (*E4* 522). Momentarily taking on the role of the *un*-dead, the observers of the eclipse are compelled to see a world in which anthropocentrism and human mastery has been dislodged for a cold, indifferent planet. It is, however, a fleeting vision, since with the returning sunlight:

> The world became more and more solid; it became populous; it became a place where an infinite number of farm-houses, of villages, of railway lines have lodgment; until the whole fabric of civilisation was modelled and moulded. But still the memory endured that the earth we stand on is made of colour; colour can be blown out; and then we stand on a dead leaf; and we who tread the earth securely now have seen it dead. (*E4* 522)

A victory for humanity, it would seem, as 'civilisation' wins out over the power of nature and those who have gathered for the historic occasion rush back to their motor cars and railway carriages to take them back to the metropolises, those seeming markers of humankind's ingenious dominion over the planet. Yet, as Woolf suggests, they have nonetheless been marked by this cosmological encounter, carrying within them a sense of their own fragility and diminutiveness in the face of what earlier in the essay has been described as an 'actor of [. . .] vast proportions' (*E4* 520).

Woolf's writings on the 1927 eclipse can be read as capturing growing anxieties around the precarity of human life and the environments which sustain it. It is a vision of a world which might wither and die, leaving behind a last generation of humans to witness the destruction, despite, or indeed *because of*, the ingenuity and advancements of modern civilisation. In the early decades of the twentieth century, those in the Global North were becoming aware of their growing ability to influence the planet. At the same time, there was an increasing sense of their absolute reliance on a complex series of interlocking biological and geological processes that, if disturbed, could bring about the end of their world. The human as all-powerful global actor and increasingly vulnerable biological species is the contradiction at the core of the Anthropocene, an era in which humans have shaped the planet in their own image and, in so doing, brought about the conditions for their potential demise. As I have written elsewhere, the early twentieth century stands as a particularly important moment in the history of the Anthropocene.[3] Knowledge and understanding of life at an individual, species and planetary scale was being revised with the emergence and modernisation of scientific fields such as ecology, ethology, quantum mechanics, climatology and geochemistry, to name but a handful. Moreover, the global environment itself was undergoing profound change. From the invention of artificial fertilisers to the rise of motor and air travel to CO_2 levels surpassing three hundred parts per million to the environmental consequences of total war, the first few decades of the twentieth century constituted a series of planetary tipping points and thresholds. These revolutions in knowledge and environmental transformations paved the way for a century of accelerated extractivism and intensifying resource use. Over the next hundred years, '[t]he human population increased from 1.5 to 6 billion, the world's economy increased fifteen-fold, energy use increased from thirteen- to fourteen-fold, freshwater use increased nine-fold, and the irrigated areas by five-fold'.[4] Such changes didn't go unrecorded. As scholars of the modernist period are increasingly showing us, growing public concern around air and water pollution, land use change, continuing imperialist expansion, fuel insecurity, growing populations and urban sprawl provoked a wide range of responses among writers, artists, philosophers and other cultural figures in the initial decades of the twentieth century.[5]

This confluence of material developments and cultural responses constitute what I have termed elsewhere the Modernist Anthropocene, a historical and aesthetic moment within the *longue durée* of the Anthropocene epoch, in which we find writers experimenting with literary form and style in response to large-scale environmental change.[6] Woolf stands out among her contemporaries as a writer particularly alert and sensitive to the Modernist Anthropocene. As Michael Rubenstein and Justin Neuman write in *Modernism and Its Environments* (2020), in contrast to other modernist writers, for whom '[c]oncern with the preservation of the natural environment from damage caused by human influence does not appear high on [the] priority list', Woolf harboured a 'deep ecological sensibility' that attuned her to the flows and forms of the nonhuman world.[7] Indeed, Woolf's willingness to suspend anthropocentrism and to push the limits of anthropomorphism, mark her out as an exceptional writer of the Anthropocene. Moreover, her writing registers an understanding that the planet was witnessing a change in kind, not in degree.

The 'Time Passes' section of *To the Lighthouse*, published a little more than a month before Woolf's trip to Barden Fell, is itself a threshold within the novel, both in form and narrative content, and is often read as the novel's *de*-humanised central portion, linking the more human-focused first and third sections.[8] This, after all, is the section of the novel in which we read of the unoccupied Ramsay dwelling gradually succumbing to the elements, as the sea air rusts the saucepans, toads make their home in the house and thistles thrust upwards between floor tiles. Here we find Woolf giving as much attention to the world beyond the human as she does to her human characters, exhibiting an acute interest in imagining a non-anthropocentric vision of the world. Yet, it is not the absence but the *presence* of human activities in 'Time Passes' that seem most significant in the context of planetary change. The section opens with very human anxieties that read all too familiarly in the Anthropocene, as Mr Bankes expresses to those gathered at the house that, in the face of uncertainty, they 'must wait for the future to show' (*TTL* 103). There is, of course, considerable irony in Bankes's sentiment, with the words portending the imminence of global war and family death, as well as the house's decline. In its articulation of the desire for the future to make itself visible and thereby known, the opening sentence is structured by what might be described as one of the Anthropocene's main affects: the sense of a present haunted and shaped by a future disaster that has not yet occurred.[9] Like 'The Sun and the Fish', 'Time Passes' presents an environment in which human ghosts appear to witness the end of the world. After '[o]ne by one, the lamps were all extinguished' (*TTL* 104) and the Ramsay house stands unoccupied, it remains haunted by 'a pair of shoes, a shooting cap, some faded skirts and coats in wardrobes' that have 'kept the human shape' and 'in the emptiness indicated how once they were filled and animated' (*TTL* 106).[10] Moreover, the ghosts in 'Time Passes' witness not only the natural decay of the house, but distinctly *un*natural processes, too. The 'intrusion' of a 'silent apparition of an ashen-coloured ship' leaves behind a 'purplish stain upon the bland surface of the sea as if something had boiled and bled, invisibly, beneath' (*TTL* 109). Conjuring an image in which it appears that the blood of dead combatants and the pollutants left behind by oil-fuelled naval warships comingle and leave an oily film in their wake, Woolf suggests that even the most remote of regions do not remain untouched by the global shifts taking place.[11]

As Derek Ryan writes, *To the Lighthouse* presents a 'supple textual framework' in which the human and the nonhuman are 'entangle[d]' rather than positioned in diametrical opposition to one another.[12] Woolf's outline for 'Time Passes', gathered along with the holograph draft of the novel when it was deposited in the Henry W. and Albert A. Berg Collection of English and American Literature at New York Public Library, reveals the degree to which this entangling was a conscious methodology:

> [T̶i̶e̶?] Ten Chapters
> Now the question of the ten years.
> [T̶i̶e̶?]
> The Seasons.
> The Skull
> The gradual dissolution of everything
> This is to be contrasted with the permanence of – what?
> Sun, moon & stars.
> Hopeless gulfs of misery.
> Cruelty.
> The War.
> Change. Oblivion. Human vitality. Old woman
> Cleaning up. The bobbed up, valorous, as of a principle
> of human life projected
> We are handed on by our children ?
> Shawls & shooting caps. A green handled brush.
> The devouringness of nature.
> But all the time, this passes, accumulates.
> Darkness.
> The welter of winds & waves
> What then is the medium through wh. we regard human beings?
> Tears. [di?]
> S̶l̶e̶e̶p̶ ̶t̶h̶ Slept through life.[13]

Stratigraphic in its lineal resemblance to sedimentary layers and reading almost like an avant-garde ode to the Anthropocene, the outline braids the cultural and the natural into a single twine, resembling what Donna Haraway would later describe as 'natureculture', in which neither constituent term can claim precedence or priority.[14]

This assemblage of nature and culture, from war to waves and from the seasons to shooting caps, becomes the 'medium' through which one understands and regards 'human beings'. Moreover, the ephemeral nature of biological life, shaped by seasonal change, stands in contrast with the cold permanence of the planets, an image which finds its correlate in the final version's memorable description of Skye's night sky lit up by planets that shine like 'plates of brightness' (*TTL* 104).

Yet, Woolf's outline for 'Time Passes' also reflects what Julia Briggs has argued is the First World War's disruption of 'the romantic vision of nature as responding to the human world or working in subtle harmony with it'.[15] 'Dissolution', 'darkness' and 'devouringness' stand out as terms that foreground threatening processes of absorption and inundation. It is unsurprising, then, that a recurring note in 'Time Passes' is that of disharmony and relationships between humans and nature as out of joint. Having described the boiling sea, itself an image of threatening dissolution, Woolf asks 'Did Nature supplement what man advanced? Did she complete what he began?' (*TTL* 110). Suggesting a hybridisation of human and nonhuman agencies, in which a personified Nature having seen humankind's 'misery' is willing to acquiesce in 'his torture' (*TTL* 110), this is an entanglement of the human and nonhuman in which natural processes bear the trace of harmful human influence. Bruno Latour has argued that while the hybridisation of human and nonhuman agencies defined modernity, the Anthropocene muddies the water further, instantiating 'utter confusion between subject and object' as it becomes impossible at times to determine what is natural and what is cultural.[16] The emerging epoch makes plain that to 'be a subject is not to act autonomously in front of an objective background, but to *share agency with other subjects that have also lost their autonomy*'.[17] Woolf's language of supplementation foreshadows Latour's description of the Anthropocene as characterised by tipping points, feedback loops and hybridisation. As the ghostly polluting ship arrives as an 'intrusion into a scene calculated to stir the most sublime reflections and lead to the most comfortable conclusions' (*TTL* 109),[18] we find that the 'dream' of nature as a 'mirror', passively reflecting human emotions or serving as a mere background, has been 'broken' (*TTL* 110). For Emma Brush, Woolf's image of nature as a shattered mirror 'forcefully voices the logic of the Anthropocene', as it decentres and recentres the human simultaneously.[19] Like Woolf's momentary vision of a dying earth in the Yorkshire Dales, the human is at once all powerful and never before so vulnerable, as it seems 'impossible that [. . .]

calm should ever return or that we should ever compose from their fragments a perfect whole' (*TTL* 105).

How Should One Read a Book (in the Anthropocene)?

To the Lighthouse can be seen as an example of what Latour describes as the ability for '[g]reat novels [to] disseminate the sources of actions in a way that the official philosophy available at their time is unable to follow'.[20] Indeed, for Latour, and others in the field of Anthropocene Studies, literary works are uniquely poised to open up new ways of thinking about, while also deepening our understanding of, the emergent planetary epoch. As Tobias Menely and Jesse Oak Taylor claim in the introduction to *Anthropocene Reading: Literary History in Geologic Times* (2017), narrative, at its most fundamental level, 'expresses a basic human imperative to understand our place in a dynamic world of water, weather, and rock'.[21] Literary history, framed as such, provides us with a record of responses to changing environmental conditions, a kind of stratigraphy in itself. Anthropocene reading, however, goes beyond simply noticing what writers record about their environments. Instead, as Menely and Taylor frame it, the Anthropocene is a geohistorical event that can 'unsettle our inherited practices of reading', as we pay attention to aspects of a text that might have previously seemed inconsequential or secondary, or perhaps only unintentionally or unconsciously present.[22] For instance, we might trace how 'literary history register[s] modes of affect and experience related to thermodynamic, geological and atmospheric processes'.[23] Moreover, as Helena Feder also argues in *Close Reading the Anthropocene* (2021), the importance of careful and critical reading practices extend beyond the field of literary studies. Not only is it the case that we find a rich repository of literary works that foreshadow or respond to the Anthropocene, but, '[f]rom the geological strata to [the] social and ecological implications [of climate change], the Anthropocene is, itself, the subject and object of close reading'.[24] Debates about the historical record, geological strata, environmental policy and nomenclature (one can think of the various 'cenes that have been proposed to either supplant or supplement the 'Anthropocene') can all be seen to foreground processes of active, attentive reading. Indeed, for Feder, even the act of creative writing should be seen as a form of close reading. Where we find a text 'articulating and delineating relations, exploring and developing connections' between human and nonhuman processes, we also find the record of a writer who has been engaged in reading the world around them.[25]

While, as I outline in the next section, critics have long highlighted how Woolf comfortably fits into the category of a writer deeply engaged with the world around her, increasing attention is also being paid to Woolf as a writer, more specifically, of the Anthropocene. Emma Brush, for instance, has situated Woolf within the 'longer conceptual lineage' of the epoch, Jesse Oak Taylor has explored how her novels bring to light the climate of modernism and Saskia McCracken has suggested that Woolf's writing on the plumage trade can help us make sense of what has been called the Sixth Mass Extinction event, an unprecedented moment of species loss.[26] As I have argued in *The Modernist Anthropocene*, we can see Woolf, alongside other modernists, as actively 'theorising' the emergent planetary epoch through experiments and innovations in literary form that give voice to new entanglements of human and nonhuman agency.[27] Yet, in addition to theorising what it means to write in the Anthropocene, we also find Woolf, much like the current wave of ecocritics mentioned above, critically examining what it means to be a *reader* in the Anthropocene, too. As critics such as Beth Rigel Daugherty, Kate Flint and Jeff Wallace have shown, for Woolf writing was always intimately connected with reading and criticism.[28] Moreover, her essays on reading frequently come back to how her relationship with literature and literary history is necessarily modulated by the ruptures and threshold moments of the early twentieth century or, as she puts it in 'How it Strikes A Contemporary' (1923), the 'shift in the scale' that has 'shaken the fabric [of society] from top to bottom' (*E3* 357). This for Woolf includes not only modern warfare and unprecedented transformations in the social order (the explicit subject of her remarks above) but broader planetary change, too. In 'Poetry, Fiction and the Future' (1927), for instance, Woolf describes a present moment defined by acceleration, 'an age' of being 'not fast anchored where we are' (*E4* 429). The essay, like the anxious Mr Bankes at the beginning of 'Time Passes', is preoccupied with what lies ahead for readers and writers alike. For the present and future generations, Woolf writes, poetry's 'lyric cry of ecstasy or despair, which is so intense, so personal, and so limited, is not enough' (*E4* 429). This is at least in part due to what we might see as an early articulation of an Anthropocene consciousness in which:

> The mind is full of monstrous, hybrid, unmanageable emotions. That the age of the earth is 3,000,000,000 years; that human life lasts but a second; that the capacity of the human mind is nevertheless boundless; that life is infinitely beautiful yet repulsive, that one's fellow

creatures are adorable but disgusting; that science and religion have between them destroyed belief; that all bonds of union seem broke, yet some control must exist – it is in this atmosphere of doubt and conflict that writers have now to create. (*E4* 429)

The individual and the planetary collide here, as Woolf suggests that the challenge of future literary works will be to make sense of competing scales of life, the geologic and the human, the personal and the impersonal, and to think on two tracks at once. Moreover, although Woolf at first appears to set up a series of irreconcilable oppositions, between the geological and the human, beauty and repulsion, science and religion, the list finishes with the assertion that bonds of union only *seem* broken. As Woolf goes on to explain in the essay, it is the job of the writer to convey the counterintuitive connections that tie together human life and geological cycles, religious belief and scientific truth, beauty and disgust. The novel of the future, Woolf suggests, will not only need to capture both scales of life but the way in which they shape one another.

To illustrate how this might be achieved, Woolf takes a polemical approach, turning to an instance of what she considers to be a failure in this regard. Notably, she turns to a particularly apt example when considering climate and fiction, singling out the storm at the end of Charlotte Brontë's *Villette* (1853). Brontë's depiction of the storm is 'eloquent, lyrical, splendid' but, Woolf suggests, in the context of the novel it is 'uncomfortable' since Brontë has 'led us to expect the rhythm, the observation, the perspective of fiction' and suddenly the reader is confronted with 'the rhythm, the observation and the perspective of poetry' (*E4* 437). Brontë's romantic imagery is 'splendid' yet wholly inappropriate: the reader feels the 'jerk' of poetry, as they are 'half woken from that trance of consent and illusion' to which one submits when reading prose (*E4* 437).[29] Woolf here prefigures Amitav Ghosh's argument in his book-length treatise on literature and climate change, *The Great Derangement: Climate Change and the Unthinkable* (2016). For Ghosh, literary novels typically struggle to accommodate 'exceptional' or 'unlikely' events such as freak storms since, as a genre, they are premised on 'the banishing of the improbable and the insertion of the everyday'.[30] They either tend to avoid depicting such events or (like Brontë) risk being faulted by critics for including the kind of 'prodigious happenings' that typically are consigned to 'romances and epic poems'.[31] Indeed, Woolf is also wary of those who take the opposite tack to Brontë and produce writing that is, as she terms it in 'Modern Fiction' (1925), deadened by the all-pervading 'air of probability' (*E4* 160). These 'materialists', as she terms them, take a workmanlike approach to the novel yet produce narratives in which 'the trivial and the transitory appear the true and the enduring' (*E4* 159).[32] At the same time, Woolf complains in 'Poetry, Fiction and the Future' that those writers who have been invested in the immaterial and the metaphysical have 'been too prone to limit psychology to the psychology of personal intercourse' and have wholly neglected the 'impersonal' (*E4* 435–6). At the heart of her argument is the conviction that readers will increasingly want literature that can engage with life on multiple scales, encompassing the human as well as the nonhuman, while maintaining the 'trance of consent and illusion' that are fundamental to a successful novel (*E4* 437). Only in 'dramatiz[ing] [. . .] those influences which play so large a part in life, yet have so far escaped the novelist' might we arrive at a form of literature that will sufficiently express 'the relations of man to nature, to fate; his imagination; his dreams' (*E4* 439).[33]

If in 'Poetry, Fiction and the Future' Woolf focuses on how writers might speak most directly to the needs of readers in the present age, in 'How Should One Read a Book' (1926) she looks at the other side of the equation, examining the obligations placed on a reader. Again, Woolf can be seen to take a planetary approach, with the opening sentence framing the essay around the question of how to approach literature in 'this late hour of the world's history' (*E4* 388). Reading in the modern world, it is implied, always takes place amid external crises that frame and shape our experience as readers, inflecting the key questions, which Woolf suggests are:

> how am I to read these books? What is the right way to set about it? [. . .] What am I to do to get the utmost possible pleasure out of them? And is it pleasure, or profit, or what is it that I should seek? (*E4* 389)

Reading literature for Woolf is primarily an aesthetic experience, associated with pleasure, immersion and illusion. It is what distinguishes literature from other forms of discourse, such as news journalism or science (as Woolf writes later in the essay, 'fact destroys fiction' [*E4* 395]). Yet, that is not to say that reading literature is hedonistic, in the sense of a withdrawal from the world, since the question of how one 'profit[s]' from what one is reading is also always at stake. Crucially for Woolf, this 'profit' cannot be separated from the aesthetic experience of the literary work. As she writes in the essay's conclusion, since 'we get nothing whatsoever except pleasure from reading' we do not need to worry about 'moralists' asking us to 'justify our love of reading' (*E4* 398). Yet, at the same time:

> That pleasure is so curious, so complex, so immensely fertilising to the mind of anyone who enjoys it, and so wide in its effects, that it would not be in the least surprising to discover, on the day of judgement when secrets are revealed and the obscure is made plain, that the reason why we have grown from pigs to men and women, and come out from our caves, and dropped our bows and arrows, and sat around the fire and talked and drunk and made merry and given to the poor and helped the sick and made pavements and houses and erected some sort of shelter and society on the waste of the world, is nothing but this: we have loved reading. (*E4* 398–9)

A tour-de-force final sentence, Woolf imagines a defence of reading at the moment of judgement, an imagined end of days, in which, reaching back into deep time (and again entwining human and geological history) reading is situated as having facilitated not only the evolution of the human but as having produced the conditions for the rise of civilisations. Yet it also invokes a curiously ambivalent tone in its penultimate clause, reflecting on literature as 'some sort of shelter and society on the waste of the world'. Up until the late nineteenth century, 'waste' typically meant 'uninhabited' or 'uncultivated' land.[34] This is nature as culture's diametrical opposite – raw material waiting to be transformed into civilisation. Yet, as Woolf knew only too well, not least from having painstakingly set by hand T. S. Eliot's *The Waste Land* (1922) when it was published by the Hogarth Press, a new understanding of 'waste' was opening up, describing the deleterious effect that modern civilisation was having on environments at a local, national and planetary level.[35] Reading, in this sense, might not only give rise to the conditions for modernity, but also, crucially, provide a refuge and place of resistance to critically reflect on the violence often done under the banner of progress.

It might not be surprising to know that Woolf wrote 'How Should One Read a Book?' while taking a short break from working on *To the Lighthouse*.[36] The essay, which stresses the importance of reading critically and self-reflectvely, while framed in its opening and closing sentences by the threat of apocalyptic end-times, resonates with the outline that Woolf wrote for 'Time Passes' in its particular emphasis on '[t]he gradual dissolution of everything'.[37] As such, what we find being articulated is not so much an environmental approach to the literary, as a literary approach to the environmental. Woolf describes how great works of literature sink into the unconscious only for a 'whole book [to float] to the top of the mind complete' when one is going about one's life and least expects it. 'Some process', Woolf writes, 'seems to have been finished without one's being aware of it' (*E4* 397). This is the 'after reading' (*E4* 397) and is just as central to our experience of the text as the initial encounter with it. The text is working within us as we go about our lives, quietly readjusting how we perceive and imagine the world around us. This also helps explain why for Woolf the experience of reading must remain primarily an aesthetic one and why literary merit remains at stake. Literature is all the more powerful for not resembling forms of cultural discourse that are premised on straightforward or direct forms of instruction; it is why, as Woolf wittily puts it in 'Poetry, Fiction and the Future', one does not go to Shakespeare for 'applied sociology' (*E4* 436). This is an anti-instrumentalist account of literature that recognises what Derek Attridge describes as the way in which literary works 'excee[d] the limits of rational accounting' and always instantiate a singular, unique encounter between reader and text.[38] It is an approach that situates the reader and text in a dynamic, open and co-participatory relationship in which literary works 'hang in the wardrobe of our mind' as we go about our lives and new meanings accumulate (*E4* 397). It offers, in sum, a way of going forward with a mode of Anthropocene reading. If, as Menely and Taylor suggest, Anthropocene reading is not so much 'a single practice or method' but instead 'the conditions under which *all* reading must henceforth proceed', then Woolf might be seen to prefigure such an insight.[39]

In essays such as 'Poetry, Fiction and the Future', 'Modern Fiction' and 'How Should One Read a Book?', Woolf offers not only a critical account of the kind of literary and theoretical questions that preoccupied her as a writer, but a series of meditations on how we might rethink reading and criticism in relation to planetary and environmental change. By no means a proto-ecocritic (not least due to the gulf in environmental knowledge between the early twentieth century and now), Woolf was nonetheless deeply preoccupied with how encounters with works of literature attune us to the world not irrespective of aesthetic merit but precisely because of it. Here we find Woolf not only foreshadowing current debates around literature, reading and the Anthropocene, but poised to intervene in crucial and timely ways. If, for Ghosh, there isn't enough direct engagement with climate change in literary fiction,[40] Woolf's theories of reading and criticism offer a counterweight, emphasising that the relationship between works of literature and our view of the world is often indirect, unconscious and surprising. That just as important as narrative content, which can risk all too easily the kind of didacticism that 'ought to have been discharged by Government officials' if it prioritises political or social considerations over all else (*E4* 159), are questions of formal and stylistic accomplishment. This is where lies the ability for a text to ignite our imaginations, our emotions and our sense of relation to other humans, animals and environments. Books are 'always overflowing their boundaries' (*E4* 390), seeping into the world and leaking into the future, with each wave of readers primed to find new dimensions and experiencing the text in unexpected, unforecastable ways. Indeed, Woolf is already thinking of the generations of readers to come in these essays, as she 'look[s] into the future' and 'trace[s] on its mist' (*E4* 429) us, her Anthropocene readers.

A Brief Environmental History of Woolf Criticism

If Woolf was ahead of her time, theorising writing, reading and criticism in such a way that speaks powerfully to our present moment, it is also the case that readers and critics of Woolf were also ahead of the curve, teasing out her ecological sensibilities long before discourse around the Anthropocene became a subject of discussion in literary studies. Indeed, one of the earliest ecocritical appraisals of Woolf came while ecocriticism was still emerging as a distinct interdisciplinary field. Writing in the Association for the Study of Literature and Environment's flagship journal, *ISLE: Interdisciplinary Studies in Literature and Environment*, in 1998, Carol Cantrell made the argument that Woolf was a writer who might be regarded as a key precursor to the kind of eco-philosophical debates taking place within the discipline of literary studies. Modernism's 'attack on dualistic thinking, the foregrounding of backgrounds, the exploration of the relation of language to alterity, and the self-referential nature of symbol-making' are flagged as ways in which the modernist corpus is rich with material through which to think about ecological questions.[41] Focusing largely on *Between the Acts* (1941), a text which it is fair to say has enjoyed the most ecocritical attention of all of Woolf's oeuvre, Cantrell draws on Maurice Merleau-Ponty's embodied phenomenology to suggest we find a landscape of more-than-human inscriptions and actors, in which 'geological, biological, and human historical processes are foregrounded as part of the weave of "the present" in which the novel takes place'.[42] Cantrell's essay is significant in a number of senses. Although it was the first explicitly ecocritical account both of Woolf *and* literary modernism, it didn't represent a modernist turn in ecocriticism nor an ecocritical turn in modernist studies as might have been imagined. Instead the false perception that, as Cantrell writes in the opening to her 1998 essay, modernism might 'seem to be a hostile territory for a student of literature and the natural environment', since it privileges the urban and the abstract over the rural and the referential, would hold fast for some time.[43] As Rubenstein and Neuman outline, although ecocriticism and the new modernist studies emerged at broadly the same time in the mid-1990s, and were forged as explicitly interdisciplinary fields of enquiry, they nevertheless 'conducted themselves in relative isolation from one another, each in their institutional silo'.[44]

While Cantrell's article was the first piece of work on Woolf to consciously situate itself as an ecocritical study, her essay in many respects represents the culmination of approaches to Woolf that from the 1980s onwards had paid attention to the relationship between the textual, material and historical dimensions of her writing.[45] Indeed, any proper environmental history of Woolf criticism would have to go back to a number of watershed publications during this period, such as Alex Zwerdling's *Virginia Woolf and the Real World* (1986), which aimed to better understand how her writing 'trace[s] the forces in the world around us that shape' one's psyche.[46] Focused on Woolf's attentiveness to external social and historical forces, the book challenged a prevalent conception of Woolf as a writer occupied only with the workings of the mind and subjectivity, insisting instead that the external and internal are always in interrelation in her novels, and that 'the relationship between the self and the world is at the heart of Woolf's social vision'.[47] Mark Hussey's *The Singing of the Real World: The Philosophy of Virginia Woolf's Fiction*, also published in 1986 and invested in reassessing the 'real' in Woolf's writing, similarly represents a moment in which the relationship between the interior subjective world and the exterior material one is examined. Although insisting that 'Woolf's art tells us not about an external, objective Reality, but about our experiences of the world',[48] Hussey's book, like Zwerdling's, reflected a growing interest in reassessing the dynamic and interrelated relationship between exteriority and interiority, materiality and subjectivity (or granite and rainbow, as Woolf might have put it) in her writing. Equally important, was the work of Gillian Beer in the same period. Her essays on Woolf and discourse around evolution, deep time, physics and anthropomorphism established the degree to which her writing was in dialogue with nineteenth- and twentieth-century scientific discourse and debates.[49]

Woolf emerged from the 1980s as a writer who was understood to have been profoundly interested in the material, historical and scientific currents shaping the world around her. In the 1990s and early 2000s, the fluid and contingent rather than oppositional and fixed relationship between the subjective and the objective in Woolf's writing continued to be explored. Susan Stanford Friedman's *Mappings: Feminism and the Cultural Geographies of Encounter* (1998) took a geopolitical approach to Woolf's feminism, situating it in a global context that foreshadowed her later more explicitly environmental concern in *Planetary Modernisms* (2015). A similar attention to geography and spatiality is present in Anna Snaith and Michael Whitworth's *Locating Woolf: The Politics of Space and Place* (2007), whose essays pay close attention to the ways in which Woolf's writing knowingly operates in a 'global space' composed of 'cultural and imperial networks'.[50] During this period, early and important ecocritical work was also being done on Woolf. Louise Westling's still-influential 1999 article on *Between the Acts* takes, like Cantrell, a Merleau-Pontian approach and argues for an 'ecological humanis[t]' undercurrent to the novel which 'restores humanity to its place within the bodily community of earth's life and refocuses attention upon the limitations and responsibilities that must humble our species if we are to survive'.[51] Caroline Webb's 2001 paper on the interplay of nature and culture in *Orlando*'s depiction of the Victorian climate, detecting a Ruskinian influence on Woolf's satire, also stands out as a forerunner of later critical accounts of the novel as, in Jesse Oak Taylor's terms, 'a formative example of what has come to be called climate fiction (or "cli-fi")'.[52]

If the Anthropocene has been marked by threshold moments and tipping points, it is also the case that the same is true of Woolf and ecocriticism. Within Woolf studies, the 2010 publication of Christina Alt's *Virginia Woolf and the Study of Nature*, the 2010 Annual International Conference on Virginia Woolf, which took as its theme 'Virginia Woolf and the Natural World', and the 2012 publication of Bonnie Kime Scott's *In The Hollow of the Wave: Virginia Woolf and Modernist Uses of Nature* all represented formative moments in the emergence of a subject that might be called ecocritical Woolf studies.[53] Alt's and Scott's monographs were particularly important in the divergent approaches they took, showing the breadth that might come under the banner of an ecocritical Woolf studies, with Alt showing how Woolf had been influenced by 'contemporary developments in the life sciences', especially the switch from taxonomical to ecological and ethological ways of knowing, in contrast to Scott's weaving of biography and ecocritical theory to present Woolf as a writer whose creative engagement 'with the natural world [. . .] makes her a resource for rethinking the sustained future of nature and culture combined'.[54] Where both studies converge, however, is in their careful positioning of Woolf not as a proto-environmentalist (not least since, as Alt points out, 'ecological thinking' in the early twentieth century was very different to present ideas of ecological-mindedness and not necessarily non-anthropocentric in its ideological underpinnings) but as a writer who is able to both help us historicise changes in how the nonhuman world was imagined and whose innovative works might speak across time to our own present moment of environmental crises.[55]

As Diana L. Swanson framed it in her introduction to a 2012 special issue of the *Virginia Woolf Miscellany* on 'Eco-Woolf', ecocritical approaches to Woolf were quickly proving 'fertile avenues' into her work.[56] Moreover, just as the 2010s saw the field of ecocriticism develop in multiform directions, broadening while also deepening how we might understand the relationship between literature and the environment, the same held true for ecocritical Woolf studies. While critics such as Karina Jakubowicz, Shilo McGiff and Elisa Kay Sparks have offered new ways of understanding the rural, the pastoral and the botanic in Woolf, especially as it intersects with questions of gender,[57] others, such as Marlene Dirschauer, Nicole Rizzuto and Laura Winkiel parallel the growing importance of the blue as well as the green in ecocriticism, in their attention to the presence of oceans and waterscapes in Woolf's writing.[58] The question of Woolf's interest (both biographically and creatively) in other species of animals also falls under the banner of the environmental and nonhuman dimensions of her work, as attested to by a number of chapters in this volume that look at Woolf and animals. This aspect of Woolf's writing, which might, following Saskia McCracken and Alex Goody, be termed her 'beastly modernism',[59] has, thanks to pathbreaking scholars such as Jeanne Dubino, Jane Goldman, Carrie Rohman and Derek Ryan, enjoyed particular uptake among Woolf studies and would well deserve to be the subject of its own critical history.[60] At the same time, the deconstruction of nature and culture as oppositional terms, and the growth of posthumanist approaches within the environmental humanities, has led scholars to consider how, even when Woolf *isn't* writing about traditionally natural subjects, she is still asking questions that have ecological or geological implications. Critics such as Ruben Borg, Aaron Jaffe, Ryan and Sultzbach have been at the forefront in considering how Woolf's writing presents a lively materiality and nonhuman agency that exceeds anthropocentric ways of seeing the world.[61] Moreover, the consequences of this explosion of critical interest in Woolf as an ecologically minded writer have not just brought her into dialogue with contemporary discourse around the environment, but fundamentally altered how we view her corpus. Certain texts have come into focus more clearly under an ecocritical lens. A once-neglected work such as *Orlando*, previously seen to 'embody the shallower aspects of Bloomsbury',[62] is now being read as presenting 'the deep interconnectedness or transmateriality of life itself' not *despite* its satire and humour but because of it.[63] Woolf's biography of Elizabeth Barrett Browning's dog, *Flush* (1933), is another text that has undergone critical revision; a once-marginal work in her oeuvre it is now widely understood to be 'a complex exploration of canine subjectivity that transgresses generic conventions and transforms the mode of biography itself'.[64] Indeed, as McCracken's contribution to this volume shows, Woolf's canine biography is more relevant than ever in the Anthropocene. Woolf's essays and short fiction are also being explored for what they show us about the nonhuman, with works such as 'The Mark on the Wall' (1917), 'Solid Objects' (1920) and 'Modern Fiction' being seen as touchstones for understanding, in Jaffe's terms, 'inhuman scenes of modernity'.[65] Simultaneous with this wave of critical revision, widely taught and studied Woolf novels, such as *Mrs Dalloway* (1925), *To the Lighthouse* and *The Waves* (1931), are also being reappraised for the degree to which, by paying attention to their ecological sensibilities, they might be better understood.[66]

With the rise of the Anthropocene concept within the humanities, Woolf's oeuvre stands ready to speak to a new wave of ecocritical enquiry. Indeed, it is notable that among the philosophers and theorists addressing our new planetary epoch head-on, Woolf's writing has been a source of influence and provided materials to think with. Donna Haraway's *Staying with the Trouble: Making Kin in the Chthulucene* (2016) appropriates Woolf's feminist call to intellectual arms, 'Think we must!', from *Three Guineas* (1938) and refashions it for the Anthropocene era. Woolf, Haraway writes,

> understood the high stakes of training the mind and imagination to go visiting, to venture off the beaten path to meet unexpected, non-natal kin, and to strike up conversations, to pose and respond to interesting questions, to propose together something unanticipated, to take up [. . .] unasked-for obligations.[67]

The concept of the Anthropocene, which insists that we think on multiple temporal and spatial scales at once so as to better understand how human processes have and continue to influence biological and geological processes, opens up new forms of ecological thought in relation to Woolf. As critics such as Paul K. Saint-Amour and Friedman have shown, Woolf was influenced by scientific and technological developments that gave rise to a sense of what Friedman calls 'planetarity', in which one becomes intensely aware of the fact that one's sense of normative scale is just a 'perception' and that there are other ways of seeing, thinking with and imagining the world.[68] Woolf was all too aware that she was living through an era of unprecedented planetary transformation. Her writing at once offers a cultural record, imprinted with the environmental history of the early twentieth century, and a space of experimental aesthetic innovation in which normative ideas about the human and nonhuman are suspended. Like the revolutions in critical approaches that have preceded it, Anthropocene studies stands to gain as much from Woolf as Woolf studies stands to gain from the ever-expanding critical discourse surrounding our emergent planetary epoch.

Chapter Summaries

The chapters in this book are structured into five sections, encompassing the various ways in which Woolf's writing helps us historicise and theorise the Anthropocene, shedding light on the epistemological, ontological, ethical and aesthetical questions that have come to the fore in recent ecocritical debates. The first section, entitled 'Imagining Climate', looks at how Woolf's writing frequently turns to a climatic imaginary. Christina Alt's essay, 'Virginia Woolf and Anticipations of the Anthropocene', examines Woolf in relation to the discourse around anthropogenic climate change that was circulating in the first few decades of the twentieth century. In the first half of the essay, Alt provides important historical depth for understanding Woolf's own climatological outlook, offering a critical overview of scientific understandings of and cultural attitudes towards climate change by figures such as Svante Arrhenius, Nils Ekholm, R. L. Sherlock, G. S. Callendar and E. Ray Lankester. In the second half of the essay, Alt shows how Woolf's writing both reflects and interrogates shifting ideas in climatological discourse. Paying particular attention to 'On Being Ill' (1926), Alt finds Woolf engaging with prevalent ideas of global cooling and glacial anxieties but, unlike her scientist contemporaries, appears critical of the instrumentalising of the Earth to narrow human ends. The question of climate also looms large in Shinjini Chattopadhyay's chapter, 'Cosmopolitan Anthropocene:

The Convergence of Transnationalism and Climatic Consciousness in Virginia Woolf's *The Years*', where the concept of modernist cosmopolitanism is brought into dialogue with ideas about the intersection of human and geological agency from the environmental humanities. Drawing on Dipesh Chakrabarty's argument that we can no longer separate human and natural histories, Chattopadhyay outlines the presence of a distinctly non-anthropocentric 'climatic consciousness' in *The Years* (1937), showing how different scales of time and space converge upon one another in the novel. This blend of human and nonhuman agency, Chattopadhyay argues, allows Woolf to fervently critique imperialism and embrace cosmopolitanism precisely because of, rather than despite, a willingness to push beyond narrow anthropocentric perspectives.

The second section is entitled 'Matter and Materialities' and explores Woolf's interest in thinking about certain material forms, as well as the category of materiality itself. As Clare Colebrook writes in her chapter, 'Outside the Anthropocene: The Subject of Virginia Woolf', Woolf's writing can be read as a precursor to the 'new materialism [that] has been crucial to the theorisation of the Anthropocene'. Woolf's radical understanding of materiality, in which the human is but one part of a vital assemblage that far exceeds one's own individual being, opens on to a new conception of the self as alive to a rich and affective more-than-human horizon. Detecting two competing 'Anthroposcenic' subjects in Woolf, one which enacts a retreat from the world, safely perceiving its vital materiality from afar and the other willing to embrace the 'radically depersonalised experience of pure difference', Colebrook suggests that Woolf's writing offers ways of thinking about the questions of race, empire and class that must remain foregrounded in our responses to the Anthropocene. Also highly alert to the ways in which Woolf's environmental imagination was shaped by materiality, but focusing on one material form in particular, is Molly Volanth Hall's '"Mud and Dung": Virginia Woolf's Environmental Mattering of War'. Situating Woolf within the historical currents and material events of the early twentieth century, Hall explores how, in the aftermath of the First World War, mud became a materiality through which Woolf could reimagine embodiment, gender and sexuality beyond humanist paradigms. Despite Woolf not having first-hand experience of the 'mudscapes' at the Front, novels such as *Jacob's Room* (1922), *Mrs Dalloway* and *The Years* are, Hall argues, splattered with muddy moments in which earthy matter is shown to be a generative and creative means of responding to conflict. Woolf's muddy-mind, Hall concludes, allowed her to understand the human and environmental costs of the war and offers a model for how we might make matter *matter* again in the present moment. The relationship between materiality, imperialism and globalism continues to be considered in 'Following the Oil: Virginia Woolf, Vita Sackville-West and Imperial Extractivism'. My contribution to the book, it explores how Woolf and her contemporaries both scrutinised and were implicated in the emergent global oil economy. Reading Woolf's 'Thunder at Wembley' (1924) and her *London Scene* essays (1931–2) alongside Vita Sackville-West's Persian travelogues, *Passenger to Teheran* (1926) and *Twelve Days* (1928), I suggest that we can trace through these works a growing preoccupation with the transformative nature of oil. While Sackville-West writes about British extractivism in modern-day Iran, including an account of a trip to the Anglo-Persian Oil Company's oilfields, in contrast, the chapter argues, Woolf attends to how this imperialist product was bringing about rapid material changes back in Britain.

The question of extinction, and particularly the challenges it brings to literary expression, has emerged as a pressing topic of discussion in Anthropocene Studies. In Part III, 'Writing Extinction', we find evidence of Woolf's own experiments and innovations in imagining the end of the world. Rasheed Tazudeen's chapter, 'Hearing Beyond Extinction: The Inhuman Comedy of Virginia Woolf's *Between the Acts*', considers how comedy has the potential to operate as an 'ecological modality' that can help us rethink, and maybe even laugh amid, extinction events. Looking at Woolf's unfinished final novel, alongside her 1905 essay 'The Value of Laughter' and her 1941 manuscript 'Anon', Tazudeen suggests we find an attention to earthy, inhumanist soundscapes that elicit a laughter that allows us to see the end of the world, and the beginnings of new ones, in less anthropocentric terms. Looking at how Woolf's writing presents instances of musicality and noise produced by nonhuman actors, as well as the Earth itself, Tazudeen argues that in her work we can hear beyond conventional humanist narratives of extinction and attune ourselves afresh to the Earth's comedy of vibrations and sounds.

Dead rats crawling with maggots might not be the first image one associates with Woolf's *The Waves*, yet Shilo McGiff focuses on exactly this in her contribution to the volume, 'The Rat or the Flower?: Decomposed Being(s) in the Holograph Draft of Virginia Woolf's *The Waves*'. Focusing on 'the poetics of the draft form' in Woolf's earliest holograph of the novel, thereby considering the text on its own terms rather than as only having value in relation to the later published version, McGiff teases out a necropastoral aesthetic that runs throughout the draft. Looking at images of death, as well as the hallucinatory and grotesque scene in which a mass of mothers give birth to innumerable 'pullulating' children amid the waves (cut from the published version of the novel), McGiff finds an aesthetic mode that deterritorialises pastoral cycles of life and death, opening up weird posthuman worldings that dislodge narrow conceptions of what it means to live and die in the Anthropocene.

The next section of the book, 'More than Human Encounters', looks at how Woolf's writing repeatedly makes recourse to scenes of encounter between humans and other-than-human life. Charles Darwin stands as an important figure in the history of the Anthropocene and, as Saskia McCracken argues in her chapter, his works had a decisive influence on Woolf's writing on animals, too. In 'Darwinism, Dogs and Significant Otherness in Virginia Woolf', McCracken brings Woolf's *Flush* into dialogue with Darwin's 'canine stories' in *The Descent of Man* (1871), showing points of confluence and offering a revisionary understanding of nonhuman agency in both. Paying particular attention to Woolf's earliest manuscript draft of *Flush*, as well as the final published novel, McCracken suggests that, even more so than in Darwin, we find a willingness to suspend anthropocentric ideas of language and literature, as Woolf gravitates towards embracing a 'doggy *logos*' that can help us rethink species relations in the Anthropocene. Flush also makes an appearance in Derek Ryan's chapter, 'Virginia Woolf's "bewildering world"'. Tracing moments of bewilderment across Woolf's essays and novels, Ryan suggests we find Woolf situating bewilderment as an affective state that unsettles processes of human meaning-making, especially in relation to the nonhuman. Beginning by looking at Woolf as a 'bewildered reader', showing how her essays on literature and criticism are often marked by questions of ambivalence and uncertainty when it comes to the relationship between the human and its others, Ryan then turns to Woolf as a 'bewildering writer' whose novels, such as *The Voyage Out* (1915), *Night and Day* (1919), *Orlando* and *Flush*, use bewilderment to explore the porous boundary between human and more-than-human life.

In Part V, 'Outsiders, Assemblages and Activism', the volume closes with two chapters that bring Woolf's writing into dialogue with twenty-first-century concerns around collectivism and community, especially as these topics relate to taking positive and hopeful action in the Anthropocene. Like the previous chapters in the collection, they show how Woolf not only offers a way of understanding the history of our epoch but also provides ideas and insights that can help us critically engage with the ongoing challenges of the present.

The Anthropocene has foregrounded the necessity of thinking about literature on a planetary scale, yet as Davi Pinho and Maria A. de Oliveira argue in their chapter, '"Suspending the Sky": Virginia Woolf and the Brazilian Indigenous Worldview of Ailton Krenak', we need to not only think about Woolf in relation to questions of planetarity, but planetary *injustice*. Bringing Woolf into 'contact' with the indigenous Brazilian writer and philosopher Ailton Krenak, Pinho and de Oliveira show how Woolf's ideas can be refashioned to critique 'contemporary myths of progress that sustain neocolonial practices'. To do so, Pinho and de Oliveira develop Woolf's idea of an 'Outsiders' Society' from *Three Guineas* as a way of thinking about being and belonging 'outside' (in multiple senses of the word). Reading Woolf with Krenak, Pinho and de Oliveira show, offers a way of thinking through the multiple power differentials that are at play when considering the Anthropocene. It also, as their reading of *The Voyage Out* shows, allows us to reassess how anticolonial and ecological aesthetics intersect in Woolf's writing. Concluding the volume is Kelly Sultzbach's 'Staging Collective Action for an Anthropocene Audience in Virginia Woolf's *Between the Acts*'. Suggesting that we can think about Woolf's final novel as it resonates with the need for action in our present moment of environmental crisis, Sultzbach finds in *Between the Acts* ideas about community and collectivism that can speak to 'Anthropocene readers'. Woolf's various assemblages of human and nonhuman beings in the novel, collectives that are contingent and precarious, help us to better understand Donna Haraway's adage of 'staying with the trouble', Sultzbach argues, and, as Pinho and de Oliveira also suggest, invite us to reflect on who or what is excluded as the 'outside' of any given community. Concluding by analysing the final scene of Woolf's final novel, Sultzbach draws the volume to a fitting close by suggesting that, in the face of bleakness and imminent destruction, Woolf nonetheless offers a sense of hope that, through 'collective work and continuance', a different future can always be forged.

Across the chapters collected in this volume, we find in Woolf a writer who both anticipates and speaks to the Anthropocene. We also find in Woolf an imagination restlessly questioning what it means to be human on a planet of finite resources upon which so many depend. Her rejection of what she dubbed in one essay an 'inveterately anthropocentric' (*E6* 446) outlook that can all too easily reduce the earth to inanimate matter blithely at the service of human ends speaks powerfully to the richness of her oeuvre in helping us understand where we are, how we got here and where the future might take us.[69]

Notes

1. Thompson, 'Reading', 144, 153. Woolf is one of the writers whom Thompson discusses in her chapter.
2. Woolf's language here foreshadows the exhortation at the conclusion of *A Room of One's Own* (1929) to 'see human beings not always in their relation to each other but in relation to reality; and the sky, too, and the trees or whatever it may be in themselves' (*AROO* 86), a passage which Davi Pinho and Maria A. de Oliveira discuss in their chapter in this volume.
3. Adkins, *Modernist Anthropocene*, 1–30.
4. John McNeill quoted in Chakrabarty, *Climate of History*, 4.
5. The 'environmental' turn within modernist studies has revealed a literary history rich with texts that speak to transformations in the environment at local, regional, national and planetary levels, and in which their literary innovations retain the potential to intervene in ongoing debates in current environmental crises. See Elizabeth Black's *The Nature of Modernism* (2017), Jeremy Diaper's *T. S. Eliot and Organicism* (2018), Matthew Griffith's *The New Poetics of Climate Change* (2017), Jon Hegglund and John McIntyre's *Modernism and the Anthropocene* (2021), Ted Howell's 'Modernism, Ecology and the Anthropocene' (2017), Andrew Kalaidjian's *Exhausted Ecologies* (2020), Jeffrey Mathes McCarthy's *Green Modernism* (2015), Michael Rubenstein and Justin Neuman's *Modernism and Its Environments* (2020), Joshua Schuster's *The Ecology of Modernism* (2015) and Kelly Sultzbach's *Ecocriticism in the Modernist Imagination* (2016).
6. Adkins, *Modernist Anthropocene*, 20. The question of exactly when the Anthropocene can be said to have begun continues to be generative in the critical and innovative responses it provokes. I offer an overview of various historical arguments about the Anthropocene in relation to modernism and modernity in *The Modernist Anthropocene* (5–10).
7. Rubenstein and Neuman, *Modernism and Its Environments*, 6. For a survey of various modernist writers' attitudes towards the natural world, see Bonnie Kime Scott, *Hollow Wave*, 13–41.
8. See, for example, Greg Garrard's essay 'Worlds without Us', Kelly Sultzbach's reading of *To the Lighthouse* in *Ecocriticism in the Modernist Imagination* (119–45) and the discussion of the novel in my essay, 'Bloomsbury and Nature'.
9. Paul K. Saint-Amour describes the inter-war period as pervaded by a sense of impending catastrophe, or 'pre-traumatic stress' (*Total War*, 7–8). As I have argued, the sense of imminent extinction became especially heightened in Woolf's late writings (*Modernist Anthropocene*, 170–96).
10. Parallels might be drawn here with the nearly imperceptible ghostly couple in 'A Haunted House' (1921) or Jacob's shoes at the end of *Jacob's Room* (1922).

11. The First World War represented an extraordinary threshold moment in the Anthropocene, both in its impact on environmental systems and its making visible of the extent to which humans could destroy entire landscapes. For more on this subject, see Molly Volanth Hall's 'Ecologies of Materiality and Aesthetics in British Modernist War-Time Literature, 1890–1939' (2020) and her chapter in this volume.
12. Ryan, *Virginia Woolf*, 77.
13. Woolf, *To the Lighthouse: The Original Holograph Draft*, 51.
14. Haraway, *Manifestly Haraway*, 104.
15. Briggs, *Reading*, 149. Brigg's assertion here somewhat overlooks the popularity of pastoral poetry in the years after the war.
16. Latour, 'Agency', 9. For Latour on hybridisation and modernity, see *We Have Never Been Modern* (1991).
17. Ibid., 5, emphasis in original.
18. In the holograph draft of the novel, Woolf describes the ship as an 'ugly snout', further blurring the distinction between the human and the non-human. Woolf, *To the Lighthouse: The Original Holograph Draft*, 222.
19. Brush, 'Inhuman', 73. For Brush, the third section of the novel, 'The Lighthouse', offers hope that 'better, more equitable' futures can follow catastrophes (82). Stefanie Heine, who also reads 'Time Passes' in the context of the Anthropocene, sees the text as resisting the apocalypticism that I have argued is the tonal keynote here. See Heine, 'Forces of Unworking'.
20. Latour, 'Agency', 9. Latour's example is Leo Tolstoy, a writer whom Woolf also greatly admired.
21. Menely and Taylor, 'Introduction', 2.
22. Ibid., 5.
23. Ibid., 12.
24. Feder, 'Introduction', 3.
25. Ibid., 5.
26. Brush, 'Inhuman', 70; Taylor, *Sky*, 188–211; McCracken, 'Virginia Woolf'; Shackleton, *British Modernism*.
27. Adkins, *Modernist Anthropocene*, 15.
28. See Daugherty, 'Readin', Writin', and Revisin'', Flint, 'Reading Uncommonly' and Wallace, 'Woolf and Criticism'.
29. For a more even-handed assessment of Brontë as a writer of the Anthropocene, see Shawna Ross's *Charlotte Brontë at the Anthropocene* (2020).
30. Ghosh, *Great Derangement*, 17. Ghosh's broad brushstroke argument reiterates the well-worn (and disputed) assertion that the novel's ascendency in the eighteenth century reflected the Enlightenment's privileging of empiricism and rationality. Ghosh approaches literary history, like Woolf, not as a professional or academic critic, but as a writer and reader of novels. At the same time he is, as Kelly Sultzbach points out in her chapter in this volume, too quick to dismiss how modernism might help us understand the Anthropocene.

31. Ibid., 26.
32. As Woolf points out at the start of the essay, in a remark that feels particularly apt in the Anthropocene, one cannot approach the writing of literature in the same way that one approaches the 'making [of] motor cars' (*E4* 157). Notably, this had been changed from the less environmentally polluting 'bicycles' in the original version of the essay in 1919 (*E3* 31).
33. Woolf's gendered language stands out here and she would soon explicitly question masculinist conventions of grammar in *A Room of One's Own*. Like the term the Anthropocene, which as Davi Pinho and Maria de Oliveira point out in their chapter in this volume, is rooted in a gendered epistemology which conflates humankind with male humans, Woolf's language brings to the surface the way in which terms like 'nature' and 'man', although seemingly *natural*, are in fact culturally constructed.
34. 'waste, n'.. *OED* Online.
35. Eliot's *The Waste Land* is increasingly being seen as offering a compelling critique of early twentieth-century environmental harms. See Matthew Griffith's *The New Poetics of Climate Change* in particular. As I argue in *The Modernist Anthropocene*, Woolf may well have had Eliot's poem in mind while penning her own critique of urban wastelands in 'The Docks of London' (1931). See Adkins, *Modernist Anthropocene*, 9.
36. See Daugherty's 'Virginia Woolf's "How Should One Read a Book?"' for a chronology of the essay's composition.
37. Woolf, *To the Lighthouse: The Original Holograph Draft*, 51.
38. Attridge, *Singularity*, 3.
39. Menely and Taylor, 'Introduction', 14, emphasis in original.
40. Ghosh, *Great Derangement*, 11.
41. Cantrell, 'Locus', 26.
42. Ibid., 35.
43. Ibid., 25.
44. Rubenstein and Neuman, *Modernism and Its Environments*, 11. The first wave of ecocriticism tended to privilege what might be broadly called 'nature writing' and literature focused on the rural rather than the urban. For a critical account of early ecocriticism and its development as a field, see Dana Phillips's *The Truth of Ecology* (2003) and Lawrence Buell's *The Future of Environmental Criticism* (2005).
45. One could go even further back in Woolf criticism to works such as Josephine O'Brien Schaefer's *The Three-Fold Nature of Reality in the Novels of Virginia Woolf* (1965). The 1980s, however, constitute a distinct and influential turn in Woolf studies to questions around the intersection of knowledge, experience and material reality that continue to inflect ecocritical studies being written today.
46. Zwerdling, *Virginia Woolf*, 3.
47. Ibid., 5.

48. Hussey, *Singing*, xiii.
49. These essays were collected in her 1996 book, *Virginia Woolf: The Common Ground*.
50. Snaith and Whitworth, 'Introduction', 2.
51. Westling, 'Virginia Woolf', 872. Merleau-Ponty's phenomenology has proven generative in ecocritical approaches to Woolf, see, for instance, Shelley Saguaro's 'The Inseminating World in the Last Writings of Virginia Woolf' and Kelly Sultzbach's *Ecocriticism in the Modernist Imagination*.
52. Webb, 'Nature and Culture'; Taylor, *Sky*, 201. Other early ecocritical accounts of Woolf include L. Elizabeth Waller's 'Writing the Real: Virginia Woolf and an Ecology of Language' and Charlotte Zoë Walker's 'Letting in the Sky: An Ecofeminist Reading of Virginia Woolf's Short Fiction'.
53. The 20th Annual International Virginia Woolf Conference was organised by Kristin Czarnecki and held at Georgetown College in the USA in June 2010. Czarnecki and Carrie Rohman's co-edited volume of selected papers from the 2010 conference give a sense of the breadth of approaches to Woolf and nature at the conference.
54. Alt, *Virginia Woolf*, 13; Scott, *Hollow Wave*, 220.
55. Alt, *Virginia Woolf*, 9–10. As Alt outlines in her study, early ecology had 'as one of its main objectives the control of the natural environment for human benefit' (66).
56. Swanson, 'Eco-Woolf', 1. In her earlier essay, 'Woolf's Copernican Shift', Swanson argued that Woolf's experimental short stories, penned between 1917 and 1921, were pivotal in her development of a modernist approach to the 'subjectivities of nonhuman beings' (54).
57. Jakubowicz, 'Nature of Post-Impressionism'; McGiff, 'Virginia Woolf and the Changing Shapes of Pastoral'. Sparks's online 'Virginia Woolf Herbarium' is an ongoing project to catalogue and examine Woolf's various references to flowers. On this topic, see also Greulich, 'Garden Work'.
58. Dirschauer, *Modernist Waterscapes*; Rizzuto, 'Maritime Modernism'; Winkiel, 'Queer Ecology'. Steve Mentz's 'After Sustainability' offers a good introduction to the importance of the blue, as well as the green, in ecocriticism.
59. McCracken and Goody, 'Introduction', 5.
60. See Dubino's 'The Bispecies Environment'; Goldman, 'Ce chien'; Rohman, 'Floating Monkeys'; Ryan, *Virginia Woolf*.
61. Borg, *Fantasies of Self-Mourning*; Jaffe, 'Inhuman Woolf'; Ryan, *Virginia Woolf*; Sultzbach, *Modernist Ecocriticism*.
62. Zwerdling, *Virginia Woolf*, 28.
63. Feder, *Ecocriticism*, 95. On *Orlando*'s satire as central to its ecological aesthetic, see Adkins, *Modernist Anthropocene*, 145–69. For the importance of comedy to Woolf's ecological aesthetics more generally, see Rasheed Tazudeen's chapter in this volume.

64. Ryan, 'Was it Flush?', 265–6.
65. Jaffe, 'Inhuman Woolf', 499. For a particularly compelling reading of 'Modern Fiction' as presenting an 'atmospheric materiality and embodiment', see Pizzo, 'Ethereal Women'.
66. See, in particular, Leanna Lostoski-Ho's 'Against Time and Sea', Scott's *In The Hollow of the Wave*, Sultzbach's *Ecocriticism in the Modernist Imagination* and Winkiel's 'A Queer Ecology of the Sea'.
67. Haraway, *Staying with the Trouble*, 130. See also Rosi Braidotti's *Posthuman Feminism* (2021) and her essay 'Virginia Woolf, Immanence and Ontological Pacifism'.
68. Friedman, 'Scaling', 119; Saint-Amour, 'Deep Time's'.
69. From the posthumously published 'Flying over London'.

Bibliography

Adkins, Peter. 'Bloomsbury and Nature'. In *The Handbook to the Bloomsbury Group*, edited by Derek Ryan and Stephen Ross, 225–38. London: Bloomsbury, 2018.
———. 'The Climate of *Orlando*: Woolf, Braidotti and the Anthropocene'. *Comparative Critical Studies* 19, no. 2 (2022): 237–57.
———. *The Modernist Anthropocene: Nonhuman Life and Planetary Change in James Joyce, Virginia Woolf and Djuna Barnes*. Edinburgh: Edinburgh University Press, 2022.
Alt, Christina. *Virginia Woolf and the Study of Nature*. Cambridge: Cambridge University Press, 2010.
Attridge, Derek. *The Singularity of Literature*. London and New York: Routledge, 2004.
Beer, Gillian. *Virginia Woolf: The Common Ground*. Ann Arbor: University of Michigan Press, 1996.
Black, Elizabeth. *The Nature of Modernism: Ecocritical Approaches to the Poetry of Edward Thomas, T. S. Eliot, Edith Sitwell and Charlotte Mew*. London: Routledge, 2017.
Borg, Ruben. *Fantasies of Self-Mourning: Modernism, the Posthuman and the Finite*. Amsterdam: Brill Rodopi, 2019.
Braidotti, Rosi. *Posthuman Feminism*. Cambridge: Polity Press, 2021.
———. 'Virginia Woolf, Immanence and Ontological Pacifism'. *Comparative Critical Studies* 19, no. 2 (June 2022): 131–48.
Briggs, Julia. *Reading Virginia Woolf*. Edinburgh: Edinburgh University Press, 2006.
Brush, Emma. 'Inhuman, All Too Human: Virginia Woolf and the Anthropocene'. *Resilience: A Journal of the Environmental Humanities* 8, no. 2 (2021): 69–87.
Buell, Lawrence. *The Future of Environmental Criticism: Environmental Crisis and Literary Imagination*. Oxford: Wiley-Blackwell, 2005.

Cantrell, Carol H. '"The locus of compossibility": Virginia Woolf, Modernism, and Place'. *Interdisciplinary Studies in Literature and Environment* 5, no. 2 (1998): 25–40.
Chakrabarty, Dipesh. *The Climate of History in a Planetary Age*. Chicago & London: University of Chicago Press, 2021.
Clark, Timothy. *Ecocriticism on the Edge: The Anthropocene as a Threshold Concept*. London: Bloomsbury, 2015.
Czarnecki, Kristin and Carrie Rohman, eds. *Virginia Woolf and the Natural World: Selected Papers from the Twentieth Annual International Conference on Virginia Woolf*. Clemson: Clemson University Press, 2011.
Daugherty, Beth Rigel. '"Readin', writin', and revisin'": Virginia Woolf's "How Should One Read a Book?"' In *Virginia Woolf and the Essay*, edited by Jeanne Dubino and Beth Carole Rosenberg, 155–79. New York: St Martin's, 1997.
——. 'Virginia Woolf's "How Should One Read a Book?"' *Woolf Studies Annual* 4 (1998): 123–85.
Diaper, Jeremy. *T. S. Eliot and Organicism*. Clemson, SC: Clemson University Press, 2018.
Dirschauer, Marlene. *Modernist Waterscapes: Water, Imagination and Materiality in the Works of Virginia Woolf*. Cham, Switzerland: Palgrave Macmillan, 2023.
Dubino, Jeanne. 'The Bispecies Environment, Coevolution and *Flush*'. In *Virginia Woolf: Twenty-First-Century Approaches*, edited by Jeanne Dubino, Gill Lowe, Vara Neverow and Kathryn Simpson, 131–47. Edinburgh: Edinburgh University Press, 2015.
Feder, Helena. *Ecocriticism and the Idea of Culture: Biology and the Bildungsroman*. Farnham: Ashgate Publishing, 2014.
——. 'Introduction: The Unbearable Closeness of Reading'. In *Close Reading the Anthropocene*, edited by Helena Feder, 1–14. Abingdon: Routledge, 2021.
Ford, Thomas H. '*Orlando*'s Romantic Climate Change'. In *Romantic Climates: Literature and Science in an Age of Catastrophe*, 173–90. Cham, Switzerland: Palgrave Macmillan, 2019.
Flint, Kate. 'Reading Uncommonly: Virginia Woolf and the Practice of Reading'. *The Yearbook of English Studies* 26 (1996): 187–98.
Friedman, Susan Stanford. *Mappings: Feminism and the Cultural Geographies of Encounter*. Princeton, NJ: Princeton University Press, 1998.
——. *Planetary Modernisms: Provocations on Modernity across Time*. New York: Columbia University Press, 2015.
——. 'Scaling Planetarity: Spacetime in the New Modernist Studies – Virginia Woolf, H. D., Hilma Af Klint, Alicja Kwade, Kathy Jetn̄il-Kijiner'. *Feminist Modernist Studies* 3, no. 2 (2020): 118–47.
Garrard, Greg. 'Worlds without Us: Some Types of Disanthropy'. *SubStance* 41, no. 1 (2012): 40–60.
Ghosh, Amitav. *The Great Derangement: Climate Change and the Unthinkable*. Chicago: University of Chicago Press, 2017.

Goldman, Jane. '"Ce chien est à moi": Virginia Woolf and the Signifying Dog'. *Woolf Studies Annual* 13 (2007): 49–86.
Greulich, Katie. 'Garden Work: Prosaic Alightments in Modern Ecology and "Kew Gardens"'. *Modernism/Modernity* 28, no. 2 (2021): 333–53.
Griffiths, Matthew. *The New Poetics of Climate Change: Modernist Aesthetics for a Warming World*. London: Bloomsbury, 2017.
Hall, Molly Volanth. 'Ecologies of Materiality and Aesthetics in British Modernist War-Time Literature, 1890–1939'. Dissertation, University of Rhode Island, 2020.
Haraway, Donna. *Manifestly Haraway*. Minneapolis: University of Minnesota Press, 2016.
———. *Staying with the Trouble: Making Kin in the Chthulucene*. Durham, NC: Duke University Press, 2016.
Hegglund, Jon, and John D. McIntyre, eds. *Modernism and the Anthropocene: Material Ecologies of Twentieth-Century Literature*. Ecocritical Theory and Practice. Lanham, MD: Lexington Books, 2021.
Heine, Stefanie. 'Forces of Unworking in Virginia Woolf's "Time Passes"'. *Textual Cultures* 12, no. 1 (2019): 120–36.
Howell, Edward. 'Modernism, Ecology, and the Anthropocene'. Dissertation, Temple University, 2017.
Hussey, Mark. *Singing of the Real World: The Philosophy of Virginia Woolf's Fiction*. Columbus: Ohio State University Press, 1986.
Jaffe, Aaron. 'Introduction: Who's Afraid of the Inhuman Woolf?' *Modernism/Modernity* 23, no. 3 (2016): 491–513.
Jakubowicz, Karina. '"A rose had flowered": Virginia Woolf and the Nature of Post-Impressionism'. In *Eco-Modernism: Ecology, Environment and Nature in Literary Modernism*, 153–68. Clemson, SC: Clemson University Press, 2022.
Kalaidjian, Andrew. *Exhausted Ecologies: Modernism and Environmental Recovery*. Cambridge: Cambridge University Press, 2020.
Latour, Bruno. 'Agency at the Time of the Anthropocene'. *New Literary History* 45, no. 1 (2014): 1–18.
———. *We Have Never Been Modern*, translated by Catherine Porter. Cambridge: Harvard University Press, 1993.
Lostoski-Ho, Leanna. '"Against time and sea": The Deep Temporality of the Interludes in The Waves'. *Woolf Studies Annual* 28 (2022): 47–68.
McCarthy, Jeffrey Mathes. *Green Modernism: Nature and the English Novel, 1900 to 1930*. Basingstoke and New York: Palgrave Macmillan, 2015.
McCracken, Saskia. 'Virginia Woolf Writes Empire and Extinction'. *Modernism/Modernity Print Plus* 7, no. 2 (2022). https://doi.org/10.26597/mod.0239.
———, and Alex Goody. 'Introduction: Beastly Modernisms'. In *Beastly Modernisms: The Figure of the Animal in Modernist Literature and Culture*, edited by Saskia McCracken and Alex Goody, 1–20. Edinburgh: Edinburgh University Press, 2023.

McGiff, Shilo. '"Out of the heart of spring": Virginia Woolf and the Changing Shapes of Pastoral 1928–1938'. Dissertation, Cornell University, 2018.

Menely, Tobias, and Jesse Oak Taylor. 'Introduction'. In *Anthropocene Reading: Literary History in Geologic Times*, edited by Tobias Menely and Jesse Oak Taylor, 1–24. University Park: Pennsylvania State University Press, 2017.

Mentz, Steve. 'After Sustainability'. *PMLA* 127, no. 3 (2012): 586–92.

Phillips, Dana. *The Truth of Ecology: Nature, Culture, Literature in America*. Oxford: Oxford University Press, 2003.

Pizzo, Justine. 'Ethereal Women: Climate and Gender from Realism to the Modernist Novel'. In *Climate and Literature*, edited by Adeline Johns-Putra, 179–95. Cambridge: Cambridge University Press, 2019.

Rizzuto, Nicole. 'Maritime Modernism: The Aqueous Form of Virginia Woolf's *The Waves*'. *Modernist Cultures* 11, no. 2 (2016): 268–92.

Rohman, Carrie. 'A Hoard of Floating Monkeys: Creativity and Inhuman Becomings in Woolf's Nurse Lugton Story'. *Deleuze Studies* 7, no. 4 (2013): 515–36.

Ross, Shawna. *Charlotte Brontë at the Anthropocene*. Studies in the Long Nineteenth Century. Albany: State University of New York Press, 2020.

Rubenstein, Michael, and Justin Neuman. *Modernism and Its Environments*. London: Bloomsbury, 2020.

Ryan, Derek. '"Was it Flush, or was it Pan?": Virginia Woolf, Ethel Smyth, and Canine Biography'. In *Reading Literary Animals: Medieval to Modern*, edited by Karen L. Edwards, Derek Ryan and Jane Spencer, 264–81. Abingdon: Routledge, 2020.

——. *Virginia Woolf and the Materiality of Theory: Sex, Animal, Life*. Edinburgh: Edinburgh University Press, 2013.

Saguaro, Shelley. '"Something that would stand for the conception": The Inseminating World in the Last Writings of Virginia Woolf'. *Green Letters* 17, no. 2 (2013): 109–20.

Saint-Amour, Paul K. 'Deep Time's Hauntings: Modernism and Alternative Chronology'. In *The New Modernist Studies*, edited by Douglas Mao, 297–313. Cambridge University Press, 2021.

——. *Tense Future: Modernism, Total War, Encyclopedic Form*. Oxford: Oxford University Press, 2015.

Schaefer, Josephine O'Brien. *The Three-Fold Nature of Reality in the Novels of Virginia Woolf*. The Hague: Mouton & Co., 1965.

Schuster, Jonathan. *The Ecology of Modernism: American Environments and Avant-Garde Poetics*. Tuscaloosa: University of Alabama Press, 2015.

Scott, Bonnie Kime. *In the Hollow of the Wave: Virginia Woolf and Modernist Uses of Nature*. Charlottesville: University of Virginia Press, 2012.

Shackleton, David. *British Modernism and the Anthropocene: Experiments with Time*. Oxford: Oxford University Press, 2023.

Snaith, Anna, and Michael Whitworth. 'Introduction: Approaches to Space and Place in Woolf'. In *Locating Woolf: The Politics of Space and Place*, edited by Anna Snaith and Michael Whitworth, 1–31. Basingstoke: Palgrave Macmillan, 2007.

Sparks, Elisa Kay. 'A Virginia Woolf Herbarium'. Accessed 15 April 2023. https://woolfherbarium.blogspot.com/

Sultzbach, Kelly. *Ecocriticism in the Modernist Imagination: Forster, Woolf, and Auden*. Cambridge: Cambridge University Press, 2016.

Swanson, Diana L. 'To the Readers: Eco-Woolf'. *Virginia Woolf Miscellany* 81 (2012): 1–2.

——. 'Woolf's Copernican Shift: Nonhuman Nature in Virginia Woolf's Short Fiction'. *Woolf Studies Annual* 18 (2012): 53–74.

Taylor, Jesse Oak. *The Sky of Our Manufacture: The London Fog in British Fiction from Dickens to Woolf*. Charlottesville: University of Virginia Press, 2016.

Thompson, Hilary. 'Reading in the Dark: The Aura of Eclipse'. In *Close Reading the Anthropocene*, edited by Helena Feder, 144–58. Abingdon: Routledge, 2021.

Walker, Charlotte Zoë. 'Letting in the Sky: An Ecofeminist Reading of Virginia Woolf's Short Fiction'. In *The Environmental Tradition in English Literature*, edited by John Parham, 172–85. Aldershot: Ashgate, 2002.

Wallace, Jeff. 'Woolf and Criticism in the Time of Post-Critique: "How Should One Read a Book?" and *The Common Reader*'. In *Virginia Woolf, Europe and Peace: Volume 2, Aesthetics and Theory*, edited by Peter Adkins and Derek Ryan, 35–50. Clemson, SC: Clemson University Press, 2020.

Waller, L. Elizabeth. 'Writing the Real: Virginia Woolf and an Ecology of Language'. In *New Essays in Ecofeminist Literary Criticism*, edited by Glynis Carr, 137–56. Lewisburg, PA: Bucknell University Press, 2000.

'waste, n'. *OED Online*. March 2023. Oxford University Press. Accessed 1 May 2023.

Webb, Caroline. '"All was dark; all was doubt; all was confusion": Nature, Culture, and Orlando's Ruskinian Storm-Cloud'. In *Virginia Woolf Out Of Bounds: Selected Papers from the Tenth Annual Conference on Virginia Woolf*, edited by Jessica Berman and Jane Goldman, 243–48. New York: Pace University Press, 2001.

Westling, Louise. 'Virginia Woolf and the Flesh of the World'. *New Literary History* 30, no. 4 (1999): 855–75.

Winkiel, Laura. 'A Queer Ecology of the Sea: Reading Virginia Woolf's *The Waves*'. *Feminist Modernist Studies* 2, no. 2 (2019): 141–63.

Woolf, Virginia. *The Diary of Virginia Woolf*, edited by Anne Olivier Bell, 5 vols. London: Penguin Books, 1979–85.

——. *The Essays of Virginia Woolf*, edited by Andrew McNeillie (vols 1–4) and Stuart N. Clarke (vols 5–6). 6 vols. London: Hogarth Press, 1986–2011.

———. *A Room of One's Own and Three Guineas*, edited by Anna Snaith. Oxford: Oxford University Press, 2015.
———. *To the Lighthouse*, edited by David Bradshaw. Oxford: Oxford University Press, 2008.
———. *To the Lighthouse: The Original Holograph Draft*, edited by Susan Dick. London: Hogarth Press, 1983.
Zwerdling, Alex. *Virginia Woolf and the Real World*. Berkeley: University of California Press, 1986.

Part I

Imagining Climate

Chapter 1

Virginia Woolf and Anticipations of the Anthropocene

Christina Alt

An essay collection on Woolf and the Anthropocene invites questions regarding the conceptions of planetary systems and human impacts upon planetary systems that were in circulation during Woolf's lifetime, the knowledge that Woolf herself had of dominant and emergent theories, and her own assessments and deployments of these ideas in her writing. This essay explores such questions in relation to one specific facet of Anthropocene discourse, that of climatic change. In the late nineteenth and early twentieth centuries, the first iterations of the theory of planetary warming due to anthropogenic CO_2 emissions found their way into scientific and, to a more limited extent, public discourse. Although these early iterations of the theory were not wholly free of errors and could not be definitively proven by the methods available at the time, they marked the introduction of the idea of the alteration of climate on a planetary scale by human impacts upon biogeochemical systems.[1] To understand the early history of this concept, it is useful to examine not only the observations and calculations that led scientists to register the possibility of a carbon-induced rise in global temperatures but also the prevailing assumptions and preoccupations that inflected the articulation and reception of this idea.

It is a fact of no little significance to the history of the theory of global warming that the research context that produced the first recognition of the possibility of planetary warming by way of anthropogenic carbon emissions was one preoccupied with the threat of cooling. In the nineteenth century, research into past fluctuations in the earth's climate and particularly into the phenomenon of ice ages generated interest in the causes of climatic change and prompted concerns regarding the possible return of ice-age conditions. In consequence, when new research suggested that CO_2 released into the atmosphere by the burning of fossil fuels was causing a rise in temperatures, this phenomenon was welcomed by some as evidence of human agency in the face of natural climatic fluctuations. In 1901, the Swedish meteorologist Nils Ekholm celebrated 'the influence of Man on climate' as 'a remarkable circumstance that has hitherto been unexampled in the history of the earth'.[2]

No evidence has yet emerged to indicate that Virginia Woolf encountered early twentieth-century iterations of the theory of anthropogenic warming by way of carbon emissions, but her work demonstrates her awareness of past climatic fluctuations on both historical and geological timescales and offers visions of the future climate of the planet that can be set in conversation with the climatic assumptions and assertions of her scientific contemporaries. Woolf's representations of climate draw upon the same background of knowledge and speculation regarding natural climatic variations that underpinned the work of her scientific contemporaries. She muses on ice ages and contemplates the prospect of the death of the sun. Her visions of future climates reflect the prevailing assumptions of the time regarding natural climatic trends – she too anticipates cooling – but she interrogates the impulse towards human mastery that fears of vulnerability to natural forces provoked.

This chapter will first review the scientific articulations of the possibility of anthropogenic climatic change due to CO_2 emissions that appeared at intervals over the course of Woolf's life – at the turn of the century, in the early 1920s and in the late 1930s – and discuss the assumptions and attitudes that led proponents of the theory to welcome, for the most part, the prospect of warming. It will then turn to examine Woolf's own visions of past and future climates, particularly her recurrent visions of the earth in future as a cold, still, ice-sheeted planet, to consider how, working from a similar underlying conceptual frame, Woolf arrives at contrasting conclusions regarding the relationship between climate and humanity.

Turn-of-the-Century Calculations: Svante Arrhenius and Nils Ekholm

In the 1890s, prompted by what he described as 'very lively discussions on the probable causes of the Ice Age' among members of the Physical Society of Stockholm and building upon earlier work by Joseph Fourier and John Tyndall on the heat-absorbing properties of atmospheric gases, Svante Arrhenius undertook to calculate the impact that a rise or fall in the concentration of atmospheric CO_2 would have upon the surface temperature of the earth.[3] In the process of this research, his attention was also drawn to an estimate of the amount of CO_2 produced annually by the burning of pit coal, and this led him in 1896 to develop, across an academic paper and a published lecture, both an estimate of the changes in the surface temperature of the earth that would accompany any increase or decrease in atmospheric CO_2 and the argument that atmospheric CO_2 levels were likely rising at the present time due to emissions produced by the burning of fossil fuels.

Arrhenius subsequently drew together his theory of anthropogenic climatic change by way of CO_2 emissions in a work written for a general readership. In *Worlds in the Making: The Evolution of the Universe* (published in Swedish in 1906 and in English translation in 1908), he traces the link between atmospheric CO_2 levels and the temperature of the earth's surface, explaining:

> [C]omparatively unimportant variations in the composition of the air have a very great influence. If the quantity of carbonic acid in the air should sink to one-half of its present percentage, the temperature would fall by about 4° [. . .] On the other hand, any doubling of the percentage of carbon dioxide in the air would raise the temperature of the earth's surface by 4°.[4]

He then highlights the significance of anthropogenic CO_2 emissions in this context. Observing that the quantity of CO_2 naturally present in the atmosphere is very low, while the quantity of CO_2 being produced artificially each year through the combustion of coal is considerable (900 million tons of coal having been burnt in 1904) and 'rapidly increasing', he declares, 'we [. . .] recognise that the slight percentage of carbonic acid in the atmosphere may by the advances of industry be changed to a noticeable degree in the course of a few centuries'.[5]

Thus far, Arrhenius's statements are striking in their familiarity, in the evidence that they offer of an awareness already at the turn of the last century of the possibility of global warming as an unintended by-product of fossil fuel emissions. However, Arrhenius's interpretation of the significance of this possibility is striking in another sense, for he embraces the prospect of warming enthusiastically and predicts:

> By the influence of the increasing percentage of carbonic acid in the atmosphere, we may hope to enjoy ages with more equable and better

climates, especially as regards the colder regions of the earth, ages when the earth will bring forth more abundant crops than at present, for the benefit of rapidly propagating mankind.[6]

Arrhenius views anthropogenically induced warming as a fortuitous by-product of industrial and technological development.

To understand this response to the prospect of anthropogenic warming, it is useful to consider the assumptions that underpinned his field of study. In his 1896 article he commented that he would 'certainly not have undertaken these tedious calculations' were it not for the 'extraordinary interest' surrounding the question of 'the probable causes of the Ice Age'.[7] The study of ice ages having begun in regions that had been under ice during the most recent period of glaciation, researchers in these locales were predisposed to regard renewed cooling as an existential threat and to welcome its opposite uncritically. The choice of terminology within the discipline registers and perpetuates this bias: climatic change was discussed in terms of the fluctuation between 'genial and glacial periods', a binary that distinctly privileges warming.[8] Further illustrating the distinctive perspectival slant that characterises climatic research in this period is Arrhenius's view of what might be termed the proper place of carbon. He depicts the atmosphere of the present age as carbon-depleted, writing that '[a] great portion of the carbonic acid has disappeared from the atmosphere of the earth' through its capture and storage in the form of 'coal, lignite, peat, petroleum, or asphalt'.[9] Regarding the present atmosphere as carbon-deficient, he argues that through the burning of fossil fuels, the store of carbon locked in the earth 'is returned to its original place in the household of nature'.[10] The language of return suggests a positive act of restoration, and this perspective shapes Arrhenius's understanding of a possible rise in CO_2 levels. Alongside a rise in temperature, he welcomes the prospect of an increase in 'the intensity of vegetable life', anticipating a renewal of the 'enormous plant growth' that characterised the earlier Carboniferous Period.[11]

The revelation of anthropogenic warming constituted, for Arrhenius, an unlooked-for solution to the anticipated threat of renewed glaciation, but while reference to the assumptions of his time, place and discipline helps to explain his outlook, his perspective also warrants criticism for its temporal short-sightedness and geographical narrowness. Arrhenius registers the rapid rate of increase in the combustion of coal – from 510 million tons in 1890 to 890 million tons in 1904 – and he reasons in response:

the percentage of carbonic acid in the air must be increasing at a constant rate as long as the consumption of coal, petroleum, etc., is maintained at its present figure, and at a still more rapid rate if this consumption should continue to increase as it does now.[12]

Yet despite his recognition of not only the present volume of emissions but also their rapid rate of increase, he does not consider the possibility that the speed of the resulting temperature increase could have a disruptive or detrimental impact. Additionally, despite his recognition of anthropogenic climatic change as a phenomenon that would raise the temperature of the earth as a whole, the narrative of climatic change that he advances is distinctly limited in the geographical scope of its concern. Observing that '[t]his age [. . .] was preceded by an age which, we are pretty certain, drove the inhabitants of northern Europe from their old abodes', he raises the question of whether similar cold periods are inevitable in the future.[13] Asking 'Is it probable that we shall in the coming geological ages be visited by a new ice period that will drive us from our temperate countries into the hotter climates of Africa?', he settles his own concern with the decisive response, 'There does not appear to be much ground for such apprehension. The enormous combustion of coal by our industrial establishments suffices to increase the percentage of carbon dioxide to a perceptible degree'.[14] It is notable that Africa – and the world beyond temperate Europe more generally – enters Arrhenius's thoughts only as a possible place of retreat for northern Europeans in the event of renewed glaciation. One might assume from Arrhenius's reference that Africa was an empty continent, for he makes no mention of the implications of a change in global temperatures for either the present inhabitants of Africa or the continent's flora, fauna and environmental systems. This narrowness of view illustrates the same 'selective perspectivism' that Kathryn Yusoff traces across the history of geology, demonstrating that regional and racial bias can affect foundational assumptions, guiding questions and resultant interpretations within the physical sciences.[15]

Cooling resulting from the depletion of atmospheric CO_2 levels was not the only scenario that concerned turn-of-the-century climatologists. There were also fears of planetary cooling resulting from changes in astronomical conditions. Writing in the *Quarterly Journal of the Royal Meteorological Society* in 1901, Arrhenius's colleague Nils Ekholm suggested that in addition to climatic changes to be expected from long-term variations in atmospheric CO_2, the planet was already in a phase of cooling – or 'deterioration' as he phrased it – as a result of natural change in the axial tilt of the earth.¹⁶ Working from this premise, Ekholm sought means of actively counteracting natural trends of planetary cooling, and he therefore welcomed Arrhenius's assertion that anthropogenic CO_2 emissions would result in a rise in global temperatures. Ekholm took the notion of anthropogenic climatic change even further than Arrhenius, looking beyond CO_2 emissions occurring as unintended by-products of the burning of fossil fuels to envision the deliberate increase in CO_2 emissions by means such as 'digging deep fountains pouring out carbonic acid' or impeding processes such as chemical weathering that withdrew CO_2 from the atmosphere.¹⁷

Ekholm's initial motivation for proposing directed intervention in biogeochemical cycles was a desire to offset anticipated climatic 'deterioration'. His imagined programme of climate engineering was guided by an interest in maintaining existing climatic conditions rather than with initiating change. Nevertheless, the notion that human beings now had the capacity to alter the global climate also led him to more ambitious musings. Looking ahead to a time when 'Man will be able efficaciously to regulate the future climate of the earth', he comments:

> It is too early to judge of how far Man might be capable of thus regulating the future climate. But already the view of such a possibility seems to me so grand that I cannot help thinking that it will afford to Mankind hitherto unforeseen means of evolution.¹⁸

This turn from the contemplation of means to maintain existing conditions to a vision of engineering improved climatic circumstances illustrates the extent to which an attitude of technological triumphalism underpinned thinking about climatic change at the beginning of the twentieth century.

Interwar Iterations: R. L. Sherlock and G. S. Callendar

Reference to the wider discourse of climatic change in this period is useful to understanding contemporary responses to the theory of anthropogenic climatic change. In 1914, W. B. Wright summarised the theories then in circulation to explain the onset of the last ice age. He discussed Arrhenius's CO_2 theory alongside theories focused on variations in the internal heat of the earth, in the intensity of solar radiation, in the distribution and elevation of land, and in the earth's rotation and orbit. Wright comments that Arrhenius's theory 'now has considerable vogue', but he also records criticisms of Arrhenius's analysis and expresses his own doubts regarding any theory that posited atmospheric changes as the primary cause of glacial periods.[19] Wright's survey is valuable as well for its assessment of the contemporary state of research into the causes of climatic change. Wright notes the existence of 'the utmost diversity of opinion' regarding the causes of ice ages and remarks that, in light of this lack of consensus, 'most glacialists at present reserve their judgement and are content to await further developments in our knowledge'.[20] Confident assertions regarding the mechanisms and consequences of climatic change emerged out of a welter of competing theories that could be neither proven nor disproven conclusively through reference to the data and methods then available.

Amid the general uncertainty that characterised the field of climate science in this period and the specific doubts articulated regarding Arrhenius's theory, the atmospheric CO_2 theory persisted throughout the interwar period as one possible explanation of the mechanisms of climatic change, and even the theory of climatic change resulting from anthropogenic CO_2 emissions remained in limited circulation. One key rearticulation of Arrhenius's theory came in R. L. Sherlock's *Man as a Geological Agent: An Account of His Action on Inanimate Nature* (1922), which refers to Arrhenius's work and revives the question of the 'probable effect on climate when the carbon of coal and petroleum is restored to the atmosphere as carbon dioxide by combustion'.[21] The overarching objective of Sherlock's study was to quantify and assess the geological impacts of human activities and to compare these impacts to the effects of other, recognised agents of geological change. Calculating, for example, the amount of material excavated in Great Britain since 1500 from mines and quarries and through excavations for railways, canals, roads, harbours and buildings, he estimates a total of 30,359,708,855m^3 of excavated material. Comparing human impacts with those of other geomorphic forces of denudation, Sherlock asserts that 'in a densely developed country like England, Man is many times more powerful, as an agent of denudation, than all the atmospheric denuding forces combined'.[22]

Turning his attention to the impact of the burning of fossil fuels, Sherlock offers an estimate of the global annual consumption of coal as well as both the annual and total combustion of petroleum since the first oil wells were sunk in the mid-nineteenth century. From this, he calculates that at the present time the combustion of coal and oil adds 'some 840 million tons of carbon to the air annually' and projects that, were consumption to continue at these rates, the carbon dioxide in the air would be doubled in about 700 years and trebled in about 1,400 years, 'bringing about the warm climate foretold by Arrhenius'.[23] Sherlock's interpretation of these findings differs in some respects from the responses to the prospect of anthropogenic warming articulated by Arrhenius and Ekholm. Most significantly, he argues that a rise in atmospheric CO_2 levels is 'likely to be in some degree inimical to the higher animals', although his concerns focus on the negative effects of a change in the composition of the atmosphere for air-breathing animals rather than on the repercussions of a rise in global temperatures.[24] Sherlock also diverges from Arrhenius and Ekholm in the sense that, while he entertains the possibility of climatic change due to anthropogenic CO_2 emissions, he remains noncommittal about the veracity of the theory, describing it as 'at present [. . .] in the speculative stage'.[25] Sherlock's hesitancy resulted in part from the impossibility of proving any theory of climatic change by the methods and data then available and in part from the unfashionability of Arrhenius's CO_2 theory by the 1920s, but it also arose in part from a tension between Sherlock's accumulated data and the wider conception he held of man as a geological agent.

On the basis of his gathered data, Sherlock finds that '[i]n spite of variations in the mode of attack, it seems that the rate of human denudation, as a whole, has been increasing rapidly until the present time'.[26] However, having arrived at this finding, he immediately poses the question of whether this rate of denudation will 'continue to increase, or even be maintained at its present level in the future', and he answers his own question firmly in the negative, declaring that 'on the whole, the prospect is that the present tendency of human interference to hasten denudation may shortly be replaced by an opposite tendency'.[27] Specifically, he predicts a shift from reliance upon coal to the utilisation of water power as a pragmatic response to the increasing scarcity and rising cost of coal. Petroleum, which he had previously discussed as an emerging energy source, does not figure in his predictions regarding future energy usage. The shift in energy regimes that Sherlock anticipates offers another partial explanation for his downplaying of the potential danger of rising atmospheric CO_2 levels: the implications of the CO_2 theory of climatic change become less concerning if one supposes an imminent turn away from reliance upon fossil fuels.

Sherlock's anticipation of an imminent reversal in the tendency of human geological impacts is based on his conviction that human activities, unlike other natural forces acting upon geology, are changeable because they are directed by human thinking, which is itself subject to change. Sherlock's recognition of 'the relation between Man's psychology and his geological activities' is astute, but his application of this principle suggests a susceptibility to oversimplified narratives of progress.[28] One illustration of this susceptibility occurs in his discussion of the history of the pollution of British rivers by chemical waste and sewage. He relates:

> The rivers became highly polluted between 1830 and 1840 and Parliament came to the rescue and suppressed much of the pollution about 1880. Hence the period of extreme pollution was probably limited to about thirty or forty years. After that time means were found to purify the streams and in many cases uses were found for the waste products.[29]

This is a triumphal and inadequate account of the history of water pollution in Britain. In the same manner, Sherlock's optimism leads him to dismiss his own painstakingly accumulated evidence of rising rates of denudation brought about by human activity in favour of predictions of an imminent shift from destructive to 'protective and renovative forces'.[30] These predictions rest on insubstantial foundations: as proof of an approaching shift from coal to water power, he offers reports of a 'scheme for damming the Severn' that was never carried out.[31] Even more fantastically, while discussing the recent 'marked increase in irrigation works' as an indication of an approaching shift from destruction to renovation, he offers as supporting evidence 'the state said to exist on Mars', which at the time was posited by figures such as Percival Lowell to be an inhabited planet 'covered by enormous canals from pole to equator', canals engineered by the dominant Martian species to counteract – if only temporarily – natural climatic trends on their cooling and drying planet.[32] Sherlock hastens to note that the question of whether engineered canals in fact exist on Mars is 'still under discussion', but this shift in the focus of his discussion from Earth to Mars, which occurs in the final paragraph of his conclusion, is strategic.[33] It redirects attention from the disquieting evidence that human activity – and particularly modern, technologically assisted human activity – exerts a destructive influence upon natural systems to an imagined scenario in which technological interventions prolong the habitability of a planet dying of natural causes. On the scale of geological and cosmological time, Sherlock judges the impacts of human – and Martian

– activities to be wholly insignificant, 'infinitesimal' in their effect on the solar system; nevertheless, when conceiving of human interventions on the scale of historical time, Sherlock's entrenched assumption of the ameliorative nature of technological progress leads him to dismiss his laboriously accumulated evidence of denuding impacts in favour of a narrative of protection and renovation.[34]

Sherlock's work makes for strange reading: to a twenty-first-century reader, he appears both prescient in his observations and wilfully oblivious to the implications of his findings. He combines almost excessive quantitative detail about the geological impact of human activity up to the present day with an ungrounded expectation of the imminent reversal of this impact. He recognises the advisability of a shift from non-renewable to renewable energy sources, but his assumptions regarding the speed and ease of such a shift suggest a complacent belief in the self-righting course of scientific progress. As Peter Adkins observes, Sherlock's work is groundbreaking in its recognition of the extent of human geological impacts but also 'exposes the gulf between early twentieth-century knowledge and that of the present day'.[35]

Early twentieth-century responses to Sherlock's study varied. Arthur Smith Woodward, Keeper of Geology at the British Museum, wrote a Foreword to Sherlock's work in which he singles out as a subject of special interest 'the question of whether man, by his prodigious combustion of coal and other carbonaceous substances, is producing more carbonic acid than can be eliminated by ordinary natural processes'.[36] Woodward forecasts, 'If this production is excessive, the result eventually may be an unwelcome change in [man's] atmospheric surroundings'.[37] This consideration then leads him to suggest that man 'may be approaching a stage when he should pause to consider whether his use and alteration of the crust of the earth itself are for future as well as for present advantage'.[38] Woodward's cautionary comments appear more continuous with Sherlock's material findings than Sherlock's own conclusions, and they constitute something of an outlier among early twentieth-century responses to the prospect of anthropogenic warming, but they demonstrate the possibility in this period of recognition of the implications of prevailing and intensifying trends of denudation and destruction.

Grenville A. J. Cole's review of Sherlock's monograph in *Nature*, titled 'The Earth Under the Rule of Man', opens with the declaration, 'The Human period of the Quaternary era has set in', a statement that foreshadows Paul Crutzen and Eugene Stoermer's proclamation of the Anthropocene three-quarters of a century later.[39] Unlike

Woodward, Cole expresses no disquiet at Sherlock's depiction of man's 'rule on the earth's surface', noting simply that Sherlock 'has brought together a large amount of curious information', that he displays a 'zeal for calculation', and that the main lines of Sherlock's inquiry suggest other 'attractive by-ways' along which the study of man's impact upon the earth might be developed.[40] Following its striking opening, Cole's review is perhaps most instructive to a twenty-first-century reader in the lack of surprise that it displays at Sherlock's findings, a response that suggests that the conception of human beings as agents of geological change aligned with prevailing perceptions of geology's potential to enhance human agency.

Arrhenius's CO_2 theory remained in limited circulation in the interwar period, though it was only one theory among many and not the most widely supported of these. In 1938, the concept of climatic change by way of anthropogenic CO_2 emissions was revived again, this time by G. S. Callendar, who supported his argument with fresh calculations and reference to fifty years of temperature records from around the globe. In 'The Artificial Production of Carbon Dioxide and Its Influence on Temperature', Callendar argued not only that human activities could in principle influence natural processes of heat exchange in the atmosphere and by so doing alter climate but also that 'such influence [. . .] is actually occurring at the present time'.[41] He offered calculations that suggested that the artificial production of CO_2 through fuel combustion was enough to cause an increase in mean temperature at a rate of 0.003°C per year and corroborated these calculations through reference to temperature records from 200 meteorological stations worldwide that showed that 'world temperatures have actually increased at an average rate of 0.005°C per year during the past half-century'.[42] In his interpretation of these figures, Callendar echoes Arrhenius and Ekholm before him, declaring:

> the combustion of fossil fuel, whether it be peat from the surface or oil from 10,000 feet below, is likely to prove beneficial to mankind in several ways, besides the provision of heat and power. For instance, the above mentioned small increases of mean temperature would be important at the northern margin of cultivation [. . .] In any case the return of the deadly glaciers should be delayed indefinitely.[43]

Callendar, like Arrhenius and Ekholm, interprets calculations and measurements indicating warming in relation to an assumption of prospective natural cooling, and he treats fossil fuel emissions as something to be perpetuated as a protective climatic measure.

Callendar also exhibits a familiar combination of planetary vision and temperate-zone bias. He draws on temperature records from around the globe – from Greenland and South Africa, Samoa and St Helena – to substantiate his claims, and he finds evidence of an increase in 'world temperatures'.[44] Yet for all his breadth of meteorological reference, he remains preoccupied with the imagined implications of anthropogenic warming for the northern temperate zone, eager for the expansion of the northern limits of cultivation, and gives no consideration to its impact elsewhere, on the tropical islands of Samoa and St Helena, for example.

Callendar's argument regarding the significance of anthropogenic CO_2 emissions did not meet with much enthusiasm in 1938. Respondents to his paper questioned the significance of the temperature changes that he registered and his status as an amateur meteorologist also inclined contemporary academic meteorologists against him.[45] Thus, the theory of climatic change by way of anthropogenic CO_2 emissions did not gain wide acceptance in the first half of the twentieth century. The iterations of the theory of global warming by way of anthropogenic CO_2 emissions that were advanced in the early twentieth century demonstrate that scientists of the period were more likely to welcome the prospect of anthropogenic warming than to consider its potential dangers. Sherlock is something of an outlier here, yet even he reflects the biases of his era in his compulsion to turn away from his accumulated evidence of the persistent and increasing destructive effects of human geological activities towards a narrative that presents technological interventions as environmentally protective, even if such a narrative depends on speculative tales of alien engineering. The perspectives that shaped the views of early twentieth-century proponents of the CO_2 theory of climatic change – the assumption of natural cooling; the conviction that scientific knowledge and technological agency would be found to be ultimately beneficial even if tangible evidence suggested otherwise; and the regional and racial bias of research conducted by white scientists in the northern temperate zone – powerfully conditioned the interpretations of anthropogenic impacts upon biogeochemical systems.

Visions of Mastery: E. Ray Lankester

Such assumptions also informed early twentieth-century conceptions of anthropogenic climatic change that did not rely on the mechanism of CO_2 emissions but that contemplated human-induced climatic change as one component of a wider vision of planetary control. In 1905, the British biologist E. Ray Lankester delivered the University of Oxford's prestigious Romanes Lecture. In his talk, later published under the title 'Nature's Insurgent Son', Lankester argues:

> What we call the will and volition of Man [. . .] has become a power in Nature, an *imperium in imperio*, which has profoundly modified not only man's own history but that of the whole living world and the face of the planet on which he exists.[46]

Lankester presents twentieth-century man as on the verge of the fulfilment of Francis Bacon's dream of a 'Regnum Hominis', possessing the knowledge and practical power to control nature that Bacon's age foresaw but did not possess.[47]

Lankester calls for the control of natural processes on a planetary scale, and this extends to the modification of climate. Like Arrhenius and others, he anticipates the natural cooling of the earth, although his allusion to the planet as a 'cooling cinder' suggests that his preoccupation is with unidirectional entropic cooling as distinct from the long-term climatic variations that occupied the scientists previously discussed.[48] Taking slow but inevitable natural cooling as a foundational assumption, Lankester contemplates means by which this cooling might be countered, even temporarily, through human intervention and posits that in future it will be possible to draw heat from the earth's interior as both an alternative energy source and a means of regulating the earth's climate. He asks:

> [M]ay we not indulge in the surmise that [. . .] [Man] may be able hereafter to deal with great planetary factors to his own advantage, [. . .] even so as to regulate, at some distant day, the climates of the earth's surface, and the winds and rains which seem now for ever beyond his control?[49]

Lankester, speaking in 1905, also anticipates Sherlock, writing in 1922, for he draws his inspiration for grand geo-engineering projects from the same speculative source: Percival Lowell's theory that surface features observed on Mars constituted 'enormous irrigation works' constructed by a technologically advanced species to transport water from Mars's polar snow caps, an artificial intervention in the planet's environmental systems upon which, Lankester states, 'the fertility and habitability of their planet, at the present time, depend'.[50] Lowell's narrative of planetary cooling and desiccation offset by vast engineering projects supports the view that an intelligent species could, through technological intervention, overcome planetary limitations. While Lankester claims to hold a 'most sceptical attitude' towards the specifics of Lowell's Martian speculations, he nevertheless welcomes 'the influence of these statements about Mars upon the imagination and hopes of Man' and the model that they offer for the 'vast manipulation of a planet'.[51]

Advancing a theory of anthropogenic climatic change was not the central purpose of Lankester's lecture: the possibility of controlling climate was simply one example that he proffered to illustrate a wider proposed programme of possession and control of natural forces and resources. He represents 'Man' as 'the heir to a vast and magnificent kingdom who has finally been educated so as to fit him to take possession of his property'.[52] Such blunt assertions of entitlement to possession of the earth and exploitation of its resources, which take on a distinctly imperialist cast in his insistence on the need 'to possess and administer this vast territory', make explicit the unspoken attitudes that led early twentieth-century climate scientists to welcome the notion of anthropogenic climatic change for the mastery of nature that it seemed to offer.[53]

'[A]n interesting theory about the age of man': Woolf's Contemplation of Climatic Change

The concept of a rise in temperatures due to anthropogenic CO_2 emissions surfaced in scientific discourse at intervals over the course of Woolf's life: around the turn of the century, in the early 1920s and in the late 1930s. Nevertheless, the theory that changes in atmospheric CO_2 levels, by either human or natural agency, could act as primary drivers of climatic change did not gain widespread support in this period, and evidence has yet to emerge that Woolf directly encountered any of the contemporary articulations of the theory of climatic warming by way of anthropogenic CO_2 emissions. However, she was undoubtedly alert to the idea of changes of climate on the scales of historical, geological and cosmological time, and her own reflections on climate can be placed in conversation with those of her scientific contemporaries.[54]

In *Orlando*, Woolf draws upon historical records to represent the 'suddenness and severity' (O 32) of climate during what is now designated the Little Ice Age, presents climate as changeable within historical timescales, and engages in an irreverent manner with the discourse of climatic determinism.[55] In *Mrs Dalloway* (1925) and

Between the Acts (1941), she offers visions of past geological ages in terms of a succession of habitats and characteristic fauna – swamp and grass, iguanodon and mammoth – that across time have occupied the space now taken up by Piccadilly and Regent's Park (*MD* 69; *BTA* 8).⁵⁶ A diary entry from September 1923 also captures her reflections on climatic fluctuations in the geological past. She records a conversation with John Maynard Keynes, who:

> talked about palaeolithic man & an interesting theory about the age of man – how the beginning of history about 5,000 B.C. is only the beginning of another lap in the race; others, many others, having been run previously & obliterated by ice ages. (*D2* 267)

Whether by this theory of 'the age of man' Keynes meant (or Woolf understood) the succession of different dominant classes of organisms – the age of amphibians succeeded by the age of reptiles, each brought to an end by a change in environmental conditions – or whether this suggests a theory of a succession of lost human cultures, rising and falling with changes in climatic conditions, this narrative stresses the impact of natural climatic fluctuations upon life on earth.

The past climates that Woolf imagines across both historical and geological timescales are varied; however, when Woolf offers descriptions of the climate of future ages, she articulates a more unvarying vision of a cold and barren planet. Repeatedly in her work, she imagines the earth 'entirely at rest' (*TTL* 30); a 'mere cinder of ice' beneath 'the last rays of the last sun' (*MD* 69); and a time when there will be 'nothing in the universe save stars and the light of stars' (*ND* 203). In 'On Being Ill', Woolf contemplates not only illness and individual mortality but also extinction on a wider scale, drawing attention to:

> what, after all, Nature is at no pains to conceal – that she in the end will conquer; heat will leave the world; stiff with frost we shall cease to drag ourselves about the fields; ice will lie thick upon factory and engine; the sun will go out [. . .] [leaving] the whole earth [. . .] sheeted and slippery. (*E4* 322)

Contemplation of the end of an individual life shades into contemplation of the end of modern, mechanised, industrialised society and further into contemplation of the end of all life on earth. In this vision of future climate, Woolf accords less with the still nascent theory of anthropogenic warming than with the more securely established and widely circulating narratives of geological time characterised by climatic fluctuations and of cosmological time following an entropic trajectory. Woolf's contemplation of the earth reduced in the long-distant future to a 'mere cinder of ice' aligns with Lankester's entropic description of 'the cooling cinder which we call the earth', demonstrating a shared imagistic and conceptual frame of reference grounded in nineteenth-century thermodynamic discourse (*MD* 69).[57]

Yet this is not to say that Woolf has nothing to contribute to discussions of anthropogenic global warming in the Anthropocene. After all, her visions of planetary cooling locate her within the same conceptual framework from within which Arrhenius and others sought to interpret the implications of novel anthropogenic warming. The common reference point of entropic cooling that Woolf shares with Lankester in particular makes it possible to set her perspective on nature and humanity in conversation with the triumphalist narrative of human possession and control of nature articulated in his conception of 'Nature's Insurgent Son'. Lankester's ambitions for planetary control can be read as an extreme form of the view that Woolf in 'On Being Ill' attributes to 'the army of the upright [that] marches to battle', a group towards whom she expresses ambivalent feelings (*E4* 322). '[W]ith the heroism of the ant or the bee', she records, 'Mrs. Jones catches her train. Mr. Smith mends his motor. The cows are driven home to be milked. Men thatch the roof. The dogs bark. The rooks, rising in a net, fall in a net upon the elm trees'; human and non-human alike are manifestations of 'the wave of life [that] flings itself out indefatigably' (*E4* 322). Yet, in humans, the indefatigable impulse of life manifests not simply as motion but as machine-assisted, coal- and oil-fuelled transportation, and even the bucolic activity of driving cows home to be milked involves the treatment of non-human animals as property and an exploitable material resource.

From her position as a recumbent 'sky-gazer', a deserter from the army of the upright, Woolf satirises the instrumentalist view of nature propounded by figures such as Lankester (*E4* 321). Observing the movement of clouds across the sky, she first articulates an impulse reminiscent of Lankester to harness natural forces for human ends. She comments:

> this interminable experiment [. . .] this endless activity, with the waste of Heaven knows how many million horse power of energy, has been left to work its will year in year out. The fact seems to call for comment and indeed for censure. Some one should write to *The Times* about it. Use should be made of it. (*E4* 321)

Quantifying the wind-driven motion of clouds in terms of the unit of measurement adopted by James Watt to describe the rate of work of steam engines situates this perspective firmly within the age of industrialism and the engine, whether coal- or oil-fuelled. However, Woolf counters this view with an alternative perspective. '[W]atch a little longer', she suggests:

> and another emotion drowns the stirrings of civic ardour. Divinely beautiful it is also divinely heartless. Immeasurable resources are used for some purpose which has nothing to do with human pleasure or human profit. If we were all laid prone, frozen, stiff, still the sky would be experimenting with its blues and golds. (*E4* 321)

Against the view of nature as human property existing for use and profit, Woolf offers a view that drastically decentres the human and satirises schemes of control and exploitation.

Yet, while Woolf contemplates the prospect of an entropic future devoid of all life, she also envisions scenes of continuance, whether for human or nonhuman life. Even in her vision of the earth covered in ice and lit only by starlight, she imagines improbable survivals:

> Even so, when the whole earth is sheeted and slippery, some undulation, some irregularity of surface will mark the boundary of an ancient garden, and there, thrusting its head up undaunted in the starlight, the rose will flower, the crocus will burn. (*E4* 322)

Although Woolf's choice of flowers suggests a garden landscape, her description also conjures up an image of alpine vegetation outlasting an age of glaciation on an isolated projection of rock amid an ice field. Such survivals disrupt the narrative of entropic death that she introduced with her allusion to the extinguishing of the sun, transforming her narrative into one less final and more cyclical, suggestive of glacial and interglacial ages and reminiscent of her discussion with Maynard Keynes of successive 'lap[s] in the race; others, many others, having been run previously & obliterated by ice ages' (*D2* 267). The uncertain focus of Keynes's discussion of 'the age of man' as recounted by Woolf in her diary leaves his theory open to multiple interpretations: it could suggest geological ages separated by mass extinction events or a conception of the human species persisting through past – and, by extension, future – glacial and interglacial periods.

Such open-endedness is also suggested by the emphasis that Woolf places on the indefatigableness of life alongside the inexorableness of death. Contemplating the future death of the sun, she declares:

> But with the hook of life still in us still we must wriggle. We cannot stiffen peaceably into glassy mounds. Even the recumbent spring up at the mere imagination of frost about the toes and stretch out to avail themselves of the universal hope – Heaven, Immortality. Surely since men have been wishing all these ages, they will have wished something into existence [. . .] But no. (E4 322–3)

Woolf's choice of glacial imagery to represent the prospect of death, whether individual or collective, and her framing of the lively impulse to persist in terms of an instinct to spring up at 'the mere imagination of frost about the toes' captures the fear at even the prospect of cooling that conditioned the responses of early twentieth-century scientists in the northern temperate zone to the notion of anthropogenic warming. At the same time, her ironic invocation of 'universal hope' highlights the wish fulfilment that underpins narratives of Heaven – or, in the case of early twentieth-century scientists, alien geo-engineering projects – promising transcendence of the limits of nature. Woolf's writing illustrates the preoccupation with the prospect of future cooling that crucially shaped early twentieth-century responses to the novel theory of anthropogenic warming by way of CO_2 emissions. Yet, while her choice of imagery reflects this contemporary concern, her arguments also interrogate the impulse of mastery and control that such fears elicited from her scientific contemporaries.

Notes

1. For discussions of the longer history of climate change theories, see James Rodger Fleming, *Historical Perspectives on Climate Change* and Adeline Johns-Putra, ed., *Climate and Literature*.
2. Ekholm, 'Variations of Climate', 61.
3. Arrhenius, 'Influence of Carbonic Acid', 267.
4. Arrhenius, *Worlds in the Making*, 53.
5. Ibid., 54.
6. Ibid., 63.
7. Arrhenius, 'Influence of Carbonic Acid', 267.
8. Ibid., 273.
9. Arrhenius, *Worlds in the Making*, 58.
10. Ibid., 58.
11. Ibid., 56.

12. Ibid., 54, 57–8.
13. Ibid., 61.
14. Ibid., 61.
15. Yusoff, *Billion Black*, xiii.
16. Ekholm, 'Variations of Climate', 60.
17. Ibid., 61.
18. Ibid., 61.
19. Wright, *Quaternary Ice Age*, 298.
20. Ibid., 293.
21. Sherlock, *Man as Geological*, 303.
22. Ibid., 333.
23. Ibid., 305.
24. Ibid., 343.
25. Ibid., 343.
26. Ibid., 345.
27. Ibid., 345–6.
28. Ibid., 343.
29. Ibid., 298.
30. Ibid., 346.
31. Ibid., 346.
32. Ibid., 347.
33. Ibid., 347.
34. Ibid., 347.
35. Adkins, *Modernist Anthropocene*, 11.
36. Woodward, 'Foreword', 7.
37. Ibid., 7–8.
38. Ibid., 8.
39. Cole, 'The Earth', 352.
40. Ibid., 352, 353.
41. Callendar, 'Artificial Production', 223.
42. Ibid., 223.
43. Ibid., 236.
44. Ibid., 223.
45. Ibid., 240.
46. Lankester, *Kingdom of Man*, 26.
47. Ibid., 30.
48. Ibid., 6.
49. Ibid., 45.
50. Ibid., 43.
51. Ibid., 45.
52. Ibid., 32.
53. Ibid., 30–1.
54. Woolf was not the only modernist writer to engage with the subjects of climate and climatic change. For further discussion of modernist engagements with climate discourse, see my essay, '"Restore to us the necessary BLIZZARDS": Early Twentieth-Century Visions of Climatic Change', 37–61.

55. For further discussion of Woolf's treatment of climate in *Orlando*, see Jesse Oak Taylor, *The Sky of Our Manufacture: The London Fog in British Fiction from Dickens to Woolf* (2016).
56. For further discussion of Woolf's depictions of prehistoric environments, see Gillian Beer, *Virginia Woolf: The Common Ground* (1996).
57. Lankester, *Kingdom of Man*, 6.

Bibliography

Adkins, Peter. *The Modernist Anthropocene: Nonhuman Life and Planetary Change in James Joyce, Virginia Woolf and Djuna Barnes*. Edinburgh: Edinburgh University Press, 2022.

Alt, Christina. '"Restore to us the necessary BLIZZARDS": Early Twentieth-Century Visions of Climatic Change'. *Modernist Cultures* 16, no. 1 (February 2021): 37–61.

Arrhenius, Svante. 'On the Influence of Carbonic Acid in the Air upon the Temperature of the Ground'. *Philosophical Magazine* 5, no. 41 (April 1896): 237–76.

——. *Worlds in the Making: The Evolution of the Universe*, translated by H. Borns. New York and London: Harper, 1908.

Beer, Gillian. *Virginia Woolf: The Common Ground*. Edinburgh: Edinburgh University Press, 1996.

Callendar, G. S. 'The Artificial Production of Carbon Dioxide and Its Influence on Temperature'. *Quarterly Journal of the Royal Meteorological Society* 64, no. 275 (April 1938): 223–40.

Cole, Grenville A. J. 'The Earth under the Rule of Man'. *Nature* 111 (17 March 1923): 352–4.

Ekholm, Nils. 'On the Variations of the Climate of the Geological and Historical Past and Their Causes'. *Quarterly Journal of the Royal Meteorological Society* 27, no. 117 (January 1901): 1–62.

Fleming, James Rodger. *Historical Perspectives on Climate Change*. Oxford: Oxford University Press, 1998.

Johns-Putra, Adeline, ed. *Climate and Literature*. Cambridge: Cambridge University Press, 2019.

Lankester, E. Ray. *The Kingdom of Man*. London: Constable, 1907.

Sherlock, R. L. *Man as a Geological Agent: An Account of His Action on Inanimate Nature*. London: H. F. & G. Witherby, 1922.

Taylor, Jesse Oak. *The Sky of Our Manufacture: The London Fog in British Fiction from Dickens to Woolf*. Charlottesville: University of Virginia Press, 2016.

Woodward, Arthur Smith. 'Foreword'. In *Man as a Geological Agent* by R. L. Sherlock, 5–8. London: H. F. & G. Witherby, 1922.

Woolf, Virginia. *Between the Acts*, edited by Frank Kermode. Oxford: Oxford University Press, 2008.

———. *The Diary of Virginia Woolf*, edited by Anne Olivier Bell. 5 vols. London: Penguin Books, 1979–85.
———. *The Essays of Virginia Woolf*, edited by Andrew McNeillie (vols 1–4) and Stuart N. Clarke (vols 5–6). 6 vols. London: Hogarth Press, 1986–2011.
———. *Mrs Dalloway*, edited by David Bradshaw. Oxford: Oxford University Press, 2000.
———. *Night and Day*, edited by Suzanne Raitt. Oxford: Oxford University Press, 1999.
———. *Orlando: A Biography*, edited by Rachel Bowlby. Oxford: Oxford University Press, 1998.
———. *To the Lighthouse*, edited by David Bradshaw. Oxford: Oxford University Press, 2000.
Wright, W. B. *The Quaternary Ice Age*. London: Macmillan, 1914.
Yusoff, Kathryn. *A Billion Black Anthropocenes or None*. Minneapolis: University of Minnesota Press, 2018.

Chapter 2

Cosmopolitan Anthropocene: The Convergence of Transnationalism and Climatic Consciousness in Virginia Woolf's *The Years*

Shinjini Chattopadhyay

In defining the Anthropocene, Paul Crutzen presents humans as a homogenous community:

> For the past three centuries, the effects of *humans* on the global environment have escalated. Because of these anthropogenic emissions of carbon dioxide, *global* climate may depart significantly from natural behaviour for many millennia to come. It seems appropriate to assign the term 'Anthropocene' to the present, in many ways [a] *human*-dominated, geological epoch, supplementing the Holocene – the warm period of the past 10–12 millennia.[1]

Crutzen's definition privileges species thinking and leads to the impression that the Anthropocene is a consequence of actions of all humans as a homogenous collective. However, one of the dangers of considering humans at the level of species and not at the level of disparate communities, Dipesh Chakrabarty points out, is that this approach disregards the socio-economic diversity of different communities. He writes in 'The Anthropocene and the Convergence of Histories' – a piece from which the title of the current chapter is partially borrowed – that considering humans as an undifferentiated agent behind the Anthropocene dismisses the perspective that developed and industrialised nations and newly industrialising countries bear disproportionate responsibility for causing climate change.[2] He further clarifies the argument in 'The Climate of History: Four Theses' and states that one may object to species thinking by claiming that the principal reasons behind the Anthropocene have been primarily contributed by Western capitalism and imperialism. He suggests that one may argue against species thinking by pointing out that, all the anthropogenic factors contributing to global warming – the burning of fossil fuel, industrialisation of animal stock, the clearing of tropical and other forests, and so on – are after all part of a larger story: the unfolding of capitalism in the West and the imperial or quasi-imperial domination by the West of the rest of the world.[3]

Such an objection would advocate for exempting the developing and formerly colonised countries from bearing the majority of responsibility for the Anthropocene:

> Why should one include the poor of the world – whose carbon footprint is small anyway – by use of such all-inclusive terms as *species* or *mankind* when the blame for the current crisis should be squarely laid at the door of the rich nations in the first place and of the richer classes in the poorer ones?[4]

Such questions disrupt the idea of the collective homogenous mankind that Crutzen imagines and prevent us from understanding how humans at the species level have become a geological force in the Anthropocene. However, adopting Crutzen's model of species thinking creates the problem of suppressing the postcolonial critique of imperial domination and colonial difference. How can we then respond to the conundrum of species thinking and engage with the idea of the Anthropocene as an epoch that all mankind experiences (and indeed brings into being) and still preserve the intrinsic heterogeneities of human civilisation? Chakrabarty proposes the solution that to grasp the meaning of the Anthropocene we need to simultaneously consider both registers of thought, i.e. we need to consider humans as a species and also examine the environmental actions of specific communities. He claims that it is only by combining the universal natural history with specific human history that we can fathom the shared sense of the climatic catastrophe of the Anthropocene that has befallen all humans.[5] In this chapter I argue that Virginia Woolf's *The Years* (1937) betrays an implicit awareness of the oncoming Anthropogenic climate catastrophe when it converges universal natural history with specific human history and that this convergence is attained through the framework of modernist cosmopolitanism.

Here the question arises of how the convergence of natural history and human history is connected with modernist cosmopolitanism. Cosmopolitanism is commonly understood as an approach to engaging with multiculturalism which privileges developing interests in cultures beyond that of one's own community and connects the local and the global. In the early to mid-twentieth century, cosmopolitan ideals encountered dual threats in the forms of fascism and colonialism. On the one hand, fascism promoted exclusionary nationalism and suppressed cosmopolitan connections beyond national borders. On the other hand, colonialism created a hierarchy between the cultures of the imperial centre and the colonial outposts where the former is seen as progressive, modern and superior and the latter is regarded as primitive, antimodern and inferior. Modernist writing dismantles these fascist and imperialist tropes and develops a particular form of cosmopolitanism which is termed as modernist cosmopolitanism. Modernist cosmopolitanism resists exclusionary nationalism and advocates for transnational interactions. It also subverts the hegemony of imperialism by displacing the hierarchy between the coloniser and the colonised and preserves the local cultural particularities of minoritarian communities. Jessica Berman elucidates how the dual movement of rejecting parochialism and subverting imperialism allows modernist cosmopolitanism to create heterogenous identities. She writes that:

> [m]odernist cosmopolitanism often posits a set of dispersed, intersecting spheres of identity, some expressly political, others less so, some more 'local' and others networked across the world. Modernist writers use their narratives to create 'cosmopolitan communities', overlapping webs of relation that narrate the story of affiliation as multiple, ever in process, and not bound by the limits of national belonging.[6]

Modernist cosmopolitanism advocates for multiple cultural affiliations where various local cultures come together to create new forms of hybridity.

Woolf's works can be read as upholding the tenets of modernist cosmopolitanism because they interrogate the limits of national boundaries and advocate for multiple cultural affiliations. Woolf's most emphatic advocacy for modernist cosmopolitanism is, of course, found in *Three Guineas* (1938) where she declares 'as a woman, I have no country. As a woman I want no country. As a woman my country is the whole world' (*TG* 229). Woolf scholars have pointed out that this statement shows a lack of awareness for intersectional identities in terms of race, class and citizenship status. Anna Snaith notes that, '[c]elebrating this desire for a global sisterhood risks obscuring those women without the luxury of belonging to an independent nation'.[7] However, Woolf's statement in *Three*

Guineas, despite its shortcomings, reveals the crux of Woolf's modernist cosmopolitanism. It shows that Woolf's modernist cosmopolitanism is premised on three principal functions – first, rejecting the limits of national belongings, second, opposing England's imperialist hegemony and, finally, forming transnational affiliations. The values of modernist cosmopolitanism that *Three Guineas* represents are unsurprisingly echoed in *The Years* since both works originate from the same novel-essay, *The Pargiters*. Woolf had initially planned to intersperse novelistic passages with essayistic explorations in *The Pargiters*. But she would later develop the essays separately in *Three Guineas* and the novel would become *The Years*. *The Years* significantly overlaps with the themes in *Three Guineas*. *The Years*, similar to *Three Guineas*, according to Snaith, encapsulates Woolf's anxiety with rising fascism in Europe[8] and, as a response to contemporary socio-political upheavals, critiques women's disempowerment within a patriarchal state, challenges England's imperial hegemony and advocates for transnational relationships across colonial boundaries.

The modernist cosmopolitanism in *The Years* can be read as a key factor in achieving the convergence between universal natural history and specific human history that Chakrabarty proposes. One of the theses that Chakrabarty puts forward in 'The Climate of History' is that 'the geological hypothesis regarding the Anthropocene requires us to put global histories of capital in conversation with the species history of humans'.[9] The modernist cosmopolitanism in *The Years* provides the critique of imperialism which Chakrabarty says is necessary for our understanding of the Anthropocene, but which is often missing from the framework of universal species thinking. *The Years* expresses an implicit awareness of how colonialism negatively impacts the environment. We can see instances of Woolf associating colonialism with environmental crisis elsewhere as well. For instance, in her essay, 'Thunder at Wembley', Woolf depicts the devastating environmental consequences of colonialism. She concludes the piece with a warning about an oncoming apocalypse,

> Humanity is rushing to destruction, but humanity is accepting its doom [. . .] Out in the open under a cloud of electric silver the bands of Empire strike up [. . .] The Empire is perishing; the bands are playing; the Exhibition is in ruins. For that is what comes of letting in the sky. (*E3* 413)

In this essay Woolf warns that colonial exploitation of the environment will ultimately become counter-productive and bring the

Empire to an end. The vision of apocalypse she invokes in the essay resembles the notion of Anthropogenic climatic catastrophe. I term Woolf's proleptic anticipation of the Anthropogenic climate crisis as her climatic consciousness. Climatic consciousness retrospectively situates the way in which Woolf depicts the relationship between humans and their environments within the context of the Anthropocene. Although Woolf does not intentionally present a causal relationship between imperial extraction of environmental resources and the phenomenon of climate change, her writings show a heightened awareness of how imperialism causes extensive environmental degradation (as exemplified in 'Thunder at Wembley'). She critiques how disparate imperialist human actions cause long-lasting and enduring environmental damage and thus anticipated the idea of Anthropogenic climate crisis before the notion of climate change entered scientific or popular discourses. Woolf, by attributing human actions as one of the major causes for environmental degradation, creates the foundation for retrospectively reading the relationship between humans and the environment in her writings within the framework of the Anthropocene. Woolf's climatic consciousness, emerging from her critique of imperialism, suggests how human actions can lead to large-scale environmental and ecological destructions at the local and transnational level. In what is to follow in this chapter, I show that Woolf's climatic consciousness in *The Years* is entwined with modernist cosmopolitanism. The modernist cosmopolitanism of the novel formulates a critique of the devastating impacts on the environment wrought by colonialism, the knowledge of which leads to the climatic consciousness about the oncoming catastrophe of the Anthropocene.

Transnationalism and the Convergence of Human History and Natural History

Recent ecocritical scholarship on Woolf has highlighted the overlap between Woolf's climatic consciousness of the Anthropocene and her modernist aesthetics. Jesse Oak Taylor terms the conjunction of Woolf's Anthropocenic consciousness and her modernist aesthetic as climatic modernism and writes that Woolf's climatic modernism offers ways of imagining futures after the end of nature as we know it.[10] Peter Adkins expands on how Woolf engages with the idea of the end of nature. He notes that Woolf's late writings in particular are especially preoccupied with the idea of human extinction. He reads this preoccupation as Woolf's response to not only the mass destructions of the Second World War but also the Anthropocene's imminent threat of inevitable human extinction as a consequence of massive climatic shifts. He shows that Woolf's meditations on the idea of human extinction leads to the emergence of a non-anthropocentric ontology and 'a pluralistic understanding of life' where 'the end of one's own world (however construed) does not amount to the end of *the* world'.[11] *The Years*, Woolf scholarship has shown, is similar to Woolf's other late works and is permeated with her climatic consciousness. The novel portrays a multiplicity of human–nonhuman relations that are at times tumultuous and at other times complementary. Bonnie Kime Scott writes that the lengthy interludes on seasons, that come at the beginning of each chapter in the novel, act as 'an objective correlative to the human drama of *The Years* – the cruellest month coming with the deaths of Eugénie and Digby; snow covers England as the family prepares to sell Abercorn Terrace, evicting their servant, Crosby'.[12] Tonya Krouse and Verita Sriratana, in their respective works, have corroborated Scott's readings and shown how nature in *The Years* reflects the personal and political upheavals experienced by the characters in the novel.[13] These readings of the human and nonhuman relations in *The Years* build the foundation for examining how Woolf's climatic consciousness in the novel is supported by her modernist cosmopolitanism.

In *The Years* Woolf's modernist cosmopolitanism evolves into her climatic consciousness when human history and natural history are no longer perceived as mutually exclusive phenomena. Chakrabarty, in 'The Climate of History', traces the origin of the separation of human and natural history to the traditional Viconian–Hobbesian notion that 'we, humans, could have proper knowledge of only civil and political institutions because we made them, while nature remains God's work and ultimately inscrutable to man'.[14] But he claims that this distinction has begun to collapse in the Anthropocene, where humans 'have reached numbers and invented technologies that are on a scale large enough to have an impact on the planet itself'.[15] Thus, it is no longer an issue of humans interacting with nature as mere biological agents, but humans impacting the planet itself as geological agents. Chakrabarty claims that the collapse between human and natural history began around the time of industrial revolution and then accelerated in the twentieth century when the impact of humans on the planet started becoming more evident.[16] The timespan of the *The Years* – from 1880 to the 1930s – is crucial for understanding how humans have become a geological force because it parallels the period when widespread colonisation creates long-lasting environmental impacts at a global scale which significantly contribute to the collapse of human and natural histories.

Some of the evident instances of the convergence of natural history and human history in *The Years* are found in the weather interludes at the beginning of each chapter. For instance, the opening description of the weather for '1880' does not merely depict the weather, it also emphasises how people react to the unpredictability of the season:

> It was an uncertain spring. The weather, perpetually changing, sent clouds of blue and of purple flying over the land. In the country farmers, looking at the fields, were apprehensive; in London umbrellas were shut by people looking up at the sky. But in April such weather was to be expected. (*TY* 3)

The above excerpt situates the idea of weather within the realm of human history by identifying a specific year, 1880, and describing how people in London and the countryside are grappling with its volatility during this particular year. But the excerpt also gestures towards the expanse of natural time when the omniscient narrator notes that 'in April such weather was to be expected'. This aside by the narrator suggests that the unpredictable spring that people are experiencing in 1880 is not an isolated event in time, rather it is part of a larger climatic phenomenon. In other words, the 'perpetually changing' spring weather is emblematic of a constant climatic pattern that repeats itself over centuries. That uncertain spring weather is part of a regular climatic pattern is re-emphasised when the spring in 1910 remains equally unpredictable with its fluctuations between sun and rain, 'an English spring day, bright enough, but a purple cloud behind the hill might mean rain' (*TY* 153). Even though the span of just three decades from 1880 to 1910 is too miniscule to determine climatic patterns across the breadth of natural history, the brief leap in time gestures towards connecting the specific moment of 1880 with natural history. The descriptions of weather at the beginning of other chapters also similarly conjoin human and natural histories by expanding a particular point in human history to the vast expanse of natural history.[17] The composition history of *The Years* also draws attention to how the weather interludes link human and natural histories in the novel. Anna Snaith, while recounting the composition history of the novel, notes how Woolf was preoccupied with reducing the length of the novel and excised entire sections when she was revising the text.[18] Woolf records in her diary her determination to curtail the length of the novel and writes,

> Just now I finished my first wild retyping & find the book comes to 740 pages: that is <174,800>148,000 words: but I think I can shorten: all the last part is still rudimentary & wants shaping; but I'm too tired in the head to do it seriously this moment. I think all the same I can reduce it. (D4 332)

The weather interludes, despite being late additions to the text, survived Woolf's concerted efforts at condensing the text and were spared from 'some bold cuts' that many other parts of the text were subjected to (D4 360). Woolf's retaining the weather interludes at the beginning of each chapter shows that these sections function as meditations on climate and natural history and prepare a segue to specific human history that is to follow.

The convergence of human and natural history in the descriptions of the weather in *The Years* intersects with some of the essential ideas of cosmopolitanism. Martha Nussbaum in 'Patriotism and Cosmopolitanism', one of the seminal texts of cosmopolitan theory, notes that the Stoics define cosmopolitanism as a socio-cultural system where the individual is surrounded by a series of concentric circles. She writes,

> [t]hey [the Stoics] suggest that we think of ourselves not as devoid of local affiliations, but as surrounded by a series of concentric circles. The first one is drawn around the self; the next takes in one's immediate family; then follows the extended family; then, in order, one's neighbors or local groups, one's fellow city-dwellers, one's fellow country-men – and we can easily add to this list groupings based on ethnic, linguistic, historical, professional, gender and sexual identities. Outside all these circles is the largest one, that of humanity as a whole.[19]

In this model, the individual develops a sense of cosmopolitanism when they move from one circle to the next and through their movement converge the local with the global. The convergence of the local and the global frees the individual of the patriotic imperative of putting one's own nation or culture ahead of other global cultures. However, Nussbaum elsewhere criticises this model of cosmopolitanism for its limitations because it considers humanity as the largest circle of belonging and does not expand its reach to include non-human entities and nature.[20] Woolf anticipates Nussbaum's critique and adapts this anthropocentric model of cosmopolitanism to the description of nonhuman weather. The weather descriptions in *The Years* expand in concentric circles and not only bring together the local and the global but also the human and the nonhuman.

The weather descriptions often begin with a focus on the local. The weather interlude of '1910' provides intricate details of London – '[m]en lay flat on the grass reading newspapers', 'mothers, squatted on the grass, watched their children play', '[o]ver Park Lane and Piccadilly the clouds kept their freedom, wandering fitfully, staining windows gold' (*TY* 153). The description of the weather focuses on the intricate human activities taking place at various locations in London. The weather description is symptomatic of modernist cosmopolitanism because it reveals the local diversity of London. The plenitude of local details in the weather interludes in *The Years* is similar to the emphasis placed on the depiction of London streets and landmarks in yet another of Woolf's works, *The London Scene* (1975). *The London Scene* is a collection of five essays – 'The Docks of London' (December 1931), 'Oxford Street Tide' (January 1932), 'Great Men's Houses' (March 1932), 'Abbeys and Cathedrals' (May 1932) and "This Is the House of Commons" (October 1932) – in which Woolf meticulously illustrates various aspects of life in London. The essays originally appeared in the transatlantic magazine *Good Housekeeping*, and included a sixth essay, 'Portrait of a Londoner' (December 1932). In these essays Woolf describes both well-known and lesser-known areas of London. For example, in 'Oxford Street Tide' Woolf depicts the relentless commercial activities on Oxford Street even though she is aware that it is not 'London's most distinguished thoroughfare' and '[m]oralists have been known to point the finger of scorn at those who buy there'. However, Woolf admits that Oxford Street, despite its alleged disrepute, 'has its fascination' (*E5* 284). Woolf, by drawing attention to Oxford Street, diverts focus from the traditional monuments of London and posh shopping areas like Bond Street which are frequented by upper-middle-class shoppers like Clarissa Dalloway. Sonita Sarker writes that in *The London Scene* Woolf intends to destabilise a masculinist nation and reconstruct a more inclusionary itinerary by describing heavily populated areas of London like Oxford Street.[21] She notes that Woolf develops this inclusive itinerary by depicting 'an infinitely various human geography' where she draws attention to ordinary people, such as the women shopping in Oxford Street or the men working at the London Docks, who are usually excluded from dominant narratives.[22] For instance, Woolf carefully describes the seedy magicians and the slumbering tortoise on Oxford Street.[23] Sarker's observation about *The London Scene* can be mapped on to *The Years* and it can be argued that the weather interludes in the novel perform a similar function of developing an inclusionary cityscape. The weather interludes draw attention to ordinary citizens like nursemaids, mothers, men reading newspapers in various parts of London. These figures, who populate the London landscape, ironically do not find a space in the saga of the Pargiters (Crosby, the Pargiters' servant, is the only exception to this trend, but she remains a minor character in the narrative nonetheless and her marginalisation is starkly highlighted when on one occasion Martin unceremoniously shuts his apartment door upon her [*TY* 212]). But the weather interludes mitigate the marginalisation of these otherwise minor figures and suggest that they are an integral part of London life. The inclusion of such marginalised local details helps Woolf reveal the internal heterogeneity of London. Woolf, by portraying the gender and class diversity of the London crowd, achieves the convergence of human and natural histories in interspersing descriptions of London life with the weather interludes.

The weather interludes also transcend the local, and echoing Nussbaum's model of concentric circles, expand to a transnational context. Although natural time precedes the formation of nations, Woolf makes national boundaries prominent in the weather interludes. She not only depicts the local weather in London, she also looks at the weather in other nations. For example, the weather interlude in '1891' begins with England – '[t]he autumn wind blew over England' – only to transcend the country's boundary. Woolf then describes how the autumn wind travels beyond England to the continent. She writes, 'Blowing behind the boat train, the wind ruffled the Channel, tossed the grapes in Provence, and made the lazy fisher boy, who was lying on his back in his boat in the Mediterranean, roll over and snatch a rope' (*TY* 86). The autumn wind blowing over England, France and the Mediterranean suggests that the season is not localised only in the region of England, rather it is part of a transnational geographical expanse. The transnational context of the weather interludes ultimately expands to a universal climatic consciousness when it describes a landscape stricken with the destruction of the First World War. The description of the landscape of England in 1917 sounds a note of desolation:

> [a] very cold winter's night, so silent that the air seemed frozen, and, since there was no moon, congealed to the stillness of glass spread over England [. . .] No light shone, save when a searchlight rayed round the sky, and stopped, here and there, as if to ponder some fleecy patch. (*TY* 266)

The emphasis on stillness, darkness and silence in the excerpt reveals the desolation of the landscape. Unlike other weather interludes, the above description has few markers of geographic specificity and local detail, except for naming the location as England. The elision of local details invokes a landscape of universal destruction that the First World War inflicts not only on England, but on the entire planet. Additionally, the elision of any particular marker of the passage of time in the excerpt produces the effect that the impacts of the war have become a permanent part of the landscape. The passage implies that it is events like the First World War that reveal the enormity that humans have assumed as a geological force on the planet. The passage thus turns an event of human history into a portal to natural history and gestures toward a climatic consciousness.

Woolf's Critique of Imperialism and Climatic Consciousness

The weather interludes are not the only locations in *The Years* where a climatic consciousness and attention to local details come together. Individual characters, such as Martin and Eleanor, also closely engage with the local details of London which inform their sense of modernist cosmopolitanism. For instance, Martin situates the local landmarks of London within a network of imperialist power and politics. Andrew Thacker notes that in Woolf's geographical imagination social space is 'intrinsically bound up' with 'questions of power and politics'.[24] Martin reveals how the social space of London is marked by the colonialist forces of the British empire. When he notices royal monuments on the streets, instead of revering them, he finds these imperialist structures absurdly funny. Temple Bar is one such monument that becomes the subject of Martin's mockery. When he walks past it, he finds it 'as ridiculous as usual' and pauses to look at the 'little flattened figures lodged so uncomfortably against the pediment of Temple Bar: Queen Victoria: King Edward' (*TY* 223). Martin challenges the imperial authority of England by scoffing at the monuments that celebrate monarchy. Especially in the context of the impending First World War Martin considers England's colonialist hegemony as particularly ephemeral. In 1913 itself Martin rightly predicts that, '[t]he war in the Balkans was over; but there was more trouble brewing – he was sure' (*TY* 210). The context of international animosity and the oncoming war makes evident for Martin the weakening of England's imperial authority. Martin himself indirectly contributes to this dilution of England's imperial power. Although he was in the colonial services in India and Africa, he eventually becomes disillusioned with the imperialist mission and admits that he was placed in the Army by his family and he 'loathed' the experience (*TY* 218). Martin's attention to local details in London thus translates into a critique of England's imperial authority. The interrogation of England's imperial hegemony that Martin develops echoes the tenets of modernist cosmopolitanism which also seeks to displace the dominance of imperial centres.

Martin's modernist cosmopolitanism also assists him to understand how the weakening of England's imperial authority is connected to the larger phenomenon of the oncoming calamity of the First World War. Martin imagines a foreshadowing of the World War in the way in which the clocks of London ominously chime together. It appears to him that the great clock and all the clocks of the city are 'gathering their forces' and they are 'whirring a preliminary warning' (*TY* 216). Although the warning fails to diminish the mirthful spirit of the London traffic; it causes a consternation among the nonhuman creatures of the city, '[a]ll the sparrows fluttered up into the air; even the pigeons were frightened; some of them made a little flight round the head of Queen Anne' (*TY* 216). The disconcerted birds portend the impending calamity of the First World War. They indicate that the War will not only cause sociopolitical chaos, it will also inflict long-lasting damage on the planet. Martin takes notice of this brooding consternation in nature. He foresees the annihilation the War is to bring upon the planet when his thoughts extend from interrogating England's imperial hegemony to an unexplained emptiness. He observes that

> [a] primal innocence seemed to brood over the scene [of spring]. The birds made a beautiful sweet chirping in the branches; [. . .] [t]he sun dappling the leaves gave everything a curious look of insubstantiality as if it were broken into separate points of light. He too, himself, seemed dispersed. His mind for a moment was a blank. (*TY* 230)

The blank in Martin's mind symbolises the oncoming destruction of the First World War. He fears that the brooding international trouble will eventually erase the scene of 'primal innocence' that he sees before him and that the World War will result in a planetary catastrophe. Martin's fear of an imminent catastrophe echoes the preoccupation with extinction in Woolf's late writing that Adkins has argued about. Adkins notes that Woolf in her late writings 'suspends normative thinking around questions of posterity and, instead, engages with an aesthetics of extinction'.²⁵ The void that momentarily consumes Martin's mind suppresses the signs of animation that immediately surrounds him and makes him aware of the imminent extinction that is to be caused by the World War. The void thus represents the aesthetics of extinction seen in Woolf's other late works. The preoccupation with extinction also destabilises traditional images of the future. Adkins points out that the Anthropocene can be considered a 'crisis for futurity' because its 'threat of massive species extinction, sea-level rise, catastrophic climate change and potential societal collapse unsettle the ontological and ethical sureties of the present, drawing into the foreground the inevitability of human extinction at *some point* in the future'.²⁶ The blank in Martin's mind is symptomatic of this Anthropogenic 'crisis for futurity'. It suggests that the eventual mass extinction that Martin fears the First World War will bring about will also invalidate the traditional notion of an Anthropocentric future. In other words, if the widespread destructions of the World War led to the eventual extinction of the human species, it will result in a future of the planet where humans are no longer central to it. Martin, in identifying the First World War and by extension European imperialism as contributing factors to the imminent climatic catastrophe, imparts an implicit awareness of how humans have become a geological force of mass annihilation. His modernist cosmopolitanism thus extends his critique of imperialism to the climatic consciousness of the Anthropocene.

Whereas Martin's modernist cosmopolitanism challenges the imperial hegemony of England, Eleanor develops a sense of transnationalism that transcends the boundaries of England. In addition to appreciating England's integral diversity – she is fond of the urban rhythms of London and also gradually develops an admiration for the English countryside – she situates the nation in a transnational context and compares it with other countries. By 1911 Eleanor has widely travelled in Spain, Greece and Italy and has become familiar with other cultures. The exposure to foreign cultures further corroborates Eleanor's modernist cosmopolitanism. She takes up an objective attitude towards England and does not allow her engagement with the country to be shrouded with unreasonable patriotism or nationalism. She forthrightly admits to herself that, 'England was disappointing, [. . .] it was small; it was pretty; she felt no affection for her native land – none whatever' (*TY* 189). In the socio-political context of rising nationalism in 1911, Eleanor's admission that she feels no particular affection for her native land emphasises her commitment to cosmopolitanism. Woolf, in *Three Guineas*, writes that when English women would compare English culture to other foreign cultures, they would find no reason to consider it superior to others. They will thus become indifferent to their native land and abandon their patriotic loyalty (*TG* 228). Eleanor exemplifies Woolf's expostulation. After her visits to various foreign lands, she decides it unconscionable to build any hierarchy between English and other cultures or to consider England superior. Kwame Anthony Appiah writes that cosmopolitanism allows one to derive pleasure from 'the presence of other, different places that are home to other, different people'.[27] Appiah's tenet of cosmopolitanism is echoed in how Eleanor engages with native and foreign cultures. She does not limit herself within England by a sense of patriotic loyalty, instead, she derives pleasure from her exposure to other foreign cultures. Her modernist cosmopolitanism allows her to appreciate the cultural particularities of countries beyond England and build flexible transnational affiliations with foreign cultures.

Eleanor's modernist cosmopolitanism leads to a climatic consciousness. Her renunciation of patriotic loyalties makes her critical of how human actions in England intervene with the environment. For instance, when she admires the beauty of the countryside in Dorset and exclaims '[h]ow lovely it is!', she is reminded by Celia, her sister-in-law, that the beauty is transient. Celia, notes that the beauty is threatened by Mr Robinson who is the 'local scourge' and who endangers the natural beauty of Dorset by threatening to build (*TY* 196). Eleanor realises that the 'pure' beauty of the countryside is only an imaginary construct and human interventions, such as building projects by the likes of Mr Robinson, puts the beauty at risk. Furthermore, Eleanor also realises that such building projects not only jeopardise the beauty of the countryside, but also have profound ecological consequences. As a result, Eleanor's appreciation of the beauty of nature is also accompanied with concerns about oncoming environmental crisis. For instance, when Celia admires the beauty of the night, '[i]t's a wonderful night, isn't it?', she quickly follows her note of admiration with anxieties about the ongoing drought. She fears that, '[i]t looks as if it would never rain again. In which case I don't know . . . ' (*TY* 197, ellipsis in original). Although Celia does not directly blame Mr Robinson's building projects for the drought, her discontent with the projects suggests that she implicitly discerns a connection between such obtrusive human projects and enduring environmental damage. Her concern with the drought reveals that unchecked building projects like those by Mr Robinson represent overdevelopment, which result in straining limited natural resources and lead to the scarcity of essential resources like water. Celia tries to abate her consternation about the drought and reassures herself by adding that, 'there's quite enough water for everybody *at present*' (*TY* 197, emphasis added). The scarcity of water and the drought in Dorset make it evident that the climatic catastrophe of the Anthropocene has already begun. Celia indirectly expresses her awareness of this catastrophe when she indicates that the future is uncertain. She admits that even though there is adequate water at present, the situation may change in the near future if the drought continues. She fears that the drought may not be a short-lived problem, instead it may be the preamble of a long-lasting environmental crisis or even the preface of a permanent shift in the climate – 'as if it would *never* rain again' (emphasis added). She leaves unsaid what the future may look like if it never rains again and the ellipsis at the end of her statement suggests her inability to envision a future engulfed in ecological issues like the water crisis she is experiencing. However, her concerns about environmental issues remain limited within Dorset and the immediate future and she does not think of the drought at an Anthropogenic scale. But in suggesting implicit connections between human actions and environmental degradation and anticipating massive climatic shifts and an uncertain future, she approaches a sense akin to Woolf's climatic consciousness.

Eleanor amplifies Celia's uncertainty for the future. She imparts an implicit understanding that the present moment of natural calamity is not nature merely taking its own course, rather it is a consequence of human actions. She suspects that the present calamity will only become worse in the future. But she is unable to envision what shape the catastrophe of the Anthropocene will assume in the future and she can only helplessly cry into the darkness, 'where are we going? Where? Where? ... ' (*TY* 203, ellipsis in original). The ellipsis at the end symbolises an ominous void. It suggests that whereas Celia is uncertain about what the future will look like, Eleanor doubts if there would be a future at all. In this Eleanor, similar to Martin, also foreshadows the preoccupation with extinction in Woolf's late writings. Eleanor, unlike Celia, does not think of the environmental crisis only in the limited context of Dorset and does not impart a myopic sense of time by thinking only of the immediate present or future. When she cries into the void, she fears an extinction of the future for all mankind. Her sense of time encompasses the epochal span of the Anthropocene. Eleanor, drawing on her sense of cosmopolitanism informed by international travels, contrasts the English countryside despoiled by human intervention with 'the great desolate mountains in Greece or in Spain, which looked as if nobody had ever set foot there since the beginning of time' (*TY* 202). The mountains in Greece or Spain make her long for an Earth unharmed by human actions. Eleanor, in approaching the present environmental crisis as a metonymic representation of an enduring ecological catastrophe caused by human actions, imparts a climatic consciousness.

Whereas modernist cosmopolitanism leads to a climatic consciousness about the Anthropocene, *The Years* also upholds instances where a lack of the sense of cosmopolitanism coexists with the absence of awareness about the Anthropocene. Abel Pargiter is an example of how the lack of cosmopolitanism also stifles any awareness of the oncoming climatic catastrophe. Colonel Pargiter holds colonialist and imperialist values and hence opposes modernist cosmopolitanism. He has significantly contributed to governing the British Empire. His body bears the marks of violence he has inflicted as a colonial official – '[h]e had lost two fingers of the right hand in the Mutiny' (*TY* 13). He has participated in forcefully suppressing the Sepoy Mutiny (1857–59), the first widespread rebellion in India against British colonial rule. He not only actively contributes to the mechanisms of colonialism he also disapproves of any anti-British and anticolonial sentiments. When he hears news of Charles Stewart Parnell's death, he feels a sense of relief and even 'a tinge of triumph'. He expresses a characteristic colonialist impulse by calling Parnell 'that agitator who had done all the mischief' (*TY* 112). Colonel Pargiter, as a flagbearer of British colonialism, predictably indulges in colonial Orientalist constructs. On one of his visits to Eugénie, he is reminded of the women in the East, 'some memory of the East came back to him; so women sat in hot countries in their doorways in the sun' (*TY* 115). It is interesting to note that the geographical locations in Colonel Pargiter's statement are identified only by 'the East' and 'hot countries'. He does not name any country in particular. This shows that the East for him is not an agglomeration of specific countries. Rather it is a nameless monolithic mass of imagined Orientalist constructs. He perceives the East as an exotic and unknowable other which is defined only in opposition to the West. In addition, conforming to Orientalist tropes, he associates the East with the idea of women whom he perceives as sexualised objects replete with a primal sensuousness. For him the 'hot' in 'hot countries' is only a vessel of sensuousness. His memory of the East is devoid of any meditation on how colonisation severely damages the ecology of colonised countries. From a twenty-first-century perspective, he remains blissfully unaware of how his contribution to colonial capitalist exploitations has accelerated the oncoming climatic catastrophe of the Anthropocene.

In *The Years* a convergence of modernist cosmopolitanism and a climatic consciousness about the Anthropocene is seen in both individual characters and the instances of the weather interludes. The weather interludes gradually expand from the concentric circles of the local, the transnational and, ultimately, to the planetary expanse of natural history. Similarly, individual consciousness in the novel also connects the transnational with the planetary. Martin and Eleanor, informed by their modernist cosmopolitanism, detect the limitations of colonialism and eventually intuit the global climatic catastrophe of the Anthropocene. However, the critique of imperialism in *The Years* is by no means comprehensive. For instance, although the weather interludes in the novel focus on marginalised Londoners, they do not portray the diversity of the London crowd. The marginalised figures, similar to their counterparts in *The London Scene*, remain racially and ethnically unmarked. The erasure of racial and ethnic diversity, according to Sarker, leads to the assumption of a homogenous identity for the London crowd and contradicts the idea of cosmopolitanism.[28] A further limitation of the cosmopolitanism of *The Years* is revealed by the fact that the novel portrays characters who sympathise with anticolonialism only from a distance but never actively participate in anti-imperialist efforts. The Pargiters produce colonial officials across generations – Colonel Pargiter, Martin and North – who willingly or unwillingly govern the Empire. Moreover, the novel only obliquely hints at the environmental exploitations of the colonies. London or England always remains the novel's centre of climatic consciousness. Although the modernist cosmopolitanism of *The Years* does not altogether displace Eurocentrism, it rejects England's imperial authority and initiates the formation of cosmopolitan connections across colonial borders. Such cosmopolitan connections create the foundation for achieving an idea of the mankind that experiences the Anthropocene as a collective but still maintains its integral heterogeneity premised on the critique of imperialism and capitalism. *The Years* thus inaugurates a new mode of climatic consciousness about the Anthropocene that is founded on the cosmopolitan critique of colonialism.

Notes

1. Crutzen, 'Geology', 23, emphasis added.
2. Chakrabarty, 'Convergence of Histories', 49.
3. Chakrabarty, 'Climate of History', 216.
4. Ibid., 216.
5. Ibid., 219.
6. Berman, 'Modernist Cosmopolitanism', 431.
7. Snaith, 'Race', 208.
8. Snaith, 'Composition History', lxxviii.
9. Chakrabarty, 'Climate of History', 212.
10. Taylor, *Sky*, 189.
11. Ibid., 177, emphasis in original.
12. Scott, *Hollow,* 209.
13. See Tonya Krouse's 'The Politics of Nature in Woolf's *The Years*' and Verita Sriratana's '"It was an uncertain spring": Reading the Weather in *The Years*'.
14. Chakrabarty, 'Climate of History', 201.
15. Ibid., 207.
16. Ibid., 207.
17. We can notice similar instances of the convergence of natural and human histories in Woolf's other works as well. Angeliki Spiropoulou uses Walter Benjamin's idea of 'natural history' and shows how Woolf's modernism 'introduces history into nature and nature into history in ways that complicate their traditional dichotomy'. Spiropoulou writes that the convergence of natural and human histories is particularly depicted in *To the Lighthouse* (1927), *The Waves* (1931), *Between the Acts* (1941) and many of Woolf's short stories. For instance, Spiropoulou analyses that the ever-changing yet repetitive waves in *The Waves* show how human and natural histories are intertwined. She shows yet another instance of the intersection of human and natural histories in *To the Lighthouse* where moments of human history, such as the Great War and the deaths in the Ramsay family, are indicated through natural decay. Spiropoulou, *Virginia Woolf,* 96–113.
18. Snaith, 'Composition History', lxxxiv.
19. Nussbaum, 'Patriotism', 4.
20. Nussbaum, *Cosmopolitan,* 17.
21. Sarker, 'Locating', 10.
22. Ibid., 15.
23. Ibid., 20.
24. Thacker, 'Geography', 423.
25. Adkins, *Modernist Anthropocene,* 171.
26. Ibid., 172, emphasis in original.
27. Appiah, 'Cosmopolitan', 618.
28. Sarker, 'Locating', 15.

Bibliography

Adkins, Peter. *The Modernist Anthropocene: Nonhuman Life and Planetary Change in James Joyce, Virginia Woolf and Djuna Barnes*. Edinburgh: Edinburgh University Press, 2022.

Appiah, Kwame Anthony. 'Cosmopolitan Patriots'. *Critical Inquiry* 23, no. 3 (1997): 617–39.

Berman, Jessica. 'Modernist Cosmopolitanism'. In *A History of the Modernist Novel*, edited by Gregory Castle, 429–48. Cambridge: Cambridge University Press, 2015.

Chakrabarty, Dipesh. 'The Climate of History: Four Theses'. *Critical Inquiry* 35, no. 2 (2009): 197–222.

——. 'The Anthropocene and the Convergence of Histories'. In *The Anthropocene and the Global Environmental Crisis: Rethinking Modernity in a New Epoch*, edited by Clive Hamilton, Christophe Bonneuil and François Gemenne, 44–56. New York: Routledge, 2015.

Crutzen, Paul. 'Geology of Mankind'. *Nature* 415 (2002): 23.

Krouse, Tonya. 'The Politics of Nature in Woolf's *The Years*'. *Virginia Woolf Miscellany* 81 (2012): 12–14.

Nussbaum, Martha. 'Patriotism and Cosmopolitanism'. *Boston Review* 19, no. 5 (1994): 3–6.

——. *The Cosmopolitan Tradition: A Noble but Flawed Ideal*. New York: Harvard University Press, 2019.

Sarker, Sonita. 'Locating a Native Englishness in Virginia Woolf's *The London Scene*'. *NWSA Journal* 13, no. 2 (Summer 2001): 1–30.

Scott, Bonnie Kime. *In the Hollow of the Wave: Virginia Woolf and Modernist Uses of Nature*. Charlottesville: University of Virginia Press, 2012.

Snaith, Anna. 'Race, Empire, and Ireland'. In *Virginia Woolf in Context*, edited by Jane Goldman and Bryony Randall, 206–18. Cambridge: Cambridge University Press, 2015.

——. 'Composition History'. In *The Years* by Virginia Woolf, edited by Anna Snaith, xlv–lxxxvi. Cambridge: Cambridge University Press, 2012.

Spiropoulou, Angeliki. *Virginia Woolf, Modernity and History: Constellations with Walter Benjamin*. London: Palgrave Macmillan, 2010.

Sriratana, Verita. 'It was an Uncertain Spring: Reading the Weather in *The Years*'. In *Virginia Woolf and the Natural World*, edited by Kristin Czarnecki and Carrie Rohman, 191–5. Liverpool: Liverpool University Press, 2011.

Taylor, Jesse Oak. *The Sky of Our Manufacture: The London Fog in British Fiction from Dickens to Woolf*. Charlottesville: University of Virginia Press, 2016.

Thacker, Andrew. 'Woolf and Geography'. In *A Companion to Virginia Woolf*, edited by Jessica Berman, 411–25. Chichester: Wiley Blackwell, 2016.

Weihman, Lisa. 'Gender and National Identity in *The Years*'. *Comparative Critical Studies* 4, no. 1 (200 7): 31–50.

Woolf, Virginia. *The Diary of Virginia Woolf*, edited by Anne Olivier Bell. 5 vols. London: Harcourt Brace Jovanovich, 1979–85.
——. *The Essays of Virginia Woolf*, edited by Andrew McNeillie (vols 1–4) and Stuart N. Clarke (vols 5–6). 6 vols. London: Hogarth Press, 1986–2011.
——. *A Room of One's Own and Three Guineas*, edited by Hermione Lee. London: Chatto & Windus, 1984.
——. *The Years*, edited by Hermione Lee. Oxford: Oxford University Press, 1992.

Part II

Matter and Materialities

Chapter 3

Outside the Anthropocene: The Subject of Virginia Woolf

Claire Colebrook

'and' the Anthropocene

Modernism, especially Virginia Woolf's modernism, seems both perfectly suited and utterly incompatible with the Anthropocene. On the one hand, of all the modernists, Woolf's sense of the complexity of consciousness was bound up with the temporality and intensity of a 'nature' that was haunted by the virtual. The mind was never its own space but always embedded and indebted to a world that bore a complexity and force that was never reducible to the private space of 'the human'. On the other hand, it is the complexity of *consciousness*, especially in its privatised form, that relays the tremors of the Earth. This is so much so that Woolf states a manifest objection to materialism. Detailing the actual world occludes the sense of things. Commenting on H. G. Wells, Arnold Bennett and John Galsworthy, Woolf notes: 'if we tried to formulate our meaning in one word we should say that these three writers are materialists. It is because they are concerned not with the spirit but with the body that they have disappointed us' (E4 158). Woolf then goes on to offer a definition: 'we mean by it that they write of unimportant things; that they spend immense skill and immense industry making the trivial and the transitory appear the true and the enduring' (E4 158).

To understand the world requires going beyond anything as distinct as mind, subjectivity or 'man'. In this sense, if Woolf rejects materialism her possible alignment with what has come to be known as *new* materialism allows us to think about the force of her work in the Anthropocene. The materialism Woolf objects to might be thought of as a contraction of scale,[1] an inability to think beyond the immediately given. *New* materialism takes many forms, but its unifying tendency lies in its recognition of the force of matters beyond the immediately given.[2] New materialism has been crucial to the theorisation of the Anthropocene. Anthropos is not man as a natural being but a historical assemblage that opens out to a history of the nonhuman and the virtual. Without the halo of sense that surrounds all events and relations it would be neither possible to discern that the Earth we live in today is the outcome of complex relations and desires, nor possible to imagine a future beyond 'the human'. This is where Woolf is at once within and beyond the Anthropocene. The subject of her modernism and the formal presupposition of her prose is something like the transcendental consciousness that was so crucial for phenomenology: the world is always the experienced world and experience is never fully present to itself but retains traces of the past and anticipations of the future.[3] The 'Anthropos' of the Anthropocene is also this virtual presupposed 'we' at the basis of the history of 'the human' – both in the journey of empire and colonialism, and in the recognition that it is this vague, unbounded, not easily delimited 'Anthropos' that marks the present. If texts such as *Orlando* (1928) give form to a consciousness that can range from inner life to the narrative of empire, Woolf also intimates a counter-Anthropos: modes of existence that do not unfold to a world and that intimate a time beyond the drama of 'the human'. It is perhaps for this reason that sexual difference operates so powerfully and so ambivalently in her work. On the one hand, the notion that genuine writing must include male and female reinforces the sense of 'the human' as a point of private complexity and difference that enables an authentic experience of the world: 'it is fatal for anyone who writes to think of their sex. It is fatal to be a man or woman pure and simple; one must be woman-manly or man-womanly' (*AROO* 75). On the other hand, within Woolf's work, moments of difference *beyond* the sexual have an apocalyptic and inhuman power. If male–female enter into relation for the sake of production, allowing the world to be narrated from a point of view rich in sense, there is something radically unworlding in events of counter-production:

> there is no limit to the horizon, [. . .] nothing – no 'method', no experiment, even of the wildest – is forbidden, but only falsity and pretence. 'The proper stuff of fiction' does not exist; everything is the proper stuff of fiction, every feeling, every thought; every quality of brain and spirit is drawn upon; no perception comes amiss. (*E4* 162)

Put more simply, the Anthropos of the Anthropocene is a being of production and sexual difference, capable of purveying and surveying the globe like a god in command of an open and dynamic whole. Beyond that Anthropos are moments of difference that do not generate a point of inclusion and coherence, but take life beyond its bounded, state and human form.

If, in the twenty-first century, philosophy has avowedly abandoned the correlationism[4] of 'subject and object and the nature of reality' (*TTL* 196), Woolf had already allowed that form of contracted humanism to appear as an impoverished mode of existence. In its place consciousness is not at all the horizon from which the world unfolds but becomes an affective intensity of an interconnected life. It would seem that the Woolf of 'Modern Fiction' (1925), *To the Lighthouse* (1927), *The Waves* (1931) and *Orlando* anticipate the forms of agential realism and new materialism that have marked Anthropocene thought. Consciousness does not picture, mirror or represent the world, but apprehends the world in its temporal complexity. The planet, also, is vibrantly material; the things we view have a force to compose us, and compose us as multiple and affected rather than singular and in a position of logical mastery. In *The Waves* we are presented with the multiplicity of consciousness. In *Orlando* the seemingly isolated individual is set within the climate of history. In 'Modern Fiction' we are given a criticism of an objectifying materialism that reduces the life of the world. Mind and world are not distinct substances but intertwined and dynamic forces that generate an experience that never fully knows itself. Sexual difference becomes crucial for this Woolfian mode of new materialism: 'the subject' is already multiple and it is this difference of inner life that is then capable of apprehending the vibrant difference of the world. The 'man' for whom the planet is so much manageable matter is the 'man' of correlational philosophy – 'subject and object and the nature of reality'. This isolated 'subject' did not survive into the twentieth century. *The Waves* will conclude with the passage from individual consciousness to an individuated moment that exists, as such, beyond its human apprehension:

> Again I see before me the usual street. The canopy of civilisation is burnt out. The sky is dark as polished whale-bone. But there is a kindling in the sky whether of lamplight or of dawn. There is a stir of some sort – sparrows on plane trees somewhere chirping. There is a sense of the break of day. I will not call it dawn. What is dawn in the city to an elderly man standing in the street looking up rather dizzily at the sky? Dawn is some sort of whitening of the sky; some sort of renewal. Another day; another Friday; another twentieth of March,

> January, or September. Another general awakening. The stars draw back and are extinguished. The bars deepen themselves between the waves. The film of mist thickens on the fields. A redness gathers on the roses, even on the pale rose that hangs by the bed-room window. A bird chirps. Cottagers light their early candles. Yes, this is the eternal renewal, the incessant rise and fall and fall and rise again. (*TW* 508)

Woolf was not alone in defining the self as a rich and affective horizon of sense, and in many ways her work is utterly compatible in its new materialist mode with the Anthropos of the twentieth and twenty-first centuries. As best exemplified in *Orlando* the subject as poet, lover and exemplary human is no longer the isolated man of reason, but a being for whom the world is an array of vibrant matter. What *Orlando* distils so powerfully is the way in which the empire of surveyed and purveyed things is inextricably intertwined with the lyric subject of modern literature (*and* the Anthropos of the Anthropocene). Orlando's journey as a poet is bound up with the journey of empire; the anonymous lives of the human poor, the head of a moor, an oak tree detached from the web of labour and subsistence, the world of so many dazzling vibrant things, can all be grasped from on high by a subject who experiences both male and female but is irreducible to either. The novel opens with a severed head, indicating the extent to which an experience of the world as a dazzling array of things follows from the brutal annihilation of other humans and other worlds:

> He – for there could be no doubt of his sex, though the fashion of the time did something to disguise it – was in the act of slicing at the head of a Moor which swung from the rafters. It was the colour of an old football, and more or less the shape of one, save for the sunken cheeks and a strand or two of coarse, dry hair, like the hair on a cocoanut. (*O* 8)

This playful relation to a single thing opens a novel that is very much about the life of things, composing a world where matters always suggest more than is present at hand:

> And so, the thought of love would be all ambered over with snow and winter; with log fires burning; with Russian women, gold swords and the bark of stags; with old King James' slobbering and fireworks and sacks of treasure in the holds of Elizabethan sailing ships. Every

single thing, once he tried to dislodge it from its place in his mind, he found thus cumbered with other matter like the lump of glass which, after a year at the bottom of the sea, is grown about with bones and dragon-flies, and coins and the tresses of drowned women. (O 59)

As others have noted,[5] *Orlando* also expresses this perceptual array with a sense of the climate and deep time:

The age was the Elizabethan; their morals were not ours; nor their poets; nor their climate; nor their vegetables even. Everything was different. The weather itself, the heat and cold of summer and winter, was, we may believe, of another temper altogether. The brilliant amorous day was divided as sheerly from the night as land from water. Sunsets were redder and more intense; dawns were whiter and more auroral. Of our crepuscular half-lights and lingering twilights they knew nothing. The rain fell vehemently, or not at all. The sun blazed or there was darkness. (O 16)

The subject of the Anthropocene is the subject of the *Anthroposcene*. The single domain of global life that can be expressed in all its rich difference is finally recognised by Anthropos who is but one fragment in a deep history. This Anthroposcenic subject is explicitly articulated in the geological claims of the Anthropocene but was always presupposed in the adventures of empire. Without the sense of 'the human' as the being capable of encompassing and comprehending difference – without the modern and modernist comportment towards history as an unsurpassable and single horizon – there could be no discourse of the Anthropocene.

Of all the modernists it was perhaps Woolf whose conception of writing, aesthetics and time connected the singularity of the private with the inhuman chaos of the cosmos.[6] The more intense the focus on inner life the less inner, human and private time becomes in Woolf's work. If György Lukács could criticise modernism for retreating into the merely psychological space of the world, he did so by way of an utterly materialist conception of the psyche (a materialism that was anathema to Woolf). For Lukács, what appeared as merely personal ought to be grasped as collective and historical, with history being the plane of economic, social and human production.[7] By contrast, with Woolf the personal is impolitic and immaterial: consciousness is partially populated by the sounds, words and events of the world, but each of those apparently material events opens out to a sense and time that is out of this world. Woolf's stream of consciousness was not the imprinting of the world on the private space of the subject but a molecular event of the infinitely small: look closely enough and all becomes impersonal. This is not the grand impersonality of the artist who is 'above and beyond' his handiwork, God-like and detached. It is the depersonalisation that occurs when the coherence of lived time, mapped onto identity and recognition, falls apart.

A modernism of elevated impersonality – where the artist is always other than any of the voices, fragments or scenes they survey – is at the heart of the temporality of Anthropocene discourse: Anthropos *is* this capacity to be everywhere and nowhere, nothing other than an apprehension of the whole. The transcendental modern subject who is *not* a thing but the condition for the possibility of apprehending things becomes – in modernism – the horizon of sense that captures a world of difference and diversity. This was why Jacques Derrida tied James Joyce to Edmund Husserl. For Joyce, the world was a single text or book requiring the synthesis of the modernist artist; for Husserl the world was a single history of sense requiring the intuition of the philosopher.[8] By the time we get to the discourse of the Anthropocene 'the human' becomes nothing other than this capacity for apprehension of the whole. It is perfectly possible and appropriate to read Woolf within this history of impersonality and elevated apprehension, where her production of a rich narrative of consciousness would extend (rather than rupture or derange) the horizons of human apprehension.

For the most part considering the Anthropocene has amounted to an expansive and extensive 'and': look at the geological events in the background; think of the year without a summer when reading *Frankenstein*;[9] note the little Ice Age in *Orlando*; look for the fossils in Romanticism.[10] Adding the Anthropocene – 'and the Anthropocene' – has predominantly been an *extensive* expansion: rather than transforming what counts as the human, or what counts as life, the Anthropocene allows 'the human' to be a grand narrative of geological scale. A modernism that is male–female and above and beyond the universe would be the penultimate moment in a history that ends with the Anthropocene, where Anthropocene man now becomes species-being in general, the human as geological agent. Dipesh Chakrabarty refers to this as negative universal history: only after witnessing what 'humanity' has done to the planet in its project of freedom can 'we' now recognise that we are held in common by that path of freedom that turns out to be a predicament with no exit.[11]

What might happen if one were to consider the Anthropocene *not* as an expansion of scale, but as a derangement? Not only would the experience of forces beyond consciousness no longer be one more step in global apprehension, one might also retroactively understand 'the human' as a history of misprision – as a grand narcissistic adventure that consumes, occludes and subsumes all difference as its own. What happens if rather than the Anthropocene becoming one more 'and' – allowing us to scale up to yet one more horizon that comprehends and complicates the whole – the Anthropocene becomes a shattering blow (after a series of shattering blows) that prompts an abandonment of human history and freedom? How long can 'we' keep holding on to the human, to the attachment to who 'we' are, dealing with blow after blow and yet each time taking that hit to our narcissism as a prompt to become more expansive in our remit? This is why I take Alexander Weheliye's *Habeas Viscus* (2014) not to be just another move in the game of theory, where one *adds* race to the production of 'man'. On the contrary, the very production of 'the human' *and* its procedures of recognising itself through ever more complex horizons of difference is a definitive racialising event.[12] Just as adding the Anthropocene – 'and the Anthropocene' – should not be the extensive moment of including more information, so thinking about race is not an event within the text but ought to be seen as its condition of possibility.

Racetime

Let us take *that* moment in *Orlando*, the opening scene of a *head* – not a face but a head – of 'a moor' (O 8). On the standard Anthropocene reading of zooming out or scaling up, it is possible to read this scene as an exemplary fragment of empire. A part of a body that is marked *only* through race – 'a moor' – is a mere plaything for a youth who has no sense of its geopolitical origin; the reader, however, can place this event within a history of racial imperialism and racial capitalism *and* the little Ice Age. The Thames that features so heavily in high modernism's understanding of the West as at once preserver and destroyer of all that is civilised becomes a point of frozen time and climate volatility that intensifies the barbarism of civilisation. It is the melting of the frozen Thames that sees property washed away while those overly attached to last things suffer and drown:

> Many perished clasping some silver pot or other treasure to their breasts; and at least a score of poor wretches were drowned by their own cupidity, hurling themselves from the bank into the flood rather than let a gold goblet escape them, or see before their eyes the disappearance of some furred gown. For furniture, valuables, possessions

> of all sorts were carried away on the icebergs. Among other strange sights was to be seen a cat suckling its young; a table laid sumptuously for a supper of twenty; a couple in bed; together with an extraordinary number of cooking utensils. Dazed and astounded, Orlando could do nothing for some time but watch the appalling race of waters as it hurled itself past him. (O 36)

Climate's slow violence is set within a narrative that opens with the immediate brutality of racial violence. We begin with the head of 'a moor' and then see the layers of property that compose the world: from severed heads to the goods of empire. At a manifest level *Orlando* is a document of racial imperialism. Body parts and the labours of the poor are listed among the spoils of empire. In this respect, *Orlando* is a perfect novel for the forms of scaled-up reading the Anthropocene seems to invite; if the novel was already a tale of empire, it can now be read as a tale of the planet. Coupling climate volatility to the violence of wealth and class allows the humanism of the novel to be not just a tale of geopolitical being, but also of species being.

What happens, though, if that scaling up or zooming out is taken *not* in the extensive sense of adding another dimension or history ('and the Anthropocene') so that 'we' have one more frame that renders this rich species life of ours stranger and more complex, but rather in the sense of cutting us off from anything like species being? Emerging from Marx, 'species being' is an exemplary Victorian concept. As Ian Baucom makes clear, 'species being' intertwines the sense of a force that precedes and forms being, with the historical contingency of that necessity: having a sense of one's 'species being' produces a range of freedom in relation to what will become 'the human'.[13] 'We' recognise ourselves as agents, *ex post facto*, of the history we unwittingly bring into being. The idea of history not simply as a line of time or chronology but a *condition* or a force that demands reckoning produces the sense of 'the human' that also marks the Anthropocene. The notion of negative universal history captures this specific mode of the human: rather than recognition of a given natural kind, the universality of the human comes through looking back and intuiting the forces that generated a present that occurred contingently but is now constitutive of who 'we' are.

Counter-time

What if one were to refuse species being *and* negative universal history? This would leave the Anthropocene *not* as an 'and' that gives the text (and history) one more dimension, but as one mode of historical existence among others.

If I opened by saying that Woolf was at once the best of modernists for connecting with the Anthropocene, she was also the worst. If we take 'and the Anthropocene' to be an extension and scaling up, rendering our species being not just biological but geological, there is the Woolf of *Orlando*, but there is also the Woolf of a form of counter-patriarchy. For this Woolf, saying something truly consequential (but perhaps not about *the human*) requires cutting oneself off from the coherence of the whole. If one seeks to do more than *understand* the Anthropocene, if one entertains the possibility of something more than (or different from) methods of coherence, it may well be that what appears as the Anthropocene opens the possibility of a destruction or derangement of the attachment to 'the human' that brought the concept and actuality of the Anthropocene into being. Thomas H. Ford has drawn attention to Woolf's own thematisation not simply of climate but of the capacity to apprehend climates. A survey of the whole is a literary, world-transforming and geopolitical event:

> Midway through Woolf's comic romance of English literary history, Orlando looks out over the city of London at midnight on the final day of the eighteenth century. Like Wordsworth upon Westminster Bridge, she applies the organising gaze of the prospect poem to the metropolis, with lyrically Romantic results. As first surveyed by her, the city embodies the eighteenth century as an age of reason.[14]

There would, then, be two Woolfs (maybe an entire pack); there would be the Woolf of *Orlando* where the space of privacy, romance, poetry and sexual difference has as its condition of possibility the racial imperialism that frames the novel. For 'a head' to appear as just one more object marked only by the racialising reduction of the body from which it has been dismembered, there needs to be all the social stratification, nobility, valour, beauty, starkly binary sexual difference and romance that the novel places at its heart. 'Anthropos' is this complex of absolutely heightened interiority and sexual difference, where all the world unfolds from the space of a single desiring subject, whose gaze allows the world to be so much backdrop. This is a world where the subject whose life pans across history can comprehend climate, politics, others and things – all as expressive fragments of a single and dynamic whole. The Anthropocene is also, essentially, the Anthropo-*scene*: history is not a straight line, but a panorama where the present looks back, synthesises the past and produces a reading and intuiting 'we' who is capable of discerning a single nature that includes 'us' all.

One can only possess a room of one's own and allow climate chaos to become a lively backdrop if there have already been social stratifications productive of something like 'the poor'. The anonymous labour that builds the spaces of private writing and grand worldly survey hums away in the background of Woolf's novels. This is what humanity is: a history in which 'man' as the being of historical, aesthetic, courtly and geopolitical grandeur emerges from the noisy rubble of the multitude:

> the couple lingered there, shouldered by apprentices; tailors; fishwives; horse dealers; cony catchers; starving scholars; maid-servants in their whimples; orange girls; ostlers; sober citizens; bawdy tapsters; and a crowd of little ragamuffins such as always haunt the outskirts of a crowd, screaming and scrambling among people's feet – all the riff-raff of the London streets indeed was there, jesting and jostling, here casting dice, telling fortunes, shoving, tickling, pinching; here uproarious, there glum; some of them with mouths gaping a yard wide; others as little reverent as daws on a house-top; all as variously rigged out as their purse or stations allowed; here in fur and broadcloth; there in tatters. (O 33)

Only with a distinction between persons of state whose romances become constitutive of the collective imagination (or the European 'mind') and the anonymous poor can there be a world of privacy, a world that can *only* be grasped if one retreats from the coherence of the whole. A room of one's own is a multivalent figure in Woolf. In *Orlando* that space of private writing is clearly marked off from, and made possible by, racial imperialism; the lyric poet has as his condition of possibility centuries of labour that produce an elevated gaze that, in turn, allows the world to appear as a dazzling array of *things*. The private room that enables the retreat of writing and an aesthetics of survey is also equiprimordial with the gaze of sexual difference; the subject of literary production purveys and surveys a world of desirable things, each thing a fragment of a single and dazzling 'nature'. 'Nature' is produced in this event of sexual difference. To be a subject is to be other than a thing, while things are there to be desired. Courtly love, writing, sexual difference, commodification, racial capitalism and empire: all assemble to produce Anthropos. There is no 'man' – Woolf knows this – without the private space of writing. From Descartes's retreat to a space to think (and therefore be) to the modernist for whom it is fatal to think of one's sex, there is an event of critical distance that allows the world to appear as so much vibrant matter. It is this event of distance that Woolf at once embraces (in the idea of a room of one's own) and then overturns: the impoverished and merely materialist writer in 'Modern Fiction' is in a sealed room incapable of seeing into the *life* of things: 'There is not so much as a draught between the frames of the windows, or a crack in the boards' (*E4* 158). She continues:

> it is possible to press a little further and wonder whether we may not refer our sense of being in a bright yet narrow room, confined and shut in, rather than enlarged and set free, to some limitation imposed by the method as well as by the mind. Is it the method that inhibits the creative power? Is it due to the method that we feel neither jovial nor magnanimous, but centred in a self which, in spite of its tremor of susceptibility, never embraces or creates what is outside itself and beyond? (*E4* 162)

What we know from *A Room of One's Own* is that there is *at least one* mode of existence that is not yet blessed with enclosed space. This cramped space generates the subject of what Woolf refers to as materialism; it is akin to the later comportment of the Anthroposcene, where a single vision can see into the life of things. In *Orlando* this lucid comprehension of the whole is depicted in competing tendencies. There is both the sovereign command of the whole, and a recognition of the elusive and vital forces that solicit the subject of any possible materialism. *Orlando* is a recognition of vibrant matter, where the dazzling array of life serves to enhance, extend and intensify the range of experience. There is also, alongside this Anthroposcenic subject, in Woolf, another modality of difference. There is another way of existing, without a room of one's own. Lily Briscoe, at the end of *To the Lighthouse* steps away from familial, domestic, private, vibrant and representational space to produce a radically depersonalised experience of pure difference: not the difference between subject and object and male and female, but a difference beyond subjective recognition: 'With a sudden intensity, as if she saw it clear for a second, she drew a line there, in the centre. It was done; it was finished' (*TTL* 334).

There is a deeply counter-Anthroposcenic force at work throughout Woolf's corpus. We can begin with 'Modern Fiction', and its refusal of materialism. Isolate yourself in a bright cramped space and what is before you will be there to be surveyed, purveyed and mastered; the space of privacy yields *the world* – a horizon with a single (if complex) sense. As the narrator of 'The Mark on the Wall' notes: 'How readily our thoughts swarm upon a new object, lifting it a little way, as ants carry a blade of straw so feverishly, and then leave it' (*CSF* 77). The cramped space of the room allows the world to be marked. *Man* is made possible by a room of one's own; there can only be 'the subject' with the spaces of privacy, introspection and sexual difference. *Orlando* situates the space of private writing as a retreat from the enabling labour of the anonymous poor, as intertwined with a world of things – including racialised persons as things – and as bound up with a drama of sexual difference. Once woman becomes that forever unattainable, mysterious, retreating and impossible object the subject becomes nothing more than the event of desire; *the subject* is not a thing within the world but the being for whom the world exists as vibrant matter.

If there is a history of Anthropos marked out in *Orlando* and criticised in 'Modern Fiction', there are also counter-Anthroposcenic events. The event of sexual transition would be but one of many moments when the difference constitutive of the subject now becomes an event within time and narrative. This is both an abstract and a concrete geopolitical gesture in Woolf's work. Abstractly or, more accurately, *immaterially* there is an affirmation of the end of the world. If one were capable of being now male, now female, now early modern, now Victorian, one would lose one's world: rather than being nothing more than one's own horizon of sense and possibility, one might imagine living beyond one's own life.

One might think of the world, as Woolf does, as the horizon of sense: the things that compose one's day-to-day existence. This is the drama of *To the Lighthouse*. The novel opens, literally, with the cutting-out of commodified things: 'James Ramsay, sitting on the floor [cut] out pictures from the illustrated catalogue of the Army and Navy Stores' (*TTL* 181). Like the room in 'Modern Fiction', *the world* is a brightly lit and limited space, a space of purpose, meaning and history. It is a space of subjects and objects and a material reality, and it is a space of sexual difference: a being who can say 'I' for whom the world is a horizon of self-making. It is only when the world breaks down that something other than the 'man' of sexual difference and the things of the world might come into being. In *To the Lighthouse* this occurs when Lily Briscoe's 'vision' takes the form *not* of representing the figure of woman (the wonderfully nurturing Mrs Ramsay) and *not* by enclosing oneself in a space that is brightly lit so that one might see the world (a lighthouse, a room of one's own). Instead, there is a cut in the real, a marker that is not between self and world but a mark as such. Abstractly, immaterially, the world ends – no longer the space of interconnected and historically meaningful things – and what comes into being is a difference *not one's own*.

More concretely, both Orlando and Lily Briscoe live through catastrophes of the Earth. Before the climate chaos of the little Ice Age interrupts the flows of commerce on the Thames, Orlando's gaze is presented as quintessentially Anthroposcenic. Elevated, sensitive to difference, aware of the order of things and ecologically attuned; this is the gaze of the modern man of poetry, for whom the world is one vast interconnected and vibrantly material system:

> Sometimes one could see the English Channel, wave reiterating upon wave. Rivers could be seen and pleasure boats gliding on them; and galleons setting out to sea; and armadas with puffs of smoke from which came the dull thud of cannon firing; and forts on the coast; and castles among the meadows; and here a watch tower; and there a fortress; and again some vast mansion like that of Orlando's father, massed like a town in the valley circled by walls. To the east there were the spires of London and the smoke of the city; and perhaps on the very sky line, when the wind was in the right quarter, the craggy top and serrated edges of Snowdon herself showed mountainous among the clouds. For a moment Orlando stood counting, gazing, recognising. That was his father's house; that his uncle's. His aunt owned those three great turrets among the trees there. The heath was theirs and the forest; the pheasant and the deer, the fox, the badger, and the butterfly.
> [. . .]
> He sighed profoundly, and flung himself – there was a passion in his movements which deserves the word – on the earth at the foot of the oak tree. (O 11)

Only with a room of one's own can one perceive and portray the complexity of a Nature that is not there as a site of collective labour, but rather appears – also – as one's own. A room of one's own creates the brightly lit space that enables the sympathetic survey of the whole. What might it be to write *without* a room of one's own? In both *Orlando* and *To the Lighthouse* there are planetary (but not global)[15] intimations of a world without the enclosed space of the subject from which the world might appear as a single horizon of sense. Taking our cue from *Orlando, and* the psychoanalytic conceptions of sexual difference that were crucial to Woolf's milieu, one might imagine that there is no woman – no ultimate being who would fulfil, conclude and overcome the distance of desire.[16] Like

Freud, Woolf depicts sexual difference as a dialectic of lost objects, substitution and possession. As a man, Orlando is a master of property, an agent of history, an author of poetry, a pursuer of women; as a woman Orlando knows what it is to be an object, to be pursued. Anticipating Lacan's reading of Freud, 'woman' is that which is never fully given.[17] The intimation of a plenitude beyond all the objects generates the feminine as an oceanic feeling, an origin prior to the vicissitudes of a desire that must seek object after object to ameliorate its necessary alienation.

As already noted, *To the Lighthouse* begins with the sexual drama of desired objects that are cut off from that which all desire tends towards – some state of plenitude beyond all the substituted objects that stand in for ultimate fulfilment (the source of light, the end of desiring difference). Lily Briscoe's final event of aesthetic 'vision' occurs after she steps outside. Rather than the subject–object grasp of reality or the brightly lit enclosed space of the lighthouse (or private room) that would give a clear, distinct and easily grasped materiality, Lily is overtaken by forces that come into being *without* perception. Vision without perception, a 'seeing' that simply *is*. Carmichael sees the journey to the lighthouse take place and includes the event in a single and sweeping vision of humanity: 'He stood there spreading his hands over all the weakness and suffering of mankind; she thought he was surveying, tolerantly, compassionately, their final destiny' (*TTL* 334). His vision is Anthroposcenic, akin to the early male Orlando's capacity to survey and grasp the world, a vision that is entwined with empire, subjectivity, the capacity to see history as a panorama of objects. After that crowning gesture, Lily produces a 'work' that neither requires the mastery of survey, nor the desire to take part in the great canon of names: 'It would be hung in the attics, she thought; it would be destroyed. But what did that matter?' (*TTL* 334). Lily's art is counter-Anthroposcenic; it neither grasps the whole, nor seeks to preserve itself. Its single line on a blurred canvas occurs after Carmichael's crowning gesture; after the grand complete vision of man, there will not be art that lasts, nor will there be art that mourns. There may be a single and fragile line beyond representation and lyricism. In *Orlando* there is also an afterlife or otherlife of art, hinted at beyond the borders of world survey and sexual difference. The male Orlando is not only master of property, pursuer of women and lord of empire, whose wistful gratitude for the anonymous poor renders him ever more kingly; he is also a poet, for whom nature seems to demand lyric expression. He knows that the English sensibility alone can feel the intensities of nature that is liberated from the needs of life. Orlando's transition from male to female is also a transition from a room of one's own to a life with empire's other. As with the novel's opening where the head of a 'moor' captures a world in which all that is other than oneself is nothing more than objects for play and poetry, so Orlando's life with the 'gipsies' [*sic*] at once takes her to a world beyond the possessive individualism of empire, even if it also has her yearning for the sensibilities in which one might have a vision of 'Nature' (that object of survey fit for poetry, if not survival):

> The pleasure of having no documents to seal, or sign, no flourishes to make, no calls to pay was enough. The gipsies followed the grass; when it was grazed down, on they moved again. She washed in streams if she washed at all; no boxes, red, blue, or green were presented to her; there was not a key, let alone a golden key in the whole camp; as for 'visiting', the word was unknown. She milked the goats; she collected brushwood; she stole a hen's egg now and then, but always put a coin or a pearl in place of it; she herded cattle; she stripped vines; she trod the grape; she filled the goat-skin and drank from it; and when she remembered how, at about this time of day, she should have been making the motions of drinking and smoking over an empty coffee cup and a pipe which lacked tobacco, she laughed aloud, cut herself another hunch of bread, and begged for a puff from old Rustum's pipe, filled though it was with cow dung.
>
> The gipsies, with whom it is obvious that she must have been in secret communication before the revolution, seem to have looked upon her as one of themselves (which is always the highest compliment a people can pay) and her dark hair and dark complexion bore out the belief that she was, by birth, one of them and had been snatched by an English Duke from a nut tree when she was a baby and taken to that barbarous land where people live in houses because they are too feeble and diseased to stand the open air. Thus, though in many ways inferior to them, they were willing to help her to become more like them; taught her their arts of cheese-making and basket-weaving, their science of stealing and bird-snaring, and were even prepared to consider letting her marry among them. (O 84–5)

As I noted at the opening of this essay, there is a Woolf of new materialism and vibrant matter: this Woolf gives herself a room of her own, looks out upon the world, sees into the life of things, can embrace within herself male and female, and can recognise art and poetry – or writing in general – as the creation of the world. Then there is the other Woolf. Let us not call her antimaterialist, or anti-new materialist but destructive of the space of 'man' that generated the problem of ontology in general. There are *no documents to sign* – we have reached the 'end of the book and the beginning of writing' (though not in the manner imagined by the Derrida who declared this to be the fragile path beyond Eurocentrism).[18] At the edge of the lyric subject who is able to include the poor, a severed head, an oak tree and things within a magisterial survey of the world, there is a writing beyond matter and matters, a writing that undoes the world: imagine being the object – even if this too emerges from a colonising fantasy, and imagine that you ever so briefly become one of *them* and no longer the all-inclusive and matter-mastering presupposed 'we': 'Thus, though in many ways inferior to them, they were willing to help her to become more like them; taught her their arts of cheese-making and basket-weaving, their science of stealing and bird-snaring, and were even prepared to consider letting her marry among them'.

After the End of the World

In both *To the Lighthouse* and *Orlando* the violence of empire is intertwined with the ways in which the history of sexual difference produces the privacy of interiority and an Anthroposcenic vision. There can only be the recognition and event of the Anthropocene – a negative universal history in which 'we' all appear as in a single planetary predicament – after the great quest of enlightenment freedom that demanded so much resource extraction and plunder. That journey of empire, in turn, requires the formation of 'man' as a subject for whom the world is Nature, a domain of production and always a private space of one's own.

Deleuze and Guattari situate Freud's oedipal family within a history of racial empire: the family of sexual difference (a fatherly authority and maternal nurturing principle) flattens and contracts the vast array of collective social forms that allow desire to attach itself to inhuman and cosmic intensities.[19] Once desire is privatised and familial, the world beyond the subject becomes nothing more than vibrant matter. Just as *Orlando* charts the lyric subject and lordly vision as equiprimoridal with the spoils of empire, so *To the Lighthouse* charts the refusal of familial sexual difference, with the refusal of the grand vision of the Earth and with the refusal of the archival fetish for the preservation of who 'we' are. Both are novels that mark the end of the world as the end of Nature and the end of sexual difference. That Orlando can transition from male to female, from empire to dispossession, from lyric poetry to a sense that there might be a world in which Nature is not an object for subjective outpouring, captures Woolf's sense of a vision that is not of this world.

There are, then, two Woolfs. One might read *Orlando* from the point of view of the Anthroposcene, such that the private space of desire and sexual difference is but one fragment of a planetary whole. The twentieth-century desire for a room of one's own is a late moment in a history of the sexual contract, which is also a global contract. The domestic privacy and the privilege of being a subject who can judge the world from the point of reason is a contraction of collective forms of existence that are increasingly annihilated by the hyperconsumption of the nuclear family and the private individual. This takes its toll on the planet, generating the condition of the twenty-first century where the *problem* is a room of one's own – both in the literal sense of privatised space and consumption, and in the figural sense as diagnosed by Woolf in 'Modern Fiction' where the brightly lit interior cramped space cuts one off from the world so that it might be surveyed and mastered (and then lost in its multiplicity). To add the planetary to the historical scale of the fiction allows us to read the adventures of Orlando within the deep history of the planet and to see the catastrophe of 'Time Passes' in *To the Lighthouse* as not simply a trauma for the family that frames the novel, but a moment of ecological rupture. The war that cuts into *To the Lighthouse* – severing one part of the novel from the other – also cuts into the planet. The nuclear bombing of Hiroshima and Nagasaki that 'ends' the next war is one of the many markers of the Anthropocene, while also opening a radical conception of annihilation in the new global order. Orlando's poem and Lily Briscoe's painting are artworks on the borders of planetary-transforming empires. Orlando, across times and sexes, is the exemplary modern subject – capable of detaching a fragment of nature in order to capture beauty in general. Lily's painting occurs as a moment of dissolution or becoming-imperceptible: no longer capturing the outside world and grasping the nature of reality, she offers a gesture that makes no claim to archival permanence. In these two works, or work and counter-work, Woolf offers two Anthropocenes. There is the magisterial, lyric, sexually differentiated drama of empire, in which events such as the little Ice Age can now be grasped as fragments of a single, global and planetary 'we'. It is when Orlando becomes a woman that the poem, 'The Oak Tree', starts to become rhizomatic, branching out into marginalia. The heightened subject of art and writing emerges from the noise and chaos of anonymous labour, experiences sexual difference as yet one more drama within the world and remains above and beyond their handiwork. The subject of *Orlando* is Anthroposcenic, a being for whom the world is one dazzling array of vibrant matter and a fragment of a negative universal history that 'we' can now recognise as planetary and capturing 'us' all. There is also another Anthropocene at the margins; what does the planet look like from the point of view of the refusal of privacy, property and a space of one's own? There are the murmuring collectives in *Orlando*, and then of course there is 'the head'. If 'Modern Fiction' berates the point of view of the cordoned-off subject into its own brightly lit space and asks us to think beyond a world of matters at hand, one might either step out – as Lily Briscoe will do – and refuse the claims of the archive, of being remembered, of taking up the task of the grand history of humanity in general. Or one might go further and ask whether the anonymous labour, wreckage, severed heads and suffering bodies would seek to save the world that has – from the point of view of grandeur – finally arrived at recognising its planetary and global force.

Notes

1. See Timothy Clark's essay 'Scale'.
2. Gamble, Hanan and Nail, 'What is New Materialism?'.
3. Marcus, 'Transcendence', 223–5.
4. See Meillassoux's *After Finitude*, 20.
5. See Brush, 'Inhuman, All Too Human'; Taylor, *The Sky of Our Manufacture*; and Adkins, 'The Climate of Orlando'.
6. Here I follow the work of Rosi Braidotti, who identifies Woolf's pacifist ontology: 'Woolf's explorations of the intensity of life go well beyond the self, the individual, and even the human' (133). In this essay I see Woolf's work pulling in two directions, at once posthuman in Braidotti's sense while remaining hyperhumanist in its historical vision.
7. Lukács, *Essays on Realism*.
8. Derrida, *Edmund Husserl's 'Origin of Geometry'*.
9. Connolly, *Climate Machines*.
10. Mitchell, 'Romanticism and the Life of Things'.
11. Chakrabarty, 'Climate of History'.
12. Weheliye, *Habeas Viscus*.
13. Baucom, *History 4°*.
14. Ford, 'Romantic Climate Change', 175.
15. In *The Climate of History in a Planetary Age*, Dipesh Chakrabarty marks a distinction between the global inclusion of human history, where nature is a backdrop, versus the planetary where forces of history exceed human agency and apprehension.
16. Copjec, *Imagine There's No Woman*.
17. Lacan, *Seminaire XX*, 75.
18. Derrida, *Of Grammatology*, 6.
19. Deleuze and Guattari, *Anti-Oedipus*.

Bibliography

Adkins, Peter. 'The Climate of *Orlando*: Woolf, Braidotti and the Anthropocene'. *Comparative Critical Studies* 19, no. 2 (2022): 237–57.
Baucom, Ian. *History 4° Celsius: Search for a Method in the Age of the Anthropocene*. Durham, NC: Duke University Press, 2020.
Braidotti, Rosi. 'Virginia Woolf, Immanence and Ontological Pacifism'. *Comparative Critical Studies* 19, no. 2 (June 2022): 131–48.
Brush, Emma. 'Inhuman, All Too Human: Virginia Woolf and the Anthropocene'. *Resilience* 8, no. 2 (2020): 69–87.
Chakrabarty, Dipesh. 'The Climate of History: Four Theses'. *Critical Inquiry* 35, no. 2 (2009): 197–222.
——. *The Climate of History in a Planetary Age*. Chicago: University of Chicago Press, 2021.
Clark, Timothy. 'Scale'. In *Telemorphosis: Theory in the Era of Climate Change*, edited by Tom Cohen, 148–66. Ann Arbor, MI: Open Humanities Press, 2012.
Connolly, William E. *Climate Machines, Fascist Drives, and Truth*. Durham, NC: Duke University Press, 2019.
Copjec, Joan. *Imagine There's no Woman: Ethics and Sublimation*. Cambridge, MA: MIT Press, 2002.
Deleuze, Gilles, and Félix Guattari. *Anti-Oedipus: Capitalism and Schizophrenia*, translated by Robert Hurley, Mark Seem and Helen R. Lane. New York: Viking Press, 1977.
Derrida, Jacques. *Edmund Husserl's Origin of Geometry: An Introduction*, translated by John P. Leavey Jr. Lincoln: University of Nebraska Press, 1989.
——. *Of Grammatology*, translated by Gayatri Chakravorty Spivak. Baltimore, MD: Johns Hopkins, 1997.
Ford, Thomas H. 'Orlando's Romantic Climate Change'. In *Romantic Climates: Literature and Science in an Age of Catastrophe*, edited by Anne Collett and Olivia Murphy, 173–90. London: Palgrave Macmillan, 2019.
Gamble, Christopher N., Joshua S. Hanan and Thomas Nail, 'What is New Materialism?' *Angelaki* 24, no. 6 (2019): 111–34.
Lacan, Jacques. *Le Seminaire XX, Encore*. Paris: Seuil, 1975.
Lukács, Georg. *Essays on Realism*, edited by Rodney Livingston, translated by David Fernbach. Cambridge, MA: MIT Press, 1980.
Marcus, Laura. 'Transcendence, Idealism and Modernity'. *History of European Ideas* 43, no. 3 (2017): 223–5.
Meillassoux, Quentin. *After Finitude: An Essay on the Necessity of Contingency,* translated by Ray Brassier. London: Continuum, 2008.
Mitchell, W. J. T. 'Romanticism and the Life of Things: Fossils, Totems, and Images'. *Critical Inquiry* 28, no. 1 (2001): 167–84.
Taylor, Jesse Oak. *The Sky of Our Manufacture: The London Fog in British Fiction from Dickens to Woolf*. Charlottesville: University of Virginia Press, 2016.

Weheliye, Alexander G. *Habeas Viscus: Racializing Assemblages, Biopolitics, and Black Feminist Theories of the Human*. Durham, NC: Duke University Press, 2014.
Woolf, Virginia. *The Complete Shorter Fiction*, edited by Susan Dick. San Diego: Harcourt Brace Jovanovich, 1985.
——. *Collected Novels of Virginia Woolf: Mrs. Dalloway, To the Lighthouse, The Waves*, edited by Stella McNichol. London: Palgrave, 1992.
——. *The Essays of Virginia Woolf*, edited by Andrew McNeillie (vols 1–4) and Stuart N. Clarke (vols 5–6). 6 vols. London: Hogarth Press, 1986–2011.
——. *Orlando: A Biography*. New York: Rosetta Books, 2008.
——. *A Room of One's Own*, edited by David Bradshaw and Stuart N. Clarke. Oxford: Wiley Blackwell, 2015.

Chapter 4

'Mud and dung': Virginia Woolf's Environmental Mattering of War

Molly Volanth Hall

According to Samuel Hynes, the First World War ushers in the 'death of landscape', producing an emergent way of perceiving the world that assumes a 'dead Nature'.[1] Though the environment itself cannot perish, interwar English literary depictions of its destruction or eulogisation are rife. Such writing registers this curious, seemingly post-natural epistemological shift. And yet, not all writers of that war opt for a dead materiality. Virginia Woolf's 'body of work', as Barbara Will notes, 'both begins and ends with the experience of war'.[2] Yet, Woolf's responses to war rely deeply on an animate, organic and elemental aesthetic.[3] She often uses a living, agential environment to stage what many consider an ontological shift – a 'break' or 'schism' – rent by the First World War, a breach that opens a perceived gap between humanity and the embedded, natural habitation of the earth.[4] Similarly to many of the writers who served on the front, Woolf's interwar work as a civilian tropes one particular environmental matter with significance. Mud, the ground-matter often most associated with First World War landscapes, appears with consistency across her interwar works. Although it might be tempting to divide postwar modernists into those who did and did not further this anthropocentric myth of nature's annihilation, Woolf does not fit easily into either camp. Acknowledging the losses wrought by the war,[5] Woolf remains aware that it is our relationship to the material world that is altered more than physical reality itself.

Because of her decentralisation of human agency within nature, Woolf's writing provides a salient arena for scholars seeking to place the First World War within an Anthropocene framework. As Peter Adkins and several contributors in this collection note, the Anthropocene as an era of climate change presents particular narratological and aesthetic challenges to humanity – both on and off the page – marking, as it does, the overlapping of modernity with the human species' ability to impact global environmental systems, primarily through the expression of CO_2 into our atmosphere at such levels that it created a change in climate patterns.[6] In addition to being smattered across Woolf's literary responses to war, mud already serves as an apt marker for the human-environmental violence wrought by the war because, as Christophe Bonneuil and Jean-Baptiste Fressoz note, mud's 'all-pervasive' presence in the 'European wars of the twentieth century is more an effect of the destruction of soil by the passage of military vehicles than a pre-existing characteristic of the terrain'.[7] Mud, then, stains the earth as a trace of human intervention in the geologic as much as it marks the pages of Woolf's interwar writing. In so doing, it suggests forms of thinking about the emergent Anthropocene.

Global Crisis, Aesthetics and Mattering

Though claims about Woolf's awareness of the Anthropocene as a distinct geologic era would be anachronistic, her quest to represent ideas and experiences that resist form (at least as it was known before the war) forecasts Anthropocene thinking. In excess of existing forms, she writes mud (and by extension the muddied mind) as a way to respond to a crisis of unprecedented scale. In the wake of the First World War, Woolf felt that 'the language of war has been deprived of the terror and horror it should inspire' to which she responded, according to Karen Levenback, with her own 'transgressive representations and an ongoing process of reorientation'.[8] Though for Woolf the crisis requiring reorientation of language to reality is global war – and the First World War in particular, inclusive of the patriarchy and fascism with which it is bound up – her crisis resembles what Timothy Morton calls a hyperobject, the term they coined to describe a different crisis: global warming. Hyperobjects 'involve profoundly different temporalities than the human-scale ones we are used to', they are 'invisible to humans for stretches of time', only 'exhibit[ing] their effects interobjectively', meaning that 'they can [only] be detected in a space that consists of interrelationships between [the] aesthetic properties of objects'.[9] In other words, hyperobjects are never directly visible but can only be perceived partially in the effects they have on more perceptible objects, such as rising sea levels, hot days, dying animals, or human refugees. Like grappling with the whole of a multiyear global conflict that stretches from trench to home front, '[t]hinking them is intrinsically tricky',[10] and our inability to see a hyperobject in toto makes it difficult to narrate the climatic problems of the Anthropocene. As I write this sentence, England and much of Europe is consumed with the tangible violence of climate change: record-setting heatwaves are endangering life directly with 42-degree-Celsius highs in the United Kingdom, while indirectly the heat has also sparked raging wildfires across the unusually dry forests of France and Spain.[11] This essay argues that moments where Woolf mediates the distributed crisis of war via an aesthetics of mud model ways for us to respond to the newly acknowledged contemporary global conflict of climate change.

This is possible for two reasons: the way in which mud represents shifts in scale and as a preference for formlessness. As an all-encompassing yet distributed event, both the First World War and climate change require scalar shifts in order to understand, represent and respond to such socio-political and ecological crises. Jesse Oak Taylor points to the way modernists are already representing a world undergoing anthropogenic climate change without being directly aware of what exactly their works register – like a fog that is actually smog. This is part of his methodological approach, suggesting we treat literary history a bit more like climate change history. Books, like ice cores, are material records containing unintentional traces of information that can, as Walter Benjamin would say, form a constellation of moments with the present, illuminating a new potential future. Taylor explains that in aestheticising the entanglement of human and environmental history, 'climatic modernism' is 'a condition in which modernity refigures our relationship to deep time, making any moment at once immediate and radically dispersed on scales that exceed human memory'.[12] This refiguring is a necessary step to depicting the 'abnatural' – both abnormal and still natural – environment emerging from a long period of imperialist and capitalist extractivism: the environment in which modernists, such as Woolf, found themselves situated. Taylor reads Woolf's work in particular as 'strikingly atmospheric, dramatizing the mutual infiltration of self and surroundings', explaining that in so doing, she 'helps to foreground the convergence of the emergence of the Anthropocene and aesthetic modernism'.[13] In addition to, or even as an extension of, extractivism, I argue that Woolf's writing also evinces formal shifts that register global war. Furthermore, these refigurations allow her literature to catch glimpses of an experience of wartime that necessitated an antirealist aesthetic, marked by the refusal of form and excess of scales that delimit this seemingly endless state of exception.

The necessity for antirealism further binds representations of the First World War and climate change together. While Amitav Ghosh largely critiques realism in order to suggest it be reconstituted differently rather than rejected for an avant-garde or magical-realist aesthetic, his recent claim that realism is unable to capture the reality of climate change mirrors the complaints made by veteran writers during and after the First World War.[14] Many of these responded to the exceptional state of war with antirealist style and forms, much like some of the best climate fiction writing today. I argue that Woolf's antirealist aesthetics, in her responses to the First World War, offer one ideal model for a late Anthropocene aesthetics and epistemology.

A further scalar similarity between world war and climate change is the global nature of both crises. In addition to the First World War's immediate destruction of warfront environs, in the 'background', the war catalysed global environmental changes via alterations to supply chains, resource extraction methods and fossil fuel economies.[15] As well as being contributing forces in the great acceleration of fuel use, which produces the atmospheric carbon levels allowing for a self-aware Anthropocene demarcation, the First *World* War (and Second), ironically become 'opportunities' for reinforcing the sense of planetarity, to borrow Susan Stanford Friedman's phrase, that marks modernisms and that will be needed to comprehend the Anthropocene framework. In other words, the First World War becomes one of the first needs for thinking globally, a morbid precursor to thinking climatically about the global phenomena of climate change. One of the abnatural effects of the First World War was the way in which it was felt on two simultaneous scales: both locally or individually and collectively or globally. As Walter Benjamin notes, 'A generation [. . .] now stood under the open sky in a countryside in which nothing remained unchanged but the clouds'.[16] And even these, we now know, are remade. Woolf's interwar work captures these diffuse, interconnected feelings, as well as the ways in which shifting global realities impacted home fronts foundationally. The way, for example, that English tree cover, already much reduced to only about ten per cent of its pre-Roman state, was further halved during the blockades of the First World War.[17] And yet, though the environs of England quickly line the trenches of France, the 'First World War continued and intensified trends' of environmental exploitation and degradation 'from the nineteenth century', explains Tait Keller, rather than 'upsetting or subverting them'.[18] Woolf's muddy aesthetics capture this combination of rupture and continuity as well. As signifier for the constitutional destabilisation and corruption of the war experience, mud is an active trope, connecting and unsettling pre- and postwar historical narratives of human–environmental epistemology. Seizing on this, Woolf's interwar work dwells often on mud and the muddled mind, drawn to its unsettling and disruptive associations and the creative potential of their deformations.

Mud, in all its viscous, sticky, distasteful qualities, was quickly associated in popular and literary discourse with the war. Santanu Das describes the 'slimescapes' of the war that confronted soldiers 'with the threat, both physical and psychic, of dissolution into formless matter at a time when modern industrial weaponry was eviscerating human form'.[19] Mud killed, as men would get stuck and expire from the fatigue of attempting to escape. Conflict anthropologist Matthew Leonard notes that

> [t]here was a feeling among the belligerents that the mud of the Front [. . .] was eroding humanity. The mudscapes that the men were forced to live in became all-consuming and the ground was like a living entity – a landscape 'alive' with the dead. It was as if the landscape was taking revenge for the destruction wrought upon it by man.[20]

In his *The Memoirs of George Sherston* (1937), for example, Siegfried Sassoon writes of his semi-autobiographical protagonist and the First World War veteran's 'mud-stained mind'.[21] Like many writers who survived the front, mud marks the stain left by the war on his psyche, even after its official end, back in England decades on.[22] While still conveying a deep and shared respect for the trauma and loss of the First World War, Woolf pushes mud to register more than just the terror of subjective and bodily dissolution. For Woolf, the destruction of the war zone abroad revealed the cracks and fissures in certain domestic structures, as she elucidates in *Three Guineas* (1938). Woolf displaces mud from this masculinist perspective, androgenising and queering mud so that this lack of form becomes generative, (non)reproductive; exposing certain things as in decline and making space for others to emerge, though these are always in an act of becoming.

Hence, for Woolf, mud is not necessarily a direct referent to the trenches, though it is in many ways borne out of that chasm in the earth. In her pages, mud coalesces around two interconnected nodes: the creative mind and primitivity. In addition to throwing systems of social, political and economic life into chaos, the war also called into question the very ability of language to articulate stable meaning in the face of such unprecedented material and epistemic disruption.

As Vincent Sherry explains, this is particularly legible in the literary experimentation of the English modernists. Woolf embraces this loss of faith in the rational and mimetic representation of reality by placing a new faith in words themselves; words do not merely describe our actuality, they are, as she notes in 'Modern Fiction', 'life or spirit, truth or reality' (*E4* 160). Ali Smith's recent piece in *The Guardian* on Woolf, Katherine Mansfield and writing in a time of crisis reminds us that 'the novel can't just leave the war out'. Smith is quoting Katherine Mansfield who herself is writing in outrage about Woolf's then latest novel, *Night and Day* (1919). According to Smith, herself often considered a Climate Fiction writer, Mansfield and Woolf shared the sense that after the First World War, not only was there a sense of loss, but that the collectively traumatic experience necessitated a shift in literary form, not just in writing about the war, but in all writing thereafter.[23] Though Woolf's *Night and Day* reverts to a sense of safety in realism in the immediate aftermath of the war, *Jacob's Room* (1922) resumes a formal innovation that would touch all subsequent writing, muddying the remainder of her life's work with the First World War despite its not always being the subject matter.

Woolf's most direct address to the immediate losses of the war, *Jacob's Room*, is marked by banal instances of mud, but also by two moments where mud is associated with the mind, in particular, an antimasculinist mind. Woolf suggests that female creation is derogatorily associated with a lack of form by male appraisers in her description of Florinda's writing:

> the impediment between Florinda and her pen was something impassable. Fancy a butterfly, gnat, or other winged insect, attached to a twig which, clogged with mud, it rolls across a page. Her spelling was abominable. Her sentiments infantile. And for some reason when she wrote she declared her belief in God. Then there were crosses – tear stains; and the hand itself rambling. (*JR* 72)

Women's writing is too full of emotion, unfocused, overly material and an abomination to human ideals in its infantile and inhuman insect associations. These all collect around the specific reference to a sort of mud-ink: lacking the masculine ideals of form and rationality, woman's writing becomes degraded, messy, primitive. When, in the end, Florinda's writing is 'redeemed' because 'she cared' (*JR* 72), one can see Woolf's attempt to redeem formlessness for female creativity, a goal we can connect with other moments through their similar evocations of a formless or primitive mud and a muddled mind operating outside patriarchal and heteronormative structures.

Beyond the metaphysical realm of writing, Jacob also juxtaposes the female spaces of the private mind with the rational male spaces of the tangible public and historical sphere of the Parthenon in Greece. Woolf writes:

> this durability exists quite independently of our admiration. Although the beauty is sufficiently humane to weaken us, to stir the deep deposit of mud – memories, abandonments, regrets, sentimental devotions – the Parthenon is separate from all that; and if you consider how it has stood out all night, for centuries, you begin to connect the blaze [. . .] with the idea that perhaps it is beauty alone that is immortal. (*JR* 116)

Using contrasting stone and mud rhetorics, The Parthenon – and the European civilisation, history and ethos it represents – is aligned with 'durability', with that which is 'separate' from the 'humane' and the human, allowing it to have 'stood [. . .] for centuries', and possess 'immortal[ity]'. Such qualities are linked to its stone materiality. In contrast, the 'us' that its 'beauty' 'weaken[s]', is characterised as 'the deep deposit of mud', our inner matter of 'memories, abandonments, regrets, sentimental devotions', and such. Mud, when contrasted to stone, is almost immaterial in its formlessness. Form has, since Aristotle, been associated with the masculine, while matter, unruly, feminine, is, like mud, lacking in form and needs to be tamed to generate value and meaning. Evoking mud as that matter which (though denigrated by Jacob) defies form and is both human and feminine makes possible something beyond the stale metaphysics of Western Civilisation. Ironically, it is that form-loving civilisation whose patriarchal ideologies birthed the war that turns our main interlocutor, Jacob, into all ghostly form and no matter, or all matter as corpse and no form, depending on your perspective. The form of the novel suggests that 'the deep deposit of mud' may be more interesting than any Grecian monuments. Like the muddy mind of *The Years* (1937), which I will discuss in more detail later in this essay, mud can also evoke a sense of 'muddle and confusion', a 'muddle – all a mystery' that is desirable or productive precisely because it lacks form (*JR* 6, 87). In addition to the feminised muddied mind, Woolf also uses mud here to distinguish between, on the one hand, the sort of antigeologic, static *longue durée* thinking that monumental stone evokes – that petrified time of human glorification which is often called progress, so popular in her day – and on the other hand, the sort of inhuman perspective, or the human in excess of the heterosexual and male subject, that Woolf explores, recommends and practises herself. Woolf's use of formless mud finds a way after the upheavals of the war to make meaning in excess of fixed, inherited forms by relying, in fact, on the inhuman. Aaron Jaffe explains that modernism's evocations of the inhuman are always entangled in efforts to 'make matter matter'.[24] This is particularly true for writing of the First World War wherein 'degraded environments of battlefields and trenches characterised by mud, filth, decaying human and animal matter, and the obliteration of plant life' gave 'authors [. . .] particular occasion to reflect on what a comingling of human and more-than-human life might look and feel like in the most appalling extreme'.[25] Inhumanist thinking is then fostered by the very environs of the First World War, modelling the necessary response to an Anthropocene where matter reasserts itself as unruly once again.

While Woolf uses mud as an image both before and after the war, one can chart outwards from *Jacob's Room* how her usage starts to accrue certain meanings in *the years* following the First World War. Not detached from an embodied, material existence, Woolf's world of words *matters*, both as materiality and meaning. As I note above, Woolf's mud is not a direct reference to the trenches, but, it appears to have arisen directly from soldiers' experience of them, especially on the Western Front. There, as Trudi Tate explains, the proximity of living, soldiering bodies to corpse-bodies and the mud and earth of the trenches themselves – especially when corpse and earth-wall began to meld – presented an ontological crisis not only of their mortality, but their materiality – the mattering of their selves. Woolf did not spend any time on the front, a phenomenon that many contributors to Mark Hussey's *Virginia Woolf and War: Fiction, Reality, and Myth* note troubled her efforts to make sense of and write the war itself and her experience of it. Yet, her post-1918 work is suffused with both references to the war and marked by the struggle to make sense of the 'new world', as it is called repeatedly in *The Years*, that emerges after the war, after its 'complete break' (*TY* 292), after what she, in 'The Leaning Tower', calls 'a chasm in a smooth road' that came like a 'crash' and 'cut into [people's] lives' (*E6* 264, 266).

Though mud does not *dominate* the pages of any one work, across and within each novel and several of her diaries and letters, mud admits the primitive, regressive associations shared with veteran war writers. Yet, it does so in a way that uses mud's resistance to fixed temporalities of progress, wherein past is past and present manifests the progress of European civilisation with no traces of so-called savagery and barbarism. In so doing, it begins to deconstruct the need for dogmatic adherence to certain formalisms and traditions. Mud's primitive associations in Woolf expose the way in which England's narrative of itself as civilised is less stable than it was possible to believe before the war, the foundations of this narrative now as loose as a puddle of mud. Into this unsettled narrative, Woolf reimagines the possibilities of form and creativity beyond the heteropatriarchy, also via the signifier of its destruction: mud. Mud in this sense comes to explore the creative potentiality of the feminine, or perhaps androgynous, but certainly antiheteronormative and antipatriarchal, mind. Furthermore, this essay argues that in centring the nonhuman matter of mud, Woolf also models a framework that is attuned to the scalar shifts needed to register and grapple with climate change in the Anthropocene.[26]

A Primordial Present: Matter, Time and Scale

Like the supposedly unevolved implications of Florinda's writing and the 'humane' emotions evoked by classical art in *Jacob's Room*, the primitive mud of Woolf's interwar work can be found also in *Mrs Dalloway* (1925), again with mixed-gendered associations. In *Mrs Dalloway*'s post-war, London world we encounter a mud linked to both an abjected but agential feminine as well as an imperialist view. This view sees the horrifying primitivity that used to evoke a colonial elsewhere emerge instead in the heart of England, as Peter, our protagonist's old love-interest, encounters a poor old woman singing. Strolling through the park, Peter's thoughts are interrupted by an 'ancient song', which:

> bubbled up opposite Regent's Park Tube station; still the earth seemed green and flowery; still, though it issued from so rude a mouth, a mere hole in the earth, muddy too, matted with root fibres and tangled grasses, still the old bubbling burbling song, soaking through the knotted roots of infinite ages, and skeletons and treasure, streamed away in rivulets over the pavement and all along the Marylebone Road, and down towards Euston, fertilising, leaving a damp stain. (*MD* 81)

This 'muddy' stain is grotesque and dirty, but also generative ('fertile'); it connects this present England to a primeval past, through its persistent materiality. The hole, from which the mud-song issues, seems to be both the woman singer and the tube station entrance at once. This opening, when considered in the larger context of the novel, is rent by the war itself. The mud connects the putrid, barbarous decay of the scene to the inarticulable female voice. While it is not a pretty association, it is one with the power to disturb, to disrupt the male mind and advancement as it does Peter. Furthermore, though old and 'rude', the mark made by the woman singer is productive. Here, in the recent aftermath of the war, Woolf stages the reclamation of mud, of disruptive formlessness, as a method for articulating (even if as 'bubbling burbling song') resistance to the imperialism (having lately arrived from India) and masculinity that Peter represents in England's war legacy.

The scene's primitivity also creates a sense of the ancient: a seemingly anachronistically geologic past in the midst of a novel very concerned with the urban present. In this sense, too, mud tropes the unsettling effects of the war in ways that resonate with the unsettling scalar shifts needed to gasp climate change and our Anthropocene status. The First World War felt both too big (global, multiyear) and too small (intimate, personal) to be easily expressed or understood in the masterful way Victorian scientism instructed the English citizenry it needs must. The out of place presence of the old mud above materialises these affective apprehensions of war felt by many to indicate a degeneration of human progress, and in its violence and destruction seeming to rend the very fabric of civilisation as such in Europe. Woolf's texts teach us to pay attention to the material markers of such hyperobjects, and to weave narrative meaning around that which can be felt but not always seen by bending language beyond reality with tropes such as the muddled mind.

Similarly, *The Years* stages a wartime encounter between the Edwardian generation whose most direct use of the image of mud is to claim that the war has revealed a decaying civilisation, and a Victorian England that falsely held itself to be a beacon of progress. Repeatedly asking us to revise history and sense time differently, Sara Pargiter, a formerly middle-class woman in her now more impoverished apartment with her sister, states theatrically of their abode, and the general state of the society: 'In time to come [. . .] people, looking into this room – this cave, this little antre, scooped out of mud and dung, will hold their fingers to their noses [. . .] and say, "Pah! They stink!"' (*TY* 189). Jed Esty includes Woolf among the authors that in the interwar years participate in what he calls the inward-looking 'Anthropological turn' in English culture amid the contraction of empire following the war and a resultant identity crisis. Standing outside both her personal perspective and her time, Sara evokes an anthropologist's reading of their present from a distant future, reducing the 'modern' to just another primitive. The phrase, 'cave of mud and dung' is then repeated by Maggie. Woolf uses mud here to evoke a perspective outside the authorised timeline of history and, furthermore, from an inhuman standpoint, taking in thousands of years at a glance.

Furthermore, betwixt mud and dung – within this inability to materially distinguish human matter and waste from the surrounding environment – Woolf orients the readers into precisely the position feared by the protagonist of most First World War memoirs and fiction: a too-close proximity to nature. In *Dark Ecology*, Timothy Morton explores this too-closeness and other weird feelings. In the Anthropocene, they declare, 'We are faced with the task of thinking at temporal and spatial scales that are unfamiliar, even monstrously gigantic'.[27] Dark Ecology describes the discomfort, terror and even depression of thinking ecologically or practicing what Morton calls 'ecognosis'.[28] 'Ecology, after all, is the thinking of beings on a number of different scales, none of which has priority over the other' – including humans.[29] The simultaneous inhumanly geologic and corporally intimate stance that Sara's depiction models resembles the 'dark ecology' which Morton suggests we need to cultivate in order to reverse the extractive mindset continuing to hurtle us towards climate-change-induced extinction: to think 'future coexistence, namely coexistence unconstrained by present concepts'.[30] Similarly, in *Between the Acts* (1941), we find the primal cave of the married couple in the novel's closing pages, Mrs Swithin reading of the muddy swamps of primeval England in her *Outline of History* and Bart's appearance to Lucy as ape-like. Each of these suggest the presence of the primitive and, as Almas Khan notes, also 'the futility of lasting serenity for' Isa and Giles's interwar 'generation'.[31] As we see in the behaviour of Bart and Giles especially, this England moves, on the eve of a second global war, closer to the masculine ideals of the military state. To evoke the affective proximity of another socially regressive war, Woolf sprinkles the text with marks of primitivity – and mud. The novel everywhere evokes a non-linearity of England's national history, a progress warped by a culture of sexism, homophobia and imperialism. In doing so via suggestions of primitive environs, mud captures these associations and harnesses again the disruptive potential of residual matters of decay in order to create possibilities for an alternative feminist, queer futurity.

Mud-Stained Mind as Muddled Mind: Creative Chaos

We see inklings of such alternatives outside her novels as well, in her struggle with her own writing process. In her letters, Woolf sometimes marks a momentarily stuck state of mind in the process of creation with images of mud. This stuckness and occlusion, its unformedness, turns out to be a crucial part of the writing process and of creativity itself. In a 1925 letter, she opens by saying: 'I was just taking up my pen when struck down by the usual old temperature, which sinks my head fathoms deep in the mud' (*L3* 5). The image clarifies itself with time. In a 1932 letter to Ethel Smyth, she explains: 'My own brain is to me the most unaccountable of machinery – always buzzing, humming, soaring roaring diving, and then buried in mud' (*L5* 140). Occurring after the First World War, both statements evoke noticeably militaristic imagery set in imaginary trenches and air raids. The writer is 'struck down' and 'sinks' – via a naval incursion – 'fathoms deep in the mud'. Then, the 'brain', is a 'machin[e]', that, like an aeroplane, makes recognisably wartime overhead sounds of 'buzzing' and 'humming', followed by motions of 'soaring' upwards towards some idea before 'diving' down, earthward, not having found a way to express itself in language, interrupted by inarticulate sound, 'roaring'.

In Woolf's own feminist mind, creativity is cast as wrestled from the mud, a drama activated by the sensorium of war. In her fiction too, stretching to give voice without the voice of traditional form, the feminine mind struggles productively. It does not always succeed, but there is much to be learned still in the failing. In *The Years*, after an air raid in London during the First World War, Sara repeats her future-anthropological assessment, suggesting they 'go upstairs' and 'leave this cellar [. . .] this cave of mud and dung' (*TY* 293). Mud, brownness, darkness and blackness proliferate across the novel, which is crowded with women stifled by men. Mud, as the mark of the regressive heteropatriarchal strictures one must wrestle with in order to produce true creativity in excess of their violent and decaying forms, stains the pages of *The Years* and the years of its female characters' lives. It is the metaphorical obstacle to certain characters' ability to bloom into expressed creativity from the chaotic 'muddle' of their muddy minds. The muddle is productive despite this. The 'muddled' mind repeatedly referenced throughout *The Years* most frequently describes Eleanor, the eldest Pargiter sister. Muddled refers in *The Years*, like in Woolf's letters, to a not being able to find the right words; it is a trailing off before finishing one's sentences or thoughts, but, most importantly, a doing so because of the mind's multiplicity. The muddy mind is multiple temporally, as it is caught between past and present, and also substantially, as it is following many hallways and making associative connections. The muddle is, then, not so much an obstacle to thought as it is a profusion of connections – almost too generative despite that being an obstacle to the linear communication demanded in their many family conversations. In her discussion of the 'Muddy Poetics' of other female wartime writers, Kate McLoughlin explains that mud is often connected with female creativity in wartime writing, as this was a time when women gained liberties due to the male exodus into the trenches. She states that mud, for the 'liberated, female, civilian imagination', 'constitutes a terrifying yet mesmerizing figure for creativity – and prohibited creativity at that', 'clearing up what appears to be a muddle, but what is, in fact, creatively chaotic'.[32]

This chaotic creativity can also be seen in *Between the Acts*, where mud is clearly associated with the feminine through the '[w]ater' that 'for hundreds of years, had silted down into the hollow, and lay there four or five feet deep over a black cushion of mud [. . .] that deep centre [. . .] that black heart' (*BTA* 43–4). This is the same water-filled hollow wherein an historic lady is said to have died of suicide in despair over the suffocating forms and restrictions of living in patriarchy. In the novel's present, however, this 'black heart' of 'mud' is reclaimed by the alternative femininity of Miss La Trobe, who herself has a muddied vision. After the productive failure of La Trobe's play, she immerses herself in the local pub chatter, 'listen[ing]', as '[w]ords of one syllable sank down into the mud. She drowsed; she nodded. The mud became fertile', like that of *Mrs Dalloway* (*BTA* 212). La Trobe exclaims 'Words rose above the intolerably laden dumb oxen plodding through the mud. Words without meaning – wonderful words' (*BTA* 212). Here, the generative capacity of mud, as a new national ground, in the mind of this uncoupled, outsider female character is revealed. Specifically, what makes them fertile and wonderful, is their being 'without meaning', and so formless. This moment begets La Trobe's next play, previewed at the end, which, despite predicting a primitive regression, also promises a rebirth from the formless mud, a starting over without the old forms of the present. As a future echo of ways of thinking the Anthropocene today, this is the bleakest. Yet, perhaps, suggests Woolf, it is only in queering the timeline, embracing a nonreproductive future,[33] that the human frame can be decentred, and a response to the climate catastrophe formed from the mud of our minds.

Woolf depicts the creative muddy mind on the cusp of a second global war and also amid the first. Published during the First World War, Woolf's 'The Mark on the Wall' (1917) tropes mud as a sign of mental antiheteropatriarchal creativity. The narrator submerges us in a river where the mind-in-thought is associated with its muddy bottom, foreshadowing both La Trobe's and Jacob's mind, where 'water-beetles slowly rais[e] domes of mud upon the bed of the river'.[34] Here, mud is able to create structure, albeit slowly, on an inhuman timescale, something Woolf's muddy mind often associates itself with as a way of escaping 'the masculine point of view which governs our lives, which sets the standard'.[35] This mud, as ever, is different from the mud of the trenches, and yet, it seems born also of them, of the caesura of the war. The war here, crashes in with masculine ways of knowing reality, as the narrator's presumable spouse interrupts her muddy mind, causing '[e]verything' to be set off 'moving, falling, slipping, vanishing' until 'There is a vast upheaval of matter' as now the husband 'stand[s] over [her] and say[s]: 'I am going out to buy a newspaper [. . .] Nothing ever happens. Curse this war; God damn this war!'[36] His interruption casually rends her ability to continue thinking creatively by identifying the mark on the wall as a 'snail', juxtaposing their two forms of thought, hers muddy and without directed form and therefore generative, fertile, and his structured and rational but also violent, like the war he draws into the narrative. The snail that links their two ways of thinking mirrors the clash. Snails are slow and inhuman like the muddy and muddled thinking Woolf performs, but in naming it as a snail the mark is now known and therefore mastered in the husband's mind, identified as an outsider. The snail also invites us to think about the war and the gendered dynamics of marriage in terms of slow violence. Like the other affinities Woolf's muddy gendered wartime thinking has with Anthropocene thinking, the muddied meandering mind of the mark on the wall, the inhumanness of Woolf's mud, can be seen as a model for registering the sort of environmental 'slow violence' explained by Rob Nixon. Nixon claims that the most pernicious environmental and social violence often occurs 'gradually and out of sight' and is usually 'dispersed across space and time', making it difficult to 'engage the representational, narrative, and strategic challenges posed by the relative invisibility of slow violence'.[37] Slow violence is the most urgent aspect of the hyperobject that is climate change. Despite its slowness, it needs to be registered and represented in the now so it can be stemmed. Though slow violence seems as if it would stand in direct contrast to the spectacle of war, it accurately describes the way in which the First World War's most traumatic elements include the unspectacular entrenchment and stagnation, as nations and soldiers waited and endured the lack of advancement that still did so much harm to individuals and landscapes. Similarly, the banal interaction between husband and wife here does not represent an act of cruel and bloody violence, and yet, it expresses the patriarchal violence of heteronormative marriage structures on the female-identified mind. The husband's interruption seems quick, like the seemingly spectacular nature of the war, but the ideologies and power structures that motivate the violence of each unfurl across a long durée. The snail is a perfect representation for this misperception as well, for just as the mark seems inanimate as a smudge or nail, it is in fact animate and agential as a snail.

Woolf's mediation of the distributed crisis of global war via an aesthetics of mud model ways for us to respond to our own crisis of climate change; reading for the muddied and muddled traces on her pages acclimates us to a life lived on multiple scales at once and trains us to be critical of the forms that claim to make sense of the Anthropocene's global weirding – forms that usually shut down alternative narratives of futurity outside extractivist systems such as capitalism. In *Three Guineas*, Woolf lays out the intersectionality of political and gendered violence, explaining that global violence, and especially British declarations of war, are intertwined with women's rights. Gender and power are inextricably bound by the link between patriarchy and fascism in the same way that environmental justice and sustainability are entwined in the Anthropocene. It is as true for us today as it was for those wanting peace in Woolf's day that we must consider the role heteropatriarchy and its attendant processes of capitalism and neocolonialism function to maintain the systems that cause environmental disfunction and keep invisible the actionable truths about our Anthropocenic present. Woolf's 'Thoughts on Peace in an Air Raid' (1940) clarifies some of the connections between global geopolitical violence and gendered inequality at home. In connecting what she calls 'Hitlerism' with men's training to be men in homes, public schools and colleges, she identifies masculinity, perhaps what we would today call toxic masculinity, as a driving force in global war (*E6* 243). Ecofeminists have long noted that the same is true for environmental destruction.[38] Woolf practises, sketches and explores the muddy mind made possible by the ruptures of the First World War, both its scale-bending primitivism and its (de)forming creativity, primarily in service of the fight against all fascisms, big and small. It is time for us too to get dirty, down in the mud, and move beyond traditional ways of thinking. We must follow Woolf's '15 May 1940' note in her diary, that: 'This idea struck me: the army is the body: I am the brain. Thinking is my fighting' (*D5* 285). We must follow it proscriptively. We, too, as both academics and everyday thinkers in the world, can fight with our ideas. Resisting and responding to the injustices of climate change is a battle of ideas not simply because we cannot fight with our bodies, for there are many things we can do: consume differently, protest in the streets, volunteer on local restorative ecology and conservation projects. Fighting with the muddied minds modelled by Woolf's wartime writing, using 'Thinking' as our 'fighting', is needed just as much in the Anthropocene, because only a shift in mind set will precipitate any true solutions to the climate crisis.

Notes

1. Hynes, *War Imagined*, 192.
2. Will, 'Silence', 95.
3. For Woolf's relationship to the elemental, see Anna Jones Abramson's 'Beyond Modernist Shock', Nicole Rizzuto's 'Maritime Modernism', Kristin Czarnecki's 'Violence against Women and the Land in Woolf's *Between the Acts* and Erdrich's *The Round House*' and Marilyn S. Samuels's 'The Symbolic Functions of the Sun in *Mrs. Dalloway*'.
4. Paul Fussell and others claim that the war constitutes a 'break' in history, though Daniel Pick and an increasing majority of scholars critique what he calls this 'schism' theory (Fussell, *Great War*, 25, 123, 347; Pick, *War Machine*, 63, 115).
5. For more on Woolf's cataloguing of war losses, see Karen Levenback's *Virginia Woolf and the Great War* (1999) and Mark Hussey's edited collection *Virginia Woolf and War: Fiction, Reality, and Myth* (1991).
6. See Crutzen and Stoermer, '"Anthropocene"'.
7. Bonneuil and Fressoz, *Shock*, 125.
8. Levenback, *Virginia Woolf*, 7–8.
9. Morton, *Hyperobjects*, 1, italics in original. They also state that one 'only sees pieces of a hyperobject at any one moment' (4).
10. Ibid., 4.
11. See Rhoden-Paul, 'UK Heatwave' and Kirby, 'Europe Heatwave'.
12. Taylor, *Sky*, 189.
13. Ibid., 188.
14. See Kate McLoughlin, *Authoring War*.
15. See, for example, Bonneuil and Fressoz's *The Shock of the Anthropocene* and Richard P. Tucker's 'The World Wars and the Globalization of Timber Cutting'.
16. Benjamin, 'Storyteller', 84.
17. See Tucker's 'The World Wars and the Globalization of Timber Cutting' and its reference in the opening to D. H. Lawrence's *Lady Chatterley's Lover* (1928).
18. Keller, 'Mobilizing', 5.
19. Das, *Touch*, 35, 37.

20. Leonard, 'Mud', 60.
21. Sassoon, *Complete Memoirs*, 435.
22. See Fussell's *The Great War and Modern Memory* (1975) and Das's *Touch and Intimacy in First World War Literature* (2005) for more on mud's prevalence in veteran First World War writing.
23. Smith, 'The Novel'.
24. Jaffe, 'Introduction', 497.
25. Walton, 'Nature Trauma', 4.
26. Jaffe agrees, writing that '[p]art of what "millions of years"', and other primitive locutions, do 'for Woolf is shift things exponentially' onto a different scale ('Introduction', 494). For more on this necessity, see Bonneuil and Fressoz's *The Shock of the Anthropocene* (2015), Taylor's *The Sky of Our Manufacture* (2016) and Chakrabarty's 'The Climate of History: Four Theses' (2009).
27. Morton, *Dark Ecology*, 25.
28. Ibid., 52.
29. Ibid., 22.
30. Ibid., 27.
31. Khan, '*Between the Acts*', 120.
32. McLoughlin, 'Muddy Poetics', 234, 225, 234.
33. I borrow this sense of nonreproductive futurity in part from Lee Edelman's *No Future: Queer Theory and the Death Drive* (2004).
34. Woolf, 'Mark', 158.
35. Ibid., 156.
36. Ibid., 159.
37. Nixon, *Slow Violence*, 2.
38. See Greta Gaard and Patrick Murphy's 'Introduction' to *Ecofeminist Literary Criticism: Theory, Interpretation, Pedagogy* (1998).

Bibliography

Abramson, Anna Jones. 'Beyond Modernist Shock: Virginia Woolf's Absorbing Atmosphere'. *Journal of Modern Literature* 38, no. 4 (2015): 39–46.
Benjamin, Walter. 'The Storyteller: Reflections on the Work of Nikoli Leskov'. In *Illuminations: Essays and Reflections,* translated by Harry Zohn, edited by Hannah Arendt, 83–109. New York: Schocken Books, 2007.
——. 'Theses on the Philosophy of History'. In *Illuminations: Essays and Reflections,* 253–64. New York: Schocken Books, 2007.
Bonneuil, Christophe, and Jean-Baptiste Fressoz. *The Shock of the Anthropocene: The Earth, History and Us,* translated by David Fernbach. London: Verso, 2015.
Chakrabarty, Dipesh. 'The Climate of History: Four Theses'. *Critical Inquiry* 35, no. 2 (2009): 197–222.
Crutzen, Paul J., and Eugene F. Stoermer. 'The "Anthropocene"'. *International Geosphere-Biosphere Programme Newsletter* 41 (2000): 17–18.

Czarnecki, Kristin. 'Violence against Women and the Land in Woolf's *Between the Acts* and Erdrich's *The Round House*'. *Virginia Woolf Miscellany* 92 (2018): 22–4.

Das, Santanu. *Touch and Intimacy in First World War Literature*. Cambridge: Cambridge University Press, 2005.

Esty, Jed. *A Shrinking Island: Modernism and National Culture in England*. Princeton, NJ: Princeton University Press, 2003.

Friedman, Susan Stanford. *Planetary Modernisms: Provocations on Modernity across Time*. New York: Columbia University Press, 2015.

Fussell, Paul. *The Great War and Modern Memory*. Oxford: Oxford University Press, 1975.

Gaard, Greta, and Patrick Murphy. 'Introduction'. In *Ecofeminist Literary Criticism: Theory, Interpretation, Pedagogy*, edited by Greta Gaard and Patrick D. Murphy, 1–13. Urbana: University of Illinois Press, 1998.

Ghosh, Amitav. *The Great Derangement: Climate Change and the Unthinkable*. Chicago: University of Chicago Press, 2016.

Hussey, Mark, ed. *Virginia Woolf and War: Fiction, Reality, and Myth*. Syracuse, NY: Syracuse University Press, 1991.

Hynes, Samuel. *A War Imagined: The First World War and English Culture*. London: Pimlico, 1990.

Jaffe, Aaron. 'Introduction: Who's Afraid of the Inhuman Woolf?' *Modernism/modernity* 23, no. 3 (2016): 491–513.

Keller, Tait. 'Mobilizing Nature for the First World War: An Introduction'. *Environmental Histories of the First World War*, edited by Richard P. Tucker, Tait Keller, J. R. McNeill and Martin Schmid, 19–37. Cambridge: Cambridge University Press, 2018.

Khan, Almas. '*Between the Acts*: A Modernist Meditation on Language, Origin Narratives, and Art's Efficacy on the Cusp of the Apocalypse'. *English Academy Review: South African Journal of English Studies* 31, no. 2 (2014): 108–24.

Kirby, Paul. 'Europe Heatwave: Thousands Escape Wildfires in France, Spain and Greece'. BBC News, 15 July 2022. Accessed 24 October 2023. https://www.bbc.com/news/world-europe-62175758.

Leonard, Matt. 'Mud: The Waterlogged Battlefields of World War I'. *Military History Monthly* (May 2012): 54–61.

Levenback, Karen L. *Virginia Woolf and the Great War*. Syracuse, NY: Syracuse University Press, 1999.

McLoughlin, Kate. 'Muddy Poetics: First World War Poems by Helen Saunders and Mary Borden'. *Women: A Cultural Review* 26, no. 3 (2015): 221–36.

Morton, Timothy. *Dark Ecology: For a Logic of Future Coexistence*. New York: Columbia University Press, 2016.

———. *Hyperobjects: Philosophy and Ecology after the End of the World*. Minneapolis: University of Minnesota Press, 2013.

Nixon, Rob. *Slow Violence and the Environmentalism of the Poor*. Cambridge, MA: Harvard University Press, 2011.

Pick, Daniel. *War Machine: The Rationalisation of Slaughter in the Modern Age*. New Haven, CT: Yale University Press, 1993.

Rhoden-Paul, Andre. 'UK Heatwave: Hottest Day of the Year Again for Third Day in a Row'. BBC News, 17 July 2022. Accessed 24 October 2023. https://www.bbc.com/news/uk-61844172.

Rizzuto, Nicole. 'Maritime Modernism: The Aqueous Form of Virginia Woolf's *The Waves*'. *Modernist Cultures* 11, no. 2 (2016): 268–292.

Samuels, Marilyn S. 'The Symbolic Functions of the Sun in *Mrs. Dalloway*'. *MFS: Modern Fiction Studies* 18 (1972): 387–99.

Sassoon, Siegfried. *The Complete Memoirs of George Sherston*. London: Faber and Faber, 1937.

Sherry, Vincent. *The Great War and the Language of Modernism*. Oxford: Oxford University Press, 2003.

Smith, Ali. '"The novel can't just leave the war out": Ali Smith on Fiction in Times of Crisis'. *The Guardian*, 26 March 2022. Accessed 24 October 2023. https://www.theguardian.com/books/2022/mar/26/the-novel-cant-just-leave-the-war-out-ali-smith-on-fiction-in-times-of-crisis.

Tate, Trudi. *Modernism, History, and the First World War*. Manchester: Manchester University Press, 1998.

Taylor, Jesse Oak. *The Sky of Our Manufacture: The London Fog in British Fiction from Dickens to Woolf*. Charlottesville: University of Virginia Press, 2016.

Tucker, Richard P. 'The World Wars and the Globalization of Timber Cutting'. In *Natural Enemy, Natural Ally: Toward an Environmental History of War*, edited by Richard P. Tucker and Edmund Russell, 110–143. Corvallis: Oregon State University Press, 2004.

Walton, Samantha. 'Nature Trauma: Ecology and the Returning Soldier in First World War English and Scottish Fiction, 1918–1932'. *Journal of Medical Humanities* (2019): 1–11.

Will, Barbara. 'Into the Silence: Hemingway, Woolf, and Beckett in the Wake of War'. *South Central Review* 35, no. 2 (2018): 90–102.

Woolf, Virginia. *Between the Acts*. London: Harcourt Brace & Company, 1970.

——. *The Diary of Virginia Woolf*, edited by Anne Olivier Bell. 5 vols. London: Penguin Books, 1979–85.

——. *The Essays of Virginia Woolf*, edited by Andrew McNeillie (vols 1–4) and Stuart N. Clarke (vols 5–6). 6 vols. London: Hogarth Press, 1986–2011.

——. *Jacob's Room*. London: Dover, 1998.

——. *The Letters of Virginia Woolf*, edited by Nigel Nicolson and Joanne Trautmann. 6 vols. London: Hogarth Press, 1975–80.

——. 'The Mark on the Wall'. In *The Virginia Woolf Reader*, edited by Mitchell A. Leaska, 151–9. London: Harcourt Brace Jovanovich, 1984.

——. *Mrs Dalloway*. London: Harcourt, Inc., 1981.

——. *The Years*. London: Harcourt, Brace, & Company, 1965.

Chapter 5

Following the Oil: Virginia Woolf, Vita Sackville-West and Imperial Extractivism

Peter Adkins

Writing to T. S. Eliot in August 1927, Virginia Woolf conveys her excitement at her and Leonard's new motor car:

> I'm glad to think that we now have another subject in common – motor cars. Did Leonard tell you how our entire life is spent driving, cleaning, dodging in and out of a shed, measuring miles on maps, planning expeditions, going expeditions, being beaten back by the rain, eating sandwiches on high roads, cursing cows, sheep, bicyclists, and when we are at rest talking of nothing but cars and petrol? Ours is a Singer. (*L3* 412–13)

It is a letter that reflects the thrills and freedoms that came with car ownership, sentiments that would make their way into the present-day section of *Orlando* (1928) which Woolf would soon begin writing. The letter also serves as a more general historical document, reflecting not just the growth in car ownership among the middle and upper classes in Britain, but an increasing dependence on oil in which, as Woolf's letter puts it, petrol had become a common talking point. The 1920s saw the number of cars in Britain surge, with vehicles on the road surpassing 1.5 million by 1925 and kerbside petrol pumps being installed for the first time, leading to an unprecedented demand for the import of oil.[1] Reading Woolf's diaries and letters from the late 1920s onwards offers a case study in Britain's nascent dependency on oil, whether in the repeated descriptions of trips to petrol pumps during various road trips or in the delight with the installation of an oil stove at Monks House in the autumn of 1929. If, as Woolf would later write in her essay, 'The Docks of London' (1931), which I look at in some detail below, the 'English language has adapted itself to the needs of commerce' (*E5* 279), then the infiltration of petroleum into daily life presents a striking example of her theory in action.

Aleksandr Etkind describes how each historical era's dominating mono-resource becomes a staple not only in terms of material production but as 'cultural imagery', producing a hegemonic cultural imaginary.[2] We see evidence of this in Woolf's writing and that of her contemporaries when, for instance, she describes her progress in writing the dinner scene in *To the Lighthouse* (1927) as 'striking oil' (*D3* 72) or when Harold Nicolson, concerned about the potential dangers of the love affair between Woolf and, his wife, Vita Sackville-West, likens the relationship to 'smoking over a petrol tank'.[3] These instances, further corroboration of Woolf's own theory of the malleability of the English language to commerce, offer linguistic traces of oil's ascendancy in early twentieth-century Britain. For Etkind, history should be understood through humankind's material, economic and political relationship with different resources, with societies and nation states experiencing growth through a reliance on particular materials, from grain to iron to sugar, with different natural resources having 'different political qualities and generat[ing] different cultural forms of reflection'.[4] The materials which a state draws on to generate wealth and power are not simply passive matter utilised in the service of a pre-existing structure but actively influence, to lesser or greater extent, the social, cultural, economic and political landscape within which they are put to work. Oil provides a clear example of how a natural resource brings about deep societal change. The first oil borehole was drilled in 1859 and by the early twentieth century its potential to radically change energy consumption was being realised.[5] In 1900, in a move that would be of great consequence in the decades to come, the Royal Navy began to use oil in its vessels instead of coal, making oil a 'vital strategic commodity, on which the security of the Empire depended'.[6] Unlike coal, oil had to be imported and the British State found itself in a position where it would need to forge special relationships with oil companies in order to ensure a reliable supply for its ships. When the British-Australian businessman William Knox D'Arcy needed financial support for a venture in Persia, where he had purchased exclusive rights to potential oil reserves in the southwest of the country, British government money provided one of the investment streams that kept the company afloat. In 1908, when Knox's oil exploration team discovered huge reserves of oil, the Anglo-Persian Oil Company was formed and in 1916 it acquired British Petroleum (BP) to operate as a subsidiary focused on selling and marketing its oil to consumers. By the 1920s, when the Woolfs were planning expeditions in their new Singer and endlessly discussing cars and petrol, BP was employing more than 3,000 British workers, running 850 supply depots and servicing a third of all demand for motor petrol. An indirect line, then, can be traced from imperial military decisions at the turn of the century to the Woolfs' ability to purchase and run a car in the late 1920s.

Yet, although Woolf might have been dazzled by the possibilities of new oil-based technologies in her personal life, from cars to stoves, she was by no means oblivious to the increasingly fossil-fuel hungry form of imperialist capitalism upon which such innovations relied. In 1928, the Woolfs published Sackville-West's, *Twelve Days*, her second Persian travelogue for the Hogarth Press, based on her time in the country visiting Nicolson, who had been posted to Teheran as a senior diplomat in 1925. *Twelve Days*, which charts Sackville-West's journey through the Bakhtiari mountains, ends at the Anglo-Persian Oil Company oilfields, a 'nightmare world' of 'mechanical structures' in the Persian landscape.[7] Moreover, although Persia was not part of the British Empire, it was embroiled in imperial politics that went beyond controlling the British Concession in the south, as Woolf knew only too well. Her cousin, Herman Norman, a British diplomat in Teheran, was involved in the 1921 coup d'état which established Reza Khan as the country's sovereign, to the advantage of British interests in the country. Woolf records discussing Norman's involvement in the 'awful mess' of the coup in her diary (*D2* 165). Furthermore, as a consumer of print media, Woolf would not have been able to avoid what Ian Wereley describes as the bombardment of BP advertisements in newspapers such as *The Times* and the *Illustrated London News* featuring 'images and stories about Persian oil'.[8] The degree to which Woolf's activities as a writer and publisher registers what might be called an oil consciousness invites qualification of what Joshua Schuster has described as the 'absent presence of oil' in modernism.[9] For Schuster, whose focus is on American modernism, oil is everywhere and nowhere. The commodities that oil enables are readily depicted in modernist writing but the black liquid itself notably eludes description, with there being little 'overt engagement with oil itself'.[10] Amitav Ghosh offers a similar argument in *The Great Derangement: Climate Change and the Unthinkable* (2017) where he suggests that thanks to the 'materiality of oil' and its mode of production (its invisible transportation and distribution in pipes and tanks) it resists the direct representation that made coal and mining so amenable to the realist novel in the nineteenth century, rendering it 'inscrutable' to the arts.[11] Yet, the strangely visible invisibility of oil, its resistance to literary depiction, did not go unnoticed during oil's rapid ascendancy. In *Twelve Days*, Sackville-West describes the uncanniness of looking out over more than a 'hundred wells [. . .] working over an area of fifty square miles, producing their four and a half million tons of oil a year' and not seeing 'a drop' of oil. A sinister secrecy, Sackville-West writes, attends the 'mysterious business of dragging it up from its lair'.[12] Moreover, Woolf's interest in oil and imperial extractivism extended beyond family connections and her role as Sackville-West's publisher. As Anna Snaith and Michael Whitworth outline, Woolf's texts 'open out into global space' and show a readiness to scrutinise the way in which British subjects are implicated 'in larger cultural and imperial networks', and her writing, in both direct and indirect forms, responds to the social, political and environmental costs of oil.[13] This chapter looks to follow the oil in Woolf's writing and literary networks, exploring how her essays document and interrogate the way in which oil was creating new social conditions both in Britain and overseas. It begins with her account of the British Empire Exhibition in 'Thunder at Wembley' (1924), originally set to be entitled 'Nature at Wembley', before moving on to look at Sackville-West's Persian travelogues that she and Leonard published at the Hogarth Press, and concludes by turning to her essays on London as a global city that she wrote for *Good Housekeeping* in 1931–2.[14] Following the oil, this chapter argues, reveals the degree to which Woolf and her contemporaries developed literary strategies to engage with the increasing complexity and pervasiveness of oil in Britain, suggesting that this planetary commodity offers a new way of understanding Woolf's political commitments and alertness to environmental changes, as well as her complicity in the imperial structures within which she was ensnared.

'Nature [. . .] is the ruin of Wembley': The British Empire Exhibition

In May 1924, Virginia Woolf attended the British Empire Exhibition in Wembley, a little over a month after its grand opening by King George V, writing about her experiences in 'Thunder at Wembley' in the *Nation and Athenaeum*. Ten miles from central London and sprawling across 220 acres, the Exhibition was the largest public event held in Britain during the interwar period, welcoming 27 million visitors over the course of the two years that it was open.¹⁵ Designed to celebrate the commercial and technological successes of the British Empire, the Exhibition featured two enormous 'Palaces' of engineering and industry built from ferro-concrete, as well as pavilions for colonies and territories that were designed to mimic the native architecture of the represented region. As Scott Cohen frames it, every 'territory of the Empire that could afford to build a pavilion had one at the exhibition', with the Exhibition organisers aiming to create a seamless 'imperial planetary vision in suburban London'.¹⁶ In its attempt to condense planetary space into a totalising representation, the Exhibition offered a microcosm of Imperial extractivism, an economic mode in which resources 'are taken out of one geographic location – often on a colonial periphery – and utilised as [. . .] inputs to industrial processes elsewhere'.¹⁷ Woolf's essay has an apocalyptic rather than celebratory tone, however. The opening sentence of Woolf's essay, which carries the trace of her original title and becomes one of the key concerns in the piece, both points to the phenomenon of extractivism and its shortcomings: 'It is nature that is the ruin of Wembley' (*E3* 410). Nature, the figurative storehouse of raw materials whose exploitation feeds the Imperial machine, is also that which stands outside of the totalising control of the exhibition's organisers. While, on one level, Woolf's opening sentence would have been recognisable to contemporary readers as an ironic comment on the torrential downpours which had dampened the first few weeks of the Exhibition, it is a statement that also opens on to what Jason W. Moore describes as the 'double internality' in the relationship between the natural world and capitalism. For Moore, extractivism should not be understood in terms of straightforward human exploitation of inert natural resources. Instead, it is vital to pay attention to the way in which there is a double movement that means the relationship between nature and capitalism is always uncertain and dynamic, or the way in which at the same time capitalism internalises and consumes nature ('nature-in-capitalism'), the biosphere internalises capitalism imposing limits, disrupting it and, in Woolf's words, bringing about its ruin ('capitalism-in-nature').¹⁸ Woolf's essay fittingly concludes by suggesting an 'impending' 'appalling catastrophe' blowing into the Exhibition, with the 'rising' wind, 'swirls' of dust, and 'livid, lurid, sulphurine' skies signifying not only the end of the day out for visitors but a broader inevitable 'doom' in the wings for the Empire (*E3* 413).

Significantly, the exhibition was keen to present Britain's growing oil economy and oil's potential for new imperial frontiers. At the Burmah [*sic*] Pavilion, a range of specially commissioned films included a documentary feature on the colony's oilfields, while at the

Newfoundland Pavilion oil and shale oil were among the proudly exhibited materials.[19] In the Sarawak Pavilion, a grand display of oil wealth was presented in the 'working model of an oil well, drilling rig and a model of the submarine pipeline at Lutong used for loading oil tankers'. At four miles, the pipeline was, at the time, the longest of its kind in the world.[20] Indeed, even the organisers behind the Exhibition had ties to the burgeoning oil industry. The idea of a grand Exhibition had been first floated in 1913 by Lord Strathcona, who was at the time the first chairman of the Anglo-Persian Oil Company. Strathcona, who died in 1914 and did not live to see the fruits of his suggestion, would have likely approved of the Exhibition's most impressive display of the wealth, utility and exoticism of oil in the form of BP's Persian Khan Pavilion. As Wereley writes, while the outside of the Pavilion resembled an 'elaborate caravanserai' of classical Persian architectural design, inside 'visitors learned about BP's products and the modern oil science and technology that had produced them', while a BP-branded delivery wagon stood in front of the exhibit (when not delivering oil to other pavilions) making clear the connection between Persian oil wells and the motor spirits that the British public were coming to recognise as an integral part of daily life.[21]

Although Woolf does not directly mention the Persian Pavilion, she is unlikely to have missed the architecturally impressive two-storey building positioned directly in front of His Majesty's Government Pavilion.[22] Moreover, one of the central concerns of her essay is the new technologies that oil was making possible. Early in the essay Woolf describes how at the Exhibition, '[y]ou look through an open door at a regiment of motor-cars aligned in avenues. They are not opulent and powerful; they are not flimsy and cheap' (*E3* 411). Woolf's description captures the importance of cars and other motor-vehicles to the Exhibition, but also the degree to which they were being democratised and made available to the middle classes through an emergent neo-imperial economy. The motor cars are of a piece with the '[d]ress fabrics, rope, table linen, [. . .] camphor, bees-wax, rattans, and the rest', in that they cost a figurative 'six and eight-pence' (*E3* 411). They are neither luxury items nor so low-priced that they appear cheap and commonplace. The British Empire's far-reaching extractivism might deplete resources abroad but at home, the British Empire Exhibition strains to suggest, these materials filter down into a democratic form of consumerism, available to many if not all. The two words that the Exhibition looks to impress on its visitors, Woolf writes, are 'democracy' and 'mediocrity' (*E3* 411).

Yet, as soon as this picture of democracy through imperialist extractivism is teased, Woolf undermines it:

> But then, just as one is beginning a little wearily to fumble with those two fine words – democracy, mediocrity – Nature asserts herself where one would least look to find her – in clergymen, school children, girls, young men, invalids in bath chairs. (*E3* 411)

As Kurt Koenigsberger writes, the 'Nature' which includes the 'world of birds and trees and sky' also includes human life, with nature serving as a general vital excess that always escapes the institutional structures that would look to circumscribe and contain it.[23] As in Moore's model of a double-internality, nature-in-capitalism and capitalism-in-nature exist in a state of disequilibrium which the essay's apocalyptic conclusion suggests will lead to both societal and environmental catastrophe. This is captured most vividly in how, despite all the planning and imperiousness of the Exhibition, the 'problem of the sky [. . .] remains' (*E3* 412). When the essay's narrator stops to ask whether it is 'the wind or [. . .] the British Empire Exhibition' that she can hear, she decides that '[i]t is both' (*E3* 413), they have become indistinguishable, with each implicated in the other in a manner that suggests not productive or democratic harmony, but terror, violence and destruction.

Cohen suggests that the tone of Woolf's essay captures a sense of time being out of joint, with the apocalyptic rather than celebratory register of the essay capturing how the Exhibition seems to be both celebrating the pre-First World War heyday of Empire *and* eulogising an Empire already in decline. For Cohen, Woolf's essay presents the Exhibition as 'the product of an empire running out of time, yet also a replica of an empire plucked out of time'.[24] Yet, the presence of oil, whether directly represented in the Persian Khan Pavilion or indirectly in the motor cars, offers a glimpse of a future that does not fit so easily within this pre-/post- model of the British Empire, suggesting a future in which imperial extractivism will take place through diplomatic manipulation and exploitative commercial arrangements rather than direct or indirect rule. Oil figures as a kind of excess at the margins in 'Thunder at Wembley', glimpsed only obliquely and yet threatening to bring about the worst kind of possible futures. It is perhaps not insignificant that Asia is one of the regions to which Woolf turns in the apocalyptic conclusion to her essay. Dreamy and pleasant reflections on 'our possessions in the East' are disturbed by the suddenly 'violent commotion' of a storm, disrupting the illusion of an extractivism without consequence (*E3* 413). Woolf, of course, would not have known of the direct correlation between imperial extractivism and the catastrophic climatic consequences that the burning of fossil fuels would engender.[25] Yet the essay nonetheless manages to intuit the environmental costs that will necessarily come from the ongoing legacies of imperialism, including the hollowness of any democracy that is derived from the materials extracted from Britain's imperialist outposts.

Petro-Narratives at the Hogarth Press

BP's Persian Khan at the British Empire Exhibition was designed to capture the imagination of a growing motoring public. As Wereley documents, the exhibit celebrated the scientific and technological ingenuity of the Anglo-Persian Oil Company, making it clear that if it was not for British intervention in the supposedly primitive regions of southern Persia then this magical resource would have remained untapped. Moreover, the British oilfields were also presented as offering a genuine contribution to the welfare and needs of the supposedly undeveloped world, encouraging motorists to not only see the benefits of the oil, but to be *proud* to use it.[26] We find evidence of this sentiment recorded in Woolf's diary when recounting dining with Sackville-West, Nicolson and Raymond Mortimer in July 1927. 'After dinner', Woolf writes, 'we discussed the Empire':

> 'The point is, Raymond, our English genius is for government' [Harold said]. 'The governed don't seem to enjoy it' said Raymond. Silly ass, said Harold. 'We do our jobs: disinterestedly; we don't think of ourselves, as the French do, as the Germans do. Take the British oil fields. There's a hospital there where they take any one, employee or not. The natives come from all over the place. Don't tell me that's not a good thing. And they trust us.' So on to the system of bribery; to the great age of England being the age of colonial expansion. (*D3* 145)

Despite Woolf's knowledge of (and familial connection to) the underhand involvement of the British in the coup that protected imperial oil interests in Persia, Woolf chooses not to challenge Nicolson's assertion of imperialist benevolence but, 'recalling the aeroplanes that had flown over us', instead suggests that 'nationality is over' and that '[a]ll divisions are rubbed out' (*D3* 145). It is not so much an anti-imperialist sentiment as an assertion of a planetary, transnational sense of identity that looks ahead to her declaration in *Three Guineas* (1938) that '[a]s a woman, I have no country [. . .] As a woman my country is the whole world' (*TG* 185). Yet, as I have written elsewhere, it is notable that Woolf does not acknowledge that this transnational vision, symbolised by air travel and a shrinking globe, is reliant on an imperial extractivism that ensures only certain global citizens have access to it.[27]

Nor was Nicolson's choice of the British oilfields an arbitrary one. As mentioned above, he was a senior diplomat in Persia between 1925 and 1927 and he and Sackville-West had visited the Persian oilfields earlier in 1927 at the conclusion of a journey on foot across the Bakhtiari mountains. Nicolson, a career diplomat but unhappy being posted so far from Sackville-West and life in England, had applied for a position within the Anglo-Persian Oil Company, hoping (unsuccessfully) to secure a desk job in London with them.[28] Sackville-West, who remained in England for the majority of Nicolson's posting, made two extended trips to visit him, one in the spring of 1926 and again in 1927. These trips were notable for generating the only two travelogues she wrote and cementing her working relationship with Virginia and Leonard Woolf's Hogarth Press. Sackville-West's first departure, in 1926, was during one of the intense periods in her love affair with Woolf and their correspondence is a valuable literary supplement to her published travel writing, pointing to both the origins of *Passenger to Teheran* (1926) and the inspiration for the Turkish sections of *Orlando*.[29] Both *Passenger to Teheran* and its sequel two years later, *Twelve Days*, present an outsider's view of Persian society, while also drawing on Sackville-West's privileged access to the upper echelons of state life (*Passenger to Teheran* includes a firsthand account of Reza Shah Pahlavi's coronation). Both books are also early examples of petro-narratives in which the motor car plays a central role, not only in literally enabling the journeys that Sackville-West takes but in mediating and shaping her experience of the region. Multiple examples could be given, but perhaps the most memorable is the description of Sackville-West arriving in Qom where the streets are 'so narrow that the car could just pass between the mud walls, lurching from rut to rut, the steering wheel half twisted out of my hands', while the city's bazaar is lit in the 'fierce and concentrated illumination' of the Ford's headlights.[30]

Both books are filled with observations and commentaries on Sackville-West's various motor cars and her experiences on the Persian roads, documenting the novelty of her mode of transport as well as the exoticism of the landscape. The car reproduces the imperialist hierarchy on the road, where those with access to motorised vehicles take precedence over those on camel or donkey, while in the towns and villages locals are described as being drawn to the motor car in an insect-like manner, 'press[ing] against the windows' of the 'brilliantly illuminat[ed]' interior.[31] Just as important to their status as petro-narratives, however, is the journey of oil and petrol being transported across the country that runs parallel to Sackville-West's own journey. On her first trip to Teheran, she overtakes 'innumerable donkeys loaded with petrol tins' from the south, later describing how 'very odd it is to see the English words on the crates: HIGHLY INFLAMMABLE'.[32] This image of donkeys and camels laden with petrol is repeated several times in both books, intended to create a jarringly anachronistic image of the primitive and the modern. The account of Persia's rural population is steeped in the racist prejudices of the period, replicating the view that the British presence, whether in a diplomatic or commercial capacity, represents a force of social amelioration for a population unable to take care of itself. As in the discussion recounted in Woolf's diary, Sackville-West discusses how oil has brought the benefits of Western medicine to the remote southern regions. The book describes how people from the nomadic population frequently approach Sackville-West and her travelling companions for medical help, since to the nomads 'all foreigners are doctors, and all doctors are omnipotent'.[33] Yet, Sackville-West's account, where she describes distributing 'lint, lotions, and medicines which at least we were sure could do no harm', also presents the limited usefulness of the Company hospital, inadvertently undermining Nicolson's argument for its benefits. When they are told of the free treatment, the nomads are said to have 'shook their heads mournfully', they already know of it but it is out of reach since the 'the Edareh – the Company – the great Anglo-Persian Oil Company – was down at Masjid-i-Suleiman, many days' journey away'.[34] The Company might provide free medical treatment but, ironically, the reality is that for most of the population you would need a car (and petrol) to access it.

The Bakhtiari region is established as a site of authentic nomadic life, a primitive foil to the Company and its oilfields, which are presented in contrast as an outpost of society and civilisation, all provided by and, importantly, justifying British control of oil. Persia is at once distant from civilisation and deeply connected to it by way of oil pipes and tankers, both a pre-modern economy and the site of a newly emerging form of planetary capitalism. While the Bakhtiari nomads would skim surface oil from puddles to 'smear on their sores and wounds', it has taken, Sackville-West writes, the ingenuity of

British capitalists like William Knox D'Arcy to hear of the 'legend of its presence' and unlock its potential.[35] In both the Orientalised romanticism of the Persian desert and the presentation of the oil industry as a civilising and improving presence, *Twelve Days* parallels the narrative strategies that BP had employed a few years earlier at the British Empire Exhibition and in their newspaper advertising campaigns, which presented the country as a 'ruggedly inhospitable space, devoid of contemporary life or culture'.[36] Indeed, the use of Company photographs as illustrations in the book present a material tie between Sackville-West's narrative and official discourse (see Figure 5.1).

Yet, *Twelve Days* offers a measure of ambivalence and caution that is missing from BP's public relations efforts. If repeated references to 'the Company' by both the travellers and the Persian population sound vaguely sinister, concealing the interests of imperialism behind an anonymous globalised capitalism, this is borne out in the description of the arrival at the oilfields. A single 'dark plume of smoke' rising straight into the sky frames the horizon of the final leg of the voyage,

Figure 5.1 Official Anglo-Persian Oil Company photograph of an oil pipeline climbing the Iman Reza Ridge included by Vita Sackville-West as an illustration for *Twelve Days*. Reproduced by the BP Archive.

an apocalyptic presence long before the oilfields are reached, with the landscape taking on further incremental changes. The 'smell of sulphur filled the air', Sackville-West writes, while the 'hills and valleys [. . .] had closed up for ever behind us'.[37] The most jarring change comes when a 'tarred road' suddenly appears in front of the party:

> The tyres of the motor ran suddenly and smoothly on a perfect surface. An English highway. What lay at the end of it? York? Cambridge? No, Sheffield rather; look at the smoke trailing out across the sky. An English highway, leading, so it seemed, straight into hell.[38]

The oilfields are 'civilisation in the most violent contrast', an 'extraordinary landscape' of 'bleached' hills that are empty apart from the 'hanging feather of smoke', pipelines and Company buildings (see Figure 5.2).[39] It is hard to overestimate how the scale of the operation would have impressed itself on a visitor. By the mid-1920s when Sackville-West visited, there were over a hundred wells in operation covering fifty square miles, employing more than a thousand European workers (in addition to local labourers) and producing more

Figure 5.2 Photograph of the Anglo-Persian Oil Company oilfields on the horizon included by Vita Sackville-West as an illustration for *Twelve Days*.

than 4.7 million tons of oil annually.[40] It is a 'perfectly organised, clanking, belching settlement' where drills are 'plunge[d] a mile down into the soil of Persia', while in the Company town, a microcosm of Englishness, you can find 'grocer's shops with the familiar tins and bottles on the counters'. This collection of shops, housing, medical buildings, schools and, even, tennis courts, surrounded by the noisy infrastructure of oil extraction, is, Sackville-West marvels, a 'hell of civilisation' in which a 'heavy smell of gas pervade[s] everything'.[41]

Like Woolf's 'Thunder at Wembley', *Twelve Days* concludes by imagining the imperial ruin and ecological apocalypse destined for Britain and its oil economy. Visiting the ruins of Palmyra after having left the oilfields, the book's final sentence imagines whether:

> in the course of centuries the Anglo-Persian oil-fields may not revert to the solitudes of the Bakhtiari hills, while London, Paris, and New York lie with [. . .] wild flowers blowing over their stones, and fields of corn bend to the breeze for the bread of the population in some distant capital whose name we do not yet know.[42]

Like Woolf's vision of colonies 'perishing' in 'inconceivable beauty and terror which some malignant power illuminates' (*E3* 414), the global metropolises and their oilfields are situated in a broader *longue durée*, in which hubristic attempts to exert control over the natural world appear to contribute to their downfall. Sackville-West, like Woolf, appears to intuit the environmental consequences to the blind all-encompassing consumption of the planet's resources. At the same time, however, Sackville-West's apocalyptic imagery stems from a much different ideological outlook. In *Twelve Days,* the tragedy of extractivism lies in its upsetting of a natural balance in which the perceived primitive authenticity of the nomadic people is to be protected. Taking an explicitly antidemocratic stance, Sackville-West argues against providing education or wage labour for the indigenous Bakhtiari, since 'the tillers of the soil [should] merely till the soil, without mixing themselves up in speculations dangerous to the half-trained mind'.[43] This approach to 'dealing with a primitive community' also has the advantage, although Sackville-West does not mention it, of ensuring that they would neither want to use the oil nor control the means of production.[44] The human population becomes akin to a natural resource to be managed and controlled. Indeed, in Sackville-West's description of the tribespeople 'winding up through the hills in a long and constant stream' they are made to resemble the oil reserves under their feet, as a natural resource to be managed and exploited.[45]

The Oil Economy and *The London Scene*

Sackville-West's Persian travelogues, with their orientalised accounts of the Middle East and implicit defence of British oil interests, were published alongside explicitly anti-imperialist titles in the Hogarth Press catalogue and speak to the broad scope of the press by the end of the 1920s. The books' politics also invite speculation on how both Virginia and Leonard Woolf received them. One indirect response, this final section argues, might be found in Woolf's 'Six Articles on London Life' published in *Good Housekeeping* magazine in 1931 and 1932, posthumously republished as *The London Scene*. The essays offer an impressionistic snapshot of London, capturing it both as an urban metropole and as a globalised city that cannot be disentangled from planetary flows of commerce and capital. In writing the first essay, 'The Docks of London', Woolf might very well have had Sackville-West's travelogues in mind, since the essay was based on a tour of the docks taken with Sackville-West, Nicolson and the Persian ambassador, Sir Robert Clive. One of the explicit contexts in which this essay developed, as such, was that of imperialist oil extraction. If in *Twelve Days* the oilfields exist at the periphery, quite literally framing the horizon in the final portion of the text and drawing the British travellers towards it, in Woolf's essay the direction of travel is reversed, with the essay presenting an image of the Thames as an 'irresistible current', funnelling resources, including oil, into London and onward elsewhere in Britain (*E5* 275).

As I have argued elsewhere, 'The Docks of London' operates on one level as an environmental polemic, pointing to the squalor and degradation of an imperialist capitalism that has reduced the city's waterways to ecologically lifeless expanses of 'flat and slimy mud', 'skeleton architecture' and fuming 'long mounds' of waste (*E5* 276–7).[46] Moreover, oil plays a central role in the image Woolf paints, both directly and indirectly. The huge ocean liners with which the essay opens, 'a thousand' of which 'anchor in the docks of London' each week (*E5* 275), stand as figures for a new, increasingly oil-dependent globalised modernity, while oil is listed among various other imported commodities (including fur, rice pudding and candles) that consumers increasingly 'demand' (*E5* 280). As Jeanette McVicker argues, Woolf's attention to consumerism in the *London Scene* essays is complex, delighting in new experiences and sensations, but situating commodities as 'double-edge[d]' in their instantiation of a liberal democratic capitalism in which individualism does not necessarily translate into freedom, especially for women.[47] The focus on consumerism and capitalism continues into the second essay, 'Oxford

Street Tide'. The essay's titular metaphor is often read as relating to the Thames, casting Oxford Street as a parallel river flowing with commodities. Yet, we might also read the title in terms of a tide of oil, flowing and seeping into the everyday space of London's commercial districts. Indeed, the opening sentence, with its use of terms like 'crudity', 'refined' and 'transformed', wears the language of oil extraction and production, while the essay's description of 'motor omnibuses' competing with 'vans' and 'cars' in 'perpetual race and disorder' points to the increasingly pervasive presence of oil in the literal transportation of goods to Oxford Street and beyond (E5 283).

As in 'The Docks of London', Woolf chooses not to moralise, acknowledging the 'excitement' and 'entertainment' of 'windows lit up by night, of banners flaunting by day' (E5 285), situating Oxford Street as a site of popular enjoyment and mass culture. It is 'gaudy, bustling [and] vulgar' (E5 287) yet fascinating and alluring, especially compared to the more exclusive Bond Street, with which Woolf perhaps expects her readers to associate her. This uncertainty as to whether Woolf is truly part of the Oxford Street masses or an observer looking on speaks to what critics have described as the essay's preoccupation with negotiating the role of insider and outsider.[48] Yet, even if Woolf does not truly belong among the masses of Oxford Street, she recognises her complicity within a growing consumerist culture. In 'The Docks of London', Woolf uses the first-person plural in describing how '[w]e demand' commodities (including oil) 'and they are brought to us', asserting that '[o]ur body is their master' (E5 280). Yet, this insistence on the sovereign mastery of the consumer is immediately undermined by the admission that '[t]rade watches us anxiously to see what new desires are beginning to grow in us, what new dislikes' (E5 280). Trade, which we have already been told is 'ingenious and indefatigable beyond the bounds of imagination' (E5 278), gives the illusion of agency and serving public wants, while in fact shaping and controlling those desires (akin to BP's aforementioned newspaper strategies around petrol). In the 'Oxford Street Tide' this idea becomes more explicit, with Woolf describing how 'the human form has adapted itself' to the commodities on offer in the street's famous department stores (E5 283). As in 'Thunder at Wembley', we find a critique of imperialist capitalism. While consumerism seems to offer new freedoms for a growing middle class, it is in fact a 'forcing house of sensation' (E5 284), a metaphor that suggests organic manipulation and environmental control.

Unlike 'Thunder at Wembley', however, Woolf opts not for an apocalyptic ending to the 'Oxford Street Tide' but something arguably worse: the extinction of conclusive thought itself. The relentless stimulation of commodities, the 'bounding, careless, remorseless tide of the street' (*E5* 287), means that until someone opens 'cells for solitary thinkers [. . .] to induce thought and reflection, it is vain to try to come to a conclusion in Oxford Street' (*E5* 287). Despite the irony, Woolf's warning is clear, suggesting that this unceasing flow of extracted materials and imported commodities, which we first encountered in 'The Docks of London', produces a social structure that precludes the conditions for thinking.[49] The explicit decision to eschew a conclusion at the end of the essay, while not an uncommon literary strategy deployed by Woolf, in this instance actively performs the kind of intellectual paralysis ushered in by an increasingly accelerated (and oil-fuelled) imperial capitalism. Straightforward refusal of the new social order is not possible, yet neither is a straightforward endorsement palatable; if conclusions usually require a degree of distance from one's subject, Woolf is clear in that she is just as implicated as the shoppers she encounters on the busy streets. The sense of resignation, perhaps even fatalism, in this non-ending articulates a common affect in the Anthropocene, in which an awareness of one's own participation in damaging and destructive practices does not easily translate into a sense of how one might respond.

Woolf's assertion that '[o]ur body is their master' in 'The Docks of London' is, on one level, a play on words, inviting itself to be understood as referring to both the individual bodies of consumers and the public body, blurring the line between individual and state responsibility in planetary capitalism. She returns to this theme in the fifth essay in the series, '"This is the House of Commons"'. If on Oxford Street Woolf observes intellectual and social paralysis, here she finds its correlative in political paralysis. The essay paints a picture of an increasingly bureaucratic and impersonal approach to government, stripped of a genuine form of politics that she associates with the individuality and integrity of 'single men and personal power' (*E5* 327). While Woolf's language contrasts here with the feminist critique of Parliament that she would later articulate in *Three Guineas*, her focus in the essay is the commercialisation of British politics. Politicians now resemble 'common hard-worked [men] of business' of the kind who have 'a small car and a villa [. . .] and play golf' (*E5* 327). Furthermore, it is these 'ordinary-looking business-like men [who] are responsible for acts which will remain when their red cheeks and top hats and check trousers are dust and ashes' (*E5* 326). Short-term commercial interests take precedence over the centuries-, perhaps millennia-long effects they will have. The decisions being made by these men, who would be more fitting in a boardroom than on the front bench, not only pave the way for the kind of thoughtless commercialism documented in 'Oxford Street Tide' but also the immediate and long-term environmental consequences outlined in 'The Docks of London'. This sense of multiple scales of time colliding, with short term interests coming at the expense of the long term, recalls the imagining of the distant future at the conclusion to Sackville-West's *Twelve Days*, where dust and ash will be all the remain of the current imperial order. If in 'Thunder at Wembley' and the earlier *London Scene* essays, Woolf insinuates that Britain's present form of democracy might not actually be very democratic, here that sentiment is made explicit: 'Down on this stuff of common humanity comes the stamp of a huge machine. And the machine itself and the man upon whom the stamp of the machine descends are both plain, featureless, impersonal' (*E5* 326–7).

One of the debates that Woolf overheard, or imagined overhearing, during her visit to Parliament was about speed limits for 'our cars' (*E5* 325) in Hyde Park. The collective pronoun is telling here, both in acknowledging *Good Housekeeping*'s middle-class audience and implicating herself in the category of car ownership. Was she thinking of her Singer, which she boasted to Eliot of, when she wrote that sentence? Christine Reynier has pointed out that car manufacturers, such as Vauxhall, were advertising in the pages of the magazine during the period the essays were published and, like Sackville-West's travelogues, Woolf's *London Scene* is a kind of petro-narrative.[50] The first metaphor in 'The Docks of London' imagines the city as a giant 'parking ground' for ships (*E5* 275), an image that seems to foresee London's future as a network of roads and car parks, while Oxford Street already roars with traffic, and road traffic legislation is debated in Parliament. Even from the calm retreat of Hampstead Heath in 'Great Men's Houses' the capital's resource-hungry extractivist economy cannot be avoided. Here, from the top of the hill, one 'sees London as a whole [. . .] its dominant domes; its guardian cathedrals; its chimneys and spires; its cranes and gasometers; and the perpetual smoke which no spring or autumn ever blows away' (*E5* 298).

Conclusion: Rags and Petrol

The 1920s were a period in which, as Wereley puts it, corporate interests were looking to 'narrativize' oil.[51] Sackville-West's travelogues and Woolf's essays might be read as offering competing narratives. Where Woolf's essays present a picture of imperialist extractivism as eroding the foundations of democracy in Britain, Sackville-West's travelogues endorse an antidemocratic future for the Persian populations who have found themselves in the crosshairs of competing global and national interests. Where they converge is in their sense of horror and fascination with an oil-dependent future, most vividly expressed in their shared apocalyptic imagery of environmental decline, and, also, in their belief of the inevitability of that future. While Sackville-West might be able to leave the hellish landscape of the Persian oilfields for country life in Kent, Woolf's *London Scene* essays suggests that the horrors happening at the imperial periphery are becoming increasingly localised in Britain. For Woolf, there is no escape from being implicated in global networks of imperial extractivism nor is there a clear solution. The idea that the answer might be found in ethical consumerism, rooted in the notion that '[o]ur body is their master' (*E5* 280), is shown to lack power in the face of a globalised capitalism that 'watches us anxiously' (*E5* 280) and has the support of an increasingly bureaucratised political class.

Following the oil in Woolf's writing and literary network shows us the narrative strategies, the elisions and innovations, that reveal both a literary history and materials to think with in the present. We find a substance that seems to get everywhere, providing Woolf with a resource that invites self-reflection and critique, as well as the acknowledgement of an impossible complicity with it. At other times, it seems to leach into the background or reveal blind spots. When, for instance, in *Three Guineas*, Woolf describes the 'rags and petrol' (*TG* 118) that might burn down the education system, clearing the ground for a different future, we might ask where that petrol comes from and who that future excludes. Etkind, in his global overview of oil, argues that it is not a coincidence that oil-producing states often have poor records on women's rights. The autocratic rule of oil states derives from the fact that oil extraction does not require the kind of labour-force that earlier industrial revolutions required, meaning, as a result, that women are offered less education and participation in professional life.[52] In December 1940, amid petrol rationing and government anxiety about protecting oil interests, Woolf invited Sackville-West to come and give a talk on Persia (by then renamed Iran) to the Rodmell Women's Institute (*L6* 448). The following summer, British forces, in agreement with the Soviets, would occupy Iran, securing the valuable oilfields for the Allies. Woolf, to be sure, would not have been blithely unaware of the contradictions in a feminism, anti-imperialism and cosmopolitanism located in an oil-fuelled colonial society, where one's intellectual and material sustenance rely on resources extracted from elsewhere. Nor does her writing suggest that she would have endorsed an environmental politics of consumerist refusal, in which you change the world by changing your purchasing habits or refusing to drive a car. Instead, we find throughout her writing an attention to the way in which the health of the planet seems to rely on the health of democracy, an attention to the narratives through which we make sense of our complicity and a willingness for critical thought even in the face of apocalyptic futures.

Notes

1. Jones, *State and Emergence*, 5–6.
2. Etkind, *Nature's Evil*, 10.
3. Quoted in Lee, *Virginia Woolf*, 503.
4. Etkind, *Nature's Evil*, 11.
5. During the nineteenth century the 'per capita consumption of energy' doubled globally. In the twentieth century it increased a hundredfold. Etkind, *Nature's Evil*, 10.
6. Jones, *State and Emergence*, 7.
7. Sackville-West, *Twelve*, 122.
8. Wereley, 'Extracting', 6.
9. Schuster, 'Where is the Oil?', 199.
10. Ibid., 200.
11. Ghosh, *Great Derangement*, 74.
12. Sackville-West, *Twelve*, 123.
13. Snaith and Whitworth, 'Introduction', 2.
14. Andrew McNeillie gives the working title of the essay in his 'Editorial Note' to volume three of Woolf's essays. See McNeillie, 'Editorial Note', xxv.
15. Wereley, 'Advertising', 26; Knight and Sabey, *Lion Roars*, 18.
16. Cohen, 'Empire', 88, 102.
17. Szeman and Wenzel, 'What Do We', 506.
18. Moore, *Capitalism*, 13.
19. Knight and Sabey, *Lion Roars*, 42, 48.
20. Ibid., 67.
21. Wereley, 'Advertising', 19.
22. Ibid., 28.
23. Koenigsberger, 'Virginia Woolf', 106.
24. Cohen, 'Empire', 89. Also see Melba Cuddy-Keane's argument that the essay functions as 'counter-discourse' to the ideology behind the Exhibition. Cuddy-Keane, *Virginia Woolf*, 47.
25. For an overview of what Woolf would probably have known about anthropogenic climate change, see my chapter on *Orlando* in *The Modernist Anthropocene* and Christina Alt's chapter in this volume.

26. Wereley, 'Advertising', 32.
27. Adkins, *Modernist Anthropocene*, 8–9.
28. Glendinning, *Vita*, 173.
29. Susan Bazargan suggests that Sackville-West was inspired by the Persian landscape to devise a poetics that could accommodate lesbian desire. See Bazargan, 'Uses of the Land'.
30. Sackville-West, *Passenger*, 93–94.
31. Sackville-West, *Twelve*, 22.
32. Sackville-West, *Passenger*, 48, 59.
33. Sackville-West, *Twelve*, 111.
34. Ibid., 93.
35. It is noticeable that Sackville-West doesn't acknowledge that Knox never personally visited Persia. Ibid., 126.
36. Wereley, 'Extracting', 6.
37. Sackville-West, *Twelve*, 115.
38. Ibid., 120.
39. Ibid., 119–20.
40. Glendinning, *Vita*, 174; Wereley, 'Advertising', 5.
41. Sackville-West, *Twelve*, 121–2.
42. Ibid., 137.
43. Ibid., 112–13.
44. Ibid., 112.
45. Ibid., 77.
46. Adkins, *Modernist Anthropocene*, 9–10.
47. McVicker, '"Six Essays"', 149. See also Christine Reynier's analysis of Woolf's making visible the 'alienating processes' of capitalism and colonialism in *Virginia Woolf's Good Housekeeping Essays* (loc. 10.43).
48. See Sarker, 'Locating' and Jeanette McVicker, '"Six Essays"'.
49. As Cuddy-Keane argues in the context of 'Thunder at Wembley', Woolf insists that space for 'critical response' is a necessary condition of 'participant democracy'. Cuddy-Keane, *Virginia Woolf*, 47.
50. Reynier, *Good Housekeeping*, loc. 10.53.
51. Wereley, 'Advertising', 37.
52. Etkind, *Nature's Evil*, 151.

Bibliography

Adkins, Peter. *The Modernist Anthropocene: Nonhuman Life and Planetary Change in James Joyce, Virginia Woolf and Djuna Barnes*. Edinburgh: Edinburgh University Press, 2022.

Bazargan, Susan. 'The Uses of the Land: Vita Sackville West's Pastoral Writing and Virginia Woolf's *Orlando*'. *Woolf Studies Annual* 5 (1999): 25–55.

Cohen, Scott. 'The Empire from the Street: Virginia Woolf, Wembley, and Imperial Monuments'. *Modern Fiction Studies* 50, no. 1 (2004): 85–109.

Cuddy-Keane, Melba. *Virginia Woolf, the Intellectual and the Public Sphere*. Cambridge: Cambridge University Press, 2003.
Etkind, Aleksandr. *Nature's Evil: A Cultural History of Natural Resources*, translated by Sara Jolly. Medford, MA: Polity Press, 2021.
Ghosh, Amitav. *The Great Derangement: Climate Change and the Unthinkable*. Chicago: University of Chicago Press, 2017.
Glendinning, Victoria. *Vita: The Life of Vita Sackville-West*. London: Penguin Books, 1984.
Jones, Geoffrey. *The State and the Emergence of the British Oil Industry*. Basingstoke: Palgrave Macmillan, 1981.
Knight, Donald R., and Alan D. Sabey. *The Lion Roars at Wembley: The British Empire Exhibition, 60th Anniversary 1924–1925*. London: D. R. Knight, 1984.
Koenigsberger, Kurt. 'Virginia Woolf and the Empire Exhibition of 1924: Modernism, Excess, and the Verandahs of Realism'. In *Locating Woolf: The Politics of Space and Place*, edited by Anna Snaith and Michael Whitworth, 99–114. Basingstoke: Palgrave Macmillan, 2007.
Lee, Hermione. *Virginia Woolf*. London: Chatto & Windus, 1996.
McNeillie, Andrew. 'Editorial Note'. In Virginia Woolf, *The Essays of Virginia Woolf, Volume III: 1919–1924*, edited by Andrew McNeillie, xxiii–xxv. London: Hogarth Press, 1988.
McVicker, Jeanette. '"Six Essays on London Life": A History of Dispersal Part I'. *Woolf Studies Annual* 9 (2003): 143–65.
Moore, Jason W. *Capitalism in the Web of Life: Ecology and the Accumulation of Capital*. New York: Verso, 2015.
Reynier, Christine. *Virginia Woolf's Good Housekeeping Essays*. New York: Routledge, 2019. eBook.
Sackville-West, Vita. *Passenger to Teheran*. London: Arrow Books, 1991.
——. *Twelve Days in Persia: Across the Mountains with Bakhtiari Tribe*. London: I. B. Tauris, 2009.
Sarker, Sonita. 'Locating a Native Englishness in Virginia Woolf's *The London Scene*'. *NWSA Journal* 13, no. 2 (July 2001): 1–30.
Schuster, Joshua. 'Where is the Oil in Modernism?' In *Petrocultures: Oil, Energy, Culture*, edited by Imre Szeman and Sheena Wilson, 197–213. Montreal: McGill Queen's University Press, 2017.
Snaith, Anna, and Michael Whitworth. 'Introduction: Approaches to Space and Place in Woolf'. In *Locating Woolf: The Politics of Space and Place*, edited by Anna Snaith and Michael Whitworth, 1–31. Basingstoke: Palgrave Macmillan, 2007.
Szeman, Imre, and Jennifer Wenzel. 'What Do We Talk about When We Talk about Extractivism?' *Textual Practice* 35, no. 3 (2021): 505–23.
Wereley, Ian. 'Advertising an Empire of Oil: The British Petroleum Company and the Persian Khan Exhibit of 1924–1925'. *MediaTropes* 7, no. 2 (5 February 2020): 19–39.

———. 'Extracting the Past from the Present: Exotic Prizes, Empty Wilderness, and Commercial Conquest in Two Oil Company Advertisements, 1925–2012'. *Humanities* 5, no. 2 (2016): 1–20.

Woolf, Virginia. *The Diary of Virginia Woolf*, edited by Anne Olivier Bell. 5 vols. London: Penguin Books, 1979–85.

———. *The Essays of Virginia Woolf*, edited by Andrew McNeillie (vols 1–4) and Stuart N. Clarke (vols 5–6). 6 vols. London: Hogarth Press, 1986–2011.

———. *The Letters of Virginia Woolf*, edited by Nigel Nicolson and Joanne Trautmann. 6 vols. London: Hogarth Press, 1975–80.

———. *A Room of One's Own and Three Guineas*, edited by Anna Snaith. Oxford: Oxford University Press, 2015.

Part III

Writing Extinction

Chapter 6

Hearing Beyond Extinction: The Inhuman Comedy of Virginia Woolf's *Between the Acts*

Rasheed Tazudeen

Tracing the disjunctive temporalities and futurities brought by the Anthropocene, as a metonym for the variegated discourses that have arisen in response to anthro-/sociogenic climate change, Elizabeth DeLoughrey writes:

> Engaging with the Anthropocene means that we must simultaneously consider the deep geological time of the planet – in comparison with previous epochs – as well as the futurity of the human as a species. Futurity is marked not just by concerns about human survival, or ameliorating species extinctions, but also by the fact that one cannot locate a stratigraphic marker for this epoch until a geologically significant period of time – such as tens of thousands of years – has passed. Thus, the Anthropocene is both forward-looking and a future retrospective, characterized by 'anticipatory logics' and anticipatory mourning.[1]

Read as proto-Anthropocenic thought, *Between the Acts* (1941) is simultaneously a proleptic elegy for the extinctions to come and an opening to the comedic unimaginability of an Earth that persists beyond humanistic possession. Comedy, I want to suggest, is also an ecological modality: the surrender of determination to forces, beings, or temporalities other than the human. In this vein, Mark McGurl has ventured 'posthuman comedy' as an umbrella term that 'draw[s] together a number of modern literary works in which scientific knowledge of the spatiotemporal vastness and numerousness of the nonhuman world becomes visible as a formal, representational, and finally existential problem'.[2] The posthuman character of comedy thus arises largely from the gap or incongruity between the vast extensive and intensive dimensions of inhuman worlds ('the inhumanly large and long') and the comparative smallness of humanistic means of thought and representation.[3] Comedy is also an opening to a yet-to-be-imagined future – or to many futures – outside of the determinate coordinates of what has historically (and scientifically, and aesthetically) been given as possible. What comes after humanism, ask Woolf's last, unfinished works – 'Anon' and 'The Reader', as well as *Between the Acts* – and how does one imagine (with) oblivion through epistemologies that have only ever been humanist? Might laughter, especially in its attunement to what is beyond human imagination, be one such means? Woolf suggests something of this possibility in the 'Time Passes' section of *To the Lighthouse* (1927). Amid the 'oblivion' or 'long night' drowning all beings in an impersonal and 'immense darkness', some gestures still persist: 'Sometimes a hand was raised as if to clutch something or ward off something, or somebody groaned, or somebody laughed aloud as if sharing a joke with nothingness' (*TTL* 126). Laughing in and with oblivion is participation in the comedic inscrutability of (individual, species and planetary) futures.

Woolf theorises the inhuman dimensions of comedy and laughter more explicitly in a 1905 essay, 'The Value of Laughter'. Laughter, according to Woolf, is the province of 'children and silly women', and 'the voice of folly and frivolity inspired neither by knowledge nor by emotion' (*E1* 58–9). Aligned with both animals and the larger domain of what we might call non-Man, laughter 'gives no message, conveys no information; it is an inarticulate utterance like the bark of a dog or the bleat of sheep, and it is beneath the dignity of a race that has made itself a language to express itself thus' (*E1* 59).[4] At the same time, however, Woolf notes that 'laughter is the one sound, inarticulate though it be, that no animal can produce' (*E1* 59). Comedy and laughter are both mediated through nonhuman beings *and* withdrawn from them, a theoretical formation that operates as well in both Mark McGurl's and Henri Bergson's accounts of the inhumanism of comedy. Of Bergson's *Laughter* (1900), McGurl writes, 'comedy can only be human, but it is also true that it arises only in the relation of humanity to something other'.[5] Further, even as Bergson locates laughter strictly within human social communities, he nonetheless inhumanises both the origin and the propagation of laughter, as uncontrollable 'reverberation' without clear beginning or end: '[Laughter] is not an articulate, clear, well-defined sound; it is something which would fain be prolonged by reverberating from one to another, something beginning with a crash, to continue in successive rumblings, like thunder in a mountain'.[6]

The Bergsonian comic, too, is only possible through an 'absence of feeling', a comportment of indifference towards the objective content of one's surrounding world: 'Indifference is [the comic's] natural environment, for laughter has no greater foe than emotion'. When we 'look upon life as a disinterested spectator', according to Bergson, 'many a drama will turn into a comedy'.[7] Yet laughter is not only removal from life, but also a more intensive means of participation in one's lived relations – including relations with the Earth itself – and one's envisioned futures. In the sociality of laughter, as Mikhail Bakhtin argues, we are both stripped of self and situated as part of an unfinished whole, one that is continually composed by our actions and our modes of being in addition to those of the vast inhuman world. Of the cultures of folk humour in the Middle Ages and the Renaissance, Bakhtin writes, 'The people do not exclude themselves from the wholeness of the world. They, too, are incomplete, they also die and are revived and renewed. [. . .] The people's ambivalent laughter [. . .] expresses the point of view of the whole world; he who is laughing also belongs to it'.[8] Laughter amid and as response to cosmic terror is a means of regenerating the world, an opening onto other futures beyond what is humanistically conceivable. What would make the Bakhtinian comedic vision into a posthuman or an inhuman[9] one might be the unimaginability of the Earth's future generation: the Bakhtinian folk laugher sees their body made incorporate with the Earth's cycles of regeneration, whereas inhuman comedy emerges as thought of Earthly generation on the other side of oblivion, growing and reverberating indifferently to human being. In other words, a 're-generation' that is not generation of the same, but rather the emergence of what cannot be known or conceptualised.

As well as elegising the extinctions to come, *Between the Acts* also modulates the spectre of extinction through comedy.[10] In line with Ancient Greek comedic conventions, as Melba Cuddy-Keane argues, both the novel and La Trobe's pageant are structured and punctuated by a 'communal chorus' or 'choric voice' that rearticulates community by inviting participation from new (human and nonhuman) voices and sounds.[11] 'The narrative act of transforming all voices into chorus', according to Cuddy-Keane, is a political and an ecological gesture that also suggests something of the subversive folk forms of festival, dance and revelry – the *kômos* of 'comedy' [*kōmōdía*] – by which existing orders of being are opened to indeterminate futures.[12] Like comedy, sound too is social. In Jean-Luc Nancy's terms, 'the visual is tendentially mimetic, and the sonorous tendentially methexic (that is, having to do with participation, sharing, or contagion)'.[13]

Included within the choric voice of *Between the Acts* are also the methexic revelries of nonhumans, or the making of worlds from sonic communions. Towards the novel's end, for example, a flock of starlings sweeps directly into a tree, 'pelt[ing] it like so many winged stones' until it becomes 'a rhapsody, a quivering cacophony, a whizz and vibrant rapture' (*BTA* 209). Lithic birds articulate new assemblages between sky and Earth – multispecied gatherings of animal, (stone) and plant – out of which are produced noises simultaneously inhuman and divine. To La Trobe, sole earwitness to this phenomenon, the choric 'syllabling' voiced by the starling-tree assemblage is also the possibility of another expressivity: the relational composition of Earth noises, or 'words of one syllable', that are not yet, and perhaps never to be assimilable into language. As La Trobe wanders the village fields, graveyard and tavern post-pageant, she hears voices acousmatically, as syllables ('words without meaning') decoupled from speaking bodies and instead planted into the earth: 'Words of one syllable sank into the mud. [. . .] The mud became fertile' (*BTA* 212).[14] What futures rise from sound-fertilised mud is neither for La Trobe nor the novel itself to give. We are left, rather, amid the comedic, revelrous generation of what Woolf calls the 'syllabling' of 'life, life, life without measure' that insists beyond the humanisms of the present and the (post)humanisms projected into the future (*BTA* 209).

Woolf's final works improvise with the impersonality of worlds still to be composed beyond the time and consciousness of humans.[15] Both La Trobe and Anon, the primordial balladeer in Woolf's eponymous, unfinished essay of 1941, sing of the ending of worlds as well as their ongoingnesses. As Woolf writes in the last line of 'The Reader' (1941), her (also unfinished) essay accompanying 'Anon': 'We are in a world where nothing is concluded'.[16] Anon, the 'common voice singing out of doors', and the sound-gatherer La Trobe both environ worlds impersonally, orienting song towards what might emerge in the absence of human consciousness: the bird song from which human art mimetically arose for Anon, the future growth of planted sounds for La Trobe. The name La Trobe, originating from the Occitan *trobador* ('troubadour'),[17] suggests La Trobe's close connection to the impersonal generativities of both Anon and the inhuman worlds ('the bird whispering reed haunted fen') that Anon sought to sing.[18] The world 'beneath our consciousness', Woolf writes in 'Anon', is 'an anonymous world', conceived both as the pre-conscious primitivity voiced by the singer and, in *Between the Acts*, as fertile ground for the comedic futures growing from humanism's ruins.[19]

In this essay, we attempt to hear towards these comedic futures – and to hear beyond extinction – through four separate, yet endlessly resonant improvisations with the Earth and its sounds. We begin with the comic-grotesque image of a gigantic ear of the Earth, which, in Lucy Swithin's imagination, serves as a hearing *and* harmonising apparatus for all wayward noises and beings. We then measure Swithin's fantasy of an all-encompassing world harmony against the impersonal songs, soundings and noises of the Earth's vast inhuman multitudes – as well as of the Earth itself – in both *Between the Acts* and 'Anon'. Cow song, in the midst of La Trobe's pageant, becomes a comedic rupture of human auditory and imaginative capacity that gestures towards another, inhumanist relation to ground or 'territory'. Similarly, the aforementioned starling-tree syllables become for La Trobe a new sonorous art form by which to both fill oblivion and to improvise with the sounds and syllables ongoingly generated by the Earth. La Trobe's bird-tree syllabary finds resonance with Anon's forestial songs, which both mourn the separation of self from bird and 'rejoice' in the modulation of all death and all loss into the 'nameless vitality' of the Earth.[20] We end with La Trobe's, Anon's and Woolf's collective desire to hear the hearing of the Earth, prior to the intrusive fiction of temporality and prior to the opening of Anon's primordial forest to the 'eye' of both Heaven and history.[21] Yet this hearing backwards is also a hearing beyond, towards the comedically unimaginable futures of an 'anonymous' Earth and the noises filling its oblivions.

A Gigantic Ear

The tensions between the novel's elegiac and comedic modalities achieve most direct expression through the reading, listening and philosophising of Lucy Swithin. Swithin is extinction-obsessed almost from the moment of her introduction, during which she is reading a book titled *Outline of History* and imagining the prehuman history of 'the entire continent' (*BTA* 8).[22] And as she later mourns, through a simultaneously familial, humanistic and geo-planetary 'we': '"That's what makes a view so sad. [. . .] And so beautiful. It'll be there," she nodded at the strip of gauze laid upon the distant fields, "when we're not"' (*BTA* 53). Yet underlying Swithin's fascination with the geohistorical indifference of land to human histories and futures is belief in a vast, multispecied comedy spanning the entire Earth, in which all beings and voices might one day be harmonised:

> Sheep, cows, grass, trees, ourselves – all are one. If discordant, producing harmony – if not to us, to a gigantic ear attached to a gigantic head. And thus – she was smiling benignly – the agony of the particular sheep, cow, or human being is necessary; and so – she was beaming seraphically at the gilt vane in the distance – we reach the conclusion that all is harmony, could we hear it. And we shall. (BTA 175)

Swithin's world-harmony, at the same time, is imaginable only in the conditional tense and in the grotesquely enfleshed form and comic dimensions of a 'gigantic ear attached to a gigantic head'. Let us dwell with (and *listen* with) this simultaneously comedic and ecological fantasy for a moment. For along with the tension between comedy and elegy, *Between the Acts* also revolves around a tension between inhuman, impersonal noise (animal, natural and machinic) and the promise of harmony, or of sound made meaningful.[23] What is the Earth hearing with its gigantic ear, and what harmony or disharmony is it making of everything methexically gathered into it ('sheep, cows, grass, trees, ourselves'), all the noises, agonies and expressions planted in its ground?

This gigantic ear might be most easily identifiable as the phonograph or gramophone, a technological prosthesis employed throughout La Trobe's pageant – including in the scene immediately preceding Swithin's musings – that enhances the capacities of the human sensorium, allowing the formerly unheard or unhearable to surface into audition.[24] In early accounts of the phonograph, as classicist and media theorist Shane Butler notes, there is an 'unmistakable slippage' between its functions as a listening device and as a medium for the reproduction and transfer of sounds.[25] 'This little instrument', as described in a *Harper's Weekly* article from March 1878, 'records the utterance of the human voice, and like a faithless confidante repeats every secret confided to it whenever requested to do so'.[26] In Butler's analysis, the '"faithless" repetition' of the phonograph actually 'depend[s] precisely on *faithful* listening to 'every secret' in earshot'.[27] We might also call these faithful comportments to tiny or secret perceptions a mode of impersonal listening. In Friedrich Kittler's analysis, such devotional listening is only possible without the mediation of a self-hearing or -organising consciousness.[28]

What separates this 'little instrument' from Mrs. Swithin's 'gigantic ear', however, is that the latter's audition is directed towards not only the reproduction but also the *harmonisation* of heard sounds. The little phonograph faithfully returns sounds in the present, while the gigantic ear hears beyond extinction, making words out of all that has been gathered or sedimented into it outside of human dictates of meaning and harmony alike. La Trobe's pageant and subsequent wanderings, as well as *Between the Acts* itself, are gathering places for sounds and for the inhuman futures of sounds. La Trobe herself imagines self and world sonically: 'Ah, but she was not merely a twitcher of individual strings', she imaginatively retorts to one of the villagers, 'she was one who seethes wandering bodies and floating voices in a cauldron, and makes rise up from its amorphous mass a re-created world' (*BTA* 153). Cauldron, pageant and novel are all sites where (multispecied) voices mingle with bodies, gathering discordantly rather than into the harmonic resolution of Swithin's imagined Earth composition.

The Comedy of the Cows

Throughout the novel, inhuman sounds have a habit of both filling and modulating the voids left in the wake of human voices. In other words, inhuman sounds tend to emerge from silences, while also transmuting these silences into new sound- or noise-scapes. For example, the novel's opening discussion among the Haineses and Olivers (itself focused on another void: the village cesspool) cedes to an emptiness filled by bovine noise: 'Then there was silence; and a cow coughed; and that led [Mrs Haines] to say how odd it was, as a child, she had never feared cows, only horses' (*BTA* 3). There is a sonic, if not a musical structure at work here – 1. voice, 2. silence, 3. inhuman noise (modulation) and 4. new soundscape – that recurs in the scene of another cow-noised punctum that emerges during the Valentine and Flavinda portion of La Trobe's pageant. As with each of the pageant's scenes, it incorporates a chorus of villagers, who play the part of field labourers here: '[D]igging and delving (they sang), hedging and ditching, we pass. [. . .] Summer and winter, autumn and spring return [. . .] All passes but we, all changes [. . .] but we remain forever the same' (*BTA* 139). However, their Earth song, which is meant to 'continue the emotion' across an interval bridging scenes of Valentine and Flavinda's courtship, goes unheard, masked by other expressivities: '(the breeze blew gaps between their words)'; '[t]hen the wind rose, and in the rustle of the leaves even the great words became inaudible; and the audience sat staring at the villagers, whose mouths opened, but no sound came' (*BTA* 139, 140). For La Trobe, the absence of choral sound is the negation of life, and death takes the form of an irremediable silence: 'Illusion had failed. "This is death," she murmured, "death"' (*BTA* 140).

Subtending the world of individualistic characters and their individualised emotions are two impersonal songs of the ground: the choral refrain of the labourers, articulating what Cuddy-Keane calls 'the life of the common people in touch with the soil' and cycles of 'repetition and recurrence in opposition to change', and the territorial refrain of the cows in the field.[29] In the interstitial sonic and vocal 'gaps' made by the breeze, the yearning-song of the cows finds a medium of expression:

> Then suddenly, as the illusion petered out, the cows took up the burden. One had lost her calf. In the very nick of time she lifted her great moon-eyed head and bellowed. All the great moon-eyed heads laid themselves back. From cow after cow came the same yearning bellow. The whole world was filled with dumb yearning. It was the primeval voice sounding loud in the ear of the present moment. Then the whole herd caught the infection. Lashing their tails, blobbed like pokers, they tossed their heads high, plunged and bellowed, as if Eros had planted his dart in their flanks and goaded them to fury. The cows annihilated the gap; bridged the distance; filled the emptiness and continued the emotion. (*BTA* 140–1)

In the absence of the 'illusion' by which humanity presents itself to itself, and amid the silencing of human voices, the cows articulate another relation to the Earth and its futures. Bellowing modulates extinction into comedy: a contagious, communal song – the *ōidē*, or song, of 'comedy' [*kōmōdía*] – of the (re)generation of the Earth.

Cow song 'annihilates the gap' between life and death, human and nonhuman being, a gap that is and has only ever been a humanistic construction. In this vein, Derek Ryan argues that the pageant's cows are best read as a Deleuzian, human–nonhuman assemblage, whose bellowing marks a new, provisional, sonic territory that is beyond the grasp of human subjectivity: the 'deterritorialization of humanity' itself.[30] With a differently articulated territory, I would add to Ryan's analysis, comes a different relation both to the ground and to what is generated from it. Louis in *The Waves* (1931) devotes a life to finding a means of domesticating the sound of a 'great beast' 'stamping' on the shore (*TW* 4). The pageant cows, on the other hand, form a comedic, 'communal chorus' that noises into being another ground that is beyond the time and hearing of humans.[31] Their world-filling, 'dumb yearning' knits together primeval and present temporalities, while also carrying the content sedimented into their song – the refrain of the labourers, the sounds of the breeze and the rustle of leaves, the emotions of Valentine and Flavinda, the aesthetic 'burden' of illusion – into an indeterminately specied future, a noisy oblivion. The comedy of cow song speaks as well to Woolf's theory of laughter as both 'beneath' language, or in our terms, Earth-oriented, and given as the message-less, information-less, 'inarticulate utterance like the bark of a dog or the bleat of sheep' (E1 59) and, we add, the bellowing of cows.

Cow song is also given as 'voice', a term generally reserved for human utterances, as well as the element that, according to a strain of sound theory most directly represented in the work of Adriana Cavarero, secures the identity of the individual amid the nonsensical, inhuman sounds, soundscapes and noises of animals, machines and animate and inanimate nature.[32] In contrast to the individualised voice, Woolf's 'primeval voice' is an aggregate, an interspecies gathering of sedimented sounds and noises sounding loud into a gigantic ear. Woolf's inhuman counter-ontology of voice resonates with media theorist Dominic Pettman's formulation of the *vox mundi*, or 'voice of the world', that imagines the voice as a non-totalisable integration of multiply sourced (human, nonhuman, machinic) sounds, 'expressed in all manner of creatures, agents, entities, objects, and phenomena'.[33] As *vox mundi* (or perhaps *vox terra*), Woolf's 'primeval voice sounding loud' is not regression to primitivity, but rather a modulation of the sonic-affective content gathered into it towards new, comedic forms by which to fill oblivion, or to continue through the impersonalised long night of human extinction. I like to think of the comedic ongoingness of this cow song, sounding through the failure of illusion and the approach of death, as a punchline accompanying *To the Lighthouse*'s aforementioned description of the drowning of every expressivity in an 'immense darkness': 'Sometimes a hand was raised as if to clutch something or ward off something, or somebody groaned, or somebody laughed aloud as if sharing a joke with nothingness' (TTL 126). By saturating the impersonality of oblivion with the overflow of powerful, world-filling yearning, cow song bridges the gap between death and life, extinction and generation, and mourning and comedy. Cow song turns the terror of night into the comedy of what persists in and beyond oblivion, where nothingness, as a medium for both insistent and unimaginable generation and the sharing of jokes, is to be laughed at and laughed with.

Yet humans remain oblivious to the joke. The primeval voice, the comedic cow song, ultimately becomes muted through another modulation, this time by the pageant's audience, to visual and conceptual apprehension: 'Suddenly the cows stopped; lowered their heads, and began browsing. Simultaneously the audience lowered their heads and read the programmes' (*BTA* 141). (In the programme, we are told, the producer has described a scene that was omitted from the Valentine and Flavinda portion due to time constraints.) This shift from gigantic, communal, interspecies voice (and the gigantic hearing ear of the landscape) to mute, individualised textual consumption also marks the (human) re-imposition of silence upon yet another inhuman noise-world. La Trobe's aesthetics of impersonality – 'she was not merely a twitcher of individual strings, she was one who seethes wandering bodies and floating voices in a cauldron, and makes rise up from its amorphous mass a re-created world' – are crafted with the fragility of these worlds in mind, which can only evade determination for so long before they are harmonically resolved into the tonality of Man (*BTA* 153).[34]

The clearest and most precise articulation of this tonality emerges perhaps from the Reverend Streatfield in his post-pageant remarks: 'Scraps, orts and fragments! Surely, we should unite?' he concludes, in an attempt to hold together what is in excess of meaning, or what the malfunctioning gramophone ongoingly insists is 'dispersed' (*BTA* 192). Even before the emergence of his voice, however, his status as 'symbol' and 'representative spokesman' for the audience, for the perpetuity of humanisms has already become drowned amid an indifferent comedy of an inhuman 'summer silent world', flowing beyond the enclosures of meaning:

> There he stood their representative spokesman; their symbol; themselves; a butt, a clod, laughed at by looking-glasses; ignored by the cows, condemned by the clouds which continued their majestic rearrangement of the celestial landscape; an irrelevant forked stake in the flow and majesty of the summer silent world. (*BTA* 190–1)

The impersonality of the (Earthly and celestial) landscape – as an indifference to or nonrepresentation of persons – opens to the regenerative laughter of and beyond oblivion. Looking-glasses laugh and a gigantic Earth ear hears: La Trobe's new language, or re-created world, must seethe mingled fragments, methexic noise, into a form that laughs with and alongside oblivion, shares a joke with the nothingnesses of a summer silent world.

Earth-(h)earing

'"A failure," she groaned, and stooped to put away the records' (*BTA* 209). Yet La Trobe's stooping is what allows her to hear the Earth differently, perhaps alongside the gigantic ear of the landscape instead of through the reconfigured sounds returned by the gramophone, that 'little instrument' which, like the Reverend Streatfield, can voice only the humanisms that have been projected into it. In stooping, however, La Trobe hears another kind of syllabling:

> Then suddenly the starlings attacked the tree behind which she was hidden. In one flock they pelted it like so many winged stones. The whole tree hummed with the whizz they made, as if each bird plucked a wire. A whizz, a buzz rose from the bird-buzzing, bird-vibrant, bird-blackened tree. The tree became a rhapsody, a quivering cacophony, a whizz and vibrant rapture, branches, leaves, birds syllabling discordantly life, life, life, without measure, without stop devouring the tree. Then up! Then off! (*BTA* 209)

Thus attacked (also a musical term, as the initiation of a sound) the tree is made co-vibrational, shaken out of the stasis that it occupied during the pageant, when trees were solidities that 'barred the music' and 'prevented what was fluid from overflowing' (*BTA* 182). The joining of bird and tree is rhapsody (from the Greek *rhapsōidía*, the sewing together [*rhaptein*] of songs [*ōidē*]), a co-composed, measureless generation of sensate, sewn-together noisings. We can hear these both as La Trobe's sought-after 'words of one syllable' and what Woolf calls in 'Anon', 'the word heard. Its solidities: its depths'.[35] Such inhuman rhapsody, songs or sounds of sewing and the dissonant gathering into which they are sown, reverberate beyond humanistic time and measure. The whizz, buzz, hum of the starling-(stone-)tree assemblage are inharmonisable syllables, units of noise joined to other noise sounding aggregately into the Earth's ear rather than 'melt[ing] into the other clouds' (*BTA* 209). Like the choric cow song 'sounding loud in the ear of the present moment', starlings and tree co-compose an ongoing sound event that fills both the oblivion of the pageant's 'failure' and the post-extinction oblivions to come.

Here, stooped to this ground planted with these inhuman sonic-affective articulations, La Trobe seeks a means of creating with the Earth noise on the other side of extinction. The starlings fly off, scared away by the passing of a villager, and La Trobe approaches the still starling-vibrant tree: 'She crossed the terrace and stopped by the tree where the starlings had gathered. It was here that she had suffered triumph, humiliation, ecstasy, despair – for nothing. Her heels had ground a hole in the grass' (*BTA* 210). La Trobe's new art, perhaps, *is* this hole: the improvised making of an ear, a modest rhyme with the gigantic ear of the landscape, through which to hear and to hear with the Earth. The hole may also be a plot for the planting of sounds into the Earth, from which new inhumanly grown relations and futures might arise.

The hole composed, La Trobe continues her wanderings through the darkening landscape where, in contrast to Swithin's earlier musings, '[t]here was no longer a view – no Folly, no spire of Bolney Minster. It was land merely, no land in particular. She put down her case and stood looking at the land. Then something rose to the surface' (*BTA* 210). This something (growing from Earth or rising from cauldron) is, most immediately, an idea for a future play: '"I should group them here," she murmured, "here." It would be midnight; there would be two figures, half concealed by a rock. The curtain would rise. What would the first words be? The words escaped her' (*BTA* 210). Midnight is no longer oblivion, but rather the time of inhumanly sounded and futured creation. La Trobe's (and Woolf's, and Anon's) impersonalisation of land is also passage to the Earth's comedic and interspecied ongoingness.

As she enters a pub – to her a site of 'shelter; voices; oblivion' – she hears through the chatter: 'Words of one syllable sank down into the mud. She drowsed; she nodded. The mud became fertile. Words rose above the intolerably laden dumb oxen plodding through the mud. Words without meaning – wonderful words' (*BTA* 212). From the soil grow non-meanings, unpossessable sonances by which to fill oblivion. La Trobe's vision is attunement to the inhuman tones generated from earth: 'There was the high ground at midnight; there the rock; and two scarcely perceptible figures. Suddenly the tree was pelted with starlings. She set down her glass. She heard the first words' (*BTA* 212).

Night ground is a rhapsodic gathering of (inharmonisable) tones by which beings – starlings, tree, stone, ground – environ worlds. Yet La Trobe can only hear such worlds obliquely, mediated through the indeterminate, 'scarcely perceptible' tonality of midnight. The first words, heard here again, are the dissonances made from thrown-together starlings and tree – a joining of sky to earth, night to ground – that modulate extinction into the clamour of an inhuman comedy.

The Green Scar Still

This comedy might have begun with Anon, who perhaps hears the same first (bird-)words at Woolf's imagined origin of human history. Woolf's 'Anon' (and history itself) begins at the end of *Between the Acts*, amid the prehistoric noise-worlds made of birds and trees:

> 'For many centuries after Britain became an island' the historian says, 'the untamed forest was king. Its moist and mossy floor was hidden from Heaven's eye by a close drawn curtain woven of innumerable tree tops'. On those matted boughs innumerable birds sang, but their song was only heard by a few skin clad hunters in the clearings.[36]

Anon's voice, given both as 'the human voice' and the androgynous, unhomed, 'common voice singing out of doors', emerges only after the trees are 'felled', after human history is instantiated by the huntsman's axe.[37] Anon's song is both mourning for the choric expressivities lost when the forest world is revealed to Heaven's eye, as well as a modulated continuity of bird-tree singing into what is imagined as the beginnings of poetic form. From Anon's first song:

>   By a bank as I lay
>   Musing myself alone, hey ho!
> A birdes voice
> Did me rejoice
>   Singing before the day;
> And me thought in her lay
> She said, winter was past, hey ho![38]

Anon's song is attempted rhyme between self and bird, sung (and only singable) after a self has already been carved from felled trees and a human dwelling made from untamed forest. The first line composes an 'I' in separation from a (disentangled) bank, an 'I' which grows even more isolate with the next line's 'myself alone'. The subsequent progression from 'me rejoice' to 'me thought' is also a movement from lost musicked touching, or co-vibration, between bird and human voice, to the imposition of concept upon the bird-given syllables. These joyful first syllables are given semantic content and placed into temporality, even as we might still hear the speaker's 'hey ho!' not as the grafting of human speech onto bird voice, but rather as a sought resonance between bodies that remain in communion even after the forests have been cleared and opened to sky.

And yet Anon can only come into existence after Heaven's eye sees the unshaped forest floor, an event leading to the differentiation of human voice from the inhumanist *poeisis* of bird-tree noise. Anon, then, is born from the touching of sky and Earth or forest, his birth leaving an unhealed 'green scar' upon the surface of the Earth, the place seen, envoiced and set into temporality by Heaven's eye. In Woolf's words, Anon journeys along 'the down and the green scar not yet healed', a green scar that persists into the Earth's present, as given more explicitly in an earlier draft of 'Anon': 'On the down is the green scar still, to mark the road along which the travellers came, past the circle where they were buried; past the stone that marks the meeting place or the burial place'.[39] The green scar, as ancient Earth-writing, a geography born of the clearing of forests and an instantiation of human history that might also be an inscription of the Anthropocene itself, also contains the histories of both Anon and the Earth, as we can still hear in the impersonal, 'common' singing of Anon.[40] Like cow song, Anon's singing allows '[e]very body' to 'share in the emotion', melding communal affect with the expressive voice of the Earth itself, a voice that is 'not self conscious', that 'can borrow', 'can repeat', and 'repeats over and over again that flowers fade; that death is the end', and 'never tire[s] of celebrating red roses and white breasts'.[41] Anon's green song is the endless, repeated modulation of death into the comedic celebration of fertility and growth, or what Woolf also calls a 'nameless vitality'.[42] As the stone near the scar marks both burial place and gathering place, so Anon's song is both proleptic mourning for the extinctions to come and celebration of the Earth's repetition of its own nameless livingness. As Earth song or *vox mundi/vox terra*, Anon's voice both gives rise to the English literary tradition and becomes silenced by its historical and formal progression towards the mute 'individuality' of the playwright (and later, in the post-Elizabethan age, by the 'man who writes a book').[43] No longer capable of gathering audiences into the terran commons formed by Anon's first words, playwright and printed word now return to the audience 'their own general life individualised in single and separate figures', amid a fully cleared forest and still scarred landscape in which 'Anon is dead'.[44]

La Trobe hearing the tree-starling syllables is perhaps also an attempt to hear the Earth that Anon heard, its first gifted words. Woolf notes the persistence of Anon and Anon's Earth into the present: 'By shutting out a chimney or factory we can still see what Anon saw'.[45] And as Woolf emphasises in an earlier draft of 'Anon': 'Nor is Anon dead in ourselves'.[46] La Trobe digs a hole in the Earth to hear the Earth. Her hearing is directed both backwards to what Anon heard and forwards to the post-extinction futures beyond humanistic imaginability, towards the oblivions filled by the inhuman *poiesis* of new Anons, singing into being new relations to Earth. In addition to hearing Anon's first words, La Trobe's backward listening may also be a means of returning to the early words of a 22-year-old Virginia Stephen written during her own communions with Earth: 'If you lie on the earth somewhere you hear a sound like a vast breath, as though it were the very inspiration of earth itself, & all the living things on her' (*PA* 203). From this already impersonalised somewhere – the gigantic breathing mouth of the Earth, perhaps? – arises a breath-like sound creatively suffused into all living things, grounding all sounds and sounding beings in the tonic of the Earth's breath. Somewhere is another voice pre-existing and continuing alongside the voice of Anon, that breathed both forests and Anon into being, and sounds still after the clearing of the forests and the death of Anon. Even when La Trobe hears the first words made from the gathered starlings and tree, first sung by Anon, she is perhaps only hearing the breath-like sound of the Earth from which all sounds are modulated. To modulate is to transfer from one mode (or in music, from one key signature) to another, but it is also to arise from pre-articulate, choric ground into mode itself. Woolf is, in this sense, attempting to hear – through co-vibration, through the touching of bodies – what is prior to modulation itself: the vast breath-like sound of the Earth, thinkable only through the obliqueness of simile, before its modal distribution into sounding beings, before the eye of Heaven scarred green the Earth. What comes after humanism and its futures, then, is perhaps the comedic, interspecied persistence of song (the *ōidē* of 'comedy') in and as the unmodulable sound of the Earth itself, and all that is sung into its gigantic ear.

Notes

1. DeLoughrey, *Allegories*, 4.
2. McGurl, 'Posthuman', 537. Similarly, Aaron Jaffe claims that one of the governing problems (if not *the* problem) for modernity is 'the discovery of inhuman scale and the technical difficulties of optimising proportional forms of access'. Jaffe, 'Who's Afraid', 505.
3. McGurl, 'Posthuman', 539.
4. See also Sam See, 'The Comedy of Nature: Darwinian Feminism in Virginia Woolf's *Between the Acts*'.
5. McGurl, 'Posthuman', 549.

6. Ibid., 5–6.
7. Ibid., 4–5.
8. Bakhtin, *Rabelais*, 12. Bakhtin, importantly, critiques Bergson's emphasis on what he calls the 'negative', mocking or satirical aspects of the comic rooted in detachment and distance: 'Let us stress once more that for the Renaissance (as for the antique sources described above) the characteristic trait of laughter was precisely the recognition of its positive, regenerating, creative meaning. This clearly distinguishes it from the later theories of the philosophy of laughter, including Bergson's conception, which bring out mostly its negative functions' (71).
9. In Claire Colebrook and Jami Weinstein's analysis, the concept of the 'posthuman' remains bound to the humanist temporal and conceptual frames that it seeks to 'surpass': posthumanism, in other words, risks becoming an extension of humanism (5). The 'inhuman', however, 'orients us to all that is not human, not just that which comes after the human. It also pushes us to scales beyond the human – temporalities and spatialities both deep and astronomical' (5). See Colebrook and Weinstein, *Posthumous Life* and Tazudeen, *Modernism's Inhuman Worlds*.
10. Smythe, 'Virginia Woolf's Elegiac Enterprise', Beer, '*Between the Acts*: Resisting the End' in *Virginia Woolf*.
11. Cuddy-Keane, 'Politics', 275. See also Christopher Ames, 'Carnivalesque Comedy in *Between the Acts*'.
12. Cuddy-Keane, 'Politics', 275, 280. Citing classical historian Jane Harrison (whose works Woolf may very well have read), Cuddy-Keane claims that 'while the chorus [in Greek drama] appears in both tragedy and comedy, it is the communal genre of comedy that provides the chorus with its true identity. Following Aristotle, Harrison traces the origins of tragedy to the *leaders* of the dithyramb, the spring dance, but the chorus, she argues, derived from the earlier stage of purely communal dance' (275).
13. Nancy, *Listening*, 10.
14. A term popularised by composer and early sound theorist Pierre Schaeffer in 1966, 'acousmatic' sound refers to 'a noise that is heard without the causes from which it comes being seen'. See *Treatise on Musical Objects*, 64. The term is said to originate from the word *akousmatikoi*, or the disciples of Pythagoras who were only allowed to listen to him lecture while he was hidden behind a curtain, thus hearing his voice without seeing his body (64). See also Brian Kane, *Sound Unseen*.
15. For compelling articulations of Woolf's theorisation of animality in *Between the Acts*, see, for example, Peter Adkins, *The Modernist Anthropocene*; Christina Alt, *Virginia Woolf and the Study of Nature*; Derek Ryan, *Virginia Woolf and the Materiality of Theory: Sex, Animal, Life*; and Vicki Tromanhauser, 'Animal Life and Human Sacrifice in Virginia Woolf's *Between the Acts*'.

16. Silver, 'Anon', 429. Both 'Anon' and 'The Reader' were potential chapters for a larger work to be titled *Reading at Random*.
17. Ellis, *British Writers*, 214.
18. Silver, 'Anon', 382.
19. Ibid., 385.
20. Ibid., 382, 398.
21. Ibid., 382.
22. Adkins and Tromanhauser both note that the work in question is likely an amalgamation of H. G. Wells's *The Outline of History* (1920) and George Macaulay Trevelyan's *History of England* (1926): see Adkins, *Modernist Anthropocene*, 194; Tromanhauser, 'Animal Life', 69.
23. Among the extensive recent theoretical and philosophical body of thought on noise, especially significant are Douglas Kahn's analysis, in *Noise, Water, Meat*, of noise as that which interferes with semantic meaning, in both auditory and visual contexts; Michel Chion's relativity argument in *Sound: An Acoulogical Treatise* that 'the assessment of noise as noise and of music as music is [. . .] a matter of cultural and individual context' (57); and Paul Valéry's claim that 'a sound makes into a semi-presence the whole system of sounds – and that is what primitively distinguishes sound from noise' (quoted in Nancy, *Listening*, 10). See also Jacques Attali, *Noise: The Political Economy of Music* (1977) and Luigi Russolo's 1913 Futurist manifesto, 'The Art of Noises'.
24. For more on the role of gramophone in *Between the Acts*, see Pamela L. Caughie, 'Virginia Woolf: Radio, Gramophone, and Broadcasting'; Michelle Pridmore-Brown, '1939–40: Of Virginia Woolf, Gramophones, and Fascism'; and Bonnie Kime Scott, 'The Subversive Mechanics of Gramophone'.
25. Butler, 'Dogs', 156, emphasis in original. See also Butler, *The Ancient Phonograph*.
26. Quoted in Butler, 'Dogs and Phonographs', 156. For more on the colonialist dimensions of phonographic inscriptive and listening practices in the late nineteenth and early twentieth centuries, see Roshanak Kheshti's *Modernity's Ear: Listening to Race and Gender in World Music*.
27. Butler, 'Dogs', 156. 'In other words', Butler continues, 'the phonograph itself models the very kind of promiscuous listening it makes available to subsequent auditors' (156).
28. Kittler, *Gramophone*, 32–3.
29. Cuddy-Keane, 'Politics', 281.
30. Ryan, '"The reality of becoming"', 549.
31. Cuddy-Keane, 'Politics', 275.
32. Cavarero, *One Voice*.
33. Pettman, *Sonic Intimacy*, 79.
34. My use of the term 'Man' here draws on Sylvia Wynter's framing of Man as the universalisation (and 'overrepresentation') of one version

of the human (as white, Western, bourgeois and male) that emerged primarily during the European encounter and ongoing conquest and imperialisation of the New World. See Wynter, 'Unsettling the Coloniality of Being/Truth/Power/Freedom'.

35. Silver, 'Anon', 377.
36. Ibid., 382.
37. Ibid., 382.
38. Ibid., 382. Woolf is borrowing these lines from an unknown poet quoted in E. K. Chambers and F. Sidgwick's collection, *Early English Lyrics*: 2 Poem No. XXXIII, as referenced in Silver, 'Anon', 402.
39. Silver, 'Anon', 382, 403.
40. Silver, in her notes to 'Anon', connects the 'green scar' more explicitly to *Between the Acts* and to the motif of the furrowing of the Earth. Silver references an earlier draft of 'Anon', in which Woolf writes,

> For when we see the great Elizabethan house – Wilton say, or Penshurst – we see the stranded relic, that has emerged from its surroundings. Could we see it as it said that the airman sees a village <field>from the air with the scars of other villages <old roads>and other houses on it. we should see the great house connected with the village. (405–6)

In Silver's gloss:

> The reference to the airman's perspective is reminiscent of Mr. Oliver's comment in *Between the Acts* that 'From an aeroplane . . . you could see, plainly marked, the scars made by the Britons; by the Romans; the plough, when they ploughed the hill to grow wheat in the Napoleonic wars'. These scars are evoked again at the end of the novel when we are told that 'The pilgrims had bruised a lane on the grass'. The antiquaries who tell us of the survival of the old roads include Trevelyan, who wrote of ancient trackways 'like the tract along the south edge of the North Downs, long afterwards known and used as the "Pilgrims Way" to Canterbury, and still at places available to the pedestrian as it was four thousand and more years ago', and of the Roman roads that in some stretches 'are reserved for the Briton or Saxon who still fares on foot; and are . . . to be traced as green lanes' (406).

41. Silver, 'Anon', 382, 397–8.
42. Ibid., 398.
43. Ibid., 398.
44. Ibid., 398.
45. Ibid., 382.
46. Ibid., 424.

Bibliography

Adkins, Peter. *The Modernist Anthropocene: Nonhuman Life and Planetary Change in James Joyce, Virginia Woolf and Djuna Barnes*. Edinburgh: Edinburgh University Press, 2022.

Alt, Christina. *Virginia Woolf and the Study of Nature*. Cambridge: Cambridge University Press, 2010.

Ames, Christopher. 'Carnivalesque Comedy in *Between the Acts*', *Twentieth-Century Literature* 44, no. 4 (Winter 1998): 394–408.

Attali, Jacques. *Noise: The Political Economy of Music*. Manchester: Manchester University Press, 1977.

Bakhtin, Mikhail. *Rabelais and His World*, translated by Helene Iswolsky. Bloomington: Indiana University Press, 1984.

Beer, Gillian. *Virginia Woolf: The Common Ground*. Edinburgh: Edinburgh University Press, 1996

Bergson, Henri. *Laughter: An Essay on the Meaning of the Comic*, translated by Cloudesly Brereton and Fred Rothwell. New York: Macmillan, 1914.

Butler, Shane. *The Ancient Phonograph*. New York: Zone Books, 2005.

——. 'Dogs and Phonographs'. *Parallax* 26, no. 2 (2020): 151–62.

Caughie, Pamela L. 'Virginia Woolf: Radio, Gramophone, and Broadcasting'. In *The Edinburgh Companion to Virginia Woolf and the Arts*, edited by Maggie Humm, 332–47. Edinburgh: Edinburgh University Press, 2010.

Cavarero, Adriana. *For More than One Voice*. Stanford, CA: Stanford University Press, 2005.

Chion, Michel. *Sound: An Acoulogical Treatise*. Durham, NC: Duke University Press, 2016.

Colebrook, Claire, and Jami Weinstein. 'Introduction: Critical Life Studies and the Problems of Inhuman Rites and Posthumous Life'. In *Posthumous Life: Theorizing Beyond the Human*, edited by Claire Colebrook and Jami Weinstein, 1–14. New York: Columbia University Press, 2017.

Cuddy-Keane, Melba. 'The Politics of Comic Modes in Virginia Woolf's *Between the Acts*'. *PMLA* 105, no. 2 (March 1990): 273–85.

DeLoughrey, Elizabeth. *Allegories of the Anthropocene*. Durham, NC: Duke University Press, 2019.

Ellis, Steve. *British Writers and the Approach of World War II*. Cambridge: Cambridge University Press, 2015.

Kahn, Douglas. *Noise, Water, Meat: A History of Sound in the Arts*. Cambridge, MA: MIT Press, 1999.

Kane, Brian. *Sound Unseen: Acousmatic Sound in Theory and Practice*. Oxford: Oxford University Press, 2014.

Kheshti, Roshanak. *Modernity's Ear: Listening to Race and Gender in World Music*. New York: New York University Press, 2015.

McGurl, Mark. 'The Posthuman Comedy'. *Critical Inquiry* 38, no. 3 (Spring 2012): 533–53.
Nancy, Jean-Luc. *Listening*, translated by Charlotte Mandell. New York: Fordham University Press, 2007.
Pettman, Dominic. *Sonic Intimacy: Voice, Species, Technics*. Stanford, CA: Stanford University Press, 2017.
Pridmore-Brown, Michelle. '1939–40: Of Virginia Woolf, Gramophones, and Fascism', *PMLA* 113, no. 3 (1998): 408–21.
Russolo, Luigi. *The Art of Noise*, translated by Robert Filliou. Unknown: Ubu Classics, 2004.
Ryan, Derek. '"The reality of becoming": Deleuze, Woolf and the Territory of Cows'. *Deleuze Studies* 7, no. 4 (2013): 537–61.
———. *Virginia Woolf and the Materiality of Theory: Sex, Animal, Life*. Edinburgh: Edinburgh University Press, 2013.
Schaeffer, Pierre. *Treatise on Musical Objects,* translated by Christine North and John Dack. Oakland, CA: University of California Press, 2017.
See, Sam. 'The Comedy of Nature: Darwinian Feminism in Virginia Woolf's Between the Acts'. *Modernism/modernity* 17, no. 3 (2010): 639–67.
Scott, Bonnie Kime. 'The Subversive Mechanics of Gramophone'. In *Virginia Woolf in the Age of Mechanical Reproduction*, edited by Pamela L. Caughie, 97–114. New York: Garland, 2000.
Silver, Brenda. '"Anon" and "The Reader": Woolf's Last Essays'. *Twentieth Century Literature* 25, nos 3–4 (1979): 356–441.
Smythe, Karen. 'Virginia Woolf's Elegiac Enterprise'. *Novel: A Forum on Fiction* 26, no.1 (Autumn 1992): 64–79.
Tazudeen, Rasheed. *Modernism's Inhuman Worlds*. Ithaca, NY: Cornell University Press, 2024.
Tromanhauser, Vicki. 'Animal Life and Human Sacrifice in Virginia Woolf's *Between the Acts*'. *Woolf Studies Annual* 15 (2009): 67–90.
Woolf, Virginia. *Between the Acts*. San Diego: Harcourt Brace Jovanovich, 1970.
———. *The Essays of Virginia Woolf*, edited by Andrew McNeillie (vols 1–4) and Stuart N. Clarke (vols 5–6). 6 vols. London: Hogarth Press, 1986–2011.
———. *A Passionate Apprentice: The Early Journals 1897–1909*, edited by Mitchell A. Leaska. San Diego: Harcourt Brace Jovanovich, 1990.
———. *To the Lighthouse*. San Diego: Harcourt Brace Jovanovich, 1989.
———. *The Waves*. San Diego: Harcourt Brace Jovanovich, 2006.
Wynter, Sylvia. 'Unsettling the Coloniality of Being/Power/Truth/Freedom: Towards the Human, After Man, Its Overrepresentation–An Argument'. *CR: The New Centennial Review* 3, no. 3 (Fall 2003): 257–337.

Chapter 7

The Rat or the Flower? Decomposed Being(s) in the Holograph Draft of Virginia Woolf's *The Waves*

Shilo McGiff

J. W. Graham begins his introduction to Virginia Woolf's *The Waves: The Two Holograph Drafts* definitively. 'From our vantage point over forty years later', he writes '*The Waves* appears as a representative text of modernism'.[1] The status that he claims for *The Waves* is one that few modernists or Woolf scholars would care to dispute. At the time of *The Two Holograph Drafts*' publication in 1976, the defining features of twentieth-century modernism included alienation, irony and the ongoing redefinition of literary and artistic form – attributes commonly associated with Woolf's text and its status as a high modernist masterpiece. Highlighting the novel's 'thematic emphasis on the dilemmas of the alienated self', Graham's editorialising situates *The Waves* with respect to dominant debates about the modernist subject, the transcendental ego and its relationship or estrangement from its environs.[2] In recommending the merits of the holograph drafts as objects of study, Graham offers a compositional history of *The Waves* as it emerges from a complex intersection of Woolf's diary entries, letters, essays, reading notes, manuscript pages and uncorrected proofs. As such, the holograph drafts provide an indispensable resource for understanding Woolf's novel *sui generis* via the 'day by day struggle with the artistic problems which confronted her, and of the gradual process by which she solved them'.[3] Compelled by the urgency of making these draft materials more widely available to scholars, Graham simultaneously contends that 'literary criticism has not yet developed approaches to the interpretation of draft material that can match the sophistication of its approaches to the contexts provided by bibliography or by the many forms of history'.[4]

Forty years and more on from the publication of the holograph drafts, despite wide innovations in modern editorial practice and the advent of genetic criticism, the fixed relationship between draft materials as historical document and published work as apotheosis of an idea continues to set the critical tempo for most considerations of Woolf's draft materials.

Scholars and editors frequently turn to the holograph texts to furnish complex histories of Woolf's literary experiment and her writing process. While many readings of the holographs are genetic, others are hermeneutic: they draw on the draft materials to develop problems endemic to the published text or to provide an interpretative counterweight to an existing claim. Others may linger in the realm of aesthetic accomplishment still captivated by the text as object of art. Even Christine Froula, whose work on genetic criticism elsewhere challenges the authority of finished forms, recentres the high modernist status of *The Waves* with a twist, when she incredulously asks 'How [. . .] did this stunning masterpiece emerge from all this bad writing?'[5]

What makes the draft material 'bad', for Froula, seems to be the problem of an intrusive and shadowy narratorial presence in the earliest drafts of *The Waves* that inhibits how she customarily experiences the novel. Once dispensed with, the novel's familiar lyric present – the pure soliloquy form of the text – is freed for emergence. A sense of a text and telos is restored despite the inherent defamiliarisation that the transcriptions themselves present. But perhaps what might also be considered 'bad' about the holograph drafts of *The Waves* is that the image reservoir within them is often stranger than anything we see in Woolf's published work and most of her life writings. In addition to landscapes of unfolding light, its pages are filled with parasites, indefinite fleshy forms, and hallucinatory terrains. They evoke phenomena visceral and gross, and sometimes fetid and festering, which may surprise a reader expecting to encounter the writer lauded for her transcendent prose and beautiful conceptions of natural and nonhuman worlds.[6] Certainly, the luminous and the tenebrous, as well as the lambent and the corpulent, can be found tangled in their pages.

Meanwhile, from the vantage point of a rapidly greening twenty-first-century modernism, we might recognise in Graham's early concerns about *The Waves* and the dilemmas of the alienated self an orientation intuitively ecological.[7] With a little finesse, the interrelated problems of estrangement and form evolving within terrains defined by the art-making subject might supply the seeds of a dynamic systems-thinking further broadened by historicist methods. Criticism of *The Waves* has expanded to take into account questions of anti-imperial and decolonial politics, critiques of the post-romantic subject, new materialism, object-oriented ontology and the ascendancy of the Anthropocene, to name just a few.[8] Reconsiderations of the boundaries between self and other, human and nonhuman tell us a story about *The Waves* and its critical contexts that is far wider and weirder than Graham might have imagined.

If the questions we ask about *The Waves* have changed, so should our orientation toward the draft materials themselves. In 'The Alfa and the *Avant-texte*: Transcribing Virginia Woolf's Manuscripts', Ted Bishop identifies 'a process of socialization' that regulates the relationship between draft form and 'final' manuscript.[9] Situating his discussion to follow Brenda Silver, Susan Stanford Friedman and Louis Hays, he observes that, in the process of becoming published and public-facing, draft materials exhibit the pressures of self-censorship and ideology. Advocating for the treatment of draft materials as simultaneously '*avant-texte*', as well as '*après-texte*', he recommends a practice of reading that circulates between draft and final work, less like a closed circle and more like a spiral – open and contingent.[10] To aid in this practice, Bishop maintains that 'material embodiments of the text', subsequent reproductions and transcriptions of draft manuscripts, must 'allow room for an imaginative engagement with the earlier stages of the work'.[11] In order to preserve the 'mood of creation', as staging ground for this engagement, he calls for transcriptions of Woolf's pre-publication texts that preserve both their 'wildness' and their 'sense of becoming'.[12]

In other words, Bishop seems to be asking, what happens if we destabilise the primary relationship between draft material and published work, invert it, or (here, we push beyond the parameters of Bishop's argument) discard it all together? What possibilities for reading emerge when we dispense with the explanatory powers of holograph drafts to show us something about a published work or a writer's development and instead read them afresh as we encounter their own various tangled and recursive forms?[13] To fully experience the vitality and wildness that Bishop ascribes to these records of composition is also to experience them as documents peculiarly open to time and their own contingent natures. If we work back along the axes of socialisation, the drafts of a text like *The Waves* might have something to tell us about ontology and metaphysics in their own right that further unravels the boundaries of modernist self and modernist text in the wider, weirder historical landscape of the Anthropocene – a landscape that enfolds the possibility of post-humanist worldings alongside visions of human extinction driven by anthropogenic forces.

What follows this preamble is still an essay about composition. But it is an essay on composition that takes as its primary object the transcribed holograph drafts of Virginia Woolf's *The Waves* and the poetics of the draft form. It is, therefore, also an essay about *de*composition. It undertakes to move freely, perhaps spiral- or looplike, between modes of composing and decomposing to ask what the holograph drafts themselves have to tell us about being and nonbeing. In order to do so, it tarries with discarded and disgusting beings in the holograph drafts – namely rats and maggots – although human children and pink rings of flesh will make an appearance, too. And it leans, perhaps surprisingly, into the idea that these phenomena might fruitfully be read within the circumference of pastoral, or more accurately antipastoral.

Why pastoral? Pastoral is, among other things, an apparatus for subject making. As Julian Yates has written, its most conventional metaphors (sheep and shepherd, for example, or pastoral *otium*) designate mechanisms by which beings are 'loaded into discourse'.[14] This constitutive process, the temporal and material coordination of its various beings, often relies on the normativity of a powerful natural imaginary. Here we might stop to think of 'natural' much in the way that Raymond Williams defines 'nature' in *Keywords*, as 'a set of laws – the constitution of the world, or an inherent, universal, primary but also recurrent force – evident in the "beauties of nature" and in the "hearts of men", teaching a singular goodness'.[15] We might also take a moment here, as we idle, to observe that what is 'natural' in Williams's definition is also subject to 'cultural' force as the arbiter of a 'nature' that might determine the essential qualities of beauty and the moral rectitude of the human subject. The scripting of nature, and of the self placed within nature, long associated with Classical and Romantic pastoral modes, invokes a sly legislative process that traces and authorises not just beings, but the conditional possibility of being, itself. If we call upon Percy Bysshe Shelley's 'A Defence of Poetry' and his claim that 'poets are the unacknowledged legislators of the world',[16] we might even name this productive entanglement with language, and its pastoral potentials, *poiesis*.[17]

As I have argued elsewhere, one way in which we might read *The Waves*, itself, is as a novel of pastoral repletion.[18] From the predawn meditation and birdsong that opens the novel to the final breaking of waves on the shore and the innumerable vegetal and animal figurations imbedded in its speaker's soliloquies, the lyrical form and self-consciously poetic diction of Woolf's play-poem evoke pastoral conventions to excess. Twentieth-century critics have commonly read the natural phenomena showcased in the interludes of Woolf's modernist experiment as representing a world without human consciousness.[19] And yet, alongside and through its dazzling descriptions of landscape, *The Waves* interleaves colonial fantasies and gender, class and racial violences. Within the chapters of *The Waves*, the pervasive iteration of Woolf's natural imaginary, read via the pastoral, highlight a subjectifying process relative to disciplinary myths of a green world – myths that encode, among other things, a determinate relationship to capitalism, patriarchy, nationalism and war.[20]

In *The Waves*, England's Arcadian empire surfaces through layers of antipastoral allegory with consequences for the citizens it thus imbricates. For example, we might understand the gorgeous pastoral lyricism of the novel's interludes as coordinating constitutive processes by which the various speakers of the interchapters achieve or do not achieve cultural legibility or power. I am less interested, however, at least for this reading, in the pastoral fashioning of England's Arcadian empire and its citizens in the finished novel, than I am in considerations of how the 'ontological choreography',[21] as Yates puts it, of the pastoral in the holograph drafts aligns with the motives of new materialist and nonhuman studies and in its capacity to disturb normative modes of reproduction, be they 'natural' or 'cultural'. I am interested in how Woolf's pastoral, as it organises and forms subjects, also dis-organises and de-forms them and, in this process, disrupts the very biopolitical ground from which any normative ethics might emerge. This seems to me to be the kind of work not just pastoral, but specifically that antipastoral and its various subspecies – the dark and necropastorals – might do.

In its long history, the pastoral poem, or the 'poor pipe', as Sir Philip Sidney once called it, has been subject to charges of idealism, artificiality and falsity.[22] If there are those who, on the one hand, reject and condemn it, there are those who also see in pastoral's utopian yearnings an ongoing and essential alternative to the ravages of industrial capitalism. For Heather Sullivan, writing on the possibilities of a material ecocriticism in an era of ongoing climate change and environmental catastrophe, 'dark pastoral' is situated between these two poles. It contains a 'sentimental attachment' to pastoral's positive valences along with a 'skeptical view' that, in her own words, provides 'a bridge between the traumatic environmental awareness of the Anthropocene' and an 'often biophilic' experience of 'natural' beauty'.[23] As both an 'ecocritical trope'[24] and a strategy for exposing the dynamics of power in an era of fossil-fuelled technologies and agriculture, Sullivan's dark pastoral might alternately be defined as the blue-green thought that emerges in and alongside the dark shades of our world's variegated apocalypses. Importantly, for Sullivan, the dark pastoral provides a means to 'frame, analyze [. . .] and re-shape'[25] human agency and ecological actions in a world overwhelmed by disaster on the one hand, and plausibly redeemed by the unrecoverable, yet still essential, idyll on the other.

For Andrew Kalaidjian, the dark pastoral appears as an environmental aesthetic that emerges in response to exhausted ecosystems of interwar modernity; it signals a breakdown or a crisis in customary modes of pastoral regeneration traditionally predicated on the centrality of the human and the plenitude of the natural world. In Kalaidjian's work, dark pastoral 'highlights the limits of human control over the environment' and, the simultaneous 'inability of nature to provide humans with any ultimate freedom or transcendence'.[26] Within the fissures created by this failure, new configurations of human and nonhuman community materialise as quintessential features of late modernist texts, providing 'progressive' models for humanity's relationship to the 'surrounding world'.[27]

If Sullivan and Kalaidjian look to their versions of 'dark pastoral' as aesthetic strategies for orienting human action and being in a wider world, they still do so in ways that largely preserve the integrity and stability of the human, even as they turn to and engage the nonhuman. Joyelle McSweeney takes a more granular, occult and uncanny approach. Her 'necropastoral' appears as an intensification of pastoral's darkest shades; its aesthetics emphasise distention, pollution and poisoned microcosms. Focusing on the intimacies of the body and its hazardous worldings, her necropastoral readings incorporate an ekphrastic attentiveness to figures of dissolution and death while also pushing the fecundity of pastoral's green metaphors into over-ripeness where they suppurate and decay. Necropastoral, McSweeney claims, provides 'a model of politics and temporality that completely denatures liberal models of the body and the state, of points and events, of agency, hierarchy, power, linearity and historical time'.[28] It is, she contends, 'released like a rat body into all edifices of hegemony'.[29] Attentiveness to these antipastoral modes primes us to read the luminous and the tenebrous, the lambent and the corpulent in the holograph texts as they oscillate between the most intimate intrasubjective encounters and visions of cosmological, and sometimes catastrophic, significance.[30]

Let us read *The Waves* and its holograph texts for these antipastoral resonances, then. Let us begin with the scene of composition.

   *   July 2nd 1929
                           The Moths?
                                       one
                 or the life of anybody.
                     life in general.
                or ⎰ Mome<u>nts of</u> Being
                or ⎱ Th<u>e Waves</u>

Figure 7.1 Virginia Woolf, *The Waves: The Two Holograph Drafts*, Holograph Draft 1.1.

Virginia Woolf composes 'The Moths? Or the life of any^{one}body. Life in general. Or Mom<u>ents of</u> Being or Th<u>e Waves</u>' (*TWHD* 1.1; Figure 7.1) in seven bound manuscripts, all written in her own hand, which together comprise the two holograph drafts of the completed book. J. W. Graham transcribed and indexed the manuscripts along with a loose-leaf notebook and a few of the Monk's House papers to give us the edition we now have of these Holograph Drafts. According to Graham, Woolf's habitual method of composition was to draft 'longhand' in the morning and then to type what she had written out later in the same day.[31] She often wrote and rewrote entire passages, repeating them serially, preferring to revise, at least in the manuscripts, by reworking the same scene in its entirety again and again before moving on.[32] Woolf's revisions in process, as transcribed, include cancellations in the form of strikethroughs, marginalia, interlineations, insertions, loops, carets and sometimes 'enigmatic squiggles'.[33]

The Holograph Drafts, and in particular the first holograph draft, have a curiously looping form. To read them straight through in sequence means to experience scenes recursively, to reread or replay them with additions, amendments, insertions, and erasures still half-visible. It is to experience alternative versions and permutations of formative scenes folded together in a changing landscape where, at least initially, even the proper names of the six characters and their identities are unstable. We might ordinarily describe this record of composition as a palimpsest. But there is something remarkably terrestrial about the holograph drafts – an unusual observation when you stop to consider that most accounts of the novel focus on the watery medium of the sea as the source for its structuring poetics. Yet, reading the holograph drafts of *The Waves* feels like digging in the dirt or playing in the garden. Sifting through the strata of its layered and various revisions mimes a process of archaeological discovery, a reading strategy recapitulated large scale in the novel as we encounter obdurate forms of lost civilisations embedded in its lines and in its frequent appeal to atavistic or prehistoric memories. Perhaps it follows then, that in the holograph drafts of *The Waves*, as we re-encounter familiar figures and vestigial forms, we experience them as sometimes abandoned, buried, struck through and left to rot, and sometimes excavated and given new life.

Reading the layered lines of even a single page of Graham's transcribed holograph manifests the wild and contingent textures to which Bishop refers. The holograph draft here demonstrates not just a writing-in-process on its way to becoming something else, but a specific opening of the text in multitemporal and material dimensions. The sedimented sentences, clauses, images, and fragments of the draft form enclose and disclose enormous snails and iridescent slime, butterflies, children, Love and Death. Its vision is stratigraphic and specific, cosmological and intimate. Freed from the constraints of linear plot or a single temporal flow, one reads backwards or forwards, lingering over a struck-through cluster here, or a cloud-like superscript there. Page 1.7 (Figure 7.2) of the holograph draft in particular calls attention to the restless movement of these poetics in one of its marginal amendments. Adjacent to the phrase 'some sense of the awful duration, & the sudden of life, and ^such the power to open the heart & close it', one finds ' to do as it liked with the heart [. . .] uncovering it, covering it again, to cover it, to uncover it, for ever & ever' (1.7). There are tremendous ontological stakes in this 'corner of a garden overshadowed by leaves' (1.7) that evoke Bergsonian and Deleuzian models of becoming and being.

Laci Mattison, for example, in a reading of a seven-sided flower that appears at Percival's farewell dinner in *The Waves*, has argued that 'Woolf's fiction calls for a new metaphysics, a redefinition of the "thing" through duration, intuition, and assemblage'.[34] For Mattison, Bergson's concept of *durée* (duration), first outlined in *Time and Free Will* (1889), but later developed in *The Creative Mind* (1934), draws attention to the presence of multiple intersecting temporalities in Woolf's writing. We might, here, understand duration as a particular experience of time as a qualitative multiplicity; that is, as one in which multiple conscious states 'permeate one another'.[35] Woolf's process-driven poetics in the garden scene of 1.7, not only reflexively name and echo *durée* in the 'awful duration [. . .] of life' but likewise enact a technique of nonlinear becoming in the presence and absence of its vital images, their doing and undoing, their composition and de-composition.

Present in these garden folds are several senses of the antipastoral that I outlined above. For example, the peacock butterfly settling on

      * ~~The~~ And there in that little crease of the napkin was a corner of a
      garden shadowed by leaves like the outstretched hands of giants.
      Here the enormous snails drew their thin track of
      iridescent slime [ ] ~~along a tiled floor~~; & the peacock butterfly
      settled on the ~~yellow~~ flowers. Here came — ~~yet~~ but none of the
broken off, children can have been ten years old yet — ~~here came~~ like
      in single phrases; ~~without a context~~. ~~This~~ Love — a growling voice;
   → Death ~~,~~ the branch of the apple tree against the moon; & ←
      ~~perh~~ though the sea was there always, now & then,
      as on a ~~summer~~ quiet day, when there had been a storm perhaps out at sea,
      & one huge wave rolls in, by itself, & crashes on the beach.
      solitary phrases, ~~about~~ interrogations, a [ ] ~~hand~~ growly voice; ~~that was~~ love;
      a ~~branch, tha toss. still~~ an extended branch — ~~that was~~ Death; &
      ~~something, leaves perhaps~~ tumult ~~never~~ [ ] of leaves — ~~shivering~~
      shivering; ~~un~~ [ ] hiding, showing, ~~fruit~~ a; something
      dazzling; as if it were the red heart laid bare.

to do as it liked ~~Among these children was one there was Louis was~~
with the heart, ~~The~~ some sense of the awful duration, ~~& the sudden~~
e: uncovering it,   such
covering it again, of life, & ~~the~~ power to open the heart & close it; &
to cover it, to   And its not my our
uncover it, for ever ~~like a~~ Yet it is ~~none of our~~ doing; — Louis said ~~that~~ in the
& ever.   corner of the garden, where the leaves ~~made a palanquin of~~
      were so prodigiously broad; ~~the~~ & the shadows of the peacock
           as black   ed
      butterflies were like clouds; & the spirally marks ~~on the~~
      ~~snails were visible to the last grain.~~ snail shells
      were visible to the last grain. ~~So saying~~ he snapped a leaf off
      viciously. ~~Far away~~ The other children hooted & catcalled,
      chasing, seeking, skimming the flower tops, all ~~gil~~
      glittering & nodding flowers, the black & gilt, with their
      nets, ~~flashing crush~~ creasing together like folds of
      ~~aethereal~~ glistery silk ~~whatever Then there was~~
      the cream, the lustre: for him shrivelled. There
      Jinny & he together ~~e killed a~~ saw the dead rat — the innumerable
               seat by the [white
      maggots.† And kissed there; ~~very~~ on the ~~board, by the greenhouse~~;

Figure 7.2 Virginia Woolf, *The Waves: The Two Holograph Drafts*, Holograph Draft 1.7.

'~~yellow~~ flowers', 'the branch of the apple tree against the moon', a storm out at sea and the 'glittering & nodding flowers', even perhaps an anthropomorphised 'Love', all activate a sense of the biophilic crucial to Heather Sullivan's sense of the dark pastoral. And yet, interlaced with the sheer vitality of the garden is also the presence of Death, Love's anthropomorphic contrary and the 'premier celebrity resident of Arcadia'.[36] The passage that houses the apple tree against the moon is multiply struck through; the peacock butterflies cast shadows 'as black like clouds;' the '~~shivering~~ shivering leaves', dance between their 'dazzling' disclosures and an evocation of fear and cold; the 'red heart' is laid bare (1.7). Finally nested at the bottom of the page, a dead rat and innumerable maggots appear.[37]

This enfolded garden is a far cry from the exhausted landscape Kalaidjian identifies with dark pastoral; it exhibits an overwhelming fecundity and presents itself as a site of almost endless generativity, both in the myriad forms that populate the scene and, in the malleability and poetic force of the language summoned to describe them. And yet, although the garden is or should be a *cultivated* natural space bearing the fruits of human design, the nonhuman takes priority in such a way as to absorb the human presence of the children. The garden nature that we encounter is wild and disorderly. The snails themselves are enormous, perhaps even larger than the children who are not yet ten years old. For most of the passage, the children themselves, save for Louis who viciously snaps a leaf, are nameless and more like butterflies and birds than human subjects as they hoot, catcall, chase and skim the flora.

None of this yet bears directly on ethics, but as we glimpse this single page of Woolf's holograph draft we are struck by the possibilities of what Kalaidjian terms the dark pastoral mode as 'an immersive force', a structuring poetics that has consequence for the multiple life-forms imbedded in its lines. In 'Entangled in Nature: Deleuze's Modernism, Woolf's Philosophy, and Spinoza's Ethology', Derek Ryan writes that 'neither Deleuze's nor Woolf's interest in the nonhuman is tied to a sentimental (anthropocentric) pastoral vision'.[38] While much of what I have written above aligns with a de-anthropocentrised vision of a 'natural' world that Ryan develops through Woolf's fiction, he is a bit quick, I think, to dismiss the pastoral as the literary mode whereby these various configuration and reconfigurations of being might occur. In *Virginia Woolf and The Materiality of Theory*, he gives a compelling rationale for reading the myriad life of the intrepid and roguish Flush as a 'naturalcultural assemblage'[39] in order to conceptualise the various human and nonhuman intermingling that compose Flush's singularised life. Yet the passage in *Flush* that best represents this intermingling for Ryan performs a decidedly conventional pastoral motif, as it refers to an anthropomorphised Nature, birdsong and the growth of spring leaves as the exuberant signs of Flush's hybridised becoming (*F* 49). The pastoral is precisely this unnamed borderzone that often occupies Ryan and in which his dynamic theorisations of the human and nonhuman take place – often with significant ethical stakes for the possibility of, what he calls, a 'posthumanist worlding'.[40]

Biological precarity along with our heightened sense of climate crises in the Anthropocene sharpens the urgencies of any posthumanist worldings that might be uncovered or discovered via the pastoral. Even as dark pastoral's sly legislative force might draw us into a simultaneous worlding and weirding – a softening of and sprouting within ontological terrains – the affective resonance of the antipastoral asserts itself. Joyelle McSweeney intuits as such when she introduces the necropastoral as 'a manifestation of the infectiousness, anxiety, and contagion occultly present in the hygienic borders of the classical pastoral'.[41] Attuned to the necropastoral as a site of 'paradoxical proliferation' and decay, McSweeney educes from it a sinister fecundity driven by 'the suspicion that the anthropocene [sic] epoch is in fact synonymous with ecological endtimes'.[42] McSweeney's necropastoral thus claims for poetry a de-naturing politics that critiques hegemonic power structures provided by liberal models of the body and the state-power structures that we might see as responsible for modes of unsustainable production driven by industrial capitalism and other impending catastrophes of the Anthropocene. For McSweeney this might look like ekphrastic attention to the 'textual landscapes' of Wilfred Owen's lyric poems as 'rife with the infectious properties and modalities of the corpse'[43] or a radical identification with insectoid timescales as a way of resisting linear, future-oriented 'historical time – imperial time – corporate time'[44] that promote illusions of progress toward a more abundant future, timescales that, in fact, tell a 'golden lie'.[45]

In *The Modernist Anthropocene*, Peter Adkins finds in Woolf's writings of the late 1930s and 1940s related preoccupations with extinction and futurity, and a critical, even radical, conception of what worlds might subsequently emerge without human life. 'Woolf', he writes, 'understood a dominant narrative of extinction to be structured by anthropocentric and heteronormative ideas of posterity that limited how the future might be imagined'.[46] Yet Woolf's own visions of extinction, prophetic, critical and informed by the spectres of anthropogenic catastrophe, appear earlier than this. In the tangled and recursive poetics of the first holograph draft, Woolf composes and decomposes golden worlds of human and nonhuman futurity, confronting and resisting visions of extinction driven by anthropogenic forces.

Let us return to *The Waves,* then, and the poetics of its draft form, this time to a scene of decomposition.

* * *

On Tuesday 29 May 1929, as Woolf contemplates the central form for her new novel, the novel that will eventually become *The Waves*, she records a moment of (de)compositional reverie:

> A mind thinking [. . .] life itself going on. The current of the moths flying strongly this way. A lamp & a flower pot in the centre. The flower can always be changing [. . .] I shall have the two different currents – the moths flying along; the flower upright in the centre; a perpetual crumbling & renewing of the plant. In its leaves she might see things happen. (*D3* 229)

Present in this early thinking about *The Waves* are at least two different, yet intersecting descriptions of time, both refracted through natural metaphor. The first is Woolf's vision of the flower, fixed and central as it crumbles and renews itself in perpetuity. The second is the flow of ephemeral moths flocking through an opened window onto a previously enclosed domestic scene. The first seems to indicate a cyclical-vegetal time that might be read in any direction; the second, a flying flock-animal time, creaturely and vulnerable, open to time's decay.

On Sunday 26 January 1930, many months into the drafting of *The Waves,* she writes a now famous entry:

> I am stuck fast in that book – I mean, glued to it, like a fly on gummed paper. Sometimes I am out of touch; but go on; then again feel that I have at last, by violent measures – like breaking through gorse – set my hands on something central. [. . .] But how to pull it together, how to compost it – press it into one – I do not know; nor can I guess the end – it might be a gigantic conversation. The interludes are very difficult, yet I think essential; so as to bridge and also to give a background – the sea; insensitive nature – I don't know. But I think, when I feel this sudden directness, that it must be right: anyhow no other form of fiction suggests itself except as a repetition at the moment. (*D3* 285)

Often cited in compositional histories of *The Waves* as the source of its interlude and soliloquy structure, this entry also sets the dominant terms for interpretations of the novel that rely on a nonhuman 'insensitive' nature counterposed to human life.[47] Here, however, I want to draw attention not just to Woolf's description of herself, immersed in the writing of *The Waves*, as a 'fly on gummed paper', nor the rhythmic accelerations, pauses, and breakthroughs of Woolf's writing process, but on 'compost' as a metaphor for Woolf's composing practice.[48] If we put this description of the novel's composition alongside the cyclical growth and decay of the flower in Woolf's 1929 reverie, we can claim for Woolf, and perhaps more particularly for *The Waves* and its holograph drafts, a poetic process that is as much *un*making as it is making, speaking to a potent ambivalence at the novel's core – one critically linked to Woolf's pastoral imagination.[49] We might further see this poetic form as tied to the holograph drafts' temporal heterogeneity, techniques of nonlinear becoming and the possibility of a posthuman worlding.

In my initial description of the holograph drafts, I mentioned their terrestrial and recursive poetics – the way in which familiar figures and vestigial forms might be left to rot or excavated and given new life. Of the many images or topoi that recur in the holograph drafts, two stand out as specifically necropastoral in nature. The first, a dead rat infested with maggots, makes its first (but not its last) appearance in the enfolded garden of 1.7. On occasion, Woolf may strike the rat through, but it multiplies throughout both holograph drafts, and survives, refracted in the novel's published version where it ultimately appears in the garden reminiscences of Bernard's final soliloquy nestled under a rhubarb leaf (*TW* 177). The second is a landscape – a hallucinatory terrain that Woolf evokes several times in the first holograph draft, but which makes no obvious appearance in the final manuscript. The landscape discloses 'many mothers' birthing 'innumerable children' out of the sea and onto a beach that subsequently dissolves into an inhospitable desert wasteland (*TWHD* 1.17). Both instances teem with life. Both instances tarry with annihilation.

Reading these figures as sites of life and decay activate the varying antipastoral registers already discussed above. While the garden scene of *TWHD* 1.7 hosts Death as one of its many denizens, Woolf's intimations of mortality within its green borders appear, at least at first glance, nascent and local. Louis, the first named human subject in the garden, appears as an obtrusive presence, snapping off leaves, as he attempts to resist the immersive de-subjectifying force of the uncanny garden. In this sense, we might read these versions of the pastoral, necropastoral and dark pastoral as roughly aligned with the tripartite processes of territorialisation, deterritorialisation, and reterritorialisation that Deleuze and Guattari develop in *Anti-Oedipus* (1972) and in *A Thousand Plateaus* (1980). If the traditional green world of pastoral authorises anthropocentric models of subjectivity discursively defined by linear models of time (historical time – imperial time – corporate time), then we might properly understand this mode of being as defined by its territorialisation. The de-naturing force of the necropastoral, then, with its emphasis on decomposition and decay, offers itself as an opportunity for deterritorialisation, a line-of-flight away from the stultifying force of pastoral's hygienic borders. The tenebrous pull of the dark pastoral, then, might be associated with a positive kind of reterritorialisation, one oriented toward a (weirder) posthuman future.

Louis, as he first enters the garden, bears the traces of a previous territorialisation. His actions are quick and finite; he acts upon the nature he finds rather than being affected or absorbed by it. He is, however, at risk. We catch an uncanny glimpse of creaturely becoming as the other children, much like the moths of Woolf's diary entry, 'skim [. . .] the flower tops [. . .] creasing together like folds of ~~aetherial~~ glistery silk' (*TWHD* 1.7). And it is here, that the rat first appears:

> There Jinny & he together ~~e killed a~~ saw the dead rat – the innumerable maggots. And kissed there; ~~very~~ on the ^{seat} ~~board,~~ $^{by\ the}$ ~~by the greenhouse~~ ^{white}' (*TWHD* 1.7)

It seems that at least initially the idea of having Jinny and Louis kill the rat together may have occurred to Woolf, a violent reminder of human hegemony in the garden, but she strikes this through and instead implicates the rat – and its 'innumerable' companion maggots in their kiss. Here, the rat, dead and yet festering with life, appears as an agent of the necropastoral, intimating its possible deterritorialisations. The rat makes its second appearance, this time sans maggots, in the description of Archie, a character who, at least in name, does not survive far into the first holograph draft:

> [Archie] never very much bothered about ~~the rat~~ [. . .] in the cradle perhaps ~~his mother he had made the circuit~~, ~~seeing~~ seen the rat $^{oh\ yes\ –oh\ yes.}$ or the flower, ~~& having considered them,~~ no longer found ~~to~~ hateful ~~in them~~; or; much amusing. It was hard to say. (*TWHD* 1.9)

Here, Archie, who has been described previously as 'curious', becomes 'never much bothered' about the rat. Having encountered the hybrid multiplicity of 'the rat ^oh yes –oh yes. or the flower' he has become estranged from a normative orientation toward the nonhuman: say, for example, one that might experience disgust for a rat or express pleasure in a flower. Like Louis and Jinny, Archie experiences a rat-assemblage – this time, a rat-flower – as it is refracted through the garden landscape, as an agent of the necropastoral which disrupts their normative acculturations.

The rat makes its third appearance, a page later, this time as part of even a larger animal-vegetable-human-nonhuman composite that implicates not just the children but other features of the landscape – snail slime and plant juice – as well:

> And it was ~~clear that~~ the bru snail slime, the sticky fluid in the ^hollow stalk & the ~~thin~~ rat heaving with maggots were all ~~embedded in the hearts of those~~ in the hearts of those ~~unhappy little creatures~~. unfortunate children (*TWHD* 1.11)

Here in the garden, snail-slime and stalk-sap and rat and maggots are all 'embedded', planted, *given territory* in the hearts of the children. And while 'unhappy little creatures' is struck through in favour of the specificity of 'unfortunate children', reading the two descriptions side by side creates ambiguity, a loss of distinction between the children and the other creatures in the garden – snails, rats, maggots, children – one that, while disturbing, is not unwelcome.

Maud Ellmann asserts that rats are 'infiltrators' that inhabit the 'netherworld', boundary crossers, representing vampiristic and capitalistic networks of modernity.[50] For McSweeney, they are agents of the necropastoral released into 'the edifices of hegemony'.[51] In Woolf's fiction, rats also are uncannily and uncomfortably tied to heteronormative modes of human reproduction. In *The Voyage Out*, as Helen Ambrose considers the marriable prospects of her niece, Rachel Vinrace, she laments the inevitable process by which clever, young English men, estranged from their own reproductive capacities by too much study, will come to view the human race as 'rats and mice squirming on the flat' (*VO* 208). In this becoming-disinterested (perhaps a little like Archie), young men who might otherwise be engaged in the enterprise of England's reproductive futurity instead achieve a perspectival clarity that alienates them from the rest of the swarm – a swarm which they are now both a part of and apart from. As we broaden our necropastoral vision, following the rat towards Woolf's many mothers, we find, within the circumference of Woolf's antipastoral poetics in *The*

Waves, not just the de-subjectifying force of death and distention on a local scale, but extinction on a planetary one.

A final alienation effect is at work in the hallucinatory vision Woolf presents in the first holograph draft in the image of: 'Many mothers, & before them many mothers & again many mothers' (*TWHD* 1.13) that rise out of the waves to toss their various 'burdens' onto the beach (*TWHD* 1.123). In Woolf's various re-workings of this scene, a few elements remain constant. The first is the sheer, almost horrifying numbers of mothers and children variously characterised as 'endlessly sinking & falling' (*TWHD* 1.125) or 'ceaseless[ly] tumbling' (*TWHD* 1.125) out of the sea. The second is the figural deformation and tenor of disgust that accompanies these representations of newly born human life. The mothers 'groan' (*TWHD* 1.13) and 'force' (*TWHD* 1.87–1.89) their children out of the waves from which they are almost indistinguishable. The children arrive on the beach and begin toddling around, variously characterised as 'little bald naked purplish rolling balls' (*TWHD* 1.121); 'little bodies', 'pinkish balls [. . .] shooting out arms & legs' (*TWHD* 1.123); 'worm like, eel like, half conscious [. . .] animals brats' (*TWHD* 1.123) and 'pinkish rings of flesh' (*TWHD* 1.125), that soon cover the beach 'with their markings' (*TWHD* 1.123). Over and over again, the text describes these babies birthed out of the waves as 'innumerable' and 'pullulating'. These descriptions repeat the adjectives commonly used by Woolf to describe the maggots that swarm on the body of the dead rat – the same dead rat that is, along with the flower (oh yes–oh yes), embedded in the hearts of the children who play in the garden. In the first holograph draft, the various pullulating polyps, as I've come to think of them, tossed up on the shore, converge on 'a vast waste, a hard illimitable beach white as a bone' (*TWHD* 1.121) where nothing grows. The only other signs of life are the remains of boats 'tarred & eaten out like the ribs of a sheep' (*TWHD* 1.125) and 'wizened trees' with 'barnacles & shellfish for fruit' (*TWHD* 1.121). If these births are origins, they are also annihilations, decidedly antipastoral figurations, weird harbingers of a (over)pullulating world.

Indeed, as Woolf recurs the topoi of many mothers and their pullulating polyps in the first holograph draft, she progressively amplifies the stakes of their distended fecundity, pushing them into scenes of mass extinction.

> But for miles there was no vegetation, no life, ~~nothing to break the desolation, until the~~ & ~~no life,~~ & ~~no~~ ship, no even, coming ~~in from~~ to shore. There was only ~~this~~ [ ]ceaseless tumbling & turning of ⌐⌐ pinkish rings of flesh; ~~some~~ such a sight as might have given to a ~~sar~~

sad mind the most dismal prognostications, & only one strong desire that the waves might cease to toss their whiffs of spray on the sand; or that another wave, as high as a prison wall & as black, might advance remorselessly & irrevocably & cover the whole mass of pullulating life with a dark ~~river~~ & a deep tide. Against that could be no struggle. (*TWHD* 1.125–1.127)

Woolf's hallucinatory terrains in the holograph drafts explicitly coordinate uncontrolled human reproduction with a vision of annihilation; they provide neither a celebration of archaic maternity nor human resiliency, but rather a recognition of the consequences of unchecked population growth located in the compulsory provisions of heteronormative reproduction. The endless generations of women and the various pullulating beings – rats, maggots, children, mothers – embedded in the strata of Woolf's holograph drafts evidence an even wider, weirder and perhaps more radical ecological consciousness than has previously been imputed to Woolf's fiction. In the holograph drafts we find a dark, wild, 'natural' imaginary released from the confines of Woolf's keen and often civilising irony. How such a radical and critical ecological awareness might be oriented towards a reconsideration of the very conditions of life in the Anthropocene remains to be determined.

In *Dark Ecology*, Timothy Morton claims that ecological awareness forces us to think and feel at multiple scales that disorient normative concepts such as 'present', 'life', 'human', 'nature', 'thing', 'thought' and 'logic'.[52] 'Ecological awareness', they say, is 'weird: it has a twisted looping form'.[53] Ecognosis, the state that emerges to accommodate all the weirdness of this ecological thinking, begins with the installation of the nonhuman at the profound level of the human.[54] I've often thought that Morton's object-oriented ontology owes an unacknowledged debt to Woolf's fiction.[55] Both the first interlude and the first soliloquy chapter of *The Waves* begin with loops of shadow and loops of light. However, it is here – in the dark corpulent loop of compost and composition, of rat and flower, of snail slime and pink flesh, of birth and death, and in the various deterritorialisations and reterritorialisations of the dark and necropastorals – that the holograph drafts ask us to reckon with the decomposed being(s) that might precede our wildest readings and weirdest posthuman worldings.

Notes

1. J. W. Graham, 'Introduction', 13.
2. Ibid., 14.

3. Ibid., 39.
4. Ibid., 39.
5. Froula, 'Unwriting', 103. For further context on Froula's work with Woolf and genetic criticism, see her essay 'Modernism, Genetic Texts and Literary Authority'. For work with Woolf's holograph texts and compositional process, see also Justyna Kostkowska, *Virginia Woolf's Experiment in Genre and Politics, 1926–1931*.
6. See, for example, Kelly Sultzbach's wonderful observation that 'depictions of momentary experiences of belonging and wholeness in Woolf's work are often associated with the nonhuman realm' in *Ecocriticism in the Modernist Imagination* (89).
7. Reference to the greening of twentieth-century modernism here includes the ongoing development of 'blue' humanistic study in environmental criticism.
8. Gillian Beer's 'Virginia Woolf and Pre-History', Laura Doyle's 'Sublime Barbarians', and Vicki Tromanhauser's 'Eating Animals' provide instructive examples of this expansion. The ongoing index project of *Woolf Studies Annual*, beginning with Volume 28, provides a cross-sectional view of critical approaches to *The Waves* since 1995.
9. Ted Bishop, 'Alfa', 152.
10. Ibid., 141.
11. Ibid., 152.
12. Ibid., 153.
13. For three novel approaches to Woolf's draft archive, see Joshua Phillips, 'How Should One Read "The Reader?"'.
14. Yates, *Sheep*, 117.
15. Williams, *Keywords*, 223.
16. Shelley, *Prose and Poetry*, 535.
17. For a treatment of 'poiesis' within the critical context of the Anthropocene, see Tobias Menely's *Climate Change and the Making of Worlds*.
18. McGiff, '"Out of the heart of spring"'.
19. See, for example, James Naremore's reading of *The Waves* in *The World without a Self* (151–89) or Frank McConnell's '"Death among the apple trees"'.
20. See Jane Marcus's reading of *The Waves* as a critical and parodic encounter with empire and the elegiac frameworks that support it in 'Britannia Rules *The Waves*'; Jane Goldman's provocations that Woolf was spectacularly capable of pastoral elegy as a poetics in *The Feminist Aesthetics of Virginia Woolf*; and Jed Esty's identification of the intimate, even essential, relationship between pastoral nostalgia and imperialist rhetoric in modernist fiction in *A Shrinking Island*.
21. Yates, *Sheep*, 118.
22. Sidney, *Major Works*, 229. Edmund Gosse, for example, a critic with whom Woolf was quite familiar, begins his 1882 'Essay on English Pastoral Poetry,' with this frank assessment of pastoral's contemporary fortunes: 'Pastoral is cold, unnatural, artificial, and the humblest

reviewer is free to cast a stone at its dishonoured grave' ('Essay', ix). For synthetic accounts of pastoral that both rehearse and challenge its classical and post-classical literary reception see Paul Alpers's *What is Pastoral?*, Thomas Hubbard's *Pipes of Pan* and Annabel Patterson's *Pastoral and Ideology*.
23. Sullivan, 'Dark Pastoral', 26.
24. Ibid., 18.
25. Ibid., 19.
26. Kalaidjian, *Exhausted*, 120.
27. Ibid., 120.
28. McSweeney, *Necropastoral*, 8.
29. Ibid., 3.
30. In *Tense Futures*, Paul Saint-Amour characterises the socio-cultural milieu of interwar Europe, the period in which *The Waves* was written, as 'the conditional space of catastrophe', wherein the anticipation of foreclosed futures produced both dire warning and forms of critique (3).
31. Graham, 'Introduction', 30.
32. Ibid., 39.
33. Ibid., 42.
34. Mattison, 'Metaphysics', 17.
35. Bergson, *Time*, 89. It is worth noting here that in describing 'the idea of duration' in 'Chapter II: The Multiplicity of Conscious States', Bergson turns to one of pastoral's constitutive figures – a flock of sheep – as a defining example of the multiplicity that constitutes a unity.
36. McSweeney, *Necropastoral*, 3.
37. The first holograph draft's 'death among the apple trees' will recur in The *Waves* (*TW* 15–16, 89, 178, 226) as will the rat (*TW* 113), maggots (*TW* 14, 50, 156) and rats wreathed with maggots (*TW* 177–8).
38. Ryan, 'Entangle', 156
39. Ryan, *Virginia Woolf*, 155. Here, Ryan combines 'natureculture' from Donna Haraway with the Deleuze's 'assemblage'.
40. Ryan, *Virginia Woolf*, 190.
41. McSweeney, *Necropastoral*, 3.
42. Ibid., 3.
43. Ibid., 4.
44. Ibid., 42.
45. Ibid., 44.
46. Adkins, *Modernist Anthropocene*, 23.
47. Leanna Lostoski-Ho's '"Against time and sea"' provides a compositional history of the interludes in *The Waves* while addressing itself to the problem of 'insensitive nature' in terms of human and nonhuman timescales.
48. For Woolf's 'composting of the literary' and the body of Woolf's work as 'global compost', see Supriya Chaudhuri's 'Virginia Woolf and Compost', 37.

49. Laura Winkiel reads Woolf's composting practice in *The Waves* as suggesting an 'intra-action of matter and form' reliant on a Woolfian representation of nature that 'rots, repulses, and mixes . . .' (148).
50. Ellmann, *Nets*, 2.
51. McSweeney, *Necropastoral*, 3.
52. Morton. *Dark Ecology*, 159.
53. Ibid., 6.
54. Ibid., 159.
55. Morton's books, from *Ecology without Nature* to *Hyposubjects*, resonate with Woolfian figurations of affective ecological awareness. In recent interviews, Morton calls Woolf one of 'the greatest realists of all time', names Woolf among their favourite authors and claims her as a stylistic reference for *Hyposubjects*. In 'Woolf's Object-Oriented Ecology', Elsa Högberg identifies a locus of shared concerns between Woolf's fiction and OOO and reads Woolf through the insights of OOO; given Morton's recent disclosure that 'Woolf is the sound things make in my head', we might prioritise reading OOO as a consequence of, rather than a lens for, Woolf's writing. See Morton, 'Reading'.

Bibliography

Adkins, Peter. *The Modernist Anthropocene: Nonhuman Life and Planetary Change in James Joyce, Virginia Woolf and Djuna Barnes*. Edinburgh: Edinburgh University Press, 2022.

Alcrim, Mitchell, Oliver Case, Jenny Ann Cuban, Niklas Fischer, Benjamin Hagen, Skylar Kovacs, Maria Trejling and Pamela Weidman, 'Index of *Woolf Studies Annual* volumes 1–10 (1995–2004)'. *Woolf Studies Annual* 28 (2022): 129–300.

Alpers, Paul. *What is Pastoral?* Chicago: University of Chicago Press, 2011.

Beer, Gillian. 'Virginia Woolf and Pre-History'. In *Virginia Woolf: A Centenary Perspective*, edited by Eric Warner, 99–123. London: Palgrave Macmillan, 1984.

Bergson, Henri. *Time and Free Will: An Essay on the Immediate Data of Consciousness*, translated by F. L. Pogson. Mineola, NY: Dover, 2001.

Bishop, Edward. 'The Alfa and the *Avant-texte*: Transcribing Virginia Woolf's Manuscripts'. In *Editing Virginia Woolf: Interpreting the Modernist Text*, edited by James M. Haule and J. H. Stape, 139–157. London: Palgrave Macmillan, 2002.

Chaudhuri, Supriya. 'Virginia Woolf and Compost'. In *Recycling Virginia Woolf in Contemporary Art and Literature*, edited by Monica Latham, Caroline Marie and Anne-Laure Rigeade, 36–52. London: Routledge, 2021.

Doyle, Laura. 'Sublime Barbarians in the Narrative of Empire: Or, Longinus at Sea in *The Waves*'. *MFS Modern Fiction Studies* 42, no. 2 (1996): 323–47.

Ellmann, Maud. *The Nets of Modernism: Henry James, Virginia Woolf, James Joyce, and Sigmund Freud*. Cambridge: Cambridge University Press, 2010.
Esty, Jed. *A Shrinking Island: Modernism and National Culture in England*. Princeton, NJ: Princeton University Press, 2009.
Froula, Christine, 'Modernism, Genetic Texts and Literary Authority in Virginia Woolf's Portraits of the Artist as the Audience'. *Romanic Review* 86, no. 3 (1995): 513–26.
———. 'Unwriting *The Waves*'. In *Genesis and Revision in Modern British and Irish Writers*, edited by Jonathan Bloom and Catherine Rovera, 101–23. London: Palgrave Macmillan, 2020.
Goldman, Jane. *The Feminist Aesthetics of Virginia Woolf: Modernism, Post-Impressionism, and the Politics of the Visual*. Cambridge: Cambridge University Press, 1998.
Gosse, Edmund. 'An Essay on English Pastoral Poetry'. In *Complete Works in Verse and Prose of Edmund Spenser Vol. III*, edited by Rev. Alexander B. Grosart, ix–xlviii. Manchester: Printed for The Spenser Society, 1882–4.
Graham, J. W. 'Introduction'. In Virginia Woolf, *The Waves: The Two Holograph Drafts*, edited by J.W. Graham, 13–48. Toronto: University of Toronto Press, 1976.
Haraway, Donna. *The Companion Species Manifesto: Dogs, People, and Significant Otherness*. Chicago: Prickly Paradigm Press, 2003.
Högberg, Elsa. 'Virginia Woolf's Object-Oriented Ecology'. In *Virginia Woolf: Writing the World: Selected Papers from the Twenty-fourth Annual International Conference on Virginia Woolf*, edited by Pamela L. Caughie and Diana L. Swanson, 148–153. Clemson, SC: Clemson University Press, 2014.
Hubbard, Thomas K. *The Pipes of Pan: Intertextuality and Literary Filiation in the Pastoral Tradition from Theocritus to Milton*. Ann Arbor: University of Michigan Press, 1998.
Kalaidjian, Andrew. *Exhausted Ecologies: Modernism and Environmental Recovery*. Cambridge: Cambridge University Press, 2020.
Kostkowska, Justyna. *Ecocriticism and Women Writers: Environmentalist Poetics of Virginia Woolf, Jeanette Winterson, and Ali Smith*. Basingstoke: Palgrave Macmillan, 2013.
———. *Virginia Woolf's Experiment in Genre and Politics, 1926–1931: Visioning and Versioning The Waves*. Lewiston, NY: Edwin Mellon Press, 2005.
Lostoski-Ho, Leanna. '"Against time and sea": The Deep Temporality of the Interludes in *The Waves*'. *Woolf Studies Annual* 28 (2022): 47–67.
McConnell, Frank. '"Death among the apple trees": "The Waves" and the World of Things'. *The Bucknell Review* 16, no. 3 (Dec 1968): 23–9.
McGiff, Shilo. '"Out of the heart of spring": Virginia Woolf and the Changing Shapes of Pastoral 1928–1938'. Dissertation, Cornell University, 2018.
McSweeney, Joyelle. *The Necropastoral: Poetry, Media, Occults*. Ann Arbor: University of Michigan Press, 2014.

Marcus, Jane. 'Britannia Rules *The Waves*'. In *Decolonizing Tradition: New Views of Twentieth Century 'British' Canons*, edited by Karen Lawrence, 136–64. Urbana and Chicago: University of Illinois Press, 1992.

Mattison, Laci. 'The Metaphysics of Flowers in *The Waves*: Virginia Woolf's Seven-Sided Flower and Henri Bergson's Intuition'. In *Virginia Woolf and the Natural World: Selected Papers from the Twentieth Annual International Conference on Virginia Woolf*, edited by Kristin Czarnecki and Carrie Rohman, 71–7. Clemson, SC: Clemson University Press, 2011.

Menely, Tobias. *Climate Change and the Making of Worlds: Toward a Geohistorical Poetics*. Chicago: University of Chicago Press, 2021.

Morton, Timothy. *Dark Ecology*. New York: Columbia University Press, 2016.

——. 'Reading with . . . Timothy Morton'. *Shelf Awareness*. 15 October 2021. Accessed 22 January 2023. https://www.shelf-awareness.com/issue.html?issue=4092#m54062.

Naremore, James. *The World without a Self: Virginia Woolf and the Novel*. New Haven, CT: Yale University Press, 1973.

Patterson, Annabel. *Pastoral and Ideology: Virgil to Valéry*. Berkeley: University of California Press, 1987.

Phillips, Joshua. 'How Should One Read "The Reader?"' *Textual Cultures* 14, no. 2 (2021): 195–219.

Ryan, Derek. 'Entangled in Nature: Deleuze's Modernism, Woolf's Philosophy, and Spinoza's Ethology'. In *Understanding Deleuze, Understanding Modernism*, edited by Paul Ardoin, S. E. Gontarski and Laci Mattison, 151–68. New York: Bloomsbury, 2014.

——. 'Posthumanist Interludes: Ecology and Ethology in *The Waves*'. In *Virginia Woolf: Twenty-First-Century Approaches*, edited by Jeanne Dubino, Gill Lowe, Vara Neverow and Kathryn Simpson, 148–68. Edinburgh: Edinburgh University Press, 2015.

——. *Virginia Woolf and the Materiality of Theory: Sex, Animal, Life*. Edinburgh: Edinburgh University Press, 2013.

Saint-Amour, Paul. *Tense Future: Modernism, Total War, Encyclopedic Form*. New York: University of Oxford Press, 2015.

Shelley, Percy Bysshe. *Shelley's Poetry and Prose*, edited by Donald H. Reiman and Neil Fraistat. New York: Norton, 2002.

Sidney, Sir Philip. *The Major Works*, edited by Katherine Duncan-Jones. Oxford: Oxford University Press, 2002.

Sullivan, Heather. 'The Dark Pastoral: Material Ecocriticism in the Anthropocene'. *Ecocene: Cappadocia Journal of Environmental Humanities* 1, no. 2 (2020): 19–31.

Sultzbach, Kelly. *Ecocriticism in the Modernist Imagination: Forster, Woolf, and Auden*. Cambridge: Cambridge University Press, 2016.

Tromanhauser, Vicki. 'Eating Animals and Becoming Meat in Virginia Woolf's *The Waves*'. *Journal of Modern Literature* 38, no. 1 (2014): 73–93.

Williams, Raymond. *Keywords: A Vocabulary of Culture and Society*. Abingdon: Routledge, 2011.
Winkiel, Laura. 'A Queer Ecology of the Sea: Reading Virginia Woolf's *The Waves*'. *Feminist Modernist Studies* 2, no. 2 (2019): 141–63.
Woolf, Virginia. *The Diary of Virginia Woolf*, edited by Anne Olivier Bell. 5 vols. New York: Harcourt Brace Jovanovich, 1979–85.
——. *Flush: A Biography*, edited by Kate Flint. Oxford: Oxford University Press, 1998.
——. *The Voyage Out*. New York: Modern Library, 2001.
——. *The Waves*, annotated with an introduction by Molly Hite. Orlando, FL: Harcourt, 2006.
——. *The Waves: The Two Holograph Drafts*, edited by J. W. Graham. Toronto: University of Toronto Press, 1976.
Yates, Julian. *Of Sheep, Oranges, and Yeast: A Multispecies Impression*. Minneapolis: University of Minnesota Press, 2017.

Part IV

More than Human Encounters

Chapter 8

Darwinism, Dogs and Significant Otherness in Virginia Woolf

Saskia McCracken

A Dog's World

Donna Haraway calls for canine stories that 'teach us to pay attention to significant otherness'[1] in the Anthropocene, or as she terms it, the 'Chthulucene' – the geological period in which humanity directly impacted climate and ecosystem change with disastrous consequences for millions of species.[2] Charles Darwin's writing on dogs in *The Descent of Man, and Selection in Relation to Sex* (1871) made the radical claim that 'there is no fundamental difference between man and the higher mammals in their mental faculties' and that 'animals do not differ in kind, although immensely in degree', which 'does not justify us placing man in a distinct kingdom'.[3] Bearing these statements in mind, this chapter will consider representations of canine agency as significant otherness in Woolf's life of Elizabeth Barrett Browning's spaniel, *Flush: A Biography* (1933), and Darwin's canine stories. Doing so will enable us to expand our understanding of Woolf's attitudes towards evolutionary theory and animal agency in the Anthropocene, particularly regarding Giorgio Agamben's concept of the anthropological machine.

I will make two key claims. First, I show that Woolf's engagement with Darwin's works was more sustained, extensive and subversive than previously recognised. Drawing on the work of Haraway and others, I show that Darwin's *Descent of Man* – specifically his work on canine ethics, language, reason and imagination – was an unacknowledged intertext for *Flush* which has been overlooked by Woolf scholars. I will support this claim with evidence from the earliest manuscript draft of *Flush*, which I have transcribed, and which contains passages excised from the published version revealing Woolf's close engagement with Darwin's work on canine faculties. Second, I show that *Flush* pushes beyond Darwin's use of canine anecdotes as evidence for furthering scientific understanding. Instead, Woolf teaches us to pay attention to significant otherness by imagining different kinds of canine agency and by blurring the boundaries between human and animal at the levels of sentence, trope and punctuation. She plays with ways of signifying significant otherness in sympathy with canine companions, using *human* language and imagination to explore ideas of *canine* language and imagination – a doggy *logos*. In sum, I will show that Woolf's canine text engages closely with Darwin's *Descent of Man*, extending and subverting his canine tropes, embracing the radical levelling of species central to evolutionary theory, and celebrating canine significant otherness. For Haraway, 'the field of evolution' and 'co-evolution' incorporates 'impressive dog fights' among scientists and writers.[4] What is at stake in taking significant canine otherness seriously is, she says, 'who and what gets to count as an actor' in post-Darwin 'dog worlds', in the Anthropocene.[5]

Woolf's *Flush* tells the fictionalised story of Flush, from his early life as companion to Mary Russell Mitford, through adventures with Barrett Browning (including a dognapping and the Barrett Browning elopement to Italy), to his death in Florence, where the Brownings settled. Woolf wrote the first draft from 21 July 1931 to April 1932, the second draft from July to October 1932 and submitted the final version in 1933, when the book was published. The first draft begins with Woolf's notes: 'human beings & dogs', only to swiftly switch her focus to 'What a dog thinks of a human being' in the following line (*FMS* 1.145).[6] From the evidence of the first draft, then, *Flush* was concerned with, and paid great attention to, 'a dog's world a spaniels [*sic*] world' (*FMS* 1.97) and shifts her focus away from anthropocentrism.

Although Woolf wrote in the first manuscript that there were 'very +few+ little authorityies for the life of Flush', she drew on a range of sources for the text, included in a postscript, titled 'Authorities' (*FMS* 1.197). This postscript refers to Barrett Browning's poems 'To Flush, My Dog' (1844) and 'Flush, or Faunus' (1850); to various Browning and Barrett Browning letters; and to Thomas Beames's *The Rookeries of London* (1850). Woolf's '*Flush: A Biography* Reading Notebook' refers to texts omitted from the 'Authorities': such as A. G. L'Estrange's *The Life of Mary Russell Mitford* (1870) and Hugh Dalziel's reference book *British Dogs: Their Varieties, History and Characteristics* (1888). The introduction to the forthcoming Cambridge edition of *Flush*, edited by Derek Ryan, Jane

Goldman and Linden Peach, identifies other intertexts not named in Woolf's 'Authorities' or notebook, including Alexandra Sutherland Orr's *Life and Letters of Robert Browning* and Nathaniel Hawthorne's *The French and Italian Notebooks*. Evidently, *Flush* was a heavily researched and intertextual book, and further sources may yet be unearthed. Woolf's copy of Darwin's *Descent of Man* 'shows some wear and dirt'[7] and was, I will show, one of these further sources.

Darwinian Dogs

The opening pages of the first edition of *Flush* draw heavily on Darwinian discourse and, as Jeanne Dubino states, 'Darwinian language and concepts appear through[out]'.[8] Woolf's use of evolutionary language was even more marked in the first draft of *Flush* than in later versions.[9] This is clear from the prevalence of words such as 'origin' which appears six times in the first draft and only once in the published version; 'descent' which appears four times in the first draft and twice in the published version; and 'inherit' and 'adapt', which appear in the first draft but do not occur in the publication. All these words were newly freighted with evolutionary significance after Darwin.[10] Woolf may have used this Darwinian language because, in February 1932, while writing this draft, she records in her diary reading *The Science of Life* (1929) by Julian Huxley, H. G. Wells and G. P. Wells (*D4* 68), which offers an introduction to evolutionary theory, a concept she was already engaged with as I, and others, have shown elsewhere.[11] Moreover, in spite of the excision of several of the above words between the first draft and publication, the opening line of the first UK edition of *Flush* retains key Darwinian terms: Flush 'claims *descent* [. . .] of the greatest antiquity' and Woolf discusses the '*origin*' of the word spaniel (*F* 7, emphasis added). She also describes the evolution of the world through natural laws: 'Ages passed; vegetation appeared', and 'where there is vegetation the *law of Nature* has decreed that there shall be rabbits' (*F* 7, emphasis added). Indeed, 'as the centuries took their way, minor branches broke off from the parent stem' with a range of breeds 'deriving from the original spaniel of prehistoric days' (*F* 9–10). Humans are said to have 'claimed descent' from esteemed families and Flush himself is described as 'descended from' a pedigree (*F* 14). This profusion of Darwinian discourse evokes the abundance of organic life that Darwin describes throughout his work. Dubino points out that the 'profusion of families, both human and spaniel, and Woolf's botanical language, recalls Darwin's famous "Tree of Life" diagram', published in *On the Origin of Species* (1859) and central to his theory of evolution.[12] Woolf's canine biography, then, is Darwinian.

Woolf scholarship on *Flush* mostly eschews the evolutionary themes of the text. As a protagonist, Flush has been read as a 'stand-in for the woman writer'[13] or 'as a stand-in for that other dogsbody, the servant'[14], while Pamela Caughie reads *Flush* as 'an allegory of canon formation and canonical value'[15] and Michael Rosenthal argues that '*Flush* is the story of Elizabeth Barrett Browning' herself, with Flush himself as a 'satiric device'.[16] Many of these readings, as Craig Smith observes, betray an 'anthropocentric bias', where *Flush* is 'accepted as a serious object of study only to the extent that it may be represented as being not really about a dog'.[17] This bias is counteracted by Jeanne Dubino, who offers the most Darwinian recent reading of *Flush*, exploring Woolf's use of 'Darwinian discourse in constructing a history of the origin of the spaniel'.[18] She explains that *Flush* is 'informed by a deep appreciation and knowledge of Darwinism'.[19] Darwinian readings of Woolf's work by scholars such as Gillian Beer, Dubino, Elizabeth Lambert and Claire Davison, tend to focus on broader evolutionary concepts such as prehistory, origins, descent and survival of the fittest. In contrast, I am arguing that Woolf does not simply '*illustrate* several Darwinian concepts, including survival of the fittest',[20] but engages directly with Darwin's work on canine faculties.

For Haraway, dogs are 'powerful figures' who have 'always been where the biological and literary or artistic come together with all the force of lived reality' and 'are at the same time creatures of imagined possibility and creatures of fierce and ordinary reality; the dimensions tangle and require response'.[21] Indeed, canine '[f]igures are not representations or didactic illustrations, but rather material-semiotic nodes or knots in which diverse bodies and meanings coshape one another'.[22] Both Darwin and Woolf draw on references to real-life dogs (Darwin's dogs, Barrett Browning's Flush, Woolf's Pinka) and create fictional dogs and tropes, working these allusions into material-semiotic nodes in which dogs and writers co-shape Darwinian theories and canine imaginaries. Woolf's dogs are not just figurative, but point towards literal dogs, too, and the ways these literal and fictional dogs are discursively entangled.

Using a phrase coined 'in honour of Virginia Woolf', Haraway calls for 'A Category of One's Own' to describe dogs, arguing that 'unregistered' and 'categorically unfixed dogs' can tell us much about 'forging new possibilities' for humans and animals in the Anthropocene.[23] Woolf, she argues, understood this, and 'understood what happens when the impure stroll over the lawns of the properly registered'.[24] Flush starts life in Britain as a properly registered dog according to the standards of the Spaniel Club, but then fathers a puppy by a spaniel who may have been 'nothing but a mongrel' (*F* 32). Flush soon sires mongrels in Italy and bonds in cross-species sympathy with the Brownings. The text follows what Derek Ryan calls 'a journey away from hierarchical, essentialist categorisations based on inclusion or exclusion, and towards a more open, entangled zone of human and animal', which allows us 'to explore a more fluid and nonanthropocentric relation between species, incorporating both the "registered and unregistered"'.[25] As such, *Flush* anticipates Haraway's call for 'stories of cross-species entanglements', in which her term, 'Companion Species', 'is less a category than a pointer to an ongoing 'becoming with'.[26] In this sense, Woolf's dogs are '[f]igures [that] help [us] grapple inside the flesh of mortal world-making entanglements'.[27]

Darwin as Source for *Flush: A Biography*

Many of Darwin's books incorporate canine themes and tropes. The central analogy in *On the Origin of Species* uses domestic breeding – particularly dogs, pigeons and farm animals – as a stand-in for, and to explain, natural selection.[28] Darwin also discusses dog breeding and canine faculties in other works, including *The Variation of Animals and Plants under Domestication* (1868), *Descent of Man* (1871) and *The Expression of the Emotions in Man and Animals* (1872). Woolf owned copies of all three books.[29] I focus here particularly on her well-thumbed copy of the *Descent of Man*,[30] which quotes her father Leslie Stephen's work on canine faculties, which she probably also read.

In *The Expression of the Emotions* and *Descent of Man*, Darwin demonstrated that various faculties considered by his contemporaries to be God-given and unique to humans – such as morality, language, reason and imagination – were shared by the 'higher' animals. His evidence that 'there is no fundamental difference between man and the higher mammals in their mental faculties' included numerous anecdotal examples involving his dogs.[31] His retriever Bob sulks and pulls a 'hot-house face'[32] whenever Darwin cuts short their walks to look at his plants and his terrier Polly recognises him after five years aboard the HMS *Beagle*.[33] The first illustration in *Descent of Man* compares human and canine embryos,[34] and the first animal illustration in *The Expression of the Emotions*[35] is probably of Polly.[36] Polly, Darwin observes, when 'scratched with a stick, will sometimes show her delight' by 'licking the air as if it were my hand' and tries to 'satisfy her instinctive maternal love by expending it on me'.[37] She later appears, torn between going for a walk and her dinner, 'presenting an unmistakable appearance of perplexed discomfort'.[38] Darwin's real companion species informed his research and explanations of evolution and animal faculties.

Darwin's numerous canine anecdotes would have been relatable to his readers. Victorian pet ownership was high in England and 'it is in the Victorian period specifically that the practise of keeping dogs as pets' developed 'most meaningfully', with dogs constructed as 'part of the family' and central to Englishness.[39] By inviting Victorian readers to look to their own pet dogs for evidence – 'we look to the hereditary varieties or races of our domestic animals'[40] – Darwin couched his radical evolutionary argument in accessible, relatable terms, domesticating his theories to soften their impact. Dogs get to count as actors here, and, as Haraway might put it, are not as significantly other as they first seem. Indeed, Darwin's dogs anticipate Haraway, 'implo[ding] nature and culture in the relentlessly historically specific, joint lives of dogs and people, who are bonded in significant otherness'.[41]

In the eighteenth century, a range of thinkers were debating questions of animal mind and emotion. Darwin's influences included the philosopher David Hume, who argued that pride and humility were 'not merely human passions' but also 'animal'.[42] Darwin's notebooks refer to Unitarian Joseph Priestley's *Observations on Man* (1749), which argues that animals 'must necessarily have, in kind, every faculty that we are possessed of'.[43] Anglican churchmen also recommended '[s]ympathy with animal feeling' in tracts and sermons, 'as part of a moral argument for the human duty of kindness to beasts'.[44] Such sermons would likely have made Darwin's radical views – for example that 'animals exhibit [. . .] qualities which in us would be called moral'[45] – more palatable to his conservative readers. Indeed, for Darwin's wide readership, 'the emotional lives of animals would have been familiar from a variety of sources, travel writing, natural histories of animal character, zoology and animal husbandry, children's stories and fables, [and] the growing culture of pet keeping'.[46] The eighteenth century also saw the rise of sentimental anthropomorphic fiction and poetry which 'encouraged readers to sympathise with the affections of beasts', were 'widely cited in later animal welfare campaigns' and 'anticipat[ed] Darwin's views on the continuity of human and animal emotions'.[47] Darwin's theories of animal mind, emotion and morality then, followed a discourse of Victorian sentimentality, animal rights movements, popularised canine domesticity and philosophical investigations into the faculties of animals.

At the same time, Darwin was writing against the traditional distinction in Western thinking between human and animal which hinged on the notion that *logos* (reason and language) is unique to humans. Derrida shows us that according to Western thought the 'animal is *alogon*', without the powers of language and reason, and therefore 'has no relation to truth'.[48] Haraway agrees that the 'history of philosophy and of science is crisscrossed with lines drawn between Human and Animal on the basis of what counts as language'.[49] According to Agamben, this distinction between the *logon* human and *alogon* animal has been maintained by what he calls the anthropological machine, whereby our humanity is separated from our animality by an internal 'caesura between the human and the animal', a caesura which disavows that animality.[50] He argues that the anthropological machine produces the 'recognition of the human' in contrast to the animal and explains that:

> the passage from animal to man [. . .] was produced by subtracting an element that [. . .] was presupposed as the identifying characteristic of the human: language. In identifying himself with language, the speaking man places his own muteness outside of himself, as already and not yet human.[51]

We shall see that, while Darwin's views on animal emotion were in keeping with Victorian sentimental thought, his arguments for animal mind, particularly animal *logos*, went against the very foundational assumptions of Western philosophy and the anthropological machine, assumptions which underpin the Anthropocene. The Anthropocene, like the anthropological machine, recognises the *anthropos* – the human – as a powerful force which requires the negation of the animal to establish human transcendence. Indeed, in dissociating the human from the nonhuman animal, the anthropological machine justifies human dominance over other species. This has enabled humanity to bring about, and continue to cause, the extinction of millions of species – the human-caused Sixth Extinction is a key characteristic of the Anthropocene. It is in this sense that the anthropological machine underpins the Anthropocene. Any destabilisation of the *logon* human / *alogon* animal binary by Darwin, Woolf and current thinkers challenges the machine which drives the Anthropocene and enables us to consider alternative discourses and futures for the planet we share with so many (dwindling) species.

Animal Faculties

While recognising 'the impossibility of judging what passes through the mind of an animal', Darwin attributes a wide range of emotions to dogs, including pleasure, pain, happiness, misery, terror, suspicion, courage and timidity.[52] The higher mammals, he adds, feel maternal affection, grief, indignation, sympathy and shame.[53] He also argues that all the higher animals feel:

> jealousy, suspicion, emulation, gratitude, and magnanimity; they practise deceit and are revengeful; they [. . .] even have a sense of humour; they feel wonder and curiosity; they possess the same faculties of imitation, attention, deliberation, choice, memory, imagination, association of ideas, and reason, though in very different degrees.[54]

This list includes momentary sensations (like terror and pleasure), practices which require intent (such as deceit and revenge) and those which depend on a sense of the distinction between self and other (jealousy, for example). Derrida points out that in the Western tradition, the *alogon* 'animal neither dissimulates nor lies, because it has no relation to truth'.[55] Indeed, he observes that scholars from Descartes to Lacan state that the animal does not have the power 'to *pretend*, to *lie*, to *cover its tracks* or *erase* its own traces'[56] or behave in ways which indicate that it could make itself the subject of the signifier of language and *logos*. Derrida takes issue with this claim, stating:

> an animal's signature might yet be able to erase or cover its traces. Or allow it to be erased, rather, be unable to prevent its being erased. And this possibility, that of tracing, effacing, or scrambling its signature, allowing it to be lost, would then have serious consequences.[57]

As such, Darwin's claims that dogs are capable of deceit and revenge are radically opposed to a Western philosophical tradition which separates humans and animals into distinct *a/logon* categories. He opens up the possibility of considering such traces, erasures and consequences. For Darwin, human and animal emotions all 'evolved from animal impulses',[58] which 'does not justify us placing man in a distinct kingdom'.[59] We will see that Darwin not only overturns this anthropocentric thinking by granting canine significant others relation to truth and deception, and therefore intent and *logos*, he also theorises an animal *logos*.

Part of Woolf's Darwinian writing involved a similar radical attribution of emotion and morality to dogs. Canine emotions – including sensations, feelings shaped by intent and emotions dependent on a sense of self (distinct from other) – are key to *Flush,* appearing across all drafts and published versions of the narrative. In the first draft Flush feels sensations such as 'momentary joy' (FMS 1.77) and 'terror' (FMS 1.97) and in the first edition he feels 'love' (*F* 67), 'loneliness' (*F* 54), 'delight' (*F* 70), 'apprehension' (*F* 58) – and so a sense of futurity – and 'despair' (*F* 125). He also feels 'emasculated, diminished, ashamed' (*F* 127). In each version of the narrative, as the Barrett Browning romance begins, Flush feels 'jealousy' (FMS 1.147) towards Robert Browning, whom he recognises as other to himself, and intentionally bites his 'usurper' in revenge (*F* 60). Darwin claims that '[e]very one has seen how jealous a dog is of his master's affection [. . .] animals not only love, but desire to be loved'.[60] This is true of Flush who, in the first edition, is distraught when he believes that his mistress, now infatuated with Browning, 'would never love him again. That shaft went to his heart' (*F* 61). Flush is also jealous in Woolf's 'Flush: A Biography Reading Notebook:' 'B respects him for his jealousy.[61] Flush's capacity for self-reflexive jealousy and deceit is consistently present from the earliest draft to the published editions and was clearly key to her depiction of Flush as *logon*. Woolf anticipates and resists the anthropological machine through Flush's Darwinian faculties.

In all versions of the text, Barrett Browning accuses Flush of 'shamming' when he injures his paw, for 'no sooner had he touched the grass [in the park] than he began to run without a thought of it' (*F* 63). Here Woolf quotes Barrett Browning's analysis of this kind of trickery in a letter to Browning (12 July 1846): 'Flush always makes the most of his misfortunes – he is of the Byronic school – il se pose en victime' (FMS 1.45, *F* 63).[62] But Woolf states that Barrett Browning has 'misjudged [Flush] completely' in this description of his behaviour: in fact, the 'dash was his answer to her mockery; I have done with you – that was the meaning he flashed at her as he ran' (*F* 63). The implication is that, in running away, Flush is not just revealing that he is not really injured, he is also *pretending* that he does not care what Barrett Browning thinks of him, despite the 'shaft' in his heart caused by her accusation (*F* 61). There are layers of pretence here, Barrett Browning's accusation (lifted from her letters) that Flush is feigning injury, the actual incident she refers to (where we cannot know if the literal Flush was pretending), and Woolf's more complex suggestion that Flush the character is *pretending to pretend*, that in the Derridean sense, Flush has a signature. In short, Woolf's Flush *does* practice deceit (though not in the way Barrett Browning thinks) and therefore has access to truth, in line with Darwin's views on canine capabilities and in opposition to the assumptions of Western philosophy outlined (and challenged) by Derrida. Flush is a Harawayan 'actor' in post-Darwin 'dog worlds'.[63]

Furthermore, every version of *Flush* contains a scene drawing on Barrett Browning's observations of Flush 'gnashing his teeth at the brown dog in the glass'.[64] Woolf's Flush 'looked at himself in the glass' and 'examined himself carefully in the looking-glass' to affirm his 'birth and breeding' (*FMS* 1.35, *F* 33). Darwin does not discuss dogs looking at mirrors in *Descent of Man*, but he does describe a canary 'singing whilst viewing itself in a mirror' and notes that '[w]hen birds gaze at themselves in a looking-glass (of which many instances have been recorded) we cannot feel sure that it is not from jealousy of a supposed rival'.[65] In this regard, Woolf's passage actually pushes Darwin's thinking one step further: Flush does not see another animal in the glass, a rival, but *himself*. These examples, and several even more striking passages below, not only suggest that Darwin's work on dogs constituted a key creative and intellectual source for *Flush*, but that Woolf engaged closely with his work on animal *logos*, exploring different ways of expressing the concept in *Flush*.

Darwin revised his sections on canine reason and language in the second edition of the *Descent of Man* (published three years after the first, in 1874) in response to Leslie Stephen's essay 'Darwinism and Divinity' (April 1872), published in *Fraser's Magazine* and republished in his collection *Freethinking and Plainspeaking* (1873). Stephen's essay acknowledges the changing attitudes of Christians towards Darwinism (from horror to acceptance) and asks, 'What possible difference can it make to me whether I am sprung from an ape or an angel?', answering that 'the philosopher's reason' is 'none the worse' in either case.[66] He demonstrates that animals, particularly dogs, have more complex faculties than previously recognised. In preparing his second edition, Darwin was partly 'expanding on [the themes of] abstraction and other mental qualities in animals'[67];

a letter written during this period refers to the influence of Stephen's 'striking article on Divinity & Darwinism' on this line of thought.[68] In the second edition of the *Descent of Man*, Darwin refers to 'Darwinism and Divinity' three times.[69] In particular, he quotes Stephen's assertion that: '[i]t is difficult to understand how anybody who has ever kept a dog [. . .] can have any doubts as to an animal's power of performing the essential process of reasoning'.[70] Stephen objects to those who have 'denied to animals even the most moderate share of our own capacities' and argues that 'a dog is constantly performing rudimentary acts of reason', such as 'testing the strength of a plank which he has to cross, or measuring the height of a jump'.[71] Dogs, Stephen says, also draw 'refined inferences', such as '[m]y master is putting on his hat, and therefore I am going to have a walk'.[72] He claims that dogs share 'what we call moral sense' with humans, and notes that he is 'heartily glad' to see animals finally 'being recognised as our relations'.[73]

Darwin's second edition of the *Descent of Man*, building on Stephen's work, also argues that dogs are rational animals, capable of 'the power of abstraction' and of 'forming general concepts'.[74] He writes that 'when a dog sees another dog at a distance [. . .] he perceives that it is a dog in the abstract', but 'his whole manner suddenly changes' when recognising the other dog as 'a friend'.[75] He adds that when he asks Polly 'where is it?' she 'takes it as a sign that something is to be hunted' and 'looks quickly all around': 'do not these actions show that she had in her mind a general idea or concept that some animal is to be discovered and hunted?'[76] Woolf's Flush is also capable of inference. 'He could read signs that nobody else could even see. He could tell by the touch of Miss Barrett's fingers that she was waiting for one thing only – for the postman's knock, for the letter on the tray' (*F* 49–50) and he 'knew perfectly well from the expression on [her] face that he was not to go with her' when she elopes (*F* 98). Furthermore, Flush senses that something is amiss as she prepares to elope – 'the signs [. . .] were unmistakable' (*F* 99) – during a passage which echoes a recollection of Darwin's son Francis Darwin's: 'when [Polly's] master was going away on a journey, she always discovered the fact by the signs of packing going on in the study, and became low-spirited accordingly'.[77] It seems highly likely, then, that both Darwin's and Stephen's well-publicised views on canine reasoning were appropriated and extended by Woolf in *Flush*.

A similar point of overlap is suggested by Stephen's and Darwin's writing on canine understanding of language. Darwin, quoting Stephen again, asserts that dogs 'fram[e] a general concept of cats or sheep, and kno[w] the corresponding words as well as a philosopher. And the capacity to understand is as good a proof of vocal intelligence, though to an inferior degree, as the capacity to speak'.[78] Darwin also notes that, while language 'has justly been considered one of the chief distinctions between man and the lower animals', 'man [. . .] is not the only animal that can make use of language'.[79] Dogs, Darwin writes, have 'the bark of eagerness, as in the chase; that of anger, as well as growling; the yelp or howl of despair, as when shut up; baying at night; the bark of joy' or of 'demand or supplication'.[80] In *The Expression of the Emotions,* he even gives his dogs quotation marks. One terrier wags his tail, 'as if to say "Never mind, it is all fun"'[81]; another dog 'would throw himself on the ground, belly upwards. By this action he seemed to say more plainly than by words, "Behold, I am your slave"'.[82] Darwin concludes that 'dogs understand many words and sentences' and vocalise their emotions.[83] In short, for both Darwin and Stephen, dogs possess the kind of *logos* which, as Haraway, Derrida and Agamben observe, Western thought has traditionally denied them. Indeed, Darwin and Stephen were making controversial claims in attributing a capacity for *logos* to dogs, one that threatened to destabilise the hierarchical boundary between human and animal.

The first edition of *Flush* embraces this acknowledgement of canine language and the consequent destabilisation of human–animal hierarchical boundaries. This is in spite of the fact that, in chapter one of the book, Woolf writes that between Flush and Barrett Browning, 'lay the widest gulf that can separate one being from another. She spoke. He was dumb. She was woman; he was dog' (*F* 27). I will discuss this caesura shortly, but the variety of ways in which Flush speaks in the text undercuts the notion that he was dumb or that the two protagonists are divided by the (human) presence and (animal) absence of *logos*. This communication includes barks, howls and other recognisably canine sounds. When Barrett Browning becomes involved in spiritualism, Flush 'did not know which way to run. What on earth was happening? What in Heaven's name possessed the drawing-room table? He lifted up his voice in a prolonged howl of interrogation' (*F* 138). Flush's empirical questions are both howled here and written as questions, focalised through Flush (although not attributed to him or framed by quotation marks) using free indirect discourse. In this passage Woolf imagines two ways into canine language: canine sounds and the imagined meaning of those sounds posed as questions. Earlier on in the narrative Barrett Browning, referring to Flush being dognapped, says: 'Poor Flush, did the naughty men take you away?' In response, Flush 'put up his head and moaned and yelled' (F 96). This appears to be a form of cross-species communication, with Flush understanding human language and speaking through canine sounds, in which he certainly gets to count as an actor. These canine sounds are not *literally* sounds, but words on the page (howl, moan, yell and so on) which *signify* sounds, drawing attention to human language as the medium through which canine language is being explored, and through which the uniqueness of human language is being destabilised. Woolf invites us to imagine ways into canine language, points up the ways in which literature always already mediates canine voice through human language, and blurs the boundaries between human and animal forms of communication, attributing *logos* to Flush.

Flush's speech is also occasionally signalled between quotation marks, as when he addresses Barrett Browning's father who sits in the chair that Browning has just vacated after a secret visit: '"Don't you know," Flush marvelled, "who's been sitting in that chair? Can't you smell him?"' (F 55). This is a striking example of Woolf granting Flush direct speech in a rare deviation from free indirect discourse in the text. She is, perhaps, ventriloquising Barrett Browning, who wrote to her friend Hugh Boyd (9 May 1843) that she has told Flush 'Mr. Boyd will soon be back again' upon which 'I think Flush said, "That's a comfort"'.[84] Woolf nods here towards Barrett Browning's sentimental style, and perhaps other Victorian first-person animal biographies such as Anna Sewell's *Black Beauty: The Autobiography of a Horse* (1877). Doing so draws attention to Woolf's prevalent stylistic methodology – free indirect discourse – in *Flush*. This methodology, where it is often ambiguous who is speaking, and difficult to distinguish speech from the shifting perspectives of the narrator and characters, opens up lacunae for the reader to fill with meaning and (non)human attribution. Woolf's technique helps us think through human–animal caesurae by drawing our attention to the unclear boundaries between speech, other forms of communication and multispecies actors, disrupting the anthropological machine. She appears to accept Darwin and Stephen's argument that dogs understand human speech and have their own kind of language. She plays with different representations of canine voice, inviting us to imagine ways into canine language. Thus Flush speaks, he is not dumb, and is not, therefore, 'separated' from Barrett Browning by the 'gulf' of language, of the *a/logon* (F 27).

Dog Dreams

The most striking parallel between the *Descent of Man* and *Flush*, which suggests most clearly that the former was a source for the latter, lies in Darwin's and Woolf's writing on canine dreams. In the *Descent of Man*, Darwin argues that dogs are capable of dreaming, and that these dreams evidence canine imagination, memory, abstract thought and self-consciousness. He argues that as dogs 'have vivid dreams, [as] is shewn by their movements and the sounds uttered, we must admit that they possess some power of imagination'.[85] How then, he adds:

> can we feel sure that an old dog with an excellent memory and some power of imagination, as shewn by his dreams, never reflects on his past pleasures or pains in the chase? And this would be a form of self-consciousness.[86]

Although the notion that dogs dream precedes Darwin, this quotation bears striking resemblance to two passages from Woolf's text in which Flush dreams of the past pains and pleasures of the chase. In chapter three:

> [Flush] dreamt as he had not dreamt since the old days at Three Mile Cross – of hares starting from the long grass; of pheasants rocketing up with long tails streaming, of partridges rising with a whirr from the stubble. He dreamt that he was hunting, that he was chasing some spotted spaniel, who fled, who escaped him. He was in Spain; he was in Wales; he was in Berkshire; he was flying before parkkeepers' truncheons in Regent's Park. (*F* 57)

Flush's dream is not 'shewn' by his movements and sounds as viewed by a human observer (such as Barrett Browning or the narrator); Woolf is not positing behaviour as scientific evidence of animal dreams and agency. Rather, she invites us to *imagine* that agency from a slippery human–canine perspective, to follow the animal following animals.

This action of *following* anticipates the title of Derrida's 'The Animal that Therefore I Am (More to Follow)' (2002), a pun on the French '*je suis*' which both means 'I am', and 'I follow'.[87] Both Woolf and Derrida question whether the human *is* animal, follows, or is followed by the animal. Woolf's third-person discourse creates a false sense of distance from Flush, yet this passage is also focalised *through* Flush, using free indirect discourse. We experience the chase as Woolf's verbs chase one another across the page. Her punctuation evokes the darting, erratic movements of the spaniel flushing wildlife from the undergrowth, as she shifts from clause to clause, from 'Spain' to 'Wales' to 'Berkshire' (F 57). She dashes off with a dash – jumping between commas, semicolons and every full stop that brings us back to the 'he', we are following, before we dash off again. As such, although 'he' dreams in the third person, the immediacy of Woolf's verbs and punctuation give the impression of first-person experience. Woolf's is an exercise in imagining the canine consciousness that Darwin speaks of, taking canine dreams beyond scientific discourse and into a place where, like Haraway, we can consider dogs as actors that count in canine stories after Darwin, and our own position as (following) animals, riding Agamben's caesura through the Anthropocene.

In her final chapter, Woolf describes Flush's 'movements and the sounds uttered' as he dreams, perhaps again of the chase.[88] This passage once again bears striking resemblance to Darwin's thoughts on dreaming dogs in the *Descent of Man*:

> He slept as dogs sleep when they are dreaming. Now his legs twitched – was he dreaming that he hunted rabbits in Spain? Was he coursing up a hot hill-side with dark men shouting 'Span! Span!' as the rabbits darted from the brushwood? Then he lay still again. And now he yelped, quickly, softly, many times in succession. Perhaps he heard Dr Mitford egging his greyhounds on to the hunt at Reading. Then his tail wagged sheepishly. Did he hear old Miss Mitford cry, 'Bad dog! Bad dog!' as he slunk back to her, where she stood among the turnips waving her umbrella? (F 147–8)

This passage is more like Darwin's than the first example of Flush dreaming, as, like Darwin, it describes canine dream behaviour and asks questions of the reader. Just as Darwin asks, 'can we feel sure that an old dog [. . .] never reflects on his past pleasures or pains in the chase?' Woolf asks, 'was he dreaming that he hunted rabbits in Spain?', and 'Did he hear old Miss Mitford' as she stood 'waving her umbrella?'(F 148). Having imagined the content of Flush's dreams in her third chapter, Woolf's questions in this last chapter remind us that that although we may follow the chase, our access to it is speculative. Her questions also invite us to consider the extent to which, and the ways in which, dogs have and experience memory, imagination, self-consciousness, the chase and agency. Do they hear shouting? Or dream of memories? To what extent do they imagine? Are canine dreams inhabited by rabbits, other dogs, humans? Or are they significantly other to human dreams? Woolf 'teach[es] us to pay attention to significant otherness as something other than a reflection of one's intentions',[89] as something we cannot directly access, but can engage with on an imaginative level, that we can follow.

Woolf embraces the radical aspects of evolutionary theory which collapse the human/animal binary and open up new ways of thinking about species and animality; she invites us to follow canine significant otherness and imagine a dog *logos* as Darwin does, to ride the caesurae between human and animal. She uses language and imagination to explore what these very things mean for dogs, and by association other animals including humans, turning to our canine companions as Darwin does, to couch her own radical approach to animal mind in relatable terms. She welcomes us into her doggy dreams about doggy dreams which help us to consider the stakes of significant otherness and agency. It matters all the more today that we take significant animal otherness seriously, that we consider 'who and what gets to count as an actor'[90] in the Anthropocene, and how we can challenge the anthropological machine, because doing so shapes who and what will exist in future.

Notes

1. Haraway, *Companion Species*, 28.
2. Haraway, *Staying*.
3. Darwin, *Descent of Man*, 86, 173.
4. Haraway, *Companion Species*, 27.
5. Ibid., 27.
6. Material from Woolf's holograph fragment and drafts is cited from transcriptions by Jane Goldman and myself, which are due to be published as part of the Cambridge Edition of *Flush*, edited by Linden Peach, Derek Ryan and Jane Goldman.
7. King, 'Darwin', np.
8. Dubino, 'Evolution', 144.
9. Light, 'Introduction', xxxviii.
10. See Gillian Beer's *Virginia Woolf: The Common Ground* (1996).
11. See Gillian Beer's *Virginia Woolf: The Common Ground*, Claire Davison's 'Hearing the World "in full orchestra": Voyaging Out with Woolf, Darwin, and Music', Elizabeth Lambert's '"and Darwin says they are nearer the cow": Evolutionary Discourse in *Melymbrosia* and *The Voyage Out*', and my doctoral thesis, '(R)evolutionary Animal Tropes in the Works of Charles Darwin and Virginia Woolf'.

12. Dubino, 'Origin of Spaniels', 145; Darwin, *Origin of Species*, 90.
13. Squier, *Virginia Woolf*, 124.
14. Light, *Mrs Woolf*, 50.
15. Caughie, *Virginia Woolf*, 146.
16. Rosenthal, *Virginia Woolf*, 206.
17. Craig Smith, 'Widest Gulf', 349.
18. Dubino, 'Origin of Spaniels', 143.
19. Ibid., 148.
20. Ibid., 147, emphasis added.
21. Haraway, *When Species Meet*, 4.
22. Ibid., 4.
23. Haraway, *Companion Species*, 88.
24. Ibid., 88.
25. Derek Ryan, 'Spaniel Club', 158, 163–4.
26. Haraway, *When Species Meet*, 16–17.
27. Haraway, *Companion Species*, 4.
28. Darwin, *Origins of Species*, 12, 16–18.
29. King and Miletic-Vejzovic, *Library*, n.p.
30. King, 'Darwin', n.p.
31. Darwin, *Descent of Man*, 86.
32. Darwin, *Expression of Emotions*, 62.
33. Darwin, *Descent of Man*, 95.
34. Ibid., 27.
35. Darwin, *Expression of Emotions*, 52.
36. White, 'Darwin's Emotions', 823.
37. Darwin, *Expression of Emotions*, 53, 114.
38. Ibid., 118.
39. Howell, *Home*, 11, 16.
40. Darwin, *Origin of Species*, 15.
41. Haraway, *Companion Species*, 16.
42. Spencer, 'Love', 32.
43. Quoted in Spencer, 'Love', 36.
44. Spencer, 'Love', 37.
45. Darwin, *Descent of Man*, 127.
46. White, 'Becoming', 122.
47. Spencer, 'Love', 27.
48. Derrida, *Beast and Sovereign*, 320–1.
49. Haraway, *When Species Meet*, 234.
50. Agamben, *The Open*, 16.
51. Ibid., 34–5.
52. Darwin, *Descent of Man*, 105, 89–90.
53. Ibid., 91–2.
54. Ibid., 100.
55. Derrida, *Beast and Sovereign*, 320–1.
56. Derrida, 'Animal', 401, emphasis in original.
57. Ibid., 401.

58. White, 'Darwin's Emotions', 813.
59. Darwin, *Descent of Man*, 173.
60. Ibid., 92.
61. Woolf, *Reading Notebooks*, 1.
62. See Barrett Browning, *The Letters of Robert Browning and Elizabeth Barrett Browning 1845–1846*. Vol. 2, 871.
63. Haraway, *Companion Species*, 27.
64. Barrett Browning, *The Letters of Robert Browning and Elizabeth Barrett Browning 1845–1846*. Vol. 1, n.p.
65. Darwin, *Descent of Man*, 418, 464.
66. Stephen, 'Darwinism', 86, 87.
67. Richardson, 'Introduction', 8.
68. Darwin, 'Letter to Chauncey Wright', n.p.
69. Darwin, *Descent of Man*, 100, 111–12, 134.
70. Stephen quoted in Darwin, *Descent of Man*, 100.
71. Stephen, 'Darwinism', 91, 92.
72. Ibid., 92.
73. Ibid., 91.
74. Darwin, *Descent of Man*, 105.
75. Ibid., 105.
76. Ibid., 105.
77. Francis Darwin, 'Reminiscences', 114.
78. Stephen quoted in Darwin, *Descent of Man*, 111–12.
79. Darwin, *Descent of Man*, 106.
80. Ibid., 107.
81. Darwin, *Expression of Emotions*, 66.
82. Ibid., 115.
83. Darwin, *Descent of Man*, 107.
84. Barrett Browning, *The Letters of Robert Browning and Elizabeth Barrett Browning 1845–1846*. Vol. 1, n.p.
85. Darwin, *Descent of Man*, 95–6.
86. Ibid., 105.
87. Derrida, 'Animal', 369.
88. Darwin, *Descent of Man*, 96.
89. Haraway, *Companion Species*, 28.
90. Ibid., 27.

Bibliography

Agamben, Giorgio. *The Open: Man and Animal*, translated by Kevin Attell. Stanford, CA: Stanford University Press, 2004.

Barrett Browning, Elizabeth. *The Letters of Elizabeth Barrett Browning with Portraits*, edited by Frederic G. Kenyon. Vol. 1. London: Smith, Elder, & Co., 1898.

———. *The Letters of Robert Browning and Elizabeth Barrett Browning 1845–1846*. Vol. 2. Cambridge, MA: Harvard University Press, 1969.
———. *The Letters of Robert Browning and Elizabeth Barrett Browning 1845–1846: with Portraits and Facsimiles*. Vol. 1. London: Smith, Elder, & Co., 1900.
Beer, Gillian. *Virginia Woolf: The Common Ground*. Edinburgh: Edinburgh University Press, 1996.
Caughie, Pamela. *Virginia Woolf and Postmodernism: Literature in Quest and Question of Itself*. Champaign: University of Illinois Press, 1991.
Darwin, Charles. 'Letter to Chauncey Wright'. 6 April 1872. Letter 8277. Darwin Correspondence Project Online. Accessed 8 November 2023. https://www.darwinproject.ac.uk/letter/?docId=letters/DCP-LETT-8277.xml.
———. *The Descent of Man, and Selection in Relation to Sex*. Second edition. London: Penguin, 2004.
———. *The Expression of the Emotions in Man and Animals*. Second edition. London: Penguin, 2009.
———. *The Origin of Species by Means of Natural Selection, or the Preservation of Favoured Races in the Struggle for Life*. Second edition. Oxford: Oxford University Press, 2008.
———. *The Variation of Animals and Plants under Domestication*. Vol. 2. London: John Murray, 1875.
Darwin, Francis. 'Reminiscences'. In *The Life and Letters of Charles Darwin: Including an Autobiographical Chapter*, vol. 1, edited by Francis Darwin, 108–62. London: John Murray, 1888.
Davison, Claire. 'Hearing the World "in full orchestra": Voyaging Out with Woolf, Darwin, and Music'. *Woolf Studies Annual* 23 (2017): 1–32.
Derrida, Jacques. 'The Animal that Therefore I Am (More to Follow)', translated by David Wills. *Critical Inquiry* 28, no. 2 (Winter 2002): 369–418.
———. *The Beast and the Sovereign*, vol. 2, translated by Geoffrey Bennington. Chicago: Chicago University Press, 2011.
Dubino, Jeanne. 'Evolution, History, and *Flush*; or, The Origin of Spaniels'. In *Virginia Woolf and the Natural World: Selected Papers from the Twentieth International Conference on Virginia Woolf*, edited by Kristin Czarnecki and Carrie Rohman, 143–50. Clemson, SC: Clemson University Press, 2011.
Haraway, Donna. *Staying with the Trouble: Making Kin in the Cthulucene*. Durham, NC: Duke University Press, 2016.
———. *The Companion Species Manifesto: Dogs, People, and Significant Otherness*. Chicago: Prickly Paradigm, 2003.
———. *When Species Meet*. Minneapolis: University of Minnesota Press, 2007.
Howell, Philip. *At Home and Astray: The Domestic Dog in Victorian Britain*. Charlottesville: University of Virginia Press, 2015.
King, Julia. 'Darwin and the Library of Leonard and Virginia Woolf'. Email correspondence, 12 December 2017.

King, Julia, and Laila Miletic-Vejzovic. *The Library of Leonard and Virginia Woolf: A Short-Title Catalogue*. Pullman, WA: Washington State University Press, 2003.

Lambert, Elizabeth. '"and Darwin says they are nearer the cow": Evolutionary Discourse in *Melymbrosia* and *The Voyage Out*'. *Twentieth Century Literature* 37, no. 1 (1991): 1–21.

Light, Alison. 'Introduction'. in *Flush: A Biography* by Virginia Woolf, ix–xli. Harmondsworth: Penguin, 2000.

——. *Mrs Woolf and the Servants*. London: Penguin Fig Tree, 2007.

McCracken, Saskia. 2021. '(R)evolutionary Animal Tropes in the Works of Charles Darwin and Virginia Woolf'. Doctoral thesis, University of Glasgow.

Peach, Linden. 'Woolf and Eugenics'. In *Virginia Woolf in Context*, edited by Bryony Randall and Jane Goldman, 439–48. Cambridge: Cambridge University Press, 2012.

Richardson, Angelique. 'Introduction: Darwin and Interdisciplinarity: A Historical Perspective'. In *After Darwin: Animals, Emotions, and the Mind*, edited by Angelique Richardson, 1–23. Amsterdam: Rodopi, 2013.

Rosenthal, Michael. *Virginia Woolf*. New York: Columbia University Press, 1979.

Ryan, Derek. 'From Spaniel Club to Animalous Society: Virginia Woolf's *Flush*'. In *Contradictory Woolf: Selected Papers from the Twenty-First Annual International Conference on Virginia Woolf*, edited by Derek Ryan and Stella Bolaki, 158–65. Clemson, SC: Clemson University Press, 2012.

Ryan, Derek, Jane Goldman and Linden Peach. 'Introduction'. *Flush: A Biography*. Cambridge: Cambridge University Press, forthcoming.

Smith, Craig. 'Across the Widest Gulf: Nonhuman Subjectivity in Virginia Woolf's *Flush*'. *Twentieth-Century Literature* 48, no. 3 (2002): 348–61.

Spencer, Jane. '"Love and hatred are common to the whole sensitive creation": Animal Feeling in the Century before Darwin'. In *After Darwin: Animals, Emotions, and the Mind*, edited by Angelique Richardson, 24–50. Amsterdam: Rodopi, 2013.

Squier, Susan. *Virginia Woolf and London: The Sexual Politics of the City*. London: North Carolina University Press, 1985.

Stephen, Leslie. 'Darwinism and Divinity'. In *Essays on Freethinking and Plainspeaking*, 82–125. London: Duckworth, 1907.

White, Paul. 'Becoming an Animal: Darwin and the Evolution of Sympathy' In *After Darwin: Animals, Emotions, and the Mind*, edited by Angelique Richardson, 112–35. Amsterdam: Rodopi, 2013.

——. 'Darwin's Emotions: The Scientific Self and the Sentiment of Objectivity'. *Isis* 100, no. 4 (2009): 811–26.

Woolf, Virginia. *The Diary of Virginia Woolf*, edited by Anne Olivier Bell. 5 vols. London: Penguin Books, 1979–85.

——. *Flush: A Biography*. London: Hogarth Press, 1933.
——. *Flush: A Biography*, edited by Derek Ryan, Jane Goldman and Linden Peach. Cambridge: Cambridge University Press, forthcoming.
——. '[Flush] Holograph draft'. Virginia Woolf collection of papers 1882–1984. The Henry W. and Albert A. Berg Collection of English and American Literature, New York Public Library.
——. *Virginia Woolf's Reading Notebooks*, edited by Brenda R. Silver. Princeton, NJ: Princeton University Press, 1983.

Chapter 9

Virginia Woolf's 'bewildering world'

Derek Ryan

In opening his 1941 Rede Lecture, E. M. Forster remarks that to read Virginia Woolf is to be transported to 'a bewildering world':

> We think of *The Waves* and say, 'Yes – that is Virginia Woolf; then we think of *The Common Reader*, where she is different, of *A Room of One's Own* or of the preface to *Life As We Have Known It*: different again. She is like a plant which is supposed to grow in a well-prepared garden bed – the bed of esoteric literature – and then pushes up suckers all over the place, through the gravel of the front drive, and even through the flagstones of the kitchen yard.[1]

If, later in the lecture, Forster's analysis of Woolf occasionally attempts to tame her writing – especially in his judgement of her 'extreme' and 'unreasonable' feminism – his botanical figuration here suggests the radical uprooting of literary conventions.[2] Forster's revisiting of Woolf's writing following her death is, as Kelly Sultzbach describes in *Ecocriticism in the Modernist Imagination* (2016), 'an experience that reminds him of organic profusion' or 'wild growth'.[3] Indeed, Forster's lecture might be read as its own experiment in bewilderment, moving as it does between domestic spaces and wild species in its engagement with Woolf's *oeuvre*. His desire to 'speak on' rather than 'sum up' branches off into various nonhuman elements that Woolf's writing brings to mind: the 'earth', 'landscape', 'a tree, a wave', 'the relation between objects', 'fresh air', 'dust and grass', 'flowers', 'the sun and waters', the 'countryside', 'dogs' and 'food', the latter of which is treated to extended reading.[4] These were all part of Woolf's fascination for what Forster calls 'the outside world', from which her senses 'were always bringing her first-hand news'.[5]

The wild and wildness have a special significance in critical approaches to the more-than-human qualities of Woolf's writing. In Woolf's unruly use of these words, she reconceptualises them as something more than the negative of domestication or civilisation. Judith Allen has, for example, written of women's 'ancient linkage with "wildness"' as well as 'the social, economic and political links of women and differing forms of the "wild"'.[6] Focusing on the symbolic 'reverberations' of wildness in her writing, and especially in *A Room of One's Own* (1929), Allen argues that Woolf 'reappropriated the word "wild" to redefine it, repossess it, and reinvent it as a strongly positive mode of being for women – a mode of resistance'.[7] In the growing body of scholarship (seen in the work of Sultzbach and others) to focus on the material presence of Woolfian wildlife, it is increasingly clear that Woolf's writing contributes to what Peter Adkins calls '[t]he Modernist Anthropocene', which is 'characterised by entanglement' of the human with nonhuman, inhuman and posthuman otherness.[8] If common conceptualisations of the Anthropocene '[speak] to the power of the human as the species that can do *so* much', in Adkins's compelling account Woolf joins the likes of James Joyce and Djuna Barnes in being concerned with the other, less aggrandising implication, that '[t]he human is the species who has been so myopic, so narrowly self-interested, so blind to its impact on the environment and other species, that it has created the conditions for its own demise'; modernists show, in other words, a 'willingness to suspend anthropocentric thinking'.[9] Adkins, too, turns to *A Room of One's Own*, opening his book with the passage in which Woolf looks a century ahead to a time when 'we escape a little from the common sitting-room and see human beings not always in their relation to each other but in relation to reality; and the sky, too, and the trees or whatever it may be in themselves' (*AROO* 86).[10]

Forster's remarks are also prescient in alerting us to the conceptual and ethical potential in the very notion of 'bewilderment', a term under renewed scrutiny by literary theorists who have been rethinking the role literature can play in probing the central tenets of the Anthropocene era. In *Wild Things: The Disorder of Desire* (2020), Jack Halberstam turns to a host of modernists – including T. S. Eliot, W. B. Yeats, Igor Stravinsky and Vaslav Nijinsky – to show the other side to a story in which modernism has not only, as has long been recognised, 'incorporated some understanding of the wild as part of a colonial sensibility that is both drawn to and repelled by expressions of wildness' (see, for example, primitivism and fauvism).[11] Bewilderment, which 'holds the wild within it' both conceptually and etymologically[12] – offers an alternative pathway, 'an immersive sense of being lost or of standing outside of a system of knowing or of merging with other systems of space and time that linger in the background to those we have selected as meaningful'.[13] A similar reappraisal of bewilderment is apparent in Nathan Snaza's *Animate Literacies: Literature, Affect, and the Politics of Humanism* (2019), where it is conceptualised as 'an affective condition of disorientation' sparked by what he calls 'the more-than-human *literacy situation*', which is to say the various nonhuman agencies that *animate* literacy events (reading, writing, teaching), but of which we are not always conscious.[14] Snaza proposes that 'this particular affective state of disorientation – bewilderment – might be the most productive way to open up possibilities for moving away from being Man toward other, incipient and furtive, ways of performing the human'.[15] Both Halberstam and Snaza acknowledge the double-edged nature of bewilderment, how it threatens 'madness' even as it promises 'escape' or invites 'anguish' as it inspires 'dreams and thinking'.[16] Crucially, however, coming to terms with the diminishment of human power initiates a process of reorienting the human toward a less partial engagement with more-than-human life.

In exploring Woolf's 'bewildering world', this chapter follows the use of the noun 'bewilderment' and its verbal and adjectival forms – 'bewilder', 'bewildered' and 'bewildering'[17] – across her writing. If the modernist Anthropocene is characterised by ontological and ethical entanglements of various kinds, then for readers of Woolf's modernism, I argue, bewilderment can be an animating force that injects affect into this entanglement, unsettling processes of human meaning-making via attunement to the nonhuman. In the first part I turn to how Woolf uses bewilderment as a critical term, from her early reviews of Edwardian fiction to her celebrated essays published in *The Common Reader*. As a reader, Woolf herself experiences bewilderment as a reorientation of the human in relation to the nonhuman. In the second part I show how bewilderment is a significant trope in Woolf's fiction, from her first novels *The Voyage Out* (1915) and *Night and Day* (1919) to *Orlando: A Biography* (1928) and *Flush: A Biography* (1933). In these texts, Woolf repeatedly draws on this term in order to expose sexist and speciesist biases that are constitutive of the human in early-twentieth-century modernity, and to imagine alternative modes of life. True to its various meanings, bewilderment does not settle into a singular concept or lead in one certain direction; instead, it is a state of potential that creates the conditions for becoming something else.

Woolf as Bewildered Reader

In exploring the relationship between writers and their readers in 'The Patron and the Crocus', first published in 1924 in the *Nation & Athenaeum* and then revised for *The Common Reader* (1925), Woolf compares the 'bewildering' contemporary scene to earlier eras:

> The Elizabethans, to speak roughly, chose the aristocracy to write for and the playhouse public. The eighteenth-century patron was a combination of coffee-house wit and Grub Street bookseller. In the nineteenth century the great writers wrote for the half-crown magazines and the leisured classes. And looking back and applauding the splendid results of these different alliances, it all seems enviably simple, and plain as a pikestaff compared with our own predicament – for whom should we write? For the present supply of patrons is of unexampled and bewildering variety. (*E4* 212)

As Woolf reels off the many audiences waiting to consume contemporary literature from the mainstream press to different reading publics (described, in her words, as 'English', 'American', 'best-seller', 'worst-seller', 'high-brow', 'red-blood'), she figures literature itself as a genus of flowering plants (appropriately comprising numerous – around 100 – different species): 'the writer who has been moved by the sight of the first crocus in Kensington Gardens' must realise that 'the crocus is an imperfect crocus until it has been shared' (*E4* 213).[18] The relationship between writer and reader is symbiotic; without a public, the writer's creations – their 'crocuses' – become 'tortured plants, beautiful and bright, but with something wry-necked about them, malformed, shrivelled on the one side, overblown on the other' (*E4* 213). Crucially, the reader does not humanise the literary creation/crocus but rather becomes part of an 'atmosphere' that hints at literature's irreducibility to the human: 'It is necessary that the patron should shed and envelop the crocus in an atmosphere which makes it appear a plant of the very highest importance' (*E4* 215). Whether the natural object that ignites the literary creation, or the artistic object that is encountered by readers, Woolf's use of the crocus here indicates literature's more-than-human significance.

Bewilderment is at the heart of Woolf's thinking about writers and readers in the first decades of the twentieth century. It is part of her optimistic, 'sanguine' vision in 'Character in Fiction' of a 'close and equal alliance' of reader and writer (*E3* 434, 436). Having explained how Mrs Brown has evaded the Edwardian writers, and has been imperfectly depicted by the Georgians, she concludes the essay by reminding readers of their responsibility to demand of literature what they may experience in life: 'You have overheard scraps of talk that filled you with amazement. You have gone to bed at night bewildered by the complexity of your feelings' (*E3* 436). While Woolf's argument is famously centred on 'human character', she also places emphasis, as in 'The Patron and the Crocus', on 'steep[ing] oneself in [Mrs Brown's] atmosphere' (*E3* 425). Moreover, just as the supposedly incidental, quotidian encounter with a flower in Kensington Gardens is key to that essay, here Mrs Brown's question, '[c]an you tell me if an oak tree dies when the leaves have been eaten for two years in succession by caterpillars?', and Mr Smith's response 'about plagues of insects' and his brother's 'fruit farm in Kent', is precisely what helps Woolf to paint that atmosphere (*E3* 424). Even where Woolf's concerns with character-making and literature-creating appear to be centred on human figures and language, she is attuned to the nonhuman life crawling and buzzing around those figures and through that language.

Woolf herself was a bewildered reader. In encountering other texts, she is quick to recognise the value of bewilderment. In a series of early reviews, she uses the word to describe admirable qualities even in writers of the Edwardian period. In 'Art and Life' (1909), a review of Vernon Lee's *Laurus Nobilis*, Woolf notes that 'although we may doubt her conclusions or admit that they bewilder us, her exposition is full of ingenuity, and has often the suggestive power of brilliant talk' (*E1* 279); if her book does not appeal to reason, it does have an 'emotional quality' and affective power to 'infect others' (*E1* 277, 279). Very similar language is used in a 1908 review of *The Red Neighbour* by W. J. Eccott, when Woolf concludes that 'the romantic atmosphere has so completely enveloped us that we ask no questions, bewildered though we are, till the book is shut. It infects us with its delightfully irresponsible spirit, and we are well content' (*E6* 365). In 'The Memoirs of Sarah Bernhardt' (1908), Woolf remarks on how the 'bewildering variety' of stories recounted by the French actress – whether 'strange and brilliant' or 'ludicrous' and 'painful' – affect the reader:

> [T]he more you are under the obsession of a book the less of articulate language you have to use concerning it. You creep along after such shocks, like some bewildered animal, whose head, struck by a flying stone, flashes with all manner of sharp lightnings. (*E1* 169)

Reading bewilders language as the reader becomes a kind of animal. The equivocal aspect of bewilderment is apparent here too; if there is a certain excitement about this more-than-human scene, it also presents a violent and disorienting image. None of these books are the masterpieces Woolf is seeking in 'Character in Fiction', but they have their own bewildering qualities that set them apart from the stolid and safe writing of Bennett, Wells and Galsworthy.

Bewilderment does not always, to be sure, succeed in opening up this new relation between reader and writer. We see this most clearly in Woolf's assessment of two other towering figures of her age, awkwardly stuck between the Edwardian and Georgian modes. Conrad's 1904 novel *Nostromo* is judged to be

> the work of a writer who has become aware that the world he writes about has changed its aspect. He has not got used to the prospect. As yet it is a world in which he does not see his way. It is a world of bewildering fullness, fineness, and intricacy. (*E2* 227)

Such bewilderment does not quite lead to a breaking with the bounds of literary convention; it results instead in 'a crowding and suffocating superabundance', plagued by 'the demon of languor, of monotony, of an inertness such as we see in the quiescence of the caged tiger' which 'broods superb, supine, but almost completely immobile' (*E2* 227). The potential wildness of Conrad's text, and of his human figures (which are 'inanimate and stationary'), has been tamed (*E2* 228). Meanwhile, a tiger of a different disposition appears in 'Cleverness and Youth', Woolf's review of Aldous Huxley's 1920 collection of short stories, *Limbo*. Here she bemoans Huxley's decision to target, in his social satire, 'the English upper middle classes' who 'lie, apparently, so open to attack, they are undoubtedly such an obstacle to vision; but their openness is the openness of the tiger's jaw which ends by swallowing you whole and leaving no trace' (*E3* 177). They are, in effect, easy meat. Woolf picks out an amusing scene from 'Farcical History of Richard Greenow', in which a Mrs Cravister 'talks to the bewildered boys now about eschatology, now about Manx cats ("No tails, no tails, like men. How symbolical everything is!"), now about the unhappy fate of the carrion crow, who mates for life', but ultimately judges that these stories do not themselves bewilder; Huxley's tiger may as well have been kept in a cage because 'as usual the upper middle classes escape unhurt' (*E3* 177) – and, by extension, certain assumptions about the human remain unharmed.

Woolf reprises and intensifies bewilderment as a critical term in her essays on the Russian masters – Anton Chekhov, Fyodor Dostoevsky and Leo Tolstoy – whom she so admired. In 'The Russian Point of View', written for *The Common Reader*, the word 'bewilderment' is introduced in relation to Chekhov's stories, when Woolf writes that '[o]ur first impressions' of them 'are not of simplicity but of bewilderment', before asking '[w]hat is the point of it, and why does he make a story out of this?' (*E4* 183–4). As she goes on to explain why English readers are so confused by Chekhov, 'bewilderment' splits into two seemingly contradictory meanings that capture its more typical everyday usage as well as its deep-rooted, wilder connotations. On the one hand it suggests being mired in confusion; on the other it represents an escape into the unknown possibilities of literary creation:

> These stories are inconclusive, we say, and proceed to frame a criticism based upon the assumption that stories ought to conclude in a way that we recognise. In so doing we raise the question of our own fitness as readers. Where the tune is familiar and the end emphatic – lovers reunited, villains discomfited, intrigues exposed – as it is in most Victorian fiction, we can scarcely go wrong, but where the tune is unfamiliar and the end a note of interrogation or merely the information that they went on talking, as it is in Tchehov [*sic*], we need a very daring and alert sense of literature to make us hear the tune, and in particular those last notes which complete the harmony. (*E4* 184)

Bewilderment is a kind of affective exercise, which allows us to prove our 'fitness as readers' and to embrace such bewilderment as far more than our first impression that Chekhov is 'rambling disconnectedly' (*E4* 185). It is, as Christine Reynier puts it, 'a call for the suspension of fixed reading habits [. . .] and for the necessity of responding fully to the alterity of the text'.[19] When we persist in our bewildered state, we gain awareness of the 'unfamiliar' and embrace a shift in scale: 'as we read these little stories about nothing at all, the horizon widens; the soul gains an astonishing sense of freedom' (*E4* 185). The effect is even greater in Dostoevsky, whose bewildering novels are described, in language that again draws from the natural world, as 'seething whirlpools, gyrating sandstorms, waterspouts which hiss and boil and suck us in' before ultimately creating 'giddy rapture' (*E4* 186). Woolf writes that 'confusion slowly settles' into a wild flow of new understanding: 'we are rushed through the water; feverishly, wildly, we rush on and on, now submerged, now in a moment of vision understanding more than we have ever understood before' (*E4* 186). As 'a new panorama of the human mind is revealed' and 'old divisions melt into each other', we are reminded of bewilderment as, in Halberstam's terminology, an 'anti-identitarian' force.[20] Finally, there is Tolstoy, who enacts another change in dimensions so that our initial 'suspicion and bewilderment' creates a more expansive vista until 'we feel that we have been set on a mountain-top and had a telescope put into our hands. Everything is astonishingly clear and absolutely sharp' (*E4* 188). Far from leading to a dead end, bewilderment is a lively if uncertain starting point for a new human and cosmic vision.

While 'The Russian Point of View' is commonly read as building on Woolf's earlier essays 'The Russian View' and 'Tchekov's Questions' (both written in 1918), its emphasis on bewilderment returns to ideas explored in 'More Dostoevsky', her 1917 *TLS* review of *The Eternal Husband and Other Stories*, translated by Constance Garnett.[21] Woolf bookends her thoughts on Dostoevsky's work with bewilderment. Near the beginning, she asserts that '[o]f all the great writers there is [. . .] none quite so surprising, or so bewildering'. Such a sense of bewilderment on the reader's part occurs due to a realisation that 'something strange and important' happens when his books, which have 'extraordinary power', are encountered by readers (*E2* 83). Woolf turns to more wild imagery to capture the deeper significance of his aesthetic. While the plot of 'The Eternal Husband' is likened merely to 'little bits of cork', these fragmented, inanimate objects 'mark a circle upon the top of the waves while the net drags the floor of the sea and encloses stranger monsters than have ever been brought to the light of day before' (*E2* 84). Even as emphasis is again placed on how Dostoevsky writes about 'the labyrinth of the soul through which we have to grope our way' (*E2* 85), his abilities to 'reconstruct[] those most swift and complicated states of mind' and 'suggest the dim and populous underworld of the mind's consciousness where desires and impulses are moving blindly beneath the sod', offers a vision of humanity always connected to 'an external reality' which might be as simple and innocuous as 'some object in the room' (*E2* 85). To be sure, where other writers – and Woolf clearly has the Edwardians in mind – merely 'reproduce all the external appearances' with surface tricks, 'the whole fabric of a book by Dostoevsky is made out of such material' – which is to say, 'the intricate maze of [his characters'] emotions' through which he 'constructs his version of life' (*E2* 85–6). This is an aesthetic of presentation and construction rather than representation and reconstruction; his writing does not reflect the world but is a world:

> In reading him, therefore, we are often bewildered because we find ourselves observing men and women from a different point of view from that to which we are accustomed. We have to get rid of the old

tune which runs so persistently in our ears, and to realise how little of our humanity is expressed in that old tune. Again and again we are thrown off the scent in following Dostoevsky's psychology (*E2* 86).

The multisensory experience of reading here becomes an encounter with what we do not yet know about the human, inside and out.

Woolf as Bewildering Writer

The affective potential of bewilderment is present in subtle but significant ways throughout Woolf's own experiments in fiction. In her debut novel *The Voyage Out*, Rachel Vinrace, who has been aligned with the nonhuman and inhuman by critics such as Claire Davison and Jeff Wallace,[22] finds herself thoroughly bewildered. At the start of Chapter VII, when the *Euphrosyne* reaches the shores of South America, the narrator informs us that 'after four weeks of silence it was bewildering to hear human speech', a comment that is heavily ironic given that the Dalloways, Ambroses and others had not stopped talking throughout the journey (*VO* 94–5). Focus soon falls on 'Rachel, to whom the end of the voyage meant a complete change of perspective' and who 'was too much bewildered by the approach of the shore' to pay much attention to what her fellow passengers were talking about (*VO* 95). Here, as later in the novel – such as Chapter XII, when Rachel 'looked bewildered' as she declared the waltz in honour of Susan's engagement to be her 'idea of hell' (*VO* 170), or Chapter XVI, when she listens to Terence Hewett's monologue about the novels he is writing 'with a certain amount of bewilderment' (*VO* 251) – Woolf's use of the term is clearly a nod to the reader that her enigmatic protagonist's potential lies elsewhere, outside the imperialist-patriarchal complacencies and privilege of her fellow travellers. Certainly, Rachel's is a more knowing state of bewilderment than that experienced by Alfred Perrott in the novel's only other use of the term, after Evelyn Murgatroyd refuses to respond to his advances; he is left with 'a bewildered expression as if he did not really understand what she was saying' (*VO* 428).

The gendered nature of alternative kinds of bewilderment is more pronounced in *Night and Day*. In Chapter IV, William Rodney's 'pause of bewilderment' and 'wild glance' as he recites his paper on 'the Elizabethan use of metaphor' is gently mocking; after all, this is the 'irresistibly ludicrous' figure who elicited in his audience (and in the readers of Woolf's novel) 'a desire to laugh' (*ND* 45). His bewilderment describes his 'discomfort' at fluffing his lines, at failing to make meaning through words: 'Rodney managed to [. . .] choose the wrong sentence [. . .] and to discover his own handwriting suddenly illegible' (*ND* 44–5). By contrast, Mary Datchet's bewilderment, in Chapter VI, is much more studied and self-possessed, expressing her conflicted feelings about her relationship with Ralph as well as her determination to continue her work for women's suffrage. After Ralph Denham and Katharine Hilbery leave the room, we read that

> her eyes rested on the door with a straightforward fierceness in which, for a moment, a certain degree of bewilderment seemed to enter; but, after a brief hesitation, she put down her cup and proceeded to clear away the tea-things. (*ND* 82)

Whereas in Mary the momentary experience of bewilderment gives way to certain action, for Ralph it signals a state of confusion about the reality he thought he knew (a false reality in men, like the one Mrs Seal calls out with her 'bewilderment' at the lack of political action to grant women the vote and 'change the lot of humanity' [*ND* 250–1]). In the following paragraph Ralph is 'bewildered by the fact that [Katharine] had nothing to do with his dream of her' (*ND* 82); it is several chapters later, after visiting Katharine's home and experiencing further 'bewilderment at finding himself among her chairs and tables', that he comes to realise 'his dream of Katherine' was false: 'in five minutes she had filled the shell of the old dream with the flesh of life' (*ND* 136).

The fraught potential in 'bewilderment' to reorient the human in relation to a more-than-human world is most fully realised in the exchanges between Katharine and Ralph in the second half of the novel. In Chapter XXIV, Katharine's search for 'a true feeling among the chaos of the unfeelings or half-feelings of life' is described as 'alternately bewildering, debasing, and exalting' (*ND* 300), which suggests any excitement in her sense of who she may become, or of her feelings for Ralph, is tempered by the acknowledgement that such bewilderment risks her sense of identity and place. Later Ralph, upon declaring to Katharine in a somewhat presumptuous manner 'I see you precisely as you are', elicits the following, wavering, response from her:

> 'That's true', she replied, 'but you can't think how I'm divided – how I'm at my ease with you, and how I'm bewildered. The unreality – the dark – the waiting outside in the wind – yes, when you look at me, not seeing me, and I don't see you either . . . But I do see', she went on quickly, changing her position and frowning again, 'heaps of things, only not you'.

'Tell me what you see', he urged.

But she could not reduce her vision to words, since it was no single shape coloured upon the dark, but rather a general excitement, an atmosphere, which, when she tried to visualize it, took form as a wind scouring the flanks of northern hills and flashing light upon cornfields and pools. (*ND* 405–6, ellipsis in original)

We again reach bewilderment as 'atmosphere' and a shift in scale so that her emotions are recomposed as an aggregate of more-than-human elements and sensations that are irreducible to language. In fact, throughout the novel Katharine has, as Benjamin Hagen persuasively argues, 'desires and needs that are coded as nonhuman: sometimes animal, sometimes vegetal, sometimes cosmic', with the effect that this 'defamiliarizes the very category of human being'.[23] When, in the penultimate chapter of the book, Ralph again visits Katharine, the realisation of their love, of 'the fact that some one shared her loneliness', causes her 'bewilderment [that] was half shame and half the prelude to profound rejoicing' (*ND* 474). Ralph, we read, 'likened her to a wild bird just settling with wings trembling to fold themselves within reach of his hand', and where bewilderment had earlier in the novel marked a divide between Katharine and William (who shared a certain 'bewilderment' about each other's feelings [*ND* 228, 230]), with Ralph she 'shared the same sense of the impending future, vast, mysterious, infinitely stored with undeveloped shapes which each would unwrap for the other to behold' (*ND* 475). As the novel progresses, then, Katharine's state increasingly resembles Halberstam's description of bewilderment as 'a rubric for passions, affects, movements, and ways of thinking' that disrupt and disorder identity categories.[24] If at home with her family Katharine feels 'like a wild animal caged in a civilized dwelling-place' (*ND* 458), her relationship with Ralph to some extent frees her 'wild, irrational, unexplained' desires (*ND* 425).

The idea of bewilderment sparking a process of becoming something else is nowhere more evident than in Woolf's fictional biographies, texts which might be thought of as her wildest experiments in crossing genders and species, as well as genres. In *Orlando: A Biography*, following the change of sex at the heart of the book, Orlando is filled with an affective force that makes her feel that she belongs to neither sex: 'for the time being, she seemed to vacillate; she was man; she was woman; she knew the secrets, shared the weaknesses of each. It was a most bewildering and whirligig state of mind to be in' (*O* 100). Here bewilderment opens queer possibilities of transformation that act against the societal conventions that wish to, in effect, domesticate Orlando.²⁵ Indeed, from the start of this chapter Orlando's bodily desires are linked to the wildness of nature. After reading that 'a delicious tremor ran through her frame' at the words of Captain Nicholas Benedict Bartolus, the next thing we are told is that '[b]irds sang; the torrents rushed' (O 98). We are witness to interspecies intimacy when 'Canute, the elk-hound [. . .] threw himself with such ardour upon his mistress that he almost knocked her to the ground' (O 108), and observe her frolicking with her spaniel Pippin (O 125).²⁶ Informed that Orlando 'looked at the garden and imagined the sleeping crocuses, the dormant dahlias' (O 110), we are reminded of Woolf's botanical bewilderment in 'The Patron and the Crocus'. Her care for animals and the land is evident, too. Unlike the male Orlando who had hunted and killed, '[s]he could not endure to see a donkey beaten or a kitten drowned'; she 'was up at dawn and out among the fields in summer before the sun had risen. No farmer knew more about crops than she did' (O 121).

It is while attuned to the nonhuman that Orlando takes up her poem 'The Oak Tree' (O 111). She writes in a state of bewilderment that is, importantly, not a return to some natural condition so much as a 'process of fabrication' (O 112). At the very point at which we are told '[c]hange was incessant, and change perhaps would never cease', we find the next use of the term:

> she went to the window, and in spite of the cold could not help unlatching it. She leant out into the damp night air. She heard a fox bark in the woods, and the clutter of a pheasant trailing through the branches. She heard the snow slither and flop from the roof to the ground. [. . .] And so bewildered as usual by the multitude of things which call for explanation and imprint their message without leaving any hint as to their meaning, she threw her cheroot out of the window and went to bed. (O 112–13)

Retiring to bed with her mind and body flooded by 'the multitude of things' – from the sensation of cold air to sounds of foxes, birds, trees and snow – Orlando wakes to begin writing 'in pursuance of these thoughts' (O 113). As she 'started afresh upon "The Oak Tree"' (O 113), this scene of writing (of both Orlando's poem and Woolf's novel) becomes, to return to Snaza's notion, a *'literacy situation*: an omnipresent, more-than-human scene of affective collisions and communications among entities and agencies'.²⁷

In Woolf's later fictional biography of Elizabeth Barrett Browning's cocker spaniel, Flush, bewilderment is, paradoxically, key to Woolf's exploration of animal domestication. The early part of *Flush:*

A Biography sets up the tension between the freeing bewilderment Flush experiences when his desires are catered for and the frightening bewilderment he is plunged into when his world-making is obstructed. At Three Mile Cross we read that Flush 'throve; he enjoyed with all the vivacity of his temperament most of the pleasures and some of the licenses natural to his youth and sex' (*F* 11). We find him 'bewildered' by the scents that help him to make meaning of his surroundings: 'smells interwoven in subtlest combination' that 'thrilled his nostrils; strong smells of earth, sweet smells of flowers; nameless smells of leaf and bramble; sour smells as they crossed the road; pungent smells as they entered bean-fields'; as well as 'a smell sharper, stronger, more lacerating than any – a smell that ripped across his brain stirring a thousand instincts, releasing a million memories – the smell of hare, the smell of fox' (*F* 11). This passage invites us to reflect on how richly scent-oriented Flush's world is. As Anna Feuerstein notes in her reading of 'Flush's canine epistemology', 'when it comes to the nose, the dog is the one with power over the human'.[28] But such an emphasis on smell has the potential to affect readers in a different way. As Snaza puts it in a chapter on olfactory aesthetics in James Joyce's *A Portrait of the Artist as a Young Man* (1916), the Freudian 'fantasy' that 'the human has to doom one of its crucial sensory capacities' in order to elevate civilisation above the lowly, smell-surrendering dogs, only 'belies the extent to which human animals too are oriented by smell' – including the smells that are 'a crucial part of any literacy situation'.[29] In reading *Flush*, therefore, we may also find our own sensory experience being redirected towards smell. Such recognition of and respect for more-than-human modes of meaning-making is, however, seldom shared by Flush's human companions. On entering the Barrett household in London, his bewilderment signals distress at his previous world being taken away from him:

> he hid himself, trembling, behind a screen. The voices ceased. A door shut. For one instant he paused, bewildered, unstrung. [. . .] Door after door shut in his face as Miss Mitford went downstairs; they shut on freedom; on fields; on hares; on grass; on his adored, his venerated mistress. (*F* 17)

Even though Flush and Miss Barrett soon form a close bond, we are told that 'they would lie and stare at each other in blank bewilderment' (*F* 26). Miss Barrett struggles to understand why Flush would 'tremble suddenly, and whimper and start and listen', or how 'he was ravaged by the alternate rages of lust and greed', or what the maid 'Wilson's wet umbrella meant to Flush; what memories it recalled, of forests and parrots and wild trumpeting elephants' (*F* 26). Meanwhile, 'Flush was equally at a loss to account for Miss Barrett's emotions', such as why her 'eyes would suddenly fill with tears' while she was writing letters, even though 'there was no sound in the room, no smell to make Miss Barrett cry' (*F* 26–7). In both settings – Three Mile Cross and Wimpole Street – Flush plays the part of domesticated dog, but his sensitivity to wildly different domestic environments is expressed through these two opposed experiences of bewilderment.

The contrast between Flush's life in London and the freedom he will later enjoy in Italy is even more pronounced. The darkest side of his experience is depicted in the 'Whitechapel' chapter when Flush is 'bewildered in the extreme' after being stolen by dog fanciers who put him through 'the most terrible experience of his life': 'One moment he was in Vere Street, among ribbons and laces; the next he was tumbled head over heels into a bag; jolted rapidly across streets, and at length was tumbled out – here. He found himself in complete darkness' (*F* 54–5). When the ransom fee is paid by Elizabeth, much to the disapproval of her father and Mr Browning, Flush returns a 'bewildered dirty dog' (*F* 67). In Italy, however, 'they were escaping; they were leaving tyrants and dog-stealers behind them'. There:

> light poured over him; he found himself alive, awake, bewildered, standing on reddish tiles in a vast bare room flooded with sunshine. He ran hither and thither smelling and touching. [. . .] Pungent and unfamiliar smells tickled his nostrils and made him sneeze. The light, infinitely sharp and clear, dazzled his eyes. He had never been in a room – if this were indeed a room – that was so hard, so bright, so big, so empty. Miss Barrett looked smaller than ever sitting on a chair by a table in the midst. (*F* 72–3)

Flush's experience alters the perspective once more. While the human figure of Miss Barrett is diminished, to Flush the room expands. To be bewildered is now aligned with being '[d]azzled, yet exhilarated' (*F* 74), and heralds the 'liberation' he feels partially in Pisa and then more fully running, chain-free, through the parks of Florence (*F* 77). If the trope of bewilderment was used earlier in the book to expose the perils of anthropocentric (mis)treatment of dogs, here Woolf invites readers to imagine a joyfully bewildering world.

Postscript: 'a bewilderment of relief'

Woolf often found herself in a state of bewilderment at responses to her writing, whether they arrived via friends or reviews. Upon the publication of *Night and Day*, she writes to Katherine Arnold-Forster of being 'pestered and blinded and bewildered' by the opinions of others, who 'give them with or without being asked and they're all different' (*L2* 410). When she publishes *The Common Reader* alongside *Mrs Dalloway* in 1925, she repeats the sentiment. Between the end of May and July we can find her referring to 'how one's friends bewilder one!', in a letter to Vita Sackville-West after discovering that Logan P. Smith did not rate *The Common Reader* (*L3* 185); reporting she is 'in a state of complete bewilderment', in a letter to Janet Case in which she complains 'everyone seems to prefer either Mrs Dalloway to the C.R. or the other way about, and implore me to write *only* novels or *only* criticism' (*L3* 191, emphases in original); and 'so bewildered by what people say that I find it difficult to go on', this time responding to Philip Morrell who wrote to praise *Mrs Dalloway* (*L3* 195). But she *does* go on. If such bewilderment suggests frustration and bemusement, it also signals a kind of unburdening or release. Even in these letters, Woolf is already looking forward to what she will write next: 'I cant stop writing' (*L3* 185); 'I want to do both [write novels and criticism]' (*L3* 191); 'I shall start again refreshed' (*L3* 195). Her description in a later diary entry, penned as she awaits responses to *Roger Fry* (1940), captures this sense that handing her books over to readers brings 'a bewilderment of relief' (*D5* 308). Whether such bewilderment is experienced in response to praise or criticism, it nonetheless propels her towards a new literary creation and her future readers.

We might hazard a guess that Woolf would have been bewildered by her work being read in relation to the Anthropocene – a term that had not yet been coined when she was alive. But I have argued that her use of bewilderment as both a critical term and creative trope reorients the human away from anthropocentrism and towards a more-than-human world that is now in more need than ever of our recognition and response. If both the premise of the Anthropocene era and promise to reduce its disastrous effects has been too focused on the aggrandisement of human agency, Woolf teaches us that reading literature can relieve the human of this fantasy and create the conditions for bewilderment to affect change.

Notes

1. Forster, 'Woolf', 253.
2. Forster, 'Woolf', 266.
3. Sultzbach, *Ecocriticism*, 82.

4. Forster, 'Woolf', 253, 254, 256, 257, 258, 259, 260, 262.
5. Forster, 'Woolf', 263.
6. Allen, *Woolf*, 69.
7. Allen, *Woolf*, 75.
8. Adkins, *Anthropocene*, 198.
9. Adkins, *Anthropocene*, 2, 20.
10. Adkins, *Anthropocene*, 1.
11. Halberstam, *Wild*, 8–9.
12. While the etymology of 'bewilderment' is uncertain, the *OED* traces the word back through 'wilder' meaning '[t]o cause or lose one's way, as in a wild or unknown place', 'to render at a loss how to act, or what to think', to 'go astray, stray, wander' (all of which were used form the seventeenth century) and '[t]o render, or become, wild or uncivilized' (which dates back to the late eighteenth century).
13. Halberstam, *Wild*, 66.
14. Snaza, *Animate*, 9.
15. Snaza, *Animate*, 81.
16. Halberstam, *Wild*, 31; Snaza, *Animate*, 81.
17. Bewilderment has been recognised as a feature of modernist aesthetics. Paul B. Armstrong explains in *Bewilderment: Understanding and Representation in James, Conrad, and Ford* (1987) how '[b]ewilderment throws into question the interpretive constructs we ordinarily take for granted as our ways of knowing the world' and takes on 'a positive value' in making us question reality (2–3). In so doing, he distinguishes them from romantic 'primordial unity of humanity and nature' or 'faith in the world's preestablished harmony' (3). In my reading, however, Woolf's bewilderment is neither a reminder of the falsity of nature and man's division from it, nor is it a reinforcement of harmonious union.
18. In her 'Virginia Woolf Herbarium', Elisa Kay Sparks notes that at 56 recorded mentions across Woolf's *oeuvre*, crocuses are 'one of her most frequently mentioned flowers' and often act figuratively as 'an igniter of imaginative creativity generated by and producing a kind of androgynously erotic excitement'.
19. Reynier, *Woolf's Ethics*, 33.
20. Halberstam, *Wild*, 30.
21. For 'The Russian View' and 'Tchekov's Questions', see *E2*, 341–4 and 244–8 respectively.
22. Claire Davison illustrates affinities between Rachel and the Darwin of *The Voyage of the Beagle* (1839) to show how both are 'listener[s] in the world, for whom panoramic settings on land and at sea are an interwoven drama of natural and aesthetic sounds'. See 'Hearing the World', 9. For Jeff Wallace, Rachel's illness signals 'the inhuman nature of human death when life is considered as a force traversing the organic and inorganic and incorporating thereby death's impersonal necessity'. See 'Inhuman Death', 153.
23. Hagen, 'Woolfian Love', 166, 168.

24. Halberstam, *Wild*, 10, 31.
25. The passage chimes with Woolf's own excitement at discovering her multiplicity in an entry dated 4 July 1935: 'But how queer to have so many selves – how bewildering!' (*D4*, 329).
26. On this scene and others of cross-species companionship, see chapter 3 in my monograph, *Bloomsbury, Beasts and British Modernist Literature*.
27. Snaza, *Animate*, 82, emphasis in original.
28. Feuerstein, 'Smell', 32–3.
29. Snaza, *Animate*, 116.

Bibliography

Adkins, Peter. *The Modernist Anthropocene: Nonhuman Life and Planetary Change in James Joyce, Virginia Woolf and Djuna Barnes*. Edinburgh: Edinburgh University Press, 2022.

Allen, Judith. *Virginia Woolf and the Politics of Language*. Edinburgh: Edinburgh University Press, 2010.

Armstrong, Paul B. *The Challenge of Bewilderment: Understanding and Representation in James, Conrad, and Ford*. Ithaca, NY and London: Cornell University Press, 1987.

'Bewilderment', *OED Online*, Oxford University Press, August 2022.

Davison, Claire. 'Hearing the World "in full orchestra": Voyaging Out with Woolf, Darwin, and Music'. *Woolf Studies Annual* 23 (2017): 1–32.

Feuerstein, Anna. 'What Does Power Smell Like? Canine Epistemology and the Politics of the Pet in Virginia Woolf's *Flush*'. *Virginia Woolf Miscellany* 84 (Fall 2013): 32–4.

Forster, E. M. 'Virginia Woolf'. In *Two Cheers for Democracy* by E. M. Forster, edited by Oliver Stallybrass, 253–69. London: Penguin, 1972.

Hagen, Benjamin. 'Woolfian Love in Aggregate: Posthuman–Queer–Feminist'. *Comparative Critical Studies* 19, no. 2 (2022): 157–83.

Halberstam, Jack. *Wild Things: The Disorder of Desire*. Durham, NC: Duke University Press, 2020.

Reynier, Christine. *Virginia Woolf's Ethics of the Short Story*. Basingstoke: Palgrave Macmillan, 2009.

Ryan, Derek. *Bloomsbury, Beasts and British Modernist Literature*. Cambridge: Cambridge University Press, 2022.

Snaza, Nathan. *Animate Literacies: Literature, Affect, and the Politics of Humanism*. Durham, NC: Duke University Press, 2019.

Sparks, Elisa Kay. 'A Virginia Woolf Herbarium'. Accessed 9 August 2022. https://woolfherbarium.blogspot.com/

Sultzbach, Kelly. *Ecocriticism in the Modernist Imagination: Forster, Woolf, and Auden*. Cambridge: Cambridge University Press, 2016.

Wallace, Jeff. 'The Inhuman Death of Rachel Vinrace'. *Comparative Critical Studies* 19, no. 2 (2022): 149–55.

Woolf, Virginia. *The Diary of Virginia Woolf*, edited by Anne Olivier Bell. 5 vols. New York: Harcourt Brace Jovanovich, 1977–84.

———. *The Essays of Virginia Woolf*, edited by Andrew McNeillie (vols 1–4) and Stuart N. Clarke (vols 5–6). 6 vols. London: Hogarth Press, 1986–2011.

———. *Flush: A Biography*, edited by Kate Flint. Oxford: Oxford University Press, 1998.

———. *The Letters of Virginia Woolf*, edited by Nigel Nicolson and Joanne Trautmann. 6 vols. London: Hogarth Press, 1975–80.

———. *Night and Day*. London: Vintage, 2005.

———. *Orlando: A Biography*. London: Vintage, 2004.

———. *A Room of One's Own and Three Guineas*, edited by Anna Snaith. Oxford: Oxford University Press, 2015.

———. *The Voyage Out*, edited by Lorna Sage. Oxford: Oxford University Press, 2009.

Part V

Outsiders, Assemblages and Activism

Chapter 10

'Suspending the sky': Virginia Woolf and the Brazilian Indigenous Worldview of Ailton Krenak

Davi Pinho and Maria A. de Oliveira

At the very end of Virginia Woolf's peroration in *A Room of One's Own*, the English writer invites her readers to think not in relation to modern paradigms of the individual in encounters with other individuals, but 'in relation to reality; and the sky, too, and the trees or whatever it may be in themselves' (*AROO* 149). The 'world of reality' includes, then, human and nonhuman actors. Hence, 'the common life which is the real life' (*AROO* 148) demands that the writers of the future frame their own lives in ethical encounters with these diverse manifestations that make any life possible on this planet. The fact that Woolf places this ethical task at the heart of a literature to come, one that would redeem 'the lives of the unknown' who are the Judith Shakespeares of the world (*AROO* 149), constitutes fertile ground for critics like Derek Ryan, who reads Woolf's evocation of the trees and the sky as her line of flight from human-centred debates of sexual difference and into a new, embodied materialist account of lived existence.[1] This 'world of reality' is also Peter Adkins's point of departure for reading Woolf as a writer who anticipates contemporary planetary concerns, as a theorist of the Anthropocene *avant la lettre*.[2] For us, Woolf's invitation to step outside a humanistic perspective and think *with* and *as* another manifestation of life is also a productive point of access to those outsides and outsiders who, in our Brazilian context, are trying to reframe the myths of progress that sustain neocolonial practices.

If, as Karen J. Warren elucidates, ecofeminist philosophies have already denounced Western practices of neocolonialism as a double helix of oppression, since they exploit women and nature in a project of civilisation that disguises its constitutive barbarism,[3] this chapter aims at first understanding Woolf's 'Outsiders' Society' from *Three*

Guineas (1938) as suggesting a methodology of outsideness that disturbs the very notion of any human society. We call it a methodology because the term 'outsider' appears differently in Woolf, who seems to expand the binding element among those who would 'join outside' modern ideas of society that are inherently patriarchal, capitalistic and human-centred (*TG* 309). In *Three Guineas*, the term includes 'daughters of educated men', but, in 'The Leaning Tower', Woolf expands it to include 'commoners' and the working class (*E6* 277). All through these occurrences, the true binding force of belonging outside 'has to do with emptying out the self, opening it out to possible encounters with the "outside"', as Rosi Braidotti elaborates while reading Woolf's 'intensive genre'.[4] Braidotti seems to be commenting precisely on what we tentatively call Woolf's methodology of outsideness, situating it as that which drives Woolf's 'intensive genre': the movement of othering herself through her ability to be affected by the human and nonhuman ecosystems she inhabits, thus displaying 'the accuracy of the cartographer with the hypersensitivity of the sensualist in apprehending the precise quality of an assemblage of elements, like the shade of the light at dusk or the curve of the wind just before the rain falls'.[5] Reading Turgenev, Woolf herself contributes to this debate when she praises the Russian writer's ability to allow his characters to remain 'profoundly conscious of their relation to things outside themselves', becoming in this sense 'not the whole of life, but only part of the whole' (*E6* 13).

Bearing this in mind, this chapter takes Woolf's movements of pushing further outside in her essays into new directions in order to bring her writing into contact with Ailton Krenak's indigenous worldview and the importance of belonging outside. Argentinian decolonial feminist thinker María Lugones affirms that, 'if we are going to make an-other construction of the self in relation, we need to bracket the dichotomous human/non-human, colonial, gender system that is constituted by the hierarchical dichotomy man/woman for European colonials+the non-gendered, non-human colonized'.[6] This outside encounter between Woolf and Krenak means exploring the way they bracket these dichotomies and opening up possibilities for bridging their different resistances to the coloniality of power and gender, without erasing the different loci of their very resistance. In our final considerations, we briefly bring Woolf's first novel, *The Voyage Out*, into this conversation with Krenak in order to show how her writing gestures towards encounters outside the 'human'. These encounters suggest a different way of occupying the world – and it is towards this difference that we write this chapter.

Towards Woolf's and Krenak's Outsides before the End of the World

Woolf's attempt to think outside her position as a woman at the end of *A Room of One's Own* is particularly relevant as an attempt to remain further outside a human-centred perspective. In the essay, Woolf writes fictional but no less true scenes that provoke still urgent critiques of oppressive gender socialisations. Judith Shakespeare is, of course, paradigmatic here, for as a woman in Early Modern England she is not inscribed as a subject in that society, being denied access to the sort of self-fashioning that marked the life and work of her brother.[7] But, in an essay that articulates questions of identity so poignantly, it is significant that Woolf chooses to end it by saying 'that our relation is to the world of reality and not only to the world of men and women' (*AROO* 149). As Ryan puts it, Woolf's closing gestures point 'towards a material reality that is more than human'[8], allowing for the deconstruction not only of gender identity binarism but also of the fundamental human/nature binary. As Woolf 'begins to de-emphasise such categorial differences based in identity'[9], she furthermore makes our attention to this world of reality a condition for the return of Judith Shakespeare: 'then the opportunity will come and the dead poet who was Shakespeare's sister will put on the body which she has so often laid down' (*AROO* 149). So, if we need to work for Judith Shakespeare, this work takes place in ethical encounters with the outside, with the trees and the sky too. In other words, the 'lives of the unknown' that return through feminist work are the fertilisers we apply to our very soil, and once this soil is fertilised, their return is also our future. This earthly temporality of Judith Shakespeare's return, then, disturbs human time – past, present and future – in favour of this soil fertilised by her body and which we occupy as bodies in a community of human and nonhuman beings, of vibrant matter, to employ Jane Bennett's term.[10] To think about things in themselves, in *A Room of One's Own*, is to think through another time (which is not just historical) and another space (which is not just the world as human culture), but earth (the tree) and cosmos (the sky) too. What Woolf proposes can be read, then, as a step towards what Bennett calls an impersonal affect, the emergence of 'thing-power' that cuts across and gathers other insurgencies that are not just human.[11]

Can we think of Virginia Woolf's 'Outsiders' Society' in *Three Guineas* in relation to this final movement in *A Room of One's Own*? That is, as an attempt to imagine bonds in more ethically responsible ways, in connection not only to the daughters and sisters of educated men but also mobilised by the shared 'outside' that is destroyed in human frames of war? After all, what the outsider says is that her country is 'the whole world' (*TG* 313). The outsider is a 'she' of an imagined future who has her roots in women's bodies' exclusion – or in their inclusion only as excluded by the State, much like another learned man's sister, Judith Shakespeare in *A Room of One's Own*. However, this 'she' who gathers in society outside Society also makes 'we' with other outsiders if we think of 'The Leaning Tower', written and read for the Workers' Educational Association in 1940. 'Are we not commoners, outsiders?' Woolf asks, placing herself alongside her audience, and ends the essay by reaffirming their collective place outside, trespassing boundaries:

> It is thus that English literature will survive this war and cross the gulf – if commoners and outsiders like ourselves make that country our own country, if we teach ourselves how to read and to write, how to preserve, and how to create. (*E6* 278)

Furthermore, the final movements of *Three Guineas* reveal once again, as in *A Room of One's Own*, the emergence of a thing-power that tries to overcome gender divisions. 'A common interest unites us; it is one world, one life. How essential it is that we should realise that unity the dead bodies, the ruined houses prove' (*TG* 365). The dead bodies and ruined houses are actants, as Bruno Latour defines them in the glossary to *Politics of Nature* and as Jane Bennett expands in *Vibrant Matter*: they are sources of vitality that Woolf mobilises to reorient our senses, to make us leave the subject of representation, and to unite us in the materiality of an interconnected world that is increasingly at risk.[12] Under the sign of women's exclusion, Woolf suggests that the outsider is an occupant of her very exclusion as a way of making bonds with other societies, always heading for the margins, always moving towards another outside. After all, the risk is that, when gathering in society, a new margin may be delimited, against which other acts of cruelty might be projected. There is a methodology of outsideness here that tries, at all costs, to make unity in the multiplicity of the outside:

> But with your letter before us we have reason to hope. For by asking our help you recognise that connection; and by reading your words we are reminded of other connections that lie far deeper than the facts on the surface. Even here, even now your letter tempts us to shut our ears to these little facts, these trivial details, to listen not to the bark

of the guns and the bray of the gramophones but to the voices of the poets, answering each other, assuring us of a unity that rubs out divisions as if they were chalk marks only; to discuss with you the capacity of the human spirit to overflow boundaries and make unity out of multiplicity. But that would be to dream – to dream the recurring dream that has haunted the human mind since the beginning of time; the dream of peace, the dream of freedom. But, with the sound of the guns in your ears you have not asked us to dream. You have not asked us what peace is; you have asked us how to prevent war. Let us then leave it to the poets to tell us what the dream is; and fix our eyes upon the photograph again: the fact. (*TG* 365–6)

The 'human spirit' in the quotation above, which breaks into the materialist argument of the writer in an impossible return to the voices of the poets, can make us think that there is still a primacy of the human here. However, we can only make this reading if we ignore that it is the abject bodies (human and nonhuman) in the photos of the Spanish Civil War that ultimately produce this sense of unity in multiplicity. The dead bodies and ruined houses are the ultimate actants that allow for gender differences to be temporarily cut across, without being erased or incorporated by a homogenising inside.

María Lugones understands 'the dichotomous hierarchy between the human and the non-human as the central dichotomy of colonial modernity'.[13] From *A Room of One's Own* to *Three Guineas*, precisely because of her awareness that, as an outsider, her human status depended on a connection with men, Woolf's writing opens itself to questions that others, outside her own position as an outsider within the Empire, have been elaborating. Brazilian indigenous reflections on how the very category of 'the natural world' depends on the 'civilised' gaze, for instance, remains outside but in connection to Woolf's outsideness if we keep on pushing her methodology. Reading Woolf alongside Ailton Krenak, the revolutionary Brazilian indigenous thinker who has been one of the leading figures of indigenous movements since the 1970s, perhaps reveals that Woolf's attempt in the final movements of *A Room of One's Own* and *Three Guineas* is to 'suspend the sky' of possibility.

According to Krenak, 'suspending the sky means to widen our horizon; not the horizon of perspective, but the existential one'.[14] Krenak's call to 'suspend the sky' refers to Davi Kopenawa, the groundbreaking Yanomami shaman who prophesied the imminent destruction of the planet. Through the cosmological knowledge of his people, Kopenawa asserts that what prevents the sky from falling, bringing about the end of the world, is the fact that there are still a few shamans alive at the heart of the Amazon rainforest. 'The white people are increasingly burning the sky's chest with their metal fumes, and the *xapiri'* (the invisible spirits that guard the forest) 'are constantly trying to cure it by pouring torrents of mountain water on it', Kopenawa says. He continues, '[y]et if there are no more shamans left in the forest, it will soon burn up until it becomes blind. Finally, it will suffocate and, becoming ghost, will suddenly start falling onto the earth'.[15] 'Suspending the sky', then, has to do with finding ways of pushing back the end of the world. But, as Krenak affirms, it has also got to do with freeing the body from social constructs through movement, 'singing, [and] dancing', which is 'common in many [indigenous] traditions' as a rite to bring bodies into closer contact with their ecosystems. Furthermore, 'it is to enrich our subjectivities, which is the matter that this time we live in wants to consume. If there is an urge to consume nature, there is also an urge to consume subjectivities – our subjectivities'.[16]

Remaining further outside than the daughters of educated men who would dance around the burning buildings of their societies (*TG* 208), Krenak's final movements in the lecture that titles the recent collection *Ideias para adiar o fim do mundo* [*Ideas to Postpone the End of the World*] also aims at making unity out of multiplicity, even if that implies dreaming across differences: 'we are definitely not the same, and it's wonderful to know that each one of us here is different from the other, like constellations'.[17] That Krenak's audience was Portuguese when he originally proffered his lecture adds another layer to this assertion.[18] In Portugal, at the place of origin for what has meant the end of certain worlds for many Brazilian original peoples, Krenak asserts that to dream, to create, to circulate as bodies in difference, is a possibility to be affirmed, now that Europe recognises that there are other ends in the horizon: 'it is important to live the experience of our own circulation around the world, not as a metaphor, but as a friction, being able to count on each other'. And he goes on: 'when you feel the sky is getting too low, just push it and breathe'.[19]

The Krenak group, to which Ailton belongs, bears in its very ethnonym the interconnected web that constitutes us as vibrant matter: *kre* (head) + *nak* (earth).[20] As 'heads of the earth', Ailton explains that the Krenak worldview understands humans as persons only in the sense that the river is also a person, just as much as the rocks, the trees and the sky too. As he concludes in 'Do Sonho e da Terra' ['Of Dream and Earth'], dreaming is, thus, not an oneiric experience, but:

> a discipline related to education, to worldview, to the tradition of different peoples that have the dream as a learning path, as self-knowledge about life, and as the application of this knowledge to one's interaction with the world and with other people.[21]

He picks up on this idea in the final lecture collected in *Ideas to Postpone the End of the World*, 'A Humanidade que Pensamos Ser' ['The Humanity We Think We Are'], telling us that before the inevitable fall – characterised as the end of the Anthropocene, for some, or as the final movements of colonisation, for others – our 'multicoloured parachutes' can only be projected from the places of vision and dreaming: 'the dream as an experience of people initiated in a tradition to dream'.[22] The postponement of the end of the world, towards which Krenak develops ideas that have been suffocated by the very civilisation that now asks for them, depends on this dream of possibility, of cohabitation, of multiplicity. The dream does not pertain to a parallel world but is rooted in this one world that we share. And speaking across differences, even if it means dreaming one's way into cohabitation, is fundamental, as Kopenawa puts it:

> This is why I would like the white people to hear our words and dream about all that they say: if the shamans' songs stop being heard in the forest, white people will not be spared any more than we will.[23]

A version of this dream breaks through in Woolf's writing. From her exclusion, she has glimpses into the interconnected nature of all lives – the fact that a flower is not a flower on its own but is 'part earth; part flower' (*MOB* 71). Woolf's outsider's feeling, as described in 'A Sketch of the Past', has its roots in her ambivalence, and ultimately resistance, towards the society into which George Duckworth insisted she must be introduced: 'Besides feeling his age and power, I felt too what I have come to call the outsider's feeling. I felt as a gypsy or a child feels who stands at the flap of the tent and sees the circus going on inside' (*MOB* 152–3). Denouncing how colonial violence is daily reproduced against indigenous peoples, Krenak expands this feeling that also constitutes Woolf's 'Outsiders' Society' in *Three Guineas* towards new outsides:

> we exclude from life, locally, those forms of organisation that are not integrated into the world of commodities, putting all other ways of living at risk – at least those that we were encouraged to think as possible, in which there was co-responsibility towards the places where we live and respect for living beings' right to live, and not just this abstraction that we have allowed ourselves to construe as humanity, which excludes all other beings.[24]

Though Woolf feels she must coin the critical term 'educated man's daughter' so as to mark, as she explains in the second note to *Three*

Guineas, women's exclusion from capital and environment in comparison to their bourgeois fathers and brothers, she is in fact denouncing her very inclusion as a commodity exchangeable among fathers and sons, as Luce Irigaray would later formulate.[25] She is also denouncing the fact that, in María Lugones's words, 'sexual purity and passivity are crucial characteristics of the white bourgeois females who reproduce the class and the colonial and racial standing of bourgeois, white men' and their constitutive exclusion 'from the production of knowledge, from most control over the means of production' in the heterosexualist gender system.[26] There is a key difference in positionality here that should be acknowledged, since Krenak and the other indigenous peoples described by Ailton Krenak are withdrawn from the very structure of exchange. Their deaths, not their lives, are profitable, for killing indigenous populations means opening up the possibility of exploiting their last remaining demarcated territories. What Woolf and Krenak share, however, is the desire not to be incorporated either into the liberal promise of democracy or the very status of 'human' in its binary separation from nature.

Part Earth, Part Human

As popularised by the Nobel Prize-winner Paul Crutzen and his colleagues to address our geological epoch, the Anthropocene recognises the central role that humans have had in the environmental degradation of the planet – a degradation that will leave its mark long beyond our existence as a species.[27] And, as Krenak puts it, 'the conclusion or understanding that we are living in an era that can be identified as the Anthropocene should ring an alarm bell in our heads'.[28] Raewyn Connell and Rebecca Pearse's etymological take on the term 'Anthropocene'[29] – which, in Greek, formally refers to a male human being through the *-os* gender inflection of the word 'anthrop*os*' – leads one to think about the role gender plays in the exploitation of the environment. Earlier, in 1938, when Woolf feels the need to coin a term that differentiates English women's positions from those of their bourgeois brothers and fathers, she does so because, as she says, our 'ideology is still so inveterately anthropocentric' (*TG* 274). So Woolf, too, brings attention to the gender dynamics in the Anthropocene. Between Connell and Pearse and Woolf, the suggestion is that ecological crises have been forged by patriarchal capitalist societies that had women and nature as sites of exploitation.

Bringing together Woolf's outsider's feeling and the indigenous worldviews of Brazilian thinkers like Ailton Krenak and Davi

Kopenawa into an ecocritical discussion of the Anthropocene is not a smooth path. The links can only be suggested, and our intention here is to let differences speak without homogenising these worldviews. After all, indigenous voices from Brazil understand that their existences are fundamental for the protection of the environment, for their very positionality within the protected areas of the Amazon rainforest and of other regions of Brazil has the potential of halting exploitation, though it is this potential that ultimately marks their lives as killable. The genocidal politics carried out by the Bolsonaro administration against the Yanomami people in order to facilitate the exploitation of their lands only reinforces this radical difference in positionally.[30] Their vulnerability is extreme, since acts of cruelty are carried out daily in the interest of the extraction of oil, minerals and wood. At the same time that the neofascist Bolsonaro administration was to blame for this recent large-scale devastation of demarcated lands, it cannot be forgotten that the capitalist enterprise, on a global scale, is involved in this machinery of exploitation of resources. This machinery has promoted the destruction of indigenous groups and their lands in Brazil through its influence on many previous governments, as the Brazilian anthropologist Eduardo Viveiros de Castro registers in 'Alguma Coisa Vai ter que Acontecer' ['Something Needs to Happen'].[31]

Describing the myth of sustainability created by world corporations to justify their assault of an indigenous idea of nature, Ailton Krenak asserts that 'we have been, for a long time, lulled with the story that we are humanity'.[32] This idea of nature, and of the human as transcendent of this very nature, produces our alienation 'from this organism which we are part of, the Earth, and we have come to think that it is one thing and we are another: the Earth and humanity'.[33] His fundamental question, then, as Eduardo Viveiros de Castro elaborates, is:

> Indeed, who are we, anyway? 'We' in relation to whom? To what? The question about 'the humanity we think we are' is a question about relations – about the relationships that constitute us as an essentially variable we, in extension as well as in understanding: for some of us [. . .] the 'we' includes, among others, the rocks, the mountains and the rivers.[34]

Though Woolf was not alive to the radical outside of Brazilian indigenous worldviews, her works are marked by interruptions of the coherent flow of the civilisational mechanism that separates humans from their ecosystems, which ultimately supports colonialist practices of destruction, as critics like Patricia Novillo-Corvalán have highlighted.[35] Because of its South-American destination, we would like to end this chapter by registering that, since the beginning of her career as a novelist, with the publication of *The Voyage Out* in 1915, Woolf opened narrative spaces for personalising the nonhuman as if she were aware that, in the words of Krenak, 'when we depersonalise the river, the mountain, when we take away their senses from them, considering that this is an exclusive attribute of humans, we allow these places to become residues of industrial and extractive activity'.[36] After all, if, in the opening chapter of the novel, Helen Ambrose has a glimpse of 'the skeleton beneath' (*VO* 6) London's imperial beauty, as the narrator qualifies the poverty and exclusion that sustains the Empire, by the time they reach Santa Marina the narrative makes room for the animals to communicate with the characters and with one another as if answering questions, filling in the gaps of silence. Birds give 'a wild laugh', monkeys chuckle 'a malicious question', and the sounds of the forest echo 'like a hall' (*VO* 312).

Furthermore, Novillo-Corvalán defends that 'the ideological discourses of taxonomy and cartography remain one of the main preoccupations of Woolf's characters' in *The Voyage Out*.[37] The vitality of the outside, of this life being carried out and registered in spite of the English travellers' discomfort or Orientalist ideas of discovering supposedly unknown lands (be it in the present time of the narrative or when the first Elizabethan expansionists came across the river), then, undoes their very positionality in these scenes. In other words, if 'their relationship with the South American landscape is always evocative of Empire, as the Amazon is constantly refashioned into a *terra incognita* awaiting colonization',[38] Woolf's narrative mocks this very relationship, showing that the forest's life was oblivious to the human differentiations of gender, race and class with which the characters struggle in the plot.

Under the weight of Richard Dalloway's patriarchal and patronising defence of women's politically inferior minds, it is relevant that Rachel Vinrace's instinct is to counter his sexist and racist stance, for whom 'the English seem, on the whole, whiter than most men, their records cleaner' (*VO* 67), by trying to think beyond the 'human': 'if one went back far enough, everything perhaps was intelligible; everything was in common; for the mammoths who pastured in the fields of Richmond High Street had turned into paving stones and boxes full of ribbon, and her aunts' (*VO* 70). Reading this passage, Lorna Sage highlights how Woolf seems to depict 'modern cultures as evolving by means of more and more elaborate codes of differentiation – race, gender, language, class, generation, and so on and on'.[39] In many ways, Rachel's untimely death brings the proliferation of these differences to a halt as Woolf suddenly breaks what otherwise seemed, as Julia Briggs affirms, to be written 'in a style of comedy and social satire inherited from a range of English examples, from Jane Austen to E. M. Forster'.[40] The impasse, then, has to do with the coloniality of power and gender, for, were Rachel to voyage back into England, the heterosexual marriage plot would potentially frame her life through gender and class performances she continuously tried to resize by paying attention to the vitality of the world outside.

Thus, the vitality of the nonhuman outside produces breaks in the colonialist and Orientalist perspective of the people in Woolf's novel, poetically contributing to her 'scathing critique of an emergent global capitalist modernity, particularly the economic impetus behind Britain's disproportionate presence in Buenos Aires and Amazonia'.[41] If, in the beginning of the novel, Helen has a glimpse into the constitutive exclusion required for Britain's emergence as a capitalist superpower in the figures of 'the poor who were unhappy and rightly malignant' in the streets of London (*VO* 6), it is relevant that these outsiders within the Empire are doubled by other outsides and outsiders in Santa Marina. In the early hours after Rachel's death, for instance, the narration contrasts human silence to another sound that did not stop all night, 'the sound of a slight but continuous breathing which never ceased, although it never rose and never fell' (*VO* 414), perhaps assimilating Rachel's last drawn breath (her ultimate silence) into the life of the planet which would soon witness the vibrant though breathless movements of her body's decomposition. As the sun is rising, the 'first sounds that were heard were little inarticulate cries, the cries, it seemed, of children or of the very poor, of people who were very weak or in pain' (*VO* 414). The ambiguity here is productive, for these may be read as referring to other than human sounds, since only after dawn these 'sounds of life' become 'bolder and more full of courage and authority' as '[b]y degrees the smoke began to ascend in wavering breaths over the houses' (*VO* 414), indicating human presence. The possibility of reading these 'inarticulate cries' as being emitted either by humans or by other animals – that is, as the sounds of children and the sick waking up, or of 'very poor' locals going to work at dawn for the English travellers, or as the sounds of birds and other animals made akin to the sounds of the most vulnerable humans of that society through an implied simile – reveals how Woolf's narrative creates poetic fissures that allow us to question both what we mean by human (are the poor included? the colonised?) and what we mean by life (is nature, as understood in its opposition to human, included?).

Though there is no room for a long survey of Woolf's novels here, this early example already reveals some form of cosmic vision of the natural world, which entails practising encounters with the outside by creating narrative fissures that allow for the nonhuman to interfere, destabilise, reflect and resize the life of her human characters. Akin to Turgenev's talent in Woolf's reading of the Russian writer, she too would strive to make readers 'hear the hum of life in the fields' (*E6* 13) and realise that we are but vibrant pieces from the vibrant whole outside a stable idea of humanity, on the one hand, and that this very idea of humanity is based on the constitutive exclusion of other (human and nonhuman) lives, on the other. After all, as we meant to show in this chapter, from her essays to her novels Woolf seems to hint at other possibilities of making 'we' with those further beyond her own marginal position as one of the English 'daughters of educated men' of her time. And, indeed, Woolf's final philosophy in 'A Sketch of the Past' shows that, behind the little separate lives we live, there is a pattern that connects the whole world. Significantly, 'we are the thing itself' (*MOB* 72) could also mean we are this matter-world in itself.

By reading Woolf alongside indigenous worldviews, then, we open her prose to the outside, offering a different perspective on decolonising the Anthropocene. Indigenous peoples can offer us many possibilities to 'postpone the end of the world', and their millenary knowledge can help us reassess modern paradigms of the self-sustaining individual. With this outside encounter in mind, we could say that, though the imperative changes, the ecological sensibility that breaks through remains the same from *A Room of One's Own* to 'A Sketch of the Past'. From *thinking of things in themselves* to *being things in themselves*, Woolf destabilises the separation between the human and nature, inviting us to occupy the thing-matter that is the world, the thing-stuff that is the body, the thing-house that is language. The invitation is to move outwards through moments like the one that took the young Virginia Stephen by storm before a vibrant body she recognised as 'part earth; part flower' (*MOB* 71). This thing that we share and that is always at risk is precisely our place as vibrant matter among other vibrant materials: the fact that we are, like young Virginia's flower, part human, but part earth – or heads of the earth, *Krenak*.

Notes

1. Ryan, *Virginia Woolf*, 75.
2. Adkins, *Modernist Anthropocene*, 20.
3. Warren, *Ecofeminist Philosophy*, XIV.
4. Braidotti, *Nomadic Theory*, 152.
5. Ibid., 152.
6. Lugones, 'Decolonial Feminism', 749.
7. Self-fashioning being, as Stephen Greenblatt puts it, 'an increased self-consciousness about the fashioning of human identity as a manipulatable, artful process' (2).
8. Ryan, *Virginia Woolf*, 75.
9. Ibid., 65.
10. Bennett is of interest here, since not only inanimate objects constitute vibrant matter in her argument, including waste and residue, which continue to live as microorganisms that change their ecosystems, but also the 'natural world' and the human body: 'I have been trying to raise the volume on the vitality of materiality per se, pursuing this task so far by focusing on nonhuman bodies, by, that is, depicting them as actants rather than as objects. But the case for matter as active needs also to readjust the status of human actants: not by denying humanity's awesome, awful powers, but by presenting these powers as evidence of our own constitution as vital materiality. In other words, human power is itself a kind of thing-power' (10). Thus, she concludes that this 'sense of a strange and incomplete commonality with the out-side may induce vital materialists to treat nonhumans – animals, plants, earth, even artifacts and commodities – more carefully, more strategically, more ecologically' (17–18). If the tree and the sky are vibrant in *A Room of One's Own*, then, so is Judith Shakespeare's body, as are the cadavers and ruins of *Three Guineas*.
11. Bennett, *Vibrant Matter*, 18.
12. In *Politics of Nature*, Bruno Latour defines 'actant' as 'a term from semiotics covering both humans and nonhumans; an actor is any entity that modifies another entity in a trial; of actors it can only be said that they act; their competence is deduced from their performances; the action, in turn, is always recorded in the course of a trial and by an experimental protocol, elementary or not' (237). For Bennett, regarding human and nonhuman bodies as *actants* – not merely actors or agents – allows for a redistribution of agency among material things in the world and for a reappraisal of how things/people are perceived, allowed to and/or made to act (9). Derek Ryan affirms that, as Bennett reads Latour, 'along with her aims to replace a focus on subjectivity with one on "developing a vocabulary and syntax for, and thus a better discernment of, the active powers issuing from nonsubjects" and to create a political analysis that includes the "contributions of nonhuman actants", Bennett, like Braidotti, is keen to dispel the onto-theological binary of life and matter' (184).

13. Lugones, 'Decolonial Feminism', 743.
14. Krenak, *Ideias*, 32. In Brazilian Portuguese: 'Suspender o céu é ampliar o nosso horizonte; não o horizonte perspectivo, mas existencial'. Quotations translated from Portuguese into English by Pinho and de Oliveira.
15. Kopenawa and Bruce Albert, *Falling Sky*, 410.
16. Krenak, *Ideias*, 32: 'Cantar, dançar e viver a experiência mágica de suspender o céu é comum em muitas tradições. Suspender o céu é ampliar o nosso horizonte; não o horizonte perspectivo, mas existencial. É enriquecer as nossas subjetividades, que é a matéria que este tempo que nós vivemos quer *consumir*. Se existe uma ânsia por consumir a natureza, existe também uma por consumir subjetividades – as nossas subjetividades'.
17. Ibid., 33: 'definitivamente não somos iguais, e é maravilhoso saber que cada um de nós que está aqui é diferente do outro, como constelações'.
18. 'Ideas to Postpone the End of the World' was originally a lecture delivered at Universidade de Lisboa, Portugal.
19. Krenak, *Ideias*, 27–8: 'é importante viver a experiência da nossa própria circulação pelo mundo, não como uma metáfora, mas como fricção, poder contar uns com os outros'/ 'quando você sentir que o céu está ficando muito baixo, é só empurrá-lo e respirar'.
20. Ibid., 48.
21. Ibid., 53: 'uma disciplina relacionada à formação, à cosmovisão, à tradição de diferentes povos que têm no sonho um caminho de aprendizado, de autoconhecimento sobre a vida, e a aplicação desse conhecimento na sua interação com o mundo e com as outras pessoas'.
22. Ibid., 65: 'O sonho como experiência de pessoas iniciadas numa tradição para sonhar'.
23. Kopenawa and Bruce Albert, *Falling Sky*, 404.
24. Krenak, *Ideias*, 47: 'excluímos da vida, localmente, as formas de organização que não estão integradas ao mundo da mercadoria, pondo em risco todas as outras formas de viver – pelo menos as que fomos animados a pensar como possíveis, em que havia corresponsabilidade com os lugares onde vivemos e o respeito pelo direito à vida dos seres, e não só dessa abstração que nos permitimos constituir como uma humanidade, que exclui todas as outras e todos os outros seres'.
25. Irigaray's argument in 'Women on the Market' is that 'the exchange of women as goods accompanies and stimulates exchanges of other "wealth" among groups of men. The economy – in both the narrow and the broad sense – that is in place in our societies thus requires that women lend themselves to alienation in consumption, and to exchanges in which they do not participate, and that men be exempt from being used and circulated like commodities' (172).
26. Lugones, 'Heterosexualism', 206.
27. For a comprehensive analysis of what is at stake in dating the Anthropocene and its implications for modernist studies, see Adkins, *Modernist Anthropocene*, 1–30.

28. Krenak, *Ideias*, 46: 'a conclusão ou compreensão de que estamos vivendo uma era que pode ser identificada como Antropoceno deveria soar como um alarme nas nossas cabeças'.
29. Connell and Pearse, *Gênero*, 222–3.
30. On the ongoing investigation, see Vinicius Sassin's news report for *Folha de São Paulo*, available at https://www1.folha.uol.com.br/internacional/en/scienceandhealth/2023/01/yanomami-genocide-prospectors-and-authorities-are-investigated.shtml
31. Viveiros de Castro, 'Alguma', 14. This is the introductory essay to *Ailton Krenak: Encontros* (2015), a collection of interviews with Krenak organised by Sergio Cohn.
32. Ailton Krenak, *Ideias*, 16: 'fomos, durante muito tempo, embalados com a história de que somos a humanidade'.
33. Ibid.: 'desse organismo de que somos parte, a Terra, e passamos a pensar que ele é uma coisa e nós, outra: a Terra e a humanidade'.
34. Viveiros de Castro, 'Perguntas Inquietantes', 77: 'Com efeito, quem somos, enfim, nós? "Nós" relativamente a quem? Ao quê? A pergunta sobre "a humanidade que pensamos ser" é uma pergunta sobre a relação – sobre as relações que nos constituem como um nós essencialmente variável, em extensão como em compreensão: para alguns de nós [. . .] o "nós" inclui, entre outros, as pedras, as montanhas e os rios . . .'
35. Reading Mr and Mrs Flushing as 'small-scale opportunists' in *The Voyage Out*, Novillo-Corvalán affirms that 'Woolf strategically uses this unscrupulous English pair as the embodiment of a deeply corrupt and unregulated system that shamelessly exploits the local indigenous communities, especially the labor produced by its women' (57).
36. Krenak, *Ideias*, 49: 'quando despersonalizamos o rio, a montanha, quando tiramos deles os seus sentidos, considerando que isso é atributo exclusivo dos humanos, nós liberamos esses lugares para que se tornem resíduos da atividade industrial e extrativista'.
37. Novillo-Corvalán, 'Empire', 37. Novillo-Corvalán makes use of the archival documents at the University of Sussex to depict the political and economic exchanges between England and Latin America, especially Argentina and Brazil, that inform Woolf's first novel. She explores how colonialist relations are clear in this novel through the construction of Willoughby Vinrace, Rachel's father, who transports dry goods to the Amazon and brings rubber back. The critic calls the reader's attention to the thorough research Woolf was undertaking as she envisioned her fictitious Santa Marina in South America, a continent she never visited. In spite of some misrepresentations, according to Novillo-Corvalán Woolf mocks the Empire's unquenchable desire for land, raw material and natural resources in the figure of Willoughby. In this case, the scholar states that Woolf was criticising the complex relation between capitalism, imperialism and modernity, especially in the context of British continued colonial exploitation of Latin America. The critic argues that Woolf places her novel in the context of the rubber

boom in Amazonia and she concludes that 'the great boom led to the destruction of the Amazonian ecosystem and to the slavery, murder and forced prostitution of the native indigenous people' (21).
38. Ibid., 37.
39. Sage, 'Introduction', xxiii.
40. Briggs, *Virginia Woolf*, 7.
41. Novillo-Corvalán, 'Empire', 58.

Bibliography

Adkins, Peter. *The Modernist Anthropocene: Nonhuman Life and Planetary Change in James Joyce, Virginia Woolf and Djuna Barnes*. Edinburgh: Edinburgh University Press, 2022.

Alt, Christina. *Virginia Woolf and the Study of Nature*. Cambridge: Cambridge University Press, 2010.

Bennett, Jane. *Vibrant Matter: A Political Ecology of Things*. Durham, NC and London: Duke University Press, 2010.

Braidotti, Rosi. *Nomadic Theory: The Portable Rosi Braidotti*. New York: Columbia University Press, 2011.

Briggs, Julia. *Virginia Woolf: An Inner Life*. Orlando, FL: Harcourt Inc., 2005.

Connell, Raewyn, and Rebecca Pearse. *Gênero: uma perspectiva global*, translated by Marília Moschkovich. São Paulo: nVersos, 2015.

Czarnecki, Kristin, and Carrie Rohman, eds. *Virginia Woolf and the Natural World. Selected Papers from the Twentieth Annual International Conference on Virginia Woolf*. Clemson, SC: Clemson University Press, 2011.

Greenblatt, Stephen. *Renaissance Self-Fashioning: From More to Shakespeare*. Chicago: Chicago University Press, 2005.

Irigaray, Luce. 'Women on the Market'. In *This Sex Which is Not One* by Luce Irigaray, translated by Catherine Porter and Carolyn Burke, 170–91. Ithaca, NY: Cornell University Press, 1985.

Kopenawa, Davi, and Bruce Albert. *The Falling Sky: Words of a Yanomami Shaman*, translated by Nicholas Elliott and Alison Dundy. Cambridge, MA: Harvard University Press, 2013.

Krenak, Ailton. *Encontros: Ailton Krenak*, edited by Sergio Cohn. Rio de Janeiro: Azougue, 2015.

——. *Ideias para adiar o fim do mundo*. São Paulo: Companhia das Letras, 2019.

Latour, Bruno. *Politics of Nature: How to Bring the Sciences into Democracy*, translated by Catherine Porter. Cambridge, MA: Harvard University Press, 2004.

Lugones, María. 'Heterosexualism and the Colonial/Modern Gender System'. *Hypatia* 22, no. 1 (Winter 2007): 186–209.

——. 'Toward a Decolonial Feminism'. *Hypatia* 25, no. 4 (Fall 2010): 742–59.

Novillo-Corvalán, Patricia. 'Empire and Commerce in Latin America: Historicizing Woolf's *The Voyage Out*'. *Woolf Studies Annual* 23 (2017): 33–62.

Ryan, Derek. *Virginia Woolf and the Materiality of Theory: Sex, Animal, Life*. Edinburgh: Edinburgh University Press, 2013.
Sage, Lorna. 'Introduction'. In *The Voyage Out*, by Virginia Woolf, edited by Lorna Sage, xii–xxix. Oxford: Oxford University Press, 2009.
Scott, Bonnie Kime. *In the Hollow of the Wave. Virginia Woolf and Modernist Uses of Nature*. Charlottesville: University of Virginia Press, 2012.
Swanson, Diana L. '"The real world": Virginia Woolf and Ecofeminism'. In *Virginia Woolf and the Natural World. Selected Papers of the Twentieth Annual International Conference on Virginia Woolf*, edited by Kristin Czarnecki and Carrie Rohman, 24–35. Clemson, SC: Clemson University Press, 2011.
Viveiros de Castro, Eduardo. '"Alguma coisa vai ter que acontecer"'. Foreword to *Encontros: Ailton Krenak*, by Ailton Krenak, edited by Sergio Cohn, 6–19. Rio de Janeiro: Azougue, 2015.
——. '"Perguntas Inquietantes"'. Afterword to *Ideias para adiar o fim do mundo*, by Ailton Krenak, 75–84. São Paulo: Companhia das Letras, 2020.
Warren, Karen J. *Ecofeminist Philosophy: A Perspective on What it is and Why it Matters*. Lanham, MD: Rowman & Littlefield, 2000.
Woolf, Virginia. *The Essays of Virginia Woolf*, edited by Andrew McNeillie (vols 1–4) and Stuart N. Clarke (vols 5–6). 6 vols. London: Hogarth Press, 1986–2011.
——. *Moments of Being*, edited by Jeanne Schulkind. London: Harcourt Brace and Company, 1985.
——. *Night and Day*, edited by Suzanne Raitt. Oxford: Oxford University Press, 2009.
——. *A Room of One's Own and Three Guineas*, edited by Morag Shiach. Oxford: Oxford University Press, 2000.
——. *The Voyage Out*, edited by Lorna Sage. Oxford: Oxford University Press, 2009.

Chapter 11

Staging Collective Action for an Anthropocene Audience in Virginia Woolf's *Between the Acts*

Kelly Sultzbach

Common Readers in the Anthropocene

Between the Acts (1941) was written at the precipice of the Second World War, yet as contemporary readers take it up amid the existential threat of global climate change, Virginia Woolf's last novel reveals unexpected correspondences across eras. In *A Field Guide to Climate Anxiety* (2020), Sarah Jaquette Ray acknowledges that 'a feeling of powerlessness to do anything to shape [the] future' inculcates 'dread'.[1] Woolf's diary acknowledges a similar struggle with a weighty political maelstrom that seemed impossible to alter: 'One ceases to think about it [Hitler and impending war] – that's all. Goes on discussing the new room, new chair, new books. What else can a gnat on a blade of grass do?' (*D5* 162). The way in which negative emotions can produce a looking away or sense of futility in relation to climate resembles the *pre-traumatic* stress disorder Paul Saint-Amour identifies as typical of interwar literature. He posits that the threat of total war and the experience of the First World War 'weaponiz[ed] anticipation, making the future seem a predetermined site for catastrophic violence' creating 'a sense that the self is futureless or the future worthless'.[2] Ray urges her twenty-first-century audience to address similar feelings through a willingness to be 'less right and more in relation' with one another.[3] *Between the Acts* represents many of these social and emotional reactions to a threat of global collapse. Further, it enacts alternative visions of collective assemblages – relations that resist anthropocentric and patriarchal models of collective action, not by promising a 'right' way forward, but by using indeterminacy and unexpected relationships as a possibility for continued survival.

In *The Great Derangement* (2016), Amitav Ghosh calls for more models of collective action, decrying the cultural idolisation of the individual that has made imagining collective action in the Anthropocene so difficult:

> at exactly the same time when it has become clear that global warming is in every sense a collective predicament, humanity finds itself in the thrall of a dominant culture in which the idea of the collective has been exiled from politics, economics, and literature alike.[4]

How we create collective action is an acute dilemma in times of crisis whether it be a world war or the closing-in of global temperature tipping points. Although Ghosh diminishes the importance of experimental modernist fiction in his account of literary history, stating that this era was when 'the literary imagination became radically centred on the human' and that 'inasmuch as the nonhuman was written about at all, it was not within the mansion of serious fiction',[5] a growing body of ecocritical modernist scholarship debunks that claim, with Woolf being a primary example.[6] The characters in *Between the Acts*, and at times perhaps even its readers, only glimpse 'parts' of the whole and question what 'roles' they play within larger dramas. The pageant is performed at Pointz Hall, a manor house surrounded by country 'views' as well as multiple viewpoints that are both shared and contested among the family who lives there, unexpected guests and local villagers, who all take centre stage in the novel's pages. A host of nonhuman life also has a voice, including 'real' swallows, cows, trees, toads, fish, ponds and cesspools, all orchestrated by the noises of the gramophone, songs and the uncertain weather, itself. With its paratactic 'scraps, orts and fragments' (*BTA* 115) scattered but often repeated within a wide range of subjective thoughts, unspoken dialogues and scripted pageant scenes, *Between the Acts* directly engages issues of unity, division and who or what constitutes a collective.

That said, examining collective action in the works of Virginia Woolf still might seem an odd choice. As Jane Marcus states in her introduction to Woolf's *Three Guineas* (1938):

> Woolf was not an activist. Neither her health nor her temperament allowed her to experience the violent demonstrations of the radical decade of feminist revolt at the beginning of the twentieth century or the equally violent anti-fascist demonstrations of the 1930s.[7]

But like Woolf, not all those in the climate movement are vehement protestors. As individuals we consume goods within systemic structures that are already scripted – what is any individual's ethical part in addressing carbon emissions or plastics? How does an Anthropocene audience advance large-scale change by joining organisations, donating money or voting? Environmentalists often struggle with the tension between their roles as private thinkers or public activists. Of course, as Marcus also points out, Woolf's wartime diary proclaims 'thinking is my fighting' (*D5* 285), reminding us there is much intellectual activity and perceptual re-vision to be done before and between acts and actions.

Woolf's own ideas were shaped by the communities she decided to be a part of, as Peter Adkins and Derek Ryan note, claiming that Woolf's 'theorizing and aestheticizing of peace [. . .] should be thought of as emerging from collective and collaborative activities'[8] including her collaborations with the Bloomsbury Group, the 'network' of fellow pacifist thinkers and writers she knew, and the Hogarth Press, founded by Virginia and Leonard as a means to amplify significant voices of their time. Yet, as will also be central to this chapter's assessment of collective action in *Between the Acts*, Woolf 'cannot be seen as a theorist of peace whose pacifist aesthetics remained static or unchanging'.[9] As Clara Jones explains, Woolf was a 'committed participant' in democratic change even as she 'interrogated her ambivalent attitudes towards this activism in her writing'.[10] The complexity with which Woolf's novels treat our uncertain membership in any community speaks to the dilemmas of an Anthropocene audience as well.

What, then, does it mean to experience a book like *Between the Acts* as an Anthropocene reader? For nature lovers, fears of extinction amid rapid commercial acceleration can stimulate a pastoral yearning for bucolic retreat that mixes uneasily with an equally passionate desire for social and multispecies justice. As a result, readers may be uncomfortably conscious of how their nostalgia for the past is tinged with an awareness of the prejudices that created it as well as a new doubt about the celebration of modern 'improvements' that spurred increased greenhouse gases: 'The value of reading climate change through Modernism, and indeed Modernism through climate change, is that both disrupt previously cherished conceptions of the world'.[11] The use of 'multiple scales and perspectives' in early twentieth-century literature allows Adkins to state that 'Planetary life, not just human life, becomes the purview of the modernist novelist'.[12] Just as the experiences of modernist form were often disorienting for readers of that era, so too are contemporary readers challenged to 'inhabit texts' in 'personally resonant ways that require intersubjective imagining and relational thinking'.[13] Perhaps what most justifies a loose, multi-scale and inquisitive Anthropocene approach to this text is the way Woolf's formal experiments invite readerly collaboration in world-making. In a draft teaching lecture for girls she wrote 'Each generation must read everything over again for itself'.[14] She recognises that the words themselves are 'the wildest, freest' (*E6* 96) of things, 'mean[ing] one thing to one person, another thing to another person; they are unintelligible to one generation, plain as a pikestaff to the next' (*E6* 97). She expects the text to adapt to changing cultural contexts. Even one's environment will nose its way into the curves and spaces that link mind and language to co-create a phenomenological experience of reading:

> Instead of being a book it seemed as if what I read was laid upon the landscape, not printed, bound, or sewn up, but somehow the product of trees and fields and the hot summer sky, like the air which swam, on fine mornings, round the outlines of things. (*E3* 142)

It is in the spirit of Woolf's own appreciation for engaging with a living text – one responsive to shifting perceptions of place and readerly perceptions of weather and feeling – that this chapter embarks on an analysis of questions an Anthropocene audience might ask about collective action in *Between the Acts*.

I/we/they/us: Personal and Plural Pronouns

As Woolf sketched her ideas for *Between the Acts* she was mulling over plural pronouns and communal identity, recording in her diary: '"I" rejected: "We" substituted . . . "We" composed of many different things . . . we all life, all art, all waifs & strays – a rambling capricious but somehow unified whole' (*D5* 135). The pageant in *Between the Acts* likewise unsettles the stability of these pronouns. Under the direction of Miss La Trobe, a queer, potentially foreign female 'outsider' who 'wasn't altogether a lady' (*BTA* 37), an outdoor drama is staged. The play features scenes from different eras of British history, including comical love plots driven by a father's 'Wills' (playing on both the literal legal document and the indomitable force of men's desires) enforcing a father's intention for his virgin daughter, and hyperbolic professions of love often motivated by a desire for money or missionary fervour, all satirising the aims of patriarchy, empire and traditional ideas of love. It concludes with the players holding up a jumble of mirrors to the audience, reflecting snatches of legs and faces back to the assemblage, creating an uncomfortable self-reflection of the 'present' era of modernity in the late 1930s. The protean nature of weather, words and identities defines the text and its characters, making any 'we' not simply a statement of group identity, but a recognition that each individual contains many selves that enrich a dynamic 'whole'. Miss La Trobe's community pageant creates a shared understanding between characters and readers *because* (not despite the fact) we have multiple identities and *because* (not despite the fact) collective creation is tensile rather than concrete. During an interval, Miss La Trobe is helping the cast with costume changes when Lucy Swithin, 'ignoring convention' (*BTA* 91), pops her head through the hedge to congratulate her on the success of the performance so far:

> Their eyes met in a common effort to bring a common meaning to birth. They failed; and Mrs. Swithin, laying hold desperately of a fraction of her meaning, said: 'What a small part I've had to play! But you've made me feel I could have played . . . Cleopatra!'
> She nodded between the trembling bushes and ambled off.
> The villagers winked. 'Batty' was the word for old Flimsy, breaking through the bushes.
> 'I might have been – Cleopatra', Miss La Trobe repeated. 'You've stirred in me my unacted part', she meant. [. . .]
> 'You've twitched the invisible strings', was what the old lady meant; and revealed – of all people – Cleopatra! Glory possessed her. Ah, but she was not merely a twitcher of individual strings; she was one who seethes wandering bodies and floating voices in a cauldron, and makes rise up from its amorphous mass a re-created world. Her moment was on her – her glory. (*BTA* 92)

Here, as in many other places in the novel, names for a single individual proliferate so that something put on an official birth record is still transformed as we act within families and local place. Lucy Swithin is 'Mrs' (a reminder of patriarchal possession), and she is also 'old Flimsy' to the younger villagers, as if old age has softened her mind or her manor-house status can be undermined by the local youth in rebellious, yet still affectionate nicknames. 'Batty' is her third moniker in this passage (though her link to swallows is more prevalent throughout), which is both a put-down and simultaneously, in this story, an apt tie to the way that nonhuman life – likewise misunderstood and stereotyped – still infiltrates human language notwithstanding anthropocentric connections. Then there is Lucy's 'unacted part', the role of Cleopatra. Gillian Beer hypothesises that the comparison might draw on 'the idea of Cleopatra as the Queen of Fertility in whose domain primeval life began in the mud of the Nile' which relates to Lucy's 'reading and ruminating on primordial life' (*BTA* 141). Interestingly, this ancient Egyptian queen (also a foil to British queens) echoes the tripartite 'Love. Hate. Peace', three emotions that 'made the ply of human life' (*BTA* 57). Cleopatra loved both Caesar and Anthony through multiple wars, as well as representing alternate feminisms and forms of power, thus subtly aligning Lucy in yet another way with the kind of community Miss La Trobe might be trying to create – one that mocks and unmakes the way collectivity has been controlled by patriarchy and violence.

As a result, even though Lucy Swithin's initial effort to communicate what the play has meant to her 'failed', her attempt to convey 'a fraction of her meaning' ultimately succeeds. Her choice of the role Cleopatra aligns her with maligned, alternate female forms of leadership, just as La Trobe casts herself as another kind of renegade feminist: a witch. Repeating Lucy's claim to the role of Cleopatra, Miss La Trobe envisions her 'glory' as being able to 'see the wandering bodies and floating voices' within a 'cauldron' that issues 'from its amorphous mass a re-created world'. Recalling multiple Shakespearian dramas with references to *Antony and Cleopatra* and witches who foretell a monarch's doom in *Macbeth*, Miss La Trobe and Lucy assert the power of art to engage audiences in cultural reimagining. The multiple vectors of association that radiate through Lucy's attempt to communicate actually convey even more meaning than she might have hoped to articulate.

By blurring the lines between pageant scenes and the characters who comprise the novel's off-stage scenes, *Between the Acts* reminds readers that we all perform multiple social and personal roles that shape lived story-worlds. Just a page after the interchange between Lucy and La Trobe, William describes Isa as 'chang[ing] dress' when she adjusts her demeanour at the arrival of her son and his nurse (*BTA* 65), which is yet another way the idea of having multiple selves is linked to the performance aspect of changing costumes and roles. Isa, herself muses about the role of collective and individual: 'But none speaks with a single voice. None with a voice free from the old vibrations. Always I hear corrupt murmurs, the chink of gold and metal. Mad music' (*BTA* 94). Here, Isa reminds us that rewriting cultural histories isn't always possible; we are challenged by the beat of selfish desires for wealth and capitalism that move within and among us as we inhabit diverse collectives and acknowledge our many-sided selves. The 'chink' of our desires for economic safety and ease are as strong as any gramophone's chuff, which can corrupt us into 'madness' and complicity with policies or lifestyles we want to resist. Even activism and protest aren't singular or static; they can be compromised by our own competing needs and desires. And yet one must still resist these 'corrupt murmurs'. Isa then:

> roused herself. She encouraged herself. 'On little donkey, patiently stumble. Hear not the frantic cries of the leaders who in that they seek to lead desert us [. . .] Hear rather the shepherd, coughing by the farmyard wall; the withered tree that sighs when the Rider gallops; the brawl in the barrack room when they stripped her naked; or the cry which in London when I thrust the window open someone cries . . . ' (BTA 94, final ellipsis in original)

Here, Isa's compositional thoughts enjoin us to hear the sounds of labour and lament in our histories – be they from human, animal or plant – and to be sensitive to tragic realities where others are cast as mere resources for the glory of others. How one collective narrative (whether it be the mainstream cultural version or even one like Miss La Trobe's) can limit the life stories of other parts of the whole (such as Isa's own poetic efforts in this passage), must be recognised if there is to be critical compassion within collective responsibility. On multiple scales, the play and the novel, itself, asks its audience to look to the past, re-cast it in the present and open up the possibility for a future cultural change in values.

As such, *Between the Acts* may not present the literary collective that Ghosh had in mind; it is not an overt appeal to collective sacrifice nor does it show readers how to enact decisive change. Yet it also seems more than 'an emergent model of the anonymous artist absorbed back into shared national traditions'.[15] Rather, it resembles Donna Haraway's idea of 'staying with the trouble' or Anna Tsing's 'third nature'.[16] Tsing's third nature eschews capitalist and mainstream understandings, taking the systems surrounding matsutake mushrooms as an example of how 'multiple futures pop in and out of possibility' both in the way the mushroom grow in cut-over landscapes and in the way their global market depends upon communities of pickers that are transitory and outside traditional economic structures. Their human and nonhuman networks disrupt orderly notions of measurable achievement: 'Progress stories have blinded us. To know the world without them, this book [*The Mushroom at the End of the World*] sketches open-ended assemblages of entangled ways of life, as these coalesce in coordination across many kinds of temporal rhythms'.[17]

Similarly, *Between the Acts* brings the past into the present, making new assemblages – Derridean traces of image and word play abound as well as mutable collectives that form and re-form across the intervals, beats and songs of the novel as characters gather and disperse into different groups. Woolf is 'staying with the trouble', which requires staying with 'generative joy, terror, and collective thinking'[18] in a way that asks us to be 'truly present, not as a vanishing pivot between awful or edenic pasts and apocalyptic or salvific futures, but as mortal critters entwined in myriad unfinished configurations of places, times, matters, meanings'.[19] The collective isn't solid but fluid – avoiding the binaries of safety or doom, or strictly political measurements of regression or progress – instead embedding humans within a larger more-than-human dynamic community which, like mushrooms with underground filaments that suddenly burst into being, might sprout up as new collectives in unexpected ways. Haraway cites Woolf specifically as a writer who 'understood the high stakes of training the mind and imagination [. . .] to venture off the beaten path to meet unexpected, non-natal kin and to strike up conversations [. . .] to propose together something unanticipated [. . .] The blackbird sings its importance, the babblers dance their shining prestige, the storytellers crack the established order'.[20]

Questions of Privilege and Prejudice Matter

While Woolf's '"I" rejected: "We" substituted' whole is fractious and multitudinous, is the 'we' still primarily Western, White and privileged? In *The Crisis of Civilization* Dipesh Chakrabarty points out the uneven burden of climate oppression in the Anthropocene asking: 'Who is the "we"?',[21] and reminding us that the responsibility for and the harms of a climate-changed planet are not equally distributed. Although Woolf may not have fully addressed issues of race and class, as a feminist and pacifist, Woolf was aware of her privilege and sensitive to some disparities in the collective 'we'. Monarchy and police powers have central roles in the pageant's scenes. But rather than reify these systems of power, La Trobe's play mocks them, using the hyperbole and parody of the genre's conventions to point up the hypocrisy of empire and the superficiality of marriage. Miss La Trobe casts working-class people from the village as her figures of mainstream authority: Budge, the owner of the pub speaking as the police, Hilda, the carpenter's daughter (*BTA* 50) and Mrs Clark, licensed to sell tobacco (*BTA* 57) are versions of the Queen. As a result, there is a slippage between those symbols of power and the more daily activities, run by those who lack class privilege, to shape what is significant in most people's lives. She is, in her own vein of humour and satire, taking down the figureheads and toppling statues. In this way the 'we' of the collective is one that plays with what Timothy Clark discusses as a Hobbesian notion of government's power – an image of the King as synecdoche for the State – conceived as a force to restrain human vices in order to promote group survival. It is this 'we' that Woolf undermines. Yet, as Clark points out, in an Anthropocene context the collective State might be more accurately figured as a brute or psychopath creating planetary chaos and ruin.[22]

Likewise, Woolf seems equally aware of the way in which socially enacted collectives can promote dangerous violence and exclusion. Isa reads a morning newspaper account of a girl 'dragged up to the barrack room' and raped by a group of soldiers (*BTA* 15), an image that will continue to haunt her throughout the day, including her aforementioned reference of a 'brawl in the barrack room when they stripped her naked' (*BTA* 94). Likewise, the policeman 'directing the traffic at 'Yde Park Corner' is metonymically enforcing the flow of empire's brutal currents, literally linking cars and commerce with what Kathryn Yusoff describes as 'weaponiz[ing] the redistribution of energy around the globe through the flesh of black bodies'.[23] The policeman's monologue is gilded with hypocrisy and genocide in describing how he does his 'duty' with 'protection and correction': 'It's a Christian country, our Empire, under the White Queen Victoria. Over thought and religion; drink; dress; manners; marriage too, I wield my truncheon' (*BTA* 97). Woolf sees the tangled knots of empire, economics and ethics, how black and brown peoples of the world have been eviscerated in body and culture under the weapon of British rule that has consumed them to produce the empire's polluting wealth – a relationship of historical abuse and privilege that still operates in climate change dynamics today.

Woolf even suggests empire's threats to the environment and non-human animals too. Mr Bart Oliver, a retired member of the Indian Civil Service (*BTA* 5) becomes a 'terrible peaked eyeless monster [. . .] brandishing arms' (*BTA* 10). Bart, disguised with a rolled-up newspaper in a misguided attempt at *play*, 'spr[ings] upon' his grandson with a 'Good morning sir' to which the maids urge George to respond as properly expected: 'Say good morning, George'. But this frightens George, who had just been seeing a flower 'entire' blazing with all its aboveground and underground parts and its 'velvet caves of lambent light', recognising that 'the flower complete' was also part of the surrounding grass and trees. Into that moment of ecological epiphany and beauty Bart appears as 'a roar and hot breath' that 'rushed between him and the flower' (*BTA* 10). Simultaneously, Mr Oliver's Afghan hound, who had been 'bounding and bouncing among the flowers' too, is called to heel by Bart, 'as if he were commanding a regiment' and the 'noose that old Oliver always carried with him' was 'slipped over his collar' as 'the hairy flanks were sucked in and out'. After this gruff capture, George 'burst[s] out crying' (*BTA* 10), upset both for himself and the pain of the hound. Mr Oliver seems to re-enact a kind of colonial violence whereby a way of holistic seeing and being is attacked under the guise of benevolence and patriarchal control. These images of exploitation, egotism and physical abuse remind the reader that in the name of control and order collectives can indeed become monstrous 'psychopaths' acting on demeaning stereotypes that serve to justify why 'other' people and animals are to be exploited as the colonial leaders please; and, in the aggregate, causing 'planetary ruin'[24] in the form of slavery, war, carbon industries and ecological devastation, all in the name of capitalism and the advancement of 'civilisation'.

As a result, Woolf's most productive communities are bands of outsiders operating in resistance to mainstream society. In *Three Guineas,* Woolf explains the idea of 'outsider societies' that we see in *Between the Acts*, referring to a loud, repetitive, malfunctioning gramophone here as well:

> It seems both wrong for us rationally and impossible for us emotionally to fill up your form and join your society. For by so doing we should merge our identity in yours; follow and repeat and score still deeper the old worn ruts in which society, like a gramophone whose needle has stuck, is grinding out with intolerable unanimity 'Three hundred million spent upon arms'. We should not give effect to a view which our own experience of 'society' should have helped us to envisage. Thus, Sir, while we respect you as a private person and prove it by giving you a guinea to spend as you choose, we believe that we can help you most effectively by refusing to join your society; by working for our common ends – justice and equality and liberty for all men and women – outside your society, not within. (*TG* 125)

While for Woolf those outsider collectives were made up of fellow feminists and pacifists, her acknowledgement that collectives who refuse to adopt the means of the dominant structure can shift cultural thinking from the periphery is acknowledging that the 'we' of her collective can and should be one that questions White, Western power. Indeed, environmentalism as a movement has its own chequered past. Today, traditional environmental organisations such as The Sierra Club and the Audubon Society have had to own up to the racism of their founding fathers and revise exclusionary practices. Yet the environmental movement created space for 'multiple futures to pop in and out of possibility'[25] with open-ended assemblages of outsiders too: scientists who risked censure and attack, social media-centred groups such as 350.org, a host of young visionaries such as Greta Thunberg, those leading Extinction Rebellion or the Sunrise Movement, citizen science organisations, bands of artists making films, as well as those writing climate literature and creating Anthropocene art. Thus, the potential dangers, limits and opportunities of the collective 'we' are always capable of dividing and re-forming. As we see in Woolf's novel, 'opportunity' can be split (as it is by the military aeroplanes overhead at the end of the Reverend Streatfield's speech (*BTA* 114–15)) into 'opp' as in opposition, the word 'or' or 'ort', and 'unity', but perhaps the point is not just that opportunity can be shattered but also that it takes a combination of words that might seem contrary in their parts but whose frictions are all needed to form 'opportunity'.

Harmony and Discord in Multispecies Movements

Multispecies communities are bound up in existential problems and anthropogenic climate change. Today, in popular books whose titles profess to unveil the 'secret' of these lives, scientists and naturalists have revealed the mycorrhizal networks of tree communication and the thoughtful lives of cows.[26] Nearly a century before these publications, Woolf's oeuvre repeatedly affirms the large and diverse sentient collective acting within and upon the human drama. As Ursula Heise writes in *Imagining Extinction* (2016), cultural stories inscribe values upon which policy decisions rest, stating that scientific efforts to save species in a climate-changed world will only 'gain sociocultural traction to the extent they become part of the stories that human communities tell about themselves: their origins, their development, their identity, and their future horizons'.[27] Louise Westling was one of the first to note that *Between the Acts*' 'giddy tangle of forms and beings' gives us the 'proper context for rethinking human destiny' by 'refocus[ing] attention upon the limitations and responsibilities that must humble our species if we are to survive'.[28]

In Woolf's multispecies collective, nonhumans are often the agents of momentary cohesion, averting the play's 'failure' or providing emotional catharsis. When Miss La Trobe's play falters and she becomes 'paralyzed' with the anxiety of failure,

> the cows took up the burden. One had lost her calf. In the very nick of time she lifted her great moon-eyed head and bellowed. [. . .] From cow after cow came the same yearning bellow. The whole world was filled with dumb yearning. It was the primeval voice sounding loud in the ear of the present moment. (*BTA* 85)

Woolf challenges her reader to hear the cows' experience of grief and comfort not as a mere 'setting' or 'props' for human plots but as fellow sentient feeling beings. As Derek Ryan points out, 'their lack of language is not seen as a privation' rather 'the privation is on the side of the human audience; what they lack is an ability to engage with the play outside the chains of rationality and recognition'.[29] Ryan decries any temptation to label this as a 'homogenous unity' of species; instead he dexterously identifies it as (in concert with the way Derrida's term is borrowed by Haraway and Tsing too) 'the proliferation of differences that do not obey hierarchical rules, the affirmation of heterogeneous assemblages'.[30] Just as the 'failure' of communication between Lucy and Miss La Trobe was nevertheless assuaged by the accrued meanings that inhered within the productive ambiguity of her claim to an unacted part of Cleopatra, 'dumb' animals only seem unable to communicate; they actually play a crucial part in creating new networks of shared experience.

These moments of interspecies being are made repeatedly visible and audible in Woolf's novel. The migrating swallows are oft noted as inserting reality into the scenes, themselves both individual birds and part of a larger movement of repeated generational rituals in their migration pattern from Africa to Europe (*BTA* 62). The trees act as 'pillars' the human actors weave themselves within, and one conjoins with starlings to create 'a whizz and vibrant rapture, branches, leaves, birds syllabling discordantly life, life, life, without measure, without stop devouring the tree. Then up! Then off!' (*BTA* 73), which Rasheed Tazudeen similarly identifies as 'the starlings creat[ing] a new kind of assemblage with the tree' which 'does not belong to any single entity, branch, leaf, or bird alike, and does not exist "for" any perceiving consciousness'.[31] Wind and weather also play their role in Woolf's larger nonhuman cast, snatching away bits of human words to edit their lines (*BTA* 49, 50, 76) and raining down in perhaps a more Romantic moment where the storm allows the audience to cry together, 'weeping for all people' (*BTA* 107).

In wondering if other lifeforms 'might think through us' Ghosh urges Anthropocene readers to consider a wider notion of nonhuman community:

> Merely to ask the question is to become aware of the multiple ways in which we are constantly engaged in patterns of communication that are not linguistic: as for example, when we try to interpret the nuances of a dog's bark; or when we listen to patterns of birdcalls; or when we try to figure out what exactly is portended by a sudden change in the sound of the wind as it blows through the trees.[32]

Understood or misunderstood, these multispecies, meteorological collaborations offer another vision of an outsider community in Woolf's work, one which humans who recognise their fate as coeval with the environment are increasingly eager to join.

Collective movements are frequently defined in the backwards glance – historians' efforts to summarise a societal narrative. Thus, Woolf's refusal to suggest a tidy, stable version of collective action represents both the unsettling experience of living through their forming and re-forming, as well as a refusal to capitulate to patriotic agendas. Instead, collectives are part of daily experience, ever apparent in various degrees of failure and success. The 'Acts' of the title evokes theatres of war and the awareness that the First World War was only one act in a longer global conflict that has a pending Second Act in the Second World War, but also suggests that 'acts' are cultural, local, creative and capable of peacefully protesting the roots of war. For an Anthropocene reader, questions about quick and slow action might reverberate in the title too, reminding one of the contrast not between war and drama, but rather explosive news soundbites, which also tend to focus on violence and immediate disasters, as opposed to the daily acts and choices that create large-scale societal action and inaction, a phenomenon discussed in Rob Nixon's *Slow Violence and the Environmentalism of the Poor* (2013). Lucy offers one of the novel's most succinct and comprehensive views of how unity is only experienced from some kind of distance, whether that be spiritual or through time:

> Sheep, cows, grass, trees, ourselves – all are one. If discordant, producing harmony – if not to us, to a gigantic ear attached to a gigantic head. And thus – she was smiling benignly – the agony of the particular sheep, cow, or human being is necessary; and so – she was beaming seraphically at the gilt vane in the distance – we reach the conclusion that all is harmony, could we hear it. (*BTA* 104)

Here the suffering of individuals in the multispecies world is promised to still make sense within the complex tonal chords that make up some larger, longer song. The inclusion of the 'gilt vane' may be a reminder (at least for today's audience) of these unseen forces: that even patterns of weather experienced by the pageant audience are themselves smaller vibrations within global atmospheric circulation and worldwide temperature zones.

Yet any 'one-making' (*BTA* 104) is never as comfortable as its associations with words like 'collective' and 'unity' might portend. All is everywhere always changing, causing individuals to adjust (perhaps even to disband and reorganise into fresh new affiliations) to the new rhythms and debates that an ongoing cultural dialogue produces:

> The tune changed. A waltz, was it? Something half known, half not. The swallows danced it [. . .] And the trees, O the trees, how gravely and sedately like senators in council, or the spaced pillars of some cathedral church [. . .] Yes, they barred the music, and massed and hoarded; and prevented what was fluid from overflowing [. . .] Homes will be built. Each flat with its refrigerator [. . .] Each of us a free man; plates washed by machinery; not an aeroplane to vex us; all liberated; made whole [. . .] The tune changed [. . .] What a cackle, what a rattle, what a yaffle – as they call the woodpecker, the laughing bird that flits from tree to tree. (*BTA* 108–9)

Nonhuman trees and swallows that Woolf might have assumed would have perpetual seasonal cycles and transnational migration patterns, are meant to 'bar' or stymie the tide of anthropogenic modern industrial change from 'overflowing'. But Anthropocene readers know that the 'refrigerator' and 'aeroplane' are profusely overflowing, creating greenhouse gases the trees can no longer regulate and rising temperatures that disrupt the looping harmonies of long-established migrations. Whether these 'advancements' have actually made 'each of us a free man' is also dependent upon where one sits on the globe. The environment's jazz-like tune seems a celebratory cacophony in its 'cackle', 'rattle' and 'yaffle' of beats and near-rhyme alliteration but might be more precariously pitched in today's orchestration of the great acceleration, without such stable bars or chords from nature. And yet, in the 'present moment' of *Between the Acts*, existential threats were just as dominant, just as seemingly poised to bomb life into oblivion, first through air raids and then catastrophic nuclear bombs. From our early twenty-first-century perspective we know that through persistent peace efforts, treaties that are regularly renegotiated, and efforts small and large on a global stage, nuclear annihilation has thus far been avoided. Each small act, even if not newsworthy or put in history books has combined in its unique, evolving way, to foster continuance and survival.

So, what is an Anthropocene reader to take from this tentative, uncertain vision of unity? Reverend Streatfield hesitantly offers some succinct themes from the play –

> 'Each is part of the whole [. . .] I thought I perceived that nature takes her part [. . .] May we not hold that there is a spirit that inspires, pervades . . . [. . .] I speak only as one of the audience, one of ourselves [. . .] Surely, we should unite?' (*BTA* 114)

But what has been the result of the pageant, itself, as a public event? Is it merely to fund (and only partially at that) electricity for the Church? Is that goal even helpful in the context of the war? Especially considering that organised religion and traditional Western faith has itself been the cause of many wars (a dynamic that Woolf also critiques in *Three Guineas*)? Do the Reverend's tobacco-juice stained fingers (*BTA* 113) redeem him in other, more common, allegiances to ordinary people in a moment of cultural precarity? Is La Trobe's vision, or any art that one might produce individually or collectively, enough? Tsing's words provide an unlikely, but helpful companion piece:

> The question of how the varied species in a species assemblage influence each other – if at all – is never settled: some thwart (or eat) each other; others work together to make life possible; still others just happen to find themselves in the same place. Assemblages are open-ended gatherings. They allow us to ask about communal effects without assuming them. They show us potential histories in the making. [. . .] Thinking through assemblages urges us to ask: How do gatherings sometimes become 'happenings', that is, greater than the sum of their parts? If history without progress is indeterminate and multidirectional, might assemblages show us its possibilities?[33]

Tsing's book deals with all the different ways communities bond unexpectedly, including war, the needs for different kinds of 'freedom' (economic, cultural, governmental or mental) and the contradictory impulses of not only the make-up of those loosely formed communities but the seeming hypocrisies of individuals among them as well. These same ideas create unexpected symbiosis in Woolf's novel too.

Further, Tsing is interested in what this reveals about capitalism, jobs and people on the large scale because 'things [like mushrooms] that seem small often turn out to be big'.[34] For Tsing 'disturbance realigns possibilities for transformative power'[35] often in interspecies encounters, but even at a global scale 'indeterminate encounters are still important'.[36] Woolf's multispecies pageant, with its disturbances, unexpected encounters and fissures of indeterminacy, does not necessarily suggest 'failure', or as Tsing might say in her context of mushrooms, forests and capitalism, 'ruin', but rather offers readers a way of understanding 'collective action' as something that is inherently precarious and transactional. But, Tsing asks, as many readers of Woolf might too, 'without progress, what is struggle?'[37] Tsing offers the idea of a 'latent commons', defined by negatives – 'it is not exclusively human, not good for everyone, resists institutionalization, and can't redeem us' – but where the 'ephemeral glimmer[s]' can be 'good-enough', in a state that is 'always imperfect and always under revision'.[38] This is a climate-change era hope that Woolf might have been aiming for as well in this, her unfinalised manuscript, which still offers readers then and now not a testament to doom nor a placating assurance that all will be well, but an insistence on some new play, some new life being born of struggle.

Facing Fear Alone Together

But such perilous hope and insistence on indeterminacy is not an easy reality to come to terms with. Climate denial, climate anxiety and solastalgia (an environmental grief and nostalgia for what you know will be lost even before it is gone) are common parlance in ecocritical scholarship and dealing with climate emotions is becoming even more of an acute need for younger generations of environmentalists. In *A Field Guide to Climate Anxiety*, Ray speaks directly to college students, helping them articulate and define the nebulous anxieties around environmental issues: 'Your generation may also be feeling profound despair about the rise of nationalism, xenophobia and authoritarianism around the globe together with a lack of progress toward a sustainable and just future'.[39] Woolf's novel gives voice to, or in a more Generation Z idiomatic, 'sees' people who are frustrated, fearful and despondent. Characters want to escape into the pastoral idyll of rural place, allowing themselves to be hypnotised by 'views'; they also vociferously resist such facile fantasies. Isa gives her fidgeting response to William's unspoken question of whether beauty is enough: '"No, not for us, who've the future", she seemed to say. The future disturbing our present' (*BTA* 51). In climate literature too, the pastoral retreat 'is unlikely to be so green or so pleasant. What once produced glib nostalgia can now trigger stress or panic',[40] whether it be because the view is overlaid with a future threat of bombs and burning planes, or the loss of birdsong and life-threatening draught or flood. Although Woolf is not sanctioning his militaristic stance, Giles also has a very 'OK, boomer' moment of intergenerational exasperation with

> old fogies who sat and looked at views over coffee and cream when the whole of Europe over there – was bristling [. . .] At any moment guns would rake that land into furrows. He, too, loved the view. And blamed Aunt Lucy, looking at views instead of – doing what? (*BTA* 34)

Woolf grappled with similar disparities between advancing social change and consistently enacting those ideals in her personal life. Even though she advocated for the breakdown of class barriers and equality for women, she still sometimes felt guilty for not being able to perfectly adhere to those goals in her daily actions. Francesca Wade surmises:

> [Woolf] had always fought to be equal with her brothers, to renounce the shackles of conventional domesticity and make her voice heard in public – but living alongside female servants [. . .] reminded her daily that she remained complicit in the very power structures she sought to critique.[41]

Reckoning with the enormity of global catastrophe and self-doubt is another way of 'staying with the trouble' and finding 'latent commons'. For Woolf also kept thinking, working and doing her own brand of fighting.

Ray also tells us that 'collective resilience and adaptation' depend on 'reframing environmentalism as a movement of abundance, connection, and well-being' so that we 'rethink it as a politics of desire rather than a politics of individual sacrifice and consumer denial'.[42] One of the ways to do that is to make visible all the work of those who are creating spaces for collective action by showing up for local events, participating in local awareness and engaging in difficult conversations about the future. Ray encourages students to 'be less right and more in relation' by focusing on the identities we share rather than the ones that polarise and stopper conversation.[43]

In the face of a second world war Woolf's social justice goals might have been easily dismissed as unattainable or lost. Even the project of writing literature and the readerly enjoyment of it may have seemed futile. Yet Woolf's last pages offer a message that resonates with Ray's, not necessarily in an affirmation of 'abundance' but in a reframing of nihilism as starting over, and a 'politics of desire' as the ability to be 'less right and more in relation' by having wider conversations where complex, but honest partnerships might grow from engaging in difficult conversations:

> Giles crumpled the newspaper and turned out the light. Left alone together for the first time that day, they were silent. Alone, enmity was bared; also love. Before they slept, they must fight; after they had fought, they would embrace. From that embrace another life might be born. But first they must fight, as the dog fox fights with the vixen, in the heart of darkness, in the fields of night. [. . .] The house had lost its shelter. It was night before roads were made, or houses. It was the night that dwellers in caves had watched from some high place among rocks.
> Then the curtain rose. They spoke. (*BTA* 129–30)

By the end of the novel, Isa and Giles, who have been silently at odds all day are 'alone together' in their entangled antagonisms and affinities. Lucy's reading of 'Prehistoric man' when England was a 'swamp' where 'thick forests covered the land' and 'birds sang' on top of their 'matted branches' (*BTA* 129) is present in the imagery of the final scene between them, as is Miss La Trobe's vision for her next play, imagined starting out 'at midnight; there the rock; and two scarcely perceptible figures. Suddenly the tree was pelted with starlings. She set down her glass. She heard the first words' (*BTA* 126). Thus, unexpected assemblages of past and future, from nonhuman interactions, and the minds of two women who aren't even in the room, mingle unexpectedly in the positive and negative energies of the novel's last paragraph to create a future third nature.

It is a final passage but also the start of a new story; it oscillates between personal and universal registers: at one level, a turning point in a marriage, and on another, a move back to figures standing in for larger processes of war and peace, or the future of the human species facing annihilation. Peter Adkins points out that the promise of a 'another life' being born from Isa and Giles's 'embrace' is a familiar move in climate literature to signal continuity through the promise of future children,[44] but suggests that Woolf's capacious wording of 'another life' rather than 'child' may portend not a new human birth, but rather some new era of nonhuman survival after human extinction.[45] Indeed, the outcome is emphatically poised and in between – not only between humanity's death or life, war or peace, scarcity or abundance, speculation and reality, or the promise within going back to go forward, but also – and perhaps most crucially – between novel and reader in the continuation of the unspoken conversation. It is Woolf's invitation to imagine and make choices about Isa and Giles's dialogue that I find most meaningful. Such an ending that is a beginning invites the reader to be part of the co-creation. Moreover, that future is one in which those who had been previously at odds, frustrated or marginalised will speak, even if mired in a process of resistance, messiness, love and compromise. It reconfigures hope as collective work and continuance as 'staying with the trouble' together, even when we feel alone. *Between the Acts* does not affirm that action will produce clear or intended effects, but it does help us realise that perhaps that is the wrong expectation – certainty and success have always been false goals. Collective effort and engagement is meant to be uneven and slippery, and it is only through making, unmaking and persistence that creativity survives.

Notes

1. Ray, *Field Guide*, 19.
2. Saint-Amour, *Tense Future*, 8, 13.
3. Ray, *Field Guide*, 97.
4. Ghosh, *Great Derangement*, 80.
5. Ibid., 66.
6. See Sultzbach, *Ecocriticism*, McCarthy, *Green Modernism* and Alt, *Virginia Woolf and the Study of Nature*.
7. Marcus, 'Introduction', xl–xli.
8. Adkins and Ryan, 'Introduction', 3. See also Christine Froula's 'Civilization and "my civilization"' in *Virginia Woolf and the Bloomsbury Avant-Garde*.
9. Ibid., 4.
10. Jones, *Virginia Woolf*, 3.
11. Griffiths, *New Poetics*, 10.
12. Adkins, *Modernist Anthropocene*, 20.
13. Marini, 'Inhabiting Words', 16.
14. Daugherty, 'Virginia Woolf's "How Should One Read a Book?"', 127.
15. Esty, *Shrinking Island*, 107.
16. Haraway, *Staying with the Trouble*; Tsing, *The Mushroom at the End of the World*.

17. Tsing, *Mushroom*, viii.
18. Haraway, *Staying*, 31.
19. Ibid., 1.
20. Ibid., 130.
21. Chakrabarty, *Crisis of Civilization*, 188.
22. Clark, *Ecocriticism*, 16.
23. Yusoff, *Billion Black*, 15.
24. Clark, *Ecocriticism*, 16.
25. Tsing, *Mushroom*, viii.
26. See *The Secret Life of Trees* by Colin Tudge, *The Hidden Life of Trees* by Peter Wohlleben, *Finding the Mother Tree* by Suzanne Simard and *The Secret Life of Cows* by Rosamund Young.
27. Heise, *Imagining Extinction*, 5.
28. Westling, 'Virginia Woolf', 867, 872.
29. Ryan, '"The reality of becoming"', 549.
30. Ibid., 550.
31. Tazudeen, '"Discordant syllabling"', 508.
32. Ghosh, *Great Derangement*, 82–3. It is worth noting that the idea that animals 'think through us' betrays some anthropocentrism, since many living things think for themselves without need of a human conduit.
33. Tsing, *Mushroom*, 22–3.
34. Ibid., 109.
35. Ibid., 152.
36. Ibid., 213.
37. Ibid., 254.
38. Ibid., 255.
39. Ray, *Field Guide*, 5.
40. Johns-Putra and Sultzbach, 'Introduction', 11.
41. Francesca Wade, *Square Haunting*, 279.
42. Ray, *Field Guide*, 7.
43. Ibid., 97.
44. Adkins, *Modernist Anthropocene*, 183.
45. Ibid., 191–2.

Bibliography

Adkins, Peter. *The Modernist Anthropocene: Nonhuman Life and Planetary Change in James Joyce, Virginia Woolf and Djuna Barnes*. Edinburgh: Edinburgh University Press, 2022.

Adkins, Peter, and Derek Ryan. 'Introduction'. In *Virginia Woolf, Europe, and Peace: Aesthetics and Theory*, edited by Peter Adkins and Derek Ryan, 1–8. Clemson, SC: Clemson University Press, 2020.

Alt, Christina. *Virginia Woolf and the Study of Nature*. Cambridge: Cambridge University Press, 2010.

Chakrabarty, Dipesh. *The Crises of Civilization: Exploring Global and Planetary Histories*. Oxford: Oxford University Press, 2018.

Clark, Timothy. *Ecocriticism on the Edge: The Anthropocene as a Threshold Concept*. London: Bloomsbury Academic, 2015.

Daugherty, Beth Rigel. 'Virginia Woolf's "How Should One Read a Book?"' *Woolf Studies Annual* vol. 4 (1998): 123–85.

Esty, Jed. *A Shrinking Island: Modernism and National Culture in England*. Princeton, NJ: Princeton University Press, 2004.

Froula, Christine. *Virginia Woolf and the Bloomsbury Avant-Garde*. New York: Columbia University Press, 2005.

Ghosh, Amitav. *The Great Derangement: Climate Change and the Unthinkable*. Chicago: University of Chicago Press, 2016.

Griffiths, Matthew. *The New Poetics of Climate Change: Modernist Aesthetics for a Warming World*. New York: Bloomsbury Academic, 2017.

Haraway, Donna Jeanne. *Staying with the Trouble: Making Kin in the Chthulucene*. Durham, NC: Duke University Press, 2016.

Heise, Ursula. *Imagining Extinction: The Cultural Meanings of Endangered Species*. Chicago: University of Chicago Press, 2016.

Johns-Putra, Adeline, and Kelly Sultzbach. 'Introduction'. In *The Cambridge Companion to Literature and Climate*, edited by Adeline Johns-Putra and Kelly Sultzbach, 1–24. New York: Cambridge University Press, 2022.

Jones, Clara. *Virginia Woolf: Ambivalent Activist*. Edinburgh: Edinburgh University Press, 2016.

McCarthy, Jeffrey Mathes. *Green Modernism: Nature and the English Novel, 1900 to 1930*. Basingstoke: Palgrave Macmillan, 2015.

Marcus, Jane. 'Introduction'. In *Three Guineas* by Virginia Woolf, edited by Mark Hussey. San Diego: Harcourt, 2006.

Marini, Amelia. 'Inhabiting Words, Inhabiting Worlds: A Case for Pragmatist Close Reading'. In *Close Reading the Anthropocene*, edited by Helena Feder, 15–29. New York: Routledge, 2021.

Ray, Sarah Jaquette. *A Field Guide to Climate Anxiety: How to Keep Your Cool on a Warming Planet*. Oakland: University of California Press, 2020.

Ryan, Derek. '"The reality of becoming": Deleuze, Woolf and the Territory of Cows'. *Deleuze Studies* 7 no. 4 (2013): 537–61.

Saint-Amour, Paul K. *Tense Future: Modernism, Total War, Encyclopedic Form*. Oxford: Oxford University Press, 2015.

Sultzbach, Kelly. *Ecocriticism in the Modernist Imagination: Forster, Woolf, and Auden*. Cambridge: Cambridge University Press, 2016.

Tazudeen, Rasheed. '"Discordant syllabling": The Language of the Living World in Virginia Woolf's *Between the Acts*'. *Studies in the Novel* 47, no. 4 (Winter 2015): 491–513.

Tsing, Anna. *The Mushroom at the End of the World: On the Possibility of Life in Capitalist Ruins*. Princeton, NJ: Princeton University Press, 2015.

Wade, Francesca. *Square Haunting: Five Women, Freedom and London between the Wars*. New York: Tim Duggan Books, 2020.

Westling, Louise. 'Virginia Woolf and the Flesh of the World'. *New Literary History* 30, no. 4 (1999): 855–72.

Woolf, Virginia. *Between the Acts*, introduction and notes by Gillian Beer. London: Penguin, 1992.

——. *The Diary of Virginia Woolf*, edited by Anne Olivier Bell. 5 vols. New York: Harcourt Brace Jovanovich, 1979–85.

——. *The Essays of Virginia Woolf*, edited by Andrew McNeillie (vols 1–4) and Stuart N. Clarke (vols 5–6). 6 vols. London: Hogarth Press, 1986–2011.

—— *Three Guineas*, edited by Mark Hussey, annotated and with introduction by Jane Marcus. San Diego: Harcourt, 2006.

Yusoff, Kathryn. *A Billion Black Anthropocenes or None*. Minneapolis: University of Minnesota Press, 2018.

Index

350.org, 258

acousmatics, 146, 158n14
activism, 249–51, 254, 263–4, 266
Adkins, Peter, 44, 60, 67–8, 99, 173, 211, 231, 250, 265
Agamben, Giorgio, 189, 195, 200, 203
Allen, Judith, 211
Alt, Christina, 15–16, 18, 26n55
Amazon rainforest, 235–6, 239–40, 245n37
Anglo-Persian Oil Company, 20, 119–20, 123, 125–30
animal emotion, 150–1, 156, 193–7, 200–1
Annual International Conference on Virginia Woolf, 15, 26n53
anthropological machine, the, 189, 195–7, 201 204
Anthroposcene, 83, 95
apocalypse, 1–2, 4, 11, 24n189, 59–61, 90–2, 94–6, 122, 124–5, 128–30, 132–3, 135–6, 167–8, 233–8, 242
Appiah, Kwame Anthony, 69
Arcadia, 167, 172
Aristotle, 105, 158n12
Armstrong, Paul B., 225n17
Arnold-Foster, Katherine, 224
Arrhenius, Svante, 18, 36–42, 45, 47, 50
Association for the Study of Literature and Environment, 13

Audubon Society, 258
Austen, Jane, 241

Bacon, Francis, 47
Bakhtiari mountains, 120, 126–7, 130
Bakhtin, Mikhail, 145, 158n8
Barden Fell, 1–2, 4
Barnes, Djuna, 211
Barrett Browning, Elizabeth, 17, 189–90, 192, 197–202, 221–3
Baucom, Ian, 86
Bazargan, Susan, 137n29
Beames, Thomas, 190
Beer, Gillian, 14, 192, 252
Benjamin, Walter, 73n17, 101–2
Bennett, Arnold, 79, 215
Bennett, Jane, 233–4, 243n10, 243n12
Bergson, Henri, 144–5, 158n8, 170, 181n35
Berman, Jessica, 58
Bernhardt, Sarah, 214
Bishop, Ted, 165, 170
Bloomsbury Group, 250
blue ecocriticism, 16, 180n7
Bob (Charles Darwin's dog), 193–4
Bolsonaro, Jair, 239
Bonneuil, Christophe, 100
Borg, Ruben, 16
Boyd, Hugh, 201
Braidotti, Rosi, 96n6, 232
Briggs, Julia, 6, 24n15, 241
British Empire Exhibition, 59, 121–5, 128

British Petroleum (BP), 119–20, 123, 125, 128, 132
Brontë, Charlotte, 9
Browning, Robert, 190–1, 193, 197, 201, 223
Brush, Emma, 6, 8, 24n19
Butler, Shane, 148, 159n27

Callendar, G. S., 18, 45–6
Cantrell, Carol, 13–15
Case, Janet, 224
Caughie, Pamela, 192
Cavarero, Adriana, 151
Chakrabarty, Dipesh, 19, 56–7, 59, 61, 84, 96n15, 255
Chekhov, Anton, 215–16
Chion, Michel, 159n23
Chthulucene, 190
Clark, Timothy, 256
climate engineering, 40, 42–3, 46–8, 52
climatic consciousness, 19, 60–1, 65–6, 70–2
climatic modernism, 8, 60, 101
Clive, Sir Robert, 131
coal, 37–44, 50–1, 119–21
Cohen, Scott, 122, 124
Cole, Grenville A. J., 44–5
Colebrook, Claire, 19, 158n9
Connell, Raewyn, 238
Conrad, Joseph, 215
correlationism, 81
Crutzen, Paul, 44, 56–7, 238
Cuddy-Keane, Melba, 136n24, 137n49, 145, 150, 158n12
Czarnecki, Kristin, 26n53

D'Arcy, William Knox, 119–20, 128, 137n35
Dalziel, Hugh, 190
dark ecology, 109, 179
dark pastoral, 167–8, 172–3, 176
Darwin, Charles, 21, 189–204, 225n22
Das, Santanu, 103
Daugherty, Beth Rigel, 8

Davison, Claire, 192, 218, 225n22
deep time, 11, 14, 83, 101
Deleuze, Gilles, 94, 150, 170, 172, 176
DeLoughery, Elizabeth, 143
democracy, 123–5, 134–6, 238
Derrida, Jacques, 84, 94, 195–6, 198, 200, 202, 254–5, 259
Descartes, René, 88, 196
deterritorialization, 21, 150, 176, 179
didacticism, 13
Dirschauer, Marlene, 16
Dostoevsky, Fyodor, 215–18
Dubino, Jeanne, 16, 191–2
Duckworth, George, 237

Eccott, W. J., 214
ecocriticism, 7–8, 12–18, 26n44, 167–8, 263
ecofeminism, 113
ecognosis, 109, 179
ecology, 3, 26n55, 109, 114
Edwardian fiction, 9–10, 79, 212–15, 217
Ekholm, Nils, 8, 36, 39–40, 42, 45
elegy, 143, 145, 147, 148, 180n20
Eliot, T. S., 25n35, 118, 134, 211
Ellmann, Maud, 177
end of the world *see* apocalypse
energy use, 3, 37–51, 118–36, 256
Esty, Jed, 108, 180n20
Etkind, Aleksandr, 119, 135
evolution, 11, 14, 40, 189–204
extinction, 1–2, 8, 20, 23n9, 49, 51, 60–1, 67–8, 70–1, 109, 132–3, 143, 145–8, 150–4, 156–7, 165, 173–4, 177–9, 195–6, 250, 258, 265–6; *see also* Sixth Mass Extinction
Extinction Rebellion, 258
extraterrestrial life, 43–4, 46–8, 52

Feder, Helena, 7
Feuerstein, Anna, 222

First World War, 4–6, 19–20, 24n11, 65–8, 95, 99–114, 124, 249, 260
Flint, Kate, 8
Flush (Elizabeth Barrett Browning's dog), 21, 172, 189–193, 197–203, 221–23; see also Virginia Woolf, Flush
Ford, Thomas H., 87
formlessness, 101, 103–6, 108, 111
Forster, E. M., 210–11, 241
Fourier, Joseph, 36
free indirect discourse, 200–3
Fressoz, Jean-Baptiste, 100
Freud, Sigmund, 91–2, 94, 222
Friedman, Susan Stanford, 15, 18, 102, 165
Froula, Christine, 164
futurity, 4, 13, 22, 36, 39–40, 42, 44, 47, 49–52, 60, 68, 70, 80, 101, 108–11, 113, 124, 135–6, 143–7, 150–1, 154, 157, 173–4, 176–7, 181n30, 197, 233–4, 248, 254–5, 258, 263–6

Galsworthy, John, 79, 215
Garnett, Constance, 217
genetic criticism, 163–6
geology, 1, 3, 7, 9, 11, 13, 16–19, 36, 39–46, 48–52, 56–7, 59, 61–2, 66, 68, 83–4, 87, 100, 105, 108–9, 143, 189, 238
geomorphology, 41
Georgian fiction, 213–15
Ghosh, Amitav, 9, 12, 24n30, 102, 120, 249, 254, 260, 267n32
ghosts, 4–6, 236
glaciation, 38–41, 45–52
global warming, 35, 37, 46, 50, 56–7, 100, 249
Goldman, Jane, 16, 180n20, 190–1
Good Housekeeping, 64, 121, 131, 134, 137n47
Goody, Alex, 16

Gosse, Edmund, 180n22
Graham, J. W., 163–5, 169–70
Greenblatt, Stephen, 243n7
Guattari, Félix, 94, 176

Hagen, Benjamin, 220
Halberstam, Jack, 211–12, 216, 220
Haraway, Donna J., 5, 17, 22, 189–90, 192–5, 198, 200, 203, 254–5, 259
Harper's Weekly, 148
Harrison, Jane, 158n12
Hawthorne, Nathaniel, 191
Hays, Louis, 165
Heine, Stefanie, 24n19
Heise, Ursula, 258
high modernism, 85, 163–4
Hobbes, Thomas, 61, 256
Hogarth Press, the, 11, 120–1, 126, 131, 250
Högberg, Elsa, 182n55
Hume, David, 194
Husserl, Edmund, 84
Hussey, Mark, 14, 106
Huxley, Aldous, 215
Huxley, Julian, 191
Hynes, Samuel, 99
hyperobjects, 100–1, 108, 112, 114n9

Ice Ages, 35–41, 48–9, 84–6, 91, 95; see also glaciation
imperialism, 3, 15, 19–20, 48, 56–60, 66–72, 80, 82–3, 85–6, 88, 92–5, 101, 107–9, 119–36, 164–5, 167, 173, 176, 180n20, 218, 235, 240–1, 245n37, 251, 255–7
impersonality, 9–10, 84, 133–4, 144, 146–8, 150–2, 154, 156–7, 233
inhumanism, 17, 20, 80, 83, 94, 104–6, 109, 112, 144–54, 156–7, 157n2, 158n9, 211, 218, 225n22
Irigaray, Luce, 238, 244n25

Jaffe, Aaron, 16–17, 106, 115n26, 157n2
Jakubowicz, Karina, 16
Jones, Clara, 250
Joyce, James, 84, 211, 222

Kahn, Douglas, 159n23
Kalaidjian, Andrew, 168, 172
Keller, Tait, 102
Keynes, John Maynard, 49, 51
Khan, Almas, 109
Khan, Reza, 120
Kittler, Friedrich, 148
Koenigsberg, Kurt, 124
Kopenawa, Davi, 235–9
Krenak, Ailton, 22, 232, 235–40, 244n16, 244n17, 244n19, 244n21, 244n2, 244n24, 245n28, 245n32, 245n36
Krouse, Tonya, 61

L'Estrange, A. G., 190
Lacan, Jacques, 92, 196
Lambert, Elizabeth, 192
Lankester, E. Ray, 18, 47–8, 50
Latour, Bruno, 6–7, 234, 243n12
laughter, 20, 144–5, 151–2, 158n8
Lee, Vernon, 214
Leonard, Matthew, 103
Little Ice Age, 48, 84–6, 91, 95
logos, 190, 195–8, 200–1, 204
Lostoski-Ho, Leanna, 181n47
Lowell, Percival, 43, 47–8
Lugones, María, 232, 235, 238
Lukács, György, 83

McCracken, Saskia, 8, 16–17, 21
McGiff, Shilo, 16, 20–1
McGurl, Mark, 143–4
McLoughlin, Kate, 111
McSweeney, Joyelle, 168, 173, 177
McVicker, Jeanette, 131
Mansfield, Katherine, 104
Marcus, Jane, 249–50
Mars, 43, 47–8

Marx, Karl, 86
materialism, 10, 79–81, 83, 89, 93–4; *see also* new materialism
materiality, 14, 16–17, 19–20, 92, 99, 105–7, 234
Mattison, Laci, 170
Menely, Tobias, 7, 12
Mentz, Steve, 26n26
Merleau-Ponty, Maurice, 13, 15, 26n51
methexis, 145–6, 148, 152
Mitford, Mary Russell, 190, 203, 222
Modernist Anthropocene, 3, 211
modernist cosmopolitanism, 19, 57–61, 64, 66–9, 71–2
modernist studies, 3–4, 13–16, 23n5, 163–5, 249–50
Moore, Jason W., 122, 124
Morrell, Philip, 224
Mortimer, Raymond, 125
Morton, Timothy, 100, 109, 114n9, 179, 182n55

Nancy, Jean-Luc, 145
Nation and Athenaeum, 121
nationalism, 58, 68–9, 167, 263
natural history, 19, 57–8, 61–3, 65–6, 72, 73n17, 194
necropastoral, 20, 167–8, 173, 175–7, 179
negative universal history, 84, 86–7, 94–6
Neuman, Justin, 3–4, 14
new materialism, 79–82, 93, 164–5, 167–8, 232, 243n10
Nicolson, Harold, 119–20, 125–7, 131
Nijinsky, Vaslav, 211
Nixon, Rob, 112, 260
Norman, Herman, 120
Novillo-Corvalán, Patricia, 239–40, 245n35, 245n7
nuclear warfare, 95, 261–2
Nussbaum, Martha, 63–5

object-orientated ontology, 165, 179
oil, 5, 20, 41–2, 45, 50–1, 118–36, 239
Owen, Wilfred, 173

Parnell, Charles Stuart, 71
pastoralism, 21, 24n15, 166–8, 172–3, 175–8, 180n20, 180n22, 250, 263–4
Pearse, Rebecca, 238
Persia, 20, 119–21, 123–31, 135–6, 137n29
petroleum *see* oil
Pettman, Dominic, 151
phenomenology, 13, 80
phonography, 148–9
Physical Society of Stockholm, 36
Pinka (Virginia Woolf's dog), 192
planetarity, 18, 22, 102
planetary cooling, 18, 35–6, 38–40, 43, 45–8, 50, 52
planetary warming *see* global warming
pollution, 3, 5–6, 25, 43, 168
Polly (Charles Darwin's dog), 193–4, 199
population growth, 3, 179
posthuman comedy, 143
posthumanism, 16, 21, 96n6, 143, 145, 158n9, 173, 175–6, 179, 211
Priestley, Joseph, 194
primitivity, 103, 107–9, 146–7, 151

race, 19, 39, 46, 58, 72, 85–8, 90, 94, 127, 167, 238, 240–1, 255, 258
Ray, Jaquette Sarah, 248, 263–5
realism, 104
Reynier, Christine, 134, 137n47, 216
Rizzuto, Nicole, 16
Rohman, Carrie, 16, 26n53
Rosenthal, Michael, 192
Royal Meteorological Society, 39

Royal Navy, 119–20
Rubenstein, Michael, 3–4, 14
Ruskin, John, 15
Ryan, Derek, 5, 16, 21, 150, 172–3, 181n39, 190–1, 193, 231, 233, 243n12, 250, 259

Sackville-West, Vita, 20, 119–21, 125–31, 134–5, 137n29, 137n35, 224
Sage, Lorna, 240–1
Saint-Amour, Paul K., 18, 23n9, 181, 248
Sarker, Sonita, 64–5, 72
Sassoon, Siegfried, 103
Schaefer, Josephine O'Brien, 25n45
Schaeffer, Pierre, 158n14
Schuster, Joshua, 120
Scott, Bonnie Kime, 15–16, 61
Second World War, 61, 95, 102, 109, 111, 135, 234, 248–9, 260, 262, 265
Sepoy Mutiny, 71
Sewell, Anna, 201
sexual difference, 80–1, 87–8, 90–2, 94–5, 231
Shakespeare, Judith, 231, 233–4, 243n10
Shakespeare, William, 12, 233, 253
Shelley, Mary, 84
Shelley, Percy Bysshe, 166
Sherlock, R. L., 18, 41–7
Sherry, Vincent, 104
Sidney, Sir Philip, 167
Sierra Club, 258
Silver, Brenda, 160n40, 165
Sixth Mass Extinction, 8, 195–6; *see also* extinction
slow violence, 86, 112–13, 260
Smith, Ali, 104
Smith, Craig, 192
Smith, Logan P., 224
Smyth, Ethel, 110
Snaith, Anna, 15, 58–9, 62, 121

Snaza, Nathan, 212, 221–2
solastalgia, 263
Spanish Civil War, 235
Sparks, Elisa Kay, 16, 225n18
species thinking, 56–7, 59
Spiropoulou, Angeliki, 73n17
Sriratana, Verita, 61
Stephen, Leslie, 193, 198–201
Stoermer, Eugene, 44
Strathcona, Lord, 123
stratigraphy, 5, 7, 170
Stravinsky, Igor, 211
Sullivan, Heather, 167–8, 172
Sultzbach, Kelly, 16, 22, 24n30, 180n6, 210–11
Sunrise Movement, 258
Sutherland, Alexandra, 191
Swanson, Diana L., 16, 26n56

Tate, Trudi, 106
Taylor, Jesse-Oak, 7–8, 12, 15, 60, 101
Tazudeen, Rasheed, 20, 26n63, 259
Thacker, Andrew, 66
Thompson, Hilary, 1
Thunberg, Greta, 258
Time and Tide, 2
Times Literary Supplement, 217
Tolstoy, Leo, 24n20, 215–16
total solar eclipse, 1–2
Tsing, Anna, 254, 259, 262–3
Turgenev, Ivan, 232, 242
Tyndall, John, 36

Valéry, Paul, 159n23
Vico, Giambattista, 61
Viveiros de Castro, Eduardo, 239, 245n34
Volanth Hall, Molly, 19

Wade, Francesca, 264
Wallace, Jeff, 8, 218, 225n22
Warren, Karen J., 231

Watt, James, 51
Webb, Caroline, 15
Weheliye, Alexander, 85
Weinstein, Jami, 158n8
Wells, G. P., 191
Wells, H. G., 79, 159n22, 191, 215
Wereley, Ian, 120, 123, 125, 134
Westling, Louise, 15, 258
Whitworth, Michael, 15, 121
Will, Barbara, 99
Williams, Raymond, 166
Winkiel, Laura, 16, 182n49
Woodward, Arthur Smith, 44–5
Woolf, Leonard, 1, 118, 121, 126, 131, 250
Woolf, Virginia
  'Abbeys and Cathedrals', 64
  'Anon', 20, 144, 146–7, 153–7, 159n16, 160n40
  'Art and Life', 214
  Between the Acts, 13, 15, 20, 22, 48–9, 73n17, 109, 111, 143–57, 160n40, 248–66
  'Character in Fiction', 213, 215
  'Cleverness and Youth', 215
  The Common Reader, 210, 212–13, 215, 224
  'The Docks of London', 64, 118, 131–4
  Flush: A Biography, 17, 21, 172–3, 189–93, 197–204, 212, 221–3
  'Great Men's Houses', 64, 134
  'A Haunted House', 23n10
  'How It Strikes a Contemporary', 8
  'How Should One Read a Book?', 10–13
  Jacob's Room, 19, 23n10, 104–7, 112
  'The Leaning Tower', 106, 232, 234
  The London Scene, 20, 64–5, 72, 131–5

Woolf, Virginia (*Cont.*)
  'The Mark on the Wall', 17, 89–90, 111–12
  'The Memoirs of Sarah Bernhardt', 214
  'Modern Fiction', 9, 12, 17, 27n65, 81, 89–90, 95–6, 104
  'More Dostoevsky', 217
  Mrs Dalloway, 17, 19, 48–50, 107, 111, 224
  Night and Day, 21, 104, 212, 218–20, 224
  'On Being Ill', 18, 49–52
  Orlando: A Biography, 15, 17, 21, 48, 80–96, 118, 126, 136n25, 212, 220–1
  'Oxford Street Tide', 64, 132–4
  The Pargiters, 59
  A Passionate Apprentice, 157
  'The Patron and the Crocus', 213–14, 221
  'Poetry, Fiction and the Future', 8–10, 12–13
  'Portrait of a Londoner', 64
  'The Reader', 144, 146, 159n16
  Roger Fry, 224
  A Room of One's Own, 23n2, 25n33, 80, 89, 210–11, 231, 233–5, 242, 243n10
  'The Russian Point of View', 215–17
  'The Russian View', 217
  Six Articles on London Life, 131
  A Sketch of the Past, 237, 242
  'Solid Objects', 17
  'The Sun and the Fish', 2, 4
  'Tchekov's Questions', 217
  '"This is the House of Commons"', 64, 133–4
  'Thoughts on Peace in an Air Raid', 113
  Three Guineas, 17, 22, 58–9, 69, 103, 113, 126, 133, 135–6, 232–8, 243n10, 249, 257, 262
  'Thunder at Wembley', 20, 59–60, 121–5, 130, 132, 134, 137n49
  To the Lighthouse, 4–7, 11, 17, 24n19, 49, 73, 81, 89–92, 94–6, 119, 144, 151
  To the Lighthouse: The Holograph Draft, 5–6
  'The Value of Laughter', 20, 144
  The Voyage Out, 21–2, 177, 212, 218, 225n22, 232, 240–1, 245n35, 245n37
  The Waves, 17, 20–1, 73n17, 81–2, 150, 164–79, 181n30, 181n37, 181n47, 182n49, 210
  The Wave: Two Holograph Drafts, 20, 163–6, 169–72, 175–9
  The Years, 19, 57, 59–72, 105–6, 108, 110
Wright, W. B., 40–1

Yates, Julian, 166–7
Yeats, W. B., 211
Yusoff, Kathryn, 39, 256

Zwerdling, Alex, 14

EU representative:
Easy Access System Europe
Mustamäe tee 50, 10621 Tallinn, Estonia
Gpsr.requests@easproject.com